MW00580603

The Schematic State

By examining the political development of racial classifications on the national censuses of the United States, Canada, and Great Britain, *The Schematic State* maps the changing nature of the census from an instrument historically used to manage and control racial populations to its contemporary purpose as an important source of statistical information, employed to monitor and rectify racial discrimination. Through a careful comparative analysis of nearly two hundred years of census-taking, it demonstrates that changes in racial schemas are driven by the interactions among shifting transnational ideas about race, the ways they are tempered and translated by nationally distinct racial projects, and the configuration of political institutions involved in the design and execution of census policy. This book argues that states seek to make their populations racially legible, turning the fluid and politically contested substance of race into stable, identifiable categories to be used as the basis of law and policy.

Debra Thompson is Assistant Professor of African American Studies at Northwestern University. She completed her PhD in the Department of Political Science at the University of Toronto in 2010 and was a SSHRC Postdoctoral Fellow with the Center for American Political Studies at Harvard University in 2010–2011. In 2011 she received the prestigious Governor General of Canada's Academic Gold Medal and her 2008 article, "Is Race Political?," won the Canadian Political Science Association's John McMenemy Prize for the best article published in the *Canadian Journal of Political Science*.

The Schematic State

Race, Transnationalism, and the Politics of the Census

DEBRA THOMPSON
Northwestern University

CAMBRIDGE
UNIVERSITY PRESS

University Printing House, Cambridge CB2 8BS, United Kingdom

Cambridge University Press is part of the University of Cambridge.

It furthers the University's mission by disseminating knowledge in the pursuit of education, learning and research at the highest international levels of excellence.

www.cambridge.org
Information on this title: www.cambridge.org/9781107130982

First published 2016

A catalogue record for this publication is available from the British Library

ISBN 978-1-107-13098-2 Hardback

Contents

Figures and Tables

FIGURES

TABLES

Acknowledgments

You can never see the end from the beginning. And from the beginning through to the bitter end, this project was shaped with the help of those whose mention here is nothing compared to the footprints they've left in the pages that follow.

This project began long ago as my dissertation in the Department of Political Science at the University of Toronto, and I cannot begin to express the enormous gratitude I have for the members of my committee. They are all scholars of the highest sort: those who ask big, interesting questions and demand complex answers from themselves as much as from me. My supervisor Jenny Nedelsky was and remains a shining light, narrowing at times to a flashlight as she asked me crucial, pointed questions that were, of course, *the point*. Melissa Williams is nothing short of an intellectual force – indeed, a force to be reckoned with, but also a force of generosity, kindness, and integrity. Many feelings of being overwhelmed dispersed while sitting across from Joe Wong, as he taught me the unspoken rules of the academic game (and the virtues of zone defense). Last, but never, ever least, Richard Iton was one of the most thoughtful and brilliant people I have ever known, truly the epitome of still waters running deep. I was heartbroken when he passed away in April 2013; I can only hope that he would be pleased that I am now at Northwestern University, where his legacy has become my moral compass. Together, my committee's encouragement, unwavering support, and inexplicable confidence in my abilities were unmatched, sometimes unwarranted, and never unappreciated.

Many others provided much needed guidance at various points. Rogers Smith has offered valuable input on this project over the years, which

I have always accepted with much appreciation and even greater awe. I owe a debt of gratitude to Joe Carens, whose astute advice permeates both my scholarly work and my navigation of sometimes turbulent academic waters. Working all too briefly with Jennifer Hochschild during a year spent at the Center for American Political Studies at Harvard University was an absolute pleasure. Special thanks to those who read various iterations or parts of the manuscript, especially Melissa Nobles, Ken Prewitt, Jennifer Hochschild, Lester Spence, Phil Triadafilopoulos, and Mara Loveman. Much was learned along the way from Yasmeen Abu-Laban, Tony Affigne, Abby Bakan, Keith Banting, Erik Bleich, Dan Carpenter, Heath Fogg-Davis, Lee Ann Fujii, Skip Gates, Peter Hall, Randall Hansen, Fred Harris, Barnor Hesse, Des King, James Moore, Charles Mills, Patrick Simon, Ed Schatz, and Linda White. I regret that I worked far too slowly for some of my most cherished advocates to see this finished product; rest in peace/power, Nick Nelson, Richard Simeon, and John Sinclair. Truly, I am humbled by these mentors, who have taught me the parallels of sword and pen. I have nothing to offer in return, except the promise to pay it forward.

Mad props to the Toronto crew that made my PhD years sparkle: my first and best ally Cheryl Auger, Seb Baglioni, Sarah Browning, Wayne Chu, Malcolm Cole, my arch nemesis Gabe Eidelman, Bill Flanik, Alanna Krowlikowski, Alex Livingston, the laudable Zack Taylor, my adopted brother Arjun Tremblay, Luc Turgeon, Ethel Tungohan, Steve White, and the unstoppable, incomparable Jenn Wallner. Brett Carter, Shauna Shames, John Munro, Scott Nelson, and the amazing network of scholars at the Du Bois Research Institute were fantastic colleagues at Harvard. I was fortunate to have my first academic job in the Department of Political Science at Ohio University, which was for the most part a very supportive environment, save for a nameless few who have less than a nodding acquaintance with the truth. My heartfelt admiration and thanks belong to Ly Burnier, Haley Duschinski, Kathryn Fisher, Judith Grant, Andrew Ross, Nukhet Sandal, Nina Sharpe, and my bestie/whiskey consultant Brandon Kendhammer. Big love to the special ones who always had my back: Erin Beck, Marcus Carney, Ty Carr, the talented James Farley, Meredith Jensen, Sara Lewkowicz, Matt Spolar, Cecil Walters, and the lovely Veladotas, Christy and Sophie. But above all, without the mentorship, support, and friendship of Susan Burgess, I surely would have gone mad. It is because of Susan that the academic traumas so often faced by we who live on the margins have left me bent but never broken, and I am eternally grateful. I love you all more than I can say, especially those I forgot to mention.

This project would not have been possible without the generous support of the Social Science and Humanities Research Council of Canada, which funded three years of my doctoral work through its Canada Graduate Scholarship and my postdoctoral fellowship at Harvard University in 2010–2011. In addition, institutional support from the College of Arts and Science at Ohio University, the Center for American Political Studies at Harvard University, and the Department of Political Science, the School of Graduate Studies, and the Centre for the Study of the United States at the University of Toronto was greatly appreciated. Thanks to Antoine Bilideau and Csaba Nikolenyi at the Department of Political Science at Concordia University for providing office space and library privileges during a nomadic summer in Montreal in 2011. I was fortunate to have the opportunity to present this research at a number of forums over the years, where critical feedback from smart people left me reinvigorated, even as I licked my wounds. Thanks to all those who spoke hard truths at the CRRES Speaker Series at Indiana University in 2015 (especially the talented Bernard Fraga and Akwasi Bempah), the 2012 meeting of the Western Political Science Association, the 2011 and 2012 meetings of the Canadian Political Science Association, the Department of Political Science at Concordia University in 2011, the History, Politics, and Institutions Workshop at Harvard University in 2011, and the School of Political Studies at Université d'Ottawa in 2010.

I'd like to thank my editor at Cambridge University Press, Lew Bateman, for his patience with this multi-year revision process. Two anonymous reviewers provided insightful feedback that made this a much, much stronger book. My former students and now friends Sarah Lilly and Michael Antonelli were fantastic research assistants. I would also like to thank the people that agreed to be interviewed for this project, some of whom spoke to me at length and multiple times, as well as Nicholas Jones at the United States Census Bureau, who has graciously kept me apprised of Bureau consultations and developments over the years. Bits and pieces of this research have been published elsewhere; thanks to: Springer Press for granting permission to use material from my chapter, "The Ethnic Question: Census Politics in Great Britain," in *Social Statistics and Ethnic Diversity: Cross-National Perspectives in Classifications and Identity Politics*, eds. Patrick Simon, Victor Piché, and Amélie A. Gagnon (2015); Cambridge University Press for granting permission to use material from my 2015 article, "What Lies

Beneath: Equality and the Making of Racial Classifications," *Social Philosophy and Policy* 31(2): 114–136; UBC Press for granting permission to use material from my chapter, "The Comparative Study of Race: Census Politics in Canada, the United States, and Great Britain," in *Comparing Canada: Methods and Perspectives on Canadian Politics*, eds. Martin Papillion, Luc Turgeon, Jennifer Wallner, and Stephen White (2014); and Taylor and Francis for granting permission to use material from my 2012 article, "Making (Mixed-)Race: Census Politics and the Emergence of Multiracial Multiculturalism in the United States, Great Britain and Canada," *Ethnic and Racial Studies* 35(8): 1409–1426.

My final words are for my loved ones. To my father, Joseph Thompson, who taught me to hold my cards close, combine ferocity with a moral center, and to speak in riddles. To my mother Ingrid Thompson, who always said that if we were for an instant to be tricked by the biological construction of race, being descended from slaves on one side and Holocaust survivors on the other would mean that, genetically speaking, we're made of the toughest stuff there is. To Jessica, my academic comrade-in-arms, Leisa, the best person I know, and Jonathan, my favorite brother, for always having my back. I'm lucky that Patrick, Christina, and Megan Byrne have given me an incredible bonus family. And finally to my pack, Jack and the Notorious Ellie B., who together and forever own my heart.

I am a work in progress. Onwards.

Abbreviations

ACS	American Community Survey
AMEA	Association of Multi-Ethnic Americans
AQE	Census Alternative Questionnaire Experiment, United States
CPS	Current Population Survey, US 1995
CRE	Commission for Racial Equality, Great Britain
GRO(S)	General Register Office for Scotland
NAACP	National Association for the Advancement of Colored People
NAC	National Archives of Canada
NHS	National Household Survey, Canada
NIRSA	Northern Ireland Statistics and Research Agency
OMB	Office of Management and Budget, United States
ONS	Office for National Statistics, Great Britain
OPCS	Office of Population Censuses and Surveys, Great Britain
PRO	Public Records Office, London, England
Project RACE	Reclassify All Children Equally
RAETT	Race and Ethnic Targeted Test, US 1996
VRA	Voting Rights Act (1965)

1

Invitation

> Not everything that can be counted counts, and not everything that counts can be counted.
>
> – *Albert Einstein*

The census seems innocuous. It exists in the realm of the mundane, an innocent exercise of state administration. For most of us, it is yet another government form to fill, file, and forget once every five or ten years, easily dismissed until we realize, a day past its due date, that it is mandated by law to complete. We peruse the question asking that we racially categorize ourselves, some of us with our eyes resting on the curious phraseology of "South Asian," some with our brows furrowing at the now-archaic descriptor "Negro." Some of us feel as though our backs are against the wall as we strategically answer in order to boost the numbers of a racial group that relies on census counts to maintain its political presence. Some of our stances are firm when we refuse to answer, believing race is a dangerous concept of an era long past. Some of our hearts sink when we are asked to pick a single race, feeling we are forced to choose between identities or even parents. Some of us respond with pride in being counted as a member of a particular racial group, and some of us never get counted at all.

As banal as it may appear to be, the census is an undeniably political enterprise. It is tied to two fundamental modalities of government: representation and redistribution. Census counts determine voting districts and the apportionment of seats in many representative democracies. Census data also help determine where government money should be spent and which programs should be created, retained, or eliminated. The census is the nation's most authoritative source of information, created to generate the statistical knowledge that the state needs to govern. At the same time, census questions and categories dictate the most relevant social and economic characteristics of a country at a given moment in time. In this way, the census plays a role in constituting the nation and its composite parts even as it is, in and of itself, an instrument of state design.

Moreover, the census is a political institution. Nowhere is this clearer than in the relationship between census politics and the politics of race. The questions of whether or not to count by race and what categories to use are political decisions requiring purposeful state action. Classification systems necessitate consistent and unique principles that underpin the method of creating order out of chaos, categories that are mutually exclusive, and an organizational structure that is complete and all-encompassing.[1] Racial categories seem so obvious, so institutionalized, so very normal, that they appear ahistorical. However, there is normative power in counting and classifying. Racial categories assume distinctive symmetry – white and black are both perceived as equally racial, but are separate races. The very act of classifying creates a connection between phenomena judged to be similar, and therefore each classification abides by the criteria that determine which items, people, or groups belong and which do not. Censuses are in the business of drawing boundaries, but category-making is a process marked by uncertainty.[2] Racial classifications give the fictitious boundaries that separate racial groups a veneer of administrative legitimacy, at times creating powerful feedback incentives for social groups to adopt the identities promoted by the census in order to converse with the state. The census does not simply reflect an objective demographic reality, but instead plays a constitutive role in its construction.[3]

The politics of the census, therefore, reveal much about the politics of race. Throughout the world, laws and policies designed to exclude and segregate populations have depended on racial classifications. From the disastrous effects of apartheid in South Africa to the marginalization of

[1] Geoffrey C. Bowker and Susan Leigh Star, *Sorting Things Out: Classification and Its Consequences* (Cambridge, MA: The MIT Press, 1999).

[2] See discussion in Debra Thompson, "What Lies Beneath: Equality and the Making of Racial Classifications," *Social Philosophy and Policy* 31, no. 2 (2015): 114–136.

[3] David I. Kertzer and Dominique Arel, "Censuses, Identity Formation, and the Struggle for Political Power," in *Census and Identity: The Politics of Race, Ethnicity and Language in National Censuses*, eds. David I. Kertzer and Dominique Arel (Cambridge: Cambridge University Press, 2002), 2.

First Nations women in Canada, race riots in Great Britain, white-only immigration policies in Australia, and the creation of an almost unique urban sub-class in the United States, state-endorsed racial classification schemas have been instrumental in shaping political, legal, normative, and vernacular conceptions of race and racial difference. And while contemporary society may now accept that claims of racial belonging are better measured by self-identification, community acceptance, or cultural idioms, the fact remains that the state is still very much involved in making racial categories – in civil rights legislation, affirmative action policies, multiculturalism programs, and the like.

We are still, in the initial decades of the twenty-first century, uncomfortable with the legacies of the racial state. Liberal democratic conceptions of equality and citizenship demand that superficial phenotypes and morphological characteristics used to distinguish supposedly distinct races matter not; the self-evident truth of the liberal ideal is that all are created equal and should be treated as such. Yet, both the historical legacy and the contemporary politics of Western societies are plagued by massive racial inequalities. We now face an unavoidable paradox: on one hand, counting by race runs contrary to dominant norms of liberal democracies; on the other, racial statistics and the classification schema they rely on provide the sole means of ascertaining and remedying the extent of racial disadvantage.

The classificatory circumstances of the past and the designating dilemmas of the present raise a number of larger questions. How are racial boundaries defined and who decides where they lie? How does the census fit with other laws and policies that implicitly or explicitly invoke race? Why do census classifications change over time? What aspects of power and privilege are at work in designing the rules that rule race? And, perhaps most importantly, why do states make and manipulate racial classification schemas, and with what effects?

This book unpacks the complicated relationships among race, the census, and the state by examining the political development of questions about race on the national censuses of the United States, Great Britain, and Canada over almost two hundred years. The rationale for choosing these cases is both theoretical and empirical. In theoretical terms, these countries are "like" cases, often compared because it is possible to control for a number of relevant factors: majority language; level of development and industrialization; legal tradition based on Anglo common law; democratic regime; social values and political culture (broadly speaking); and ideological commitments to the principle of individual rights.

Comparisons of Great Britain, Canada, and the United States – or some combination thereof – have been used to study a wide array of political phenomena, including the welfare state, health care, immigration policies, pension reform, and electoral change.[4] These countries also share contemporary challenges of race relations and diversity governance: struggles to address increased immigration from non-European source countries; challenges to decades-old approaches to race relations, particularly from the political right and national minorities; the continued existence of racial inequality in social and economic factors such as housing, employment, and education; multiracial populations that are likely to grow exponentially in coming decades.

In empirical terms, the purposes of racial enumeration have shifted over time within each country, raising questions about the causes of change and stability in the racial politics of the census. The United States has consistently asked a question on race or color on every national census since 1790. Early censuses encoded race into the distinction between the free and slave populations, but by the mid-nineteenth century the census employed unsettled and fluctuating racial taxonomies alongside the persistent staples of black and white. American racial classifications stabilized after 1930 and were standardized in 1977 into what David Hollinger calls the ethno-racial pentagon:[5] White, Black, American Indian, Asian or Pacific Islander, and Hispanic. In the year 2000, the American census made history by allowing respondents, for the first time, to mark one or more racial category. In Canada, a question on race existed on the pre-Confederation censuses of the nineteenth century and was included on virtually every census through 1941. In 1951, the terminology of race was

[4] Julia S. O'Connor, Ann Shola Orloff, and Sheila Shaver, *States, Markets, Families: Gender, Liberalism and Social Policy in Australia, Canada, Great Britain, and the United States* (Cambridge: Cambridge University Press, 1999); Jacob Hacker, "The Historical Logic of National Health Insurance: Structure and Sequence in the Development of British, Canadian, and U.S. Medical Policy," *Studies in American Political Development* 12, no. 1 (1998): 57–130; Christian Joppke, *Immigration and the Nation-State: The United States, Germany, and Great Britain* (Oxford and New York: Oxford University Press, 1999); Ann Shola Orloff, *The Politics of Pensions: A Comparative Analysis of Britain, Canada, and the United States, 1880–1940* (Madison: University of Wisconsin Press, 1993); Pradeep Chhibber and Ken Kollman, *The Formation of National Party Systems: Federalism and Party Competition in Canada, Great Britain, India, and the United States* (Princeton: Princeton University Press, 2004).

[5] David Hollinger, *Postethnic America: Beyond Multiculturalism*, rev. edn (New York: Basic Books, 2000).

abandoned, eventually replaced by the less ominous term "ethnicity." When it included a redesigned question intended to measure the "visible minority" population in 1996, Canada adopted the same multiple response approach that had long been in effect for its ethnic question. Unlike the United States and Canada, the decision to include a question on race is fairly recent in Great Britain; after several failed attempts to include a question in 1971 and 1981, the census of England and Wales first introduced its "ethnic question" in 1991 and modified several elements for the 2001 Census.

Comparatively, there are also puzzling differences among these circumstances at various points in time. Counting by race was an integral state imperative in the United States and Canada throughout the nineteenth and early twentieth centuries; this was not the case in Britain, though the imperial power retained a vested interest in counting by race in its colonies. In the post-war era, the United States continued its tradition of racial enumeration while Canada altered its trajectory and Great Britain made several failed attempts to begin to count by race. By the 1990s, all three cases implemented a direct question on race, and a decade later all made efforts to count mixed-race as never before. However, within this recent convergence to allow mixed-race people to identify as mixed-race if they so choose, the cases diverge in their distinctive approaches for doing so: the United States and Canada accept multiple responses ("mark one or more"), while Great Britain provides three single-response options under the heading "Mixed" alongside a free-text field.

The principal aim of this book is to explain how and why these transformations in counting and classifying by race occurred, and, in doing so, to contribute to our understanding of the complicated and contradictory ways that the bureaucratic exercises of state administration abet the construction of racial schematics and shape racial orders. Obvious racial politics – Jim Crow, apartheid, the struggle for civil rights – are always supported by obscure, yet governing, racial practices. The census requires a simple check-mark beside a predetermined box on a standardized government form; and yet, census counts also narrate the composition of the nation in the aggregate, simultaneously masking and concretizing racial categories and the boundaries that separate them, making the contested, constructed, unstable, and uncontainable nature of race and racial identities appear natural and immutable. To this end, I explore two interrelated questions across time and space. First, why count by race? What factors lead governments to develop and implement a question on race?[6] Similarly, why do governments sometimes amend or abandon these questions? Second, who counts as what? What are the classification rules governing the enumeration of racial identities, and how did they come to pass? Who decides, and with what consequences?

In brief, I argue that the census is an evolving race-making instrument, shaped by transnational ideas, domestic-level institutions, and their interactions. First, I suggest that census politics in a given time period will reflect macro-level worldviews about the nature of race and racial difference and meso-level programmatic beliefs about whether racial statistics are a viable or problematic policy instrument. Here, I draw from a growing body of literature in the social sciences that affords causal significance to the role of ideas, but expand upon its empirical application to racial politics by focusing on the development and evolution of the idea of race itself. This involves two conceptual claims. First, race is a transnational phenomenon that exists in excess of national boundaries, and second, the meaning and reverence of race have changed substantially over time, often because of forces beyond the control of any one nation-state. I trace the evolution and impact of these global ideas on the racial politics of the census over four periods: the dominance of biological racialism in the nineteenth and early twentieth centuries; the invalidation

[6] I make an analytical distinction between census questions that identify populations according to race and those that focus on ethnic origin, ancestry, nationality, birthplace, or other proximate signifiers of racial identity, for three reasons. First, race and ethnicity are not reducible to one another. Ethnicity, which can overlap and intersect with race, often describes a collectivity with common ancestry, a shared past, culture, and language, and a sense of peoplehood or community. However, the origins of race are in assignment and categorization, and while ethnicity can have similar beginnings it is more often associated with the assertions of group members. More importantly, as Cornell and Hartmann argue, "power is almost invariably an aspect of race; it may or may not be an aspect of ethnicity." See Stephen Cornell and Douglas Hartmann, *Ethnicity and Race: Making Identities in a Changing World*, 2nd edn (Thousand Oaks: Pine Forge Press, 2007), 31, Michael Omi and Howard Winant, *Racial Formation in the United States: From the 1960s to the 1990s*, 2nd edn (New York and London: Routledge, 1994), chapter 1, and Howard Winant, "Race, Ethnicity, and Social Science," *Ethnic and Racial Studies* 38, no. 12 (2015): 2176–2185. Second, proximate indicators of race are not the same as directly tabulating race – that is, race and ethnicity do not necessarily line up. For example, before the implementation of a direct question on race in Canada, Haitians identified their ethnic origins as "French" and Jamaicans identified as "English" or "British." And finally, this differentiation is particularly justified given that two of the three cases – Canada and the United States – have distinct questions on race and ethnicity in their censuses. Britain's "ethnic question" conflates racial, ethnic, and national signifiers, but as the Office of Population Censuses and Surveys (OPCS) itself noted, "the census ethnic categories are essentially racial." OPCS, *Looking Towards the 2001 Census*, Occasional Paper 46 (London: OPCS, 1996), 40.

of exclusionary paradigms and the emergence of race as a socio-cultural construct in the post-war era; the "multicultural moment" of the 1980s and 1990s; and, most recently, the reframing of race to include a recognition of mixed-race identities at the turn of the twenty-first century. These shifts in the conceptualization of race were particularly powerful in the Anglosphere, transforming the politics of the census in sometimes subtle and sometimes pronounced ways by informing the legitimate ends of race policies and the appropriate means of achieving those ends.

Second, I identify two types of domestic-level institutions that constrain and enable the development of racial census taxonomies. The first is racial projects of the state – slavery, colonialism, immigration, civil rights, multiculturalism, post-racialism – that operate alongside the census. Each racial project possesses its own causes, internal dynamics, and political consequences, but also influences census politics by creating incentives for counting or not counting by race, inflating racial taxonomies, and imbuing racial worldviews of a given time period with nationally specific cultural, legal, and political repertoires. In nineteenth-century America, biological racialism was tied to political contestation over slavery and emancipation; census categories both informed and were derived from these debates. The worldview also shaped immigration and Indian affairs policy regimes in North America from the 1870s onwards. Racial classifications proved useful to measure the success of indigenous assimilation and to monitor the influx of "Orientals" on the western seaboard. Both sides of the political spectrum looked to the census to derive estimates of non-white immigrants to Great Britain after the Second World War, either to provide or dispel wild estimates about the size of this growing population. The multicultural moment legitimized race-conscious policies with egalitarian ends, though different civil rights regimes were adopted in each country. The recognition of multiracialism in the late twentieth century questioned the validity of discrete racial categories, at times providing ammunition for political actors to dismantle civil rights in the name of moving toward a post-racial world. These racial projects create the categorical imperatives for counting by race – not in the Kantian sense, but literally the ways that other areas of law and policy operating alongside the census create institutional imperatives for including (or avoiding) particular racial categories. At times, the various imperatives arising from these racial projects are incoherent; race-making can be a contradictory process.

Political institutions, broadly defined as "the rules of the game,"[7] are the second domestic factor. Though other scholars have explored census bureaus as political actors in themselves, the most notable of which is Melissa Nobles' trailblazing comparative study of census politics in the United States and Brazil,[8] I build on and depart from this and other important accounts by examining the census as a policy sphere where outcomes are often victories on political battlefields that involve multiple players and interests within and outside statistical agencies. By engaging with the insights of new institutionalism and American Political Development, I examine the ways that institutional arrangements frame the relationships between state and society, particularly in terms of venue access points and participants in the policy process. What Britain, Canada, and the United States hold in common is the nature of the census, an institution in its own right. Census policy effectiveness is measured by the quality of data produced and high response rates – this means that racial categories must be constructed in ways that are cognizable to both government and society. I identify three specific institutions that enable and constrain policy change: (1) the *centralization* of authority, especially as it relates to federalism and the horizontal organization of the statistical system; (2) the *autonomy* of statistical agencies to operate free of influence from above (that is, partisan politics) or below (for example, social movements), largely determined by system of government; and (3) the protocols of *census administration* for conducting censuses and the policy feedback that arises from traditions of racial enumeration. These institutions shape the contours of decision-making power – who gets a seat at the table, how they articulate their interests, and the relative power and influence they have in doing so – but are not static; not only do institutional arrangements vary between the United States, Great Britain, and Canada, but they

[7] Peter A. Hall, *Governing the Economy: The Politics of State Intervention in Britain and France* (Oxford: Oxford University Press, 1986); Kathleen Thelen and Sven Steinmo, eds., *Structuring Politics: Historical Institutionalism in Comparative Politics* (Cambridge: Cambridge University Press, 1992); Kathleen Thelen, "Historical Institutionalism in Comparative Politics," *Annual Review of Political Science* 2 (1999): 369–404.

[8] Melissa Nobles, *Shades of Citizenship: Race and the Census in Modern Politics* (Stanford: Stanford University Press, 2000); see also Margo J. Anderson and Stephen E. Fienberg, *Who Counts? The Politics of Census-Taking in Contemporary America* (New York: Russell Sage Foundation, 1999); Peter Skerry, *Counting on the Census? Race, Group Identity, and the Evasion of Politics* (Washington D.C.: Brookings Institution Press, 2000); Kertzer and Arel, *Census and Identity*; Jean-Louis Rallu, Victor Piché, and Patrick Simon, "Démographie et Ethnicité: Une Relation Ambiguë," in *Démographie: Analyse et Synthèse*, eds. G. Caselli, J. Vallin, and G. Wunsch (Paris: Institut National d'Etudes Démographiques, 2004), 481–515.

have each evolved substantially over time, as well. The story of the census is in part a story of institutional development.

Finally, I argue that the state interactively mediates between transnational and domestic influences. Transnational ideas about race may never be adopted, influential, or institutionalized in domestic contexts and, if they are, norms are often modified to produce similar but idiosyncratic outcomes. Using the scholarship from constructivist international relations and studies of policy diffusion as a guide, I analyze the processes of cultural and institutional translation through which racial ideas are obstructed, mediated, filtered, or refracted. These interpretive processes depend on the internal characteristics of racial norms (whether they resonate with domestic norms already in place or create ideational conflict), how transnational ideas are framed by domestic-level actors (whether they can be localized or whether actors have incentives for doing so, as well as the power, resources, and institutional position of those doing the framing), and the institutional context in which the idea operates (the extent to which these ideas are rendered as politically and administratively viable). Political actors and policymakers are important agents in this analysis, but they do not have a monopoly on these processes; social actors and harder-to-measure influences from, for example, diasporic consciousness can also play potent roles.

The incorporation, circumvention, or modification of transnational racial ideas in domestic policy is not the end of the story. Simply put, *racial ideas are not static.* National-level developments in race relations often have transnational reverberations, and sometimes global ideas about race morph precisely because of the ways that they have been adopted in domestic racial projects. Global ideas about race are therefore not simply "out there," ready and waiting to be adopted by political actors. Rather, the development of these ideas is an ongoing, discordantly melodic constitutive process. However, not all developments have the same influence on global racial norms. Some circumstances have caught the world's attention – decolonization, the American civil rights movement, the end of apartheid in South Africa – and have influenced both the transnational conception of race and the operationalization of racial projects elsewhere. The United States has been highly influential, perhaps more so than any other nation, but itself has consumed racial lessons from South Africa.[9] Incentives for action can thus be either positive, through

[9] Audie Klotz, *Norms in International Relations: The Struggle against Apartheid* (Ithaca: Cornell University Press, 1995).

social learning and lesson-drawing from the politics of race in other places, or negative, as states make efforts to avoid racial practices gone awry. In sum, there is a circuitry of racial ideas, and causal arrows point in many directions. The metaphor of a circulatory system is apt, with all its limitations: racial ideas are reused, recycled, and changed through the course of their travel, their influence thinner in some parts and thicker in others; not all contributing factors to the proliferation, maintenance, or alteration of racial ideas carry the same weight; some components of the circulatory system bear a heavier burden than others; and there is constant risk of obstruction as these ideas navigate or are forced through levels of abstraction.

The empirical focus on three Anglophone countries to explore the interaction of transnational norms and domestic institutions is useful in some ways and limiting in others. It is particularly useful in that the "Anglosphere," defined as "a grouping of English-speaking states, nations and societies united by the language, values, and institutions associated with the historical experience of England/Britain and its empire," is a pervasive discourse that pertains to the Anglophone presence in post-1945 global governance structures.[10] Since Anglosphere identity is defined not simply by language, but also culture, political institutions, liberal market economies, and long-standing but controversial "broader scientific and vernacular claims of the exceptionality and superiority of the English-speaking peoples," these characteristics are poised to enable the transmission of global racial ideas.[11] The relationships among these countries, which politicians often describe in familial, friendly, or at least neighborly terms, also provide traceable and detailed sequences of policy learning and diffusion.[12] In many ways, the focus on the United States, Great Britain, and Canada makes those circumstances when transnational racial ideas were obstructed or refuted all the more curious.

However, this Anglosphere angle also raises questions about the generalizability of the overarching argument. Though I am careful throughout the text not to overgeneralize from these cases to wider populations,

[10] Srdjan Vucetic, "Anglobal Governance?" *Cambridge Review of International Affairs* 23, no. 3 (2010): 456.

[11] Vucetic, "Anglobal Governance?" 460; George and Bennett also note that cases can be selected with a view towards being the most likely to provide the strongest possible inferences on particular theories. See Alexander L. George and Andrew Bennett, *Case Studies and Theory Development in the Social Sciences* (Cambridge, MA: MIT Press, 2005), 31–32.

[12] George and Bennett, *Case Studies*, 33–34.

the ideal of social scientific inquiry is to specify conditions under which propositions should hold universally.[13] Here, the selection of three similar national cases limits the findings somewhat, as it is difficult to know, without careful research a priori, the pervasiveness of global ideas about race in racially homogenous societies or the aspects of translative processes that would be most consequential for mediating transnational racial norms in the substantially different cultural context of, for example, continental Europe. At a minimum, however, the theoretical framework inductively developed here provides a compelling analytical background against which new investigations can be launched and more generalizable results ascertained. Recent work by Mara Loveman, for example, suggests that the administrative practices of racially classifying populations in Latin America are tied to the influence of international norms and actors on national census-taking and large-scale political and cultural projects that defined the boundaries and progress of the national community, seemingly separate but in fact highly interrelated issues ultimately bound together by and through the exercise of state power.[14] Her analysis, which similarly argues that the political field of struggle involved in the definition of racial classification schemas is not confined by national borders, at least provides a preliminary check on the theoretical value of examining the interaction effects of transnational and domestic spheres.

The theoretical objective of this book is to reorient our understandings of race and the politics of the census by thinking through and, somewhat paradoxically, beyond the state, which has been a pivotal site of the definition and manipulation of racial classification schema. In the classic Weberian definition the modern state is premised on domination, as it claims, monopolizes, and legitimates the use of force in the territory over which it presides. The state is also much more than this. It is a conceptual abstraction that dominates while simultaneously conjuring ideas of loyalty in its organic connection to and representation of the people and the nation as a whole. The state monopolizes the legitimate use of violence through institutions such as the police and military, but the cartel is never fully without competition from multiple forms and loci of authority, themselves often fragmented and contested by both internal and external

[13] Dietrich Rueschemeyer, "Can One or a Few Cases Yield Theoretical Gains?" in *Comparative Historical Analysis in the Social Sciences*, eds. James Mahoney and Dietrich Rueschemeyer (New York: Cambridge University Press, 2003), 309.

[14] Mara Loveman, *National Colors: Racial Classification and the State in Latin America* (New York: Oxford University Press, 2014).

forces.[15] In comparative politics, we often speak of weak states and strong states, though weak states rarely appear weak to those fleeing from state-sanctioned violence and strong states sometimes seem helpless to counter the whims of the global market.

The nature of state power is equally as complicated. The universal image of the state exists in tandem with a diverse array of state practices that have structuring effects on racial orders, with both racist and emancipatory potentialities. State interventions can be used to create, maintain, reinforce, or upset racial hierarchies. They also routinize our everyday lives: we apply for marriage licenses, birth certificates, and passports, celebrate national holidays, brake for pedestrians, and pay taxes. The state does not simply wield one type of power based on either coercion or consent.[16] Given a particular theoretic lens or a specific set of practices, however, it is all too tempting to anthropomorphize the state. The idea of the Nanny State, for example, suggests the state has a duty of care toward its citizenry premised on maternal principles of distribution and compassion; proponents of neoliberalism use this gendered metaphor to condemn the excessively protective and interventionist use of state power to unduly regulate the lives of individuals who would otherwise be free to not wear seat belts or smoke cigarettes in office buildings.[17] In political science, pluralist theory is premised on the Neutral State, contending that all interests, represented by elites or groups, compete against one another for power (or causal influence) in the government; because of the nature of the competition, outcomes are generally compromises around different interests.[18] Some radical feminist theories define the Patriarchal State as coercively and authoritatively constituting the social order to enact, sustain, and represent masculine power and dominance through laws, policies, norms, and societal relations.[19] Scholarship in critical race theory often implies that the Racial State is the willing promoter of laws and regulations that, for all claims to being value-free

[15] Joel Migdal, *State in Society: Studying How States and Societies Transform and Constitute One Another* (Cambridge and New York: Cambridge University Press, 2001).

[16] Wendy Brown, *States of Injury: Power and Freedom in Late Modernity* (Princeton: Princeton University Press, 1995), 166–196.

[17] Marian Sawer, "Gender, Metaphor and the State," *Feminist Review* 52 (1996): 118–134.

[18] Robert A. Dahl, *Who Governs? Democracy and Power in an American City* (New Haven: Yale University Press, 1961).

[19] Catharine A. MacKinnon, *Toward a Feminist Theory of the State* (Cambridge, MA: Harvard University Press, 1989).

and appearances to the contrary, are heavily laden with norms that are deceitfully designed to maintain white hegemony.[20]

How might we characterize state power as it operates in census politics? Historically, censuses functioned to institutionalize the idea of race as biological truth, abet the management and control of racialized populations, promote classificatory structures that legitimated exclusionary racial projects, and protect the shifting boundaries of whiteness. In contemporary times, we no longer believe that the color of one's skin dictates intelligence, behavior, or human potential. The state's reliance on the racial categories it once used to demarcate, order, and exclude remains, however, now employed to remedy instances of racial discrimination through civil rights legislation and affirmative action programs. The data produced by the census are a crucial source of information that allows governments to make policies and provide benefits, academics to conduct research, advertising agencies to market products, political parties to tailor their campaigns, and non-profit agencies to reach their target audiences. Bureaucrats employed by statistical agencies see themselves as public servants and professionals, not race-makers. Accordingly, political elites and policymakers think of the census as a benign instrument of governance rather than a potentially sinister instrument of statecraft. Censuses are also a technological feat, requiring a mass mobilization of national resources – people, time, and money – in order to sketch the image and shape the imaginaries of the nation. How can we understand these multiple and contradictory faces of state power, some of which exist in the same time and space?

The central theoretical axiom of this book conceptualizes the state as neither sinister nor benign, but inherently *schematic*. As an instrument of statecraft, the consistent purpose of the census is to make the population legible. Legibility is a process that entails a preliminary, implicit acknowledgment that racial identities are unruly, transgressive, or amiss, a deciphering of these identities into a more familiar language, followed by a purposeful recoding of race using a comprehensible, standardized,

[20] Peter Fitzpatrick, "Racism and the Innocence of Law," *Journal of Law and Society* 14, no. 1 (1987): 119–132; Lucius Outlaw, "Toward a Critical Theory of 'Race'," in *Anatomy of Racism*, ed. David Theo Goldberg (Minneapolis: University of Minnesota Press, 1990), 58–82; Kimberlé Crenshaw, Neil Gotanda, Gary Peller, and Kendall Thomas, eds., *Critical Race Theory: The Key Writings that Formed the Movement* (New York: The New Press, 1995); Charles Mills, *The Racial Contract* (Ithaca: Cornell University Press, 1997); David Theo Goldberg, *The Racial State* (Malden: Blackwell Publishing, 2002).

easier-to-understand syntax. Though making a population legible may appear to be, in the words of James Scott, a project of simplification,[21] in reality it is complicated and contested, tacitly involving normative assertions about what characteristics are most important for determining racial similarity and difference and what criteria should be used to evaluate claims to identity. Race must be calibrated with dominant ideational and institutional paradigms; that which is fundamentally immeasurable, declaratory, experiential, and performative must be made quantifiable. The end result is a convenient though spurious shorthand that takes on a path-dependent life of its own as the schematic vernacular of the legible displaces the complexities of the original form and seeps into political, economic, and social realms by mandate and osmosis. Supported by the power of a standard lexicon, racial categories appear bound, immutable, impermeable, and nationally specific. A glimmer of the nearly-lost disruptive potential of a more nuanced dialect remains harbored in the fact that the fixed nature of categories will always fail to encapsulate the muddled and evasive fluidity of their substance. Racial legibility, therefore, involves taking the changing, unruly, and politically contested concept of race and creating stable, identifiable categories to be used as the basis of law and policy.

Legibility occurs in a myriad of ways, as the basic function of the modern state is to create and thereby legitimize distinctions that become meaningful in the body politic: between those who can access the rights of citizenship and foreigners; between those who earn enough to provide a certain standard of living and those who require government assistance; between those whose domestic partnerships are legally recognized and those whose are not. The census may not confer rights and privileges on its own, but as an administrative hub it is both an instrument and an end, operating as an institution and in service of other institutions while presenting itself as external, uninvolved, and neutral with regards to power. The schematic created through and employed by the census embeds realms of meaning as it orders and binds. Conversely, sometimes the state's willingness not to know and its use of omission as method and silence as meaning can be just as powerful as cataloged articulation[22] – here we need only think of France,

[21] James C. Scott, *Seeing Like a State: How Certain Schemes to Improve the Human Condition Have Failed* (New Haven and London: Yale University Press, 1998).

[22] I am indebted to my mentor, the late Richard Iton, for pointing out that in studying race it is imperative to "acknowledge meaning in those spaces where speechlessness is the common currency." Richard Iton, *In Search of the Black Fantastic: Politics and Popular Culture in the Post-Civil Rights Era* (New York: Oxford University Press, 2008), 11.

where critics charge that the color-blind approach to race is a "choice of ignorance" that has contributed to the trivialization, denial, and concealment of widespread racial discrimination.[23] Much like the multiple traditions that Rogers Smith argues have simultaneously, and sometimes discordantly, shaped America's cultural assumptions and political outcomes,[24] there are many systems of meaning operating at the same time, often signifying racial boundaries that differ dramatically from the ones promoted by the official schematic. Contestation over rules of racial classification implies a continuing struggle over the meaning-making function of the census.

The theoretical conundrum of the schematic state is that it is both an incoherent, multifaceted, tension-ridden ensemble of institutions and power relations whose being and effects are complex and contradictory *and* a vehicle of racial domination with (often unrealized) emancipatory potential. The state has neither intentions nor agency, but state actions drive social, economic, and political change and profoundly shape a society's normative, legal, discursive, and political racial order. State power is ubiquitous, cumulative, and unsystematic; parsimonious claims about cause and effect, therefore, will nearly always be insufficient for understanding interconstitutive relationships.[25] Bearing this in mind, as a framework, the schematic state is useful for tracing the operation of state power, which works concurrently on two fronts.

First, to invoke "schematic" as an adjective implies the state – or, at least, the "image" of the state[26] – is an actor responsible for putting the underlying organizational pattern of race into place. When an individual receives a census form or opens her door to an enumerator, the state appears to be a dominant, singular, integrated entity that determines and controls the official racial schematic. It is more entrenched and stable than government in that the census occurs every decade, regardless of which party controls what part of the legislative branch. Through the

[23] Patrick Simon, "The Choice of Ignorance: The Debate on Ethnic and Racial Statistics in France," *French Politics, Culture & Society* 26, no. 1 (2008): 7–31.

[24] Rogers M. Smith, "Beyond Tocqueville, Myrdal and Hartz: The Multiple Traditions in America," *American Political Science Review* 87, no. 3 (1993): 549–566; Rogers M. Smith, *Civic Ideals: Conflicting Visions of Citizenship in U.S. History* (New Haven: Yale University Press, 1997). See also Jacqueline Stevens, "Beyond Tocqueville, Please!" *American Political Science Review* 89, no. 4 (1995): 987–995; Mark Stears, "The Liberal Tradition and the Politics of Exclusion," *Annual Review of Political Science* 10 (2007): 85–101.

[25] Brown, *States of Injury*, 183.

[26] Migdal, *State in Society*.

census, the state draws boundaries: between separate races, each with a box to be checked or space to be filled in; between itself (with the power to create a measurement system and take dimensions according to it) and society (those who must stand still and be quiet until the measuring is finished); and between its established schematic and those of other states. To create the racial schematic, the state draws from transnational racial ideas, a global-level cultural code that provides a normative touchstone of acceptable behavior in racial politics, and the racial meanings that underpin other domestic racial projects and configure the racial order. For example, whereas mixed-race people were once perceived as a degenerate population, by the year 2000 interracial relationships were heralded as indicative of an increasingly diverse and less racially segregated society. The categories and classification rules in the census reflect and refract these ideas.

But as an underlying pattern the schematic is something of a plan that has yet to come to fruition. Race exists beyond the reach of the state, in terms of its transnational nature and its activation through everyday practices and individuals' subjectivities. The meaning of race is fluid and often in flux, and state fictions backed by bureaucratic administration, jurisprudence, laws, and policies transform the reality they claim to simply observe, although "never so thoroughly as to precisely fit the grid."[27] The schematic state cannot fully contain the meaning of race, nor control its actualization. The British state did not foresee mass opposition to its proposed ethnic question in 1979, when racial minorities believed Thatcher's Conservative government was only counting by race to keep tabs on the non-white population and to, one day, mandate repatriation to the far-flung edges of the British Empire. The Canadian state could not predict that the "Count me Canadian!" campaign, a neoconservative backlash against multiculturalism and hyphenated identities, would corrupt the ethnic origin data derived from the 1991 Census so much that the bureaucracy would be unable to tell which "Canadians" were racial minorities and which were not. Though the schematic state maintains control over the original design of the prototype, it cannot predetermine its final formulation. Sometimes the scheme unexpectedly, unpredictably goes awry.

Second, interpreting "the schematic state" as a noun suggests the state is an arena where policy alternatives are contested and where the state itself participates among other actors. Though practices and outcomes can reinforce (and sometimes undermine) the mythologized image of the

[27] Scott, *Seeing Like a State*, 24.

monolithic state, the state is also a field of power and a site of struggle. Simply put, the state is not a unified entity. It is comprised of many different parts, each moving to its own drumbeat. Moreover, political institutions are populated by actors who bargain, form coalitions, interpret ideas, and negotiate constraints. Political decisions about race are contested ground in multiple policymaking arenas, and the meaning of race has rarely been monopolized by state power.

Analyzing the role of political institutions brings three realities of the disaggregated state into focus. First, the different government bodies, agencies, and departments in the census policy sphere have varying and potentially conflicting goals, agendas, and interests. Statistical agencies are embedded in larger institutional structures with vertical lines of accountability, and while impartiality is now a fundamental principle of official statistics,[28] the ideal of independence can only go as far as legislative mandates, executive authority, parliamentary responsibility, congressional oversight, and budgetary procurements permit. Horizontal coordination and collaboration within and beyond the statistical system should not be mistaken for automatic consensus. Rather than being an indicator of dysfunction in the ideal-type Weberian bureaucracy, intra-institutional conflict is both normal and central to the institutional organization and function of the state apparatus. But once the schematic is established, it renders invisible the work, conflict, discord, and uncertainty undertaken in the process of its creation. Second, the boundaries of state and society are rarely clearly delineated. The independence of statistical agencies partially rests on the idea that the census exists autonomously from the society it purports to record; methodologically speaking, there is an implicit presumption of unbiased observation. If the state is a conceptual abstraction, however, then so too is the dividing line between state and society. The very appearance of the state's ability to create racial taxonomies and apply them to society is a "structural effect" of processes of spatial organization, temporal arrangement, function specification, and supervision and surveillance. The assumed distinction between state and society therefore generates resources of power that determine authority, convey legitimacy, and reinforce the racial order.[29] Further, the constructed boundaries between

[28] United Nations Statistics Division, *Fundamental Principles of Official Statistics* (New York: United Nations Statistical Division, 2013), accessed September 25, 2013, http://unstats.un.org/unsd/dnss/gp/FP-New-E.pdf

[29] Here, I draw insight from efforts to denaturalize and dehistoricize the state, from: Timothy Mitchell, "The Limits of the State: Beyond Statist Approaches and Their Critics," *American Political Science Review* 85, no. 1 (1991): 77–96; Aradhana Sharma

state and society are clouded by the recent increase in public participation in the census design process. Though "race classification is a type of necessary decision-making that is *most conveniently* done in the shadows,"[30] advisory groups, public consultations, and targeted social engagement are now institutionalized procedures of census administration. And, third, race-making processes in the schematic state are, somewhat ironically, far more contradictory than coherent. Racial classification schemas in the census do not always align with the racial categories used in other areas of law, policy, or jurisprudence. The many and simultaneous racial projects of the state may each encompass internally consistent ideas about the meaning of race and mechanisms for organizing society along racial lines, but together, the conglomerate is rather dissonant. The idea of the state as a singular entity works to both hide and enshrine these contradictions, just as schematic outcomes make the state appear coherent, unabridged, and static.

Finally, in implicating the root-word "scheme," I want to suggest that at times the state is duplicitous or may act in insidious ways. There is a normative bent to race-making processes that cannot be ignored: in its schematizing, the state determines spaces of legality and illegality, acceptability and abnormality. Racial dominance and white supremacy were once explicit goals of most Western democracies; the census has been used to manage and control racial populations, to restrict undesired immigration from non-white or not-white-enough countries, to reinforce and compound the effects of the one-drop rule, to promote a racially invisible version of multiculturalism, and to diminish the claims of racial minorities to citizenship and belonging. In more recent times, state power is still no more race-neutral than it is gender- or class-neutral. The features of the state that enact and sustain white supremacy, masculine power, elitism, and/or heteronormativity, however, are often submerged, largely invisible to the general public.[31] With the audacity of hope (or the hope for audacity) of a post-racial world, neoliberal principles demand an expanse of the private sector at the expense of the public, making racially driven

and Akhil Gupta, eds., *The Anthropology of the State: A Reader* (Malden: Blackwell Publishing, 2006); and Akhil Gupta, *Red Tape: Bureaucracy, Structural Violence and Poverty in India* (Durham and London: Duke University Press, 2012).

[30] Christopher Ford, "Administering Identity: The Determination of 'Race' in Race-Conscious Law," *California Law Review* 82 (1994): 1283–1284.

[31] On the concept of the submerged state, see Suzanne Mettler, *The Submerged State: How Invisible Government Policies Undermine American Democracy* (Chicago: University of Chicago Press, 2011).

exclusions in both spheres off-limits to state intervention.[32] In census politics, the quantification of race supports laws and policies that are designed (however ineffectually) to lessen circumstances of racial disadvantage; indeed, the data produced by the census have been critical in proving that racial inequalities remain entrenched. But, in doing so, the state portrays itself as the defender of liberal principles of equality and justice, absolving itself of its responsibility for creating and enabling these circumstances in the first place and taking comfort in its contradictory role of combating racism in some ways while supporting it in others. The theoretical implications of state schemes, which I will return to in the concluding chapter, must seriously question whether racial classifications designed through state power can truly be used as instruments of egalitarian change and emancipatory action.

A LOOK AHEAD

The approach developed in this book follows Ira Katznelson's configurative understanding of causality, which considers the ways that actors are constituted by the structures within which they are located,[33] while paying heed to the isomorphic nature of ideas, institutions, and their interactions. Time and space are therefore important elements of this comparative project – both are taken seriously. Each chapter is organized by overlapping temporal periods in order to augment the central argument concerning the transnational nature of racial ideas and their global circuitry. The evidence is derived from extensive archival research, internal government documents, official records of congressional and parliamentary debates, census and survey data, and secondary sources. I also conducted semi-structured interviews and follow-ups with political elites and

[32] On race and neoliberalism, see Loïc Wacquant, *Punishing the Poor: The Neoliberal Government of Social Insecurity* (Durham: Duke University Press, 2009), David Theo Goldberg, *The Threat of Race: Reflections on Racial Neoliberalism* (Malden: Blackwell Publishing, 2009), Joe Soss, Richard C. Fording, and Sanford F. Schram, *Disciplining the Poor: Neoliberal Paternalism and the Persistent Power of Race* (Chicago: University of Chicago Press, 2011), and Lester K. Spence, *Knocking the Hustle: Against the Neoliberal Turn in Black Politics* (Brooklyn: Punctum books, 2015).

[33] Ira Katznelson, "Strong Theory, Complex History: Structure and Configuration in Comparative Politics Revisited," in *Comparative Politics: Rationality, Culture, and Structure*, 2nd edn, eds. Mark Irving Lichbach and Alan S. Zuckerman (New York: Cambridge University Press, 2009), 100.

policymakers in each country between 2009 and 2011.[34] In addition, each within-case analysis uses process-tracing techniques in order to pay careful attention to the sequencing of events in each country. This way, the comparison takes into account the potential effects of long causal processes, even from the distant past, that shape the viable alternatives of the present. Rather than situating *The Schematic State* in a single paradigm, I choose instead to embark on a mission of analytical eclecticism[35] that bridges literatures, theories, and audiences in order to understand the pragmatic, conceptual, and normative consequences of race-making through the census.

Chapter 2 expands upon the arguments and analytic framework sketched in this invitation to rethink the substance of and relationships among race, the state, and the census. I begin by unpacking my arguments about the transnational nature of race and the causal influence of racial ideas. I then contextualize the role of racial projects and domestic-level institutions. Finally, I detail my understanding of the interactions between transnational racial ideas and domestic institutional contexts, focusing on processes of institutional and cultural translation.

Chapter 3 begins by emphasizing the transnational underpinnings of racial discourses in the nineteenth and early twentieth centuries, in which race was understood as a biological and naturally hierarchical phenomenon. At the same time, the international rise of statistical science and the political development of census bureaus allowed the schematic state to "see" race, both in terms of categories and population groups, as something that ought to be managed and controlled. The census was one means, among many others, for doing so. The classification schemes – especially the rules applied to determine who was white and who was not – employed in the early censuses of the United States and Canada and the colonial censuses of the British Empire aligned with other racial projects of the state, though at times these racial imperatives were contradictory in content. The battles within the state apparatus over census policy were often between political elites and the bureaucracy. There was little societal participation in the determination of census classifications, though expert communities of scientists played a pivotal role in the

[34] See Appendix for a list of interviewees and a discussion of access and positionality in interviewing and archival research.

[35] Rudra Sil and Peter J. Katzenstein, "Analytic Eclecticism in the Study of World Politics: Reconfiguring Problems and Mechanisms across Research Traditions," *Perspectives on Politics* 8, no. 2 (2010): 411–431.

United States, especially in developing categories that would provide information to supplement, and later supplant, their pseudo-scientific theories about the nature of race.

Chapter 4 examines the global invalidation of biological racialism following the Second World War and its implications for census politics. It argues that this monumental shift in the macro-level idea of race, intensified by American developments in race relations, reframed a transnational norm surrounding the legitimacy of state action and inaction with regards to racial discrimination. In particular, legislation in the United States demonstrated to watchful governments elsewhere how census data could be used to support civil rights. However, processes of institutional and cultural translation were consequential. The British and Canadian governments viewed race as overly divisive and chose, in the Canadian case, to abandon the terminology of race in the census, and in the British case, to purposely avoid counting by race in order to maintain social cohesion.

Chapter 5 argues that ramifications of (and backlash against) civil rights regimes throughout the 1970s and 1980s helped reframe the global politics of race as the tension between color-blindness and race-consciousness. In census politics, this reframing supported a burgeoning transnational norm that gave primacy to racial self-declaration and recognized racial statistics as an acceptable policy instrument. As lobbies in the United States formed to capitalize on the incentives to being counted, bureaucrats and elites in Canada and Great Britain acknowledged that their color-blind stance of not counting by race was unsustainable. Though both countries put anti-discrimination laws into place, it was only when elite-level support was combined with unexpected policy contingencies that these governments moved to change the status quo. The approach to racial enumeration in all three cases converged: counting was necessary to justify positive action and to promote harmonious race relations. Institutional developments were also quite important. When self-administered census forms replaced trained enumerators in the 1970s, statistical agencies needed to ensure that questions were understandable to the public. Focus groups and extensive census field tests became part of the institutional business of the schematic state, though not all consultative processes are created equal – while some involved institutionalized minority participation, others were closer to a public relations campaign than to deliberative decision-making.

Chapter 6 considers the political development of the enumeration of the multiracial populations of Canada, Great Britain, and the United

States at the end of the twentieth century. The convergent outcomes of "counting" mixed-race was a marked normative ideational shift from just two decades earlier, when census designers believed that mixed-race posed a problem to accurate census counts. By the 1990s, however, multiraciality was becoming a viable and recognizable identity. Three factors with transnational undercurrents, which together were reframed as programmatic beliefs about how counting by race could be used to promote national diversity as a positive value, contributed to this development. First, these countries witnessed similar demographic trajectories that stemmed from changing immigration and intermarriage patterns. These produced a small, but growing, population that claimed to be multiracial in exactly a normative timeframe when mixed-race people were beginning to be recognized *as mixed-race*. Second, the burgeoning transnational norm of racial self-declaration was internalized in epistemic communities. Policymakers became uncomfortable with assigning identities and expressed concern that respondents be brought "closer to the measure." This entailed giving respondents the ability to identify as mixed-race if they so desired, and policymakers were willing to adjust previously successful census categories in order to accommodate these issues of identity and recognition. Lastly, the census became a more potent instrument of diversity governance used by the schematic state to promote multiculturalism and diversity as positive national values. Multiraciality became a discursive weapon that could be promoted by policy entrepreneurs – at times, strategically and in varying ways – as a corollary of multicultural discourse. At the same time, each country's particular approach to multiracial enumeration was mediated by political institutions. Canada permitted multiple responses to its race question because of the path-dependent constraints that arose from its policy of encouraging respondents to "mark all that apply" on its ethnic ancestry question. In Britain, the relatively closed structure of the policy network made its choice of stand-alone multiracial categories uncontroversial, while the open nature of the American federal review of racial classification in the 1990s necessitated that state and non-state actors form coalitions and bargain for their preferred outcome.

In Chapter 7, I conclude by exploring the most recent census round, including President Barack Obama's choice to identify as black rather than mixed-race and the proposals for significantly changing how the 2020 American census will count by race; the Canadian government's announcement in July 2010 that the census long-form would be replaced with a voluntary survey, thereby jeopardizing the accuracy of the ethnic and racial data produced; and recent discussions in Great Britain about eliminating the census altogether. Given these circumstances, the retrenchment of anti-discrimination policies, and the rising mixed-race populations in these countries, the book ends by examining the most critical question of racial census politics: what is the future of counting by race?

2

Orientation

RACIAL IDEAS IN GLOBAL CONTEXT

For most of its conceptual history, race has been understood as rooted in biology. Phenotypes and morphological characteristics such as skin color, eye shape and size, nose width, and hair texture – what W.E.B. Du Bois called the "grosser physical differences of color, hair and bone"[1] – were the tell-tale signs that distinguished races from one another. In its biological construction, race was considered determinative – one's moral worth and human potential were a corollary of his or her racial identity, and race could account for every type of difference in attitude, ability, and achievement. The calamitous history of race is one of assignment and hierarchy. While the paradigm of biological racialism was far from static or coherent, the rankings of mankind in terms of physical, intellectual, temperamental, behavioral, and moral traits were dependent upon the maintenance of impermeable racial boundaries. Biology, however, was always an insufficient and inaccurate container with which to capture race. It is now generally recognized that race is a social construct, "a concept that signifies and symbolizes socio-political conflicts and interests in reference to different types of human bodies."[2] But, as political theorist Barnor Hesse has warned, the bodily identification of race is just a privileged metonym for a larger idea of the constructed differences between Europeans and non-Europeans, intimately tied to both modernity and

[1] W.E.B Du Bois, *The Conservation of Races*, The American Negro Academy Occasional Papers, No. 2 (Washington D.C.: American Negro Academy, 1897).

[2] Omi and Winant, *Racial Formation*, 55.

colonial rule.[3] In other words, not only are skin color and other physiological characteristics inadequate to delineate between different races, but *their invocation is fundamentally part of the construct itself.*

Following this logic, I suggest that rather than being an indicator of corporeal difference or an objective social fact, race is more like a powerful set of ideas or norms about identity, difference, and the organization of a society and its constituents. At base, ideas are causal beliefs that posit connections between people and things in the world and provide cognitive and normative maps that guide – though do not predetermine – action.[4] Racial ideas, then, are ways of knowing, understanding, perceiving, and interpreting human difference. Deep-seated and so cognitively ingrained that they are often taken for granted, racial ideas reflect understandings of social, political, cultural, and economic environments; provide explanations for social values, forces, and conditions; organize information and knowledge in accordance with historical and cultural circumstance; and masquerade as truth while obscuring the power relations that sustain them. As many scholars acknowledge, race is a distinctively modern idea that emerged over several centuries as a result of the need to create sharp divisions between Europeans and non-Europeans in the Atlantic slave trade, the spread of European colonial rule throughout Africa and Asia, and, eventually, pseudo-scientific racial ideologies of the nineteenth and early twentieth centuries.[5] It is not,

[3] Barnor Hesse, "Racialized Modernity: An Analytics of White Mythologies," *Ethnic and Racial Studies* 30, no. 4 (2007): 643–663; Barnor Hesse, "Self-Fulfilling Prophecy: The Postracial Horizon," *South Atlantic Quarterly* 110, no. 1 (2011):155–178.

[4] Daniel Béland and Robert Henry Cox, "Introduction: Ideas and Politics," in *Ideas and Politics in Social Science Research*, eds. Daniel Béland and Robert Henry Cox (New York: Oxford University Press, 2011), 3–4. See also Grace Skogstad, ed., *Policy Paradigms, Transnationalism, and Domestic Politics* (Toronto: University of Toronto Press, 2011).

[5] See William Stanton, *The Leopard's Spots: Scientific Attitudes towards Race in America, 1815–1859* (Chicago: University of Chicago Press, 1960); Winthrop D. Jordan, *White over Black: American Attitudes toward the Negro, 1550–1812* (Chapel Hill: University of North Carolina Press, 1968); George M. Fredrickson, *The Black Image in the White Mind: The Debate on Afro-American Character and Destiny, 1817–1914* (New York: Harper & Row Publishers, 1971); Stephen J. Gould, *The Mismeasure of Man* (New York and London: W.W. Norton & Company, 1981); Nancy Stepan, *The Idea of Race in Science: Great Britain, 1800–1960* (Oxford: Macmillan, 1982); Elazar Barkan, *The Retreat of Scientific Racism: Changing Concepts of Race in Britain and the United States between the World Wars* (Cambridge: Cambridge University Press, 1992); Robert Young, *Colonial Desire: Hybridity in Theory, Culture and Race* (London and New York: Routledge, 1995); Thomas F. Gossett, *Race: The History of an Idea in America*, new edn (New York: Oxford University Press, 1997); George M. Fredrickson, *Racism: A Short History* (Princeton: Princeton University Press, 2002); Charles Hirschman, "The Origins and Demise of the

however, an autonomous, easily distinguishable, static, or "free-floating" signifier. Race is obstinately embedded in and reproduced by socio-historical contexts, cultural matrices, material forces,[6] and (importantly) political institutions – a point I examine further below. Racial ideas are also normatively engraved with cognitive beliefs that proscribe and regulate behavior, define the parameters of acceptability, and opine about how the world ought to be.[7]

Race is therefore clearly more than supposed biological differences or state-derived modes of classification. It is enveloped in ideas and ideologies about how society should operate and how social order should be maintained, animated through the many and varied practices and relationships of power.[8] Race operates on multiple scales and criss-crossing planes of social signification at the macro-level of social structures, the micro-level experiences of identity formation, and the intersection of gender, class, and sexuality.[9] Any number of focal points can inform

Concept of Race," *Population and Development Review* 30, no. 3 (2004): 385–415; Bruce Baum, *The Rise and Fall of the Caucasian Race: A Political History of Racial Identity* (New York and London: New York University Press, 2006); Audrey Smedley, *Race in North America: Origin and Evolution of a Worldview*, 3rd edn (Boulder: Westview Press, 2007); Marilyn Lake and Henry Reynolds, *Drawing the Global Colour Line: White Men's Countries and the International Challenge of Racial Equality* (Cambridge: Cambridge University Press, 2008); Manfred Berg and Simon Wendt, eds., *Racism in the Modern World: Historical Perspectives on Cultural Transfer and Adaptation* (New York and Oxford: Berghahn Books, 2011).

6 Race is, of course, far more than simply and solely an idea; it is also both constitutive of and created by material and structural social relations. An emphasis on the idea of race must not ignore or minimize the stubborn endurance of racialized power, inequalities, and oppression on national and global scales. See Branwen Gruffydd Jones, "Race in the Ontology of International Order," *Political Studies* 56, no. 4 (2008): 907–927.

7 The precise distinction between "ideas" and "norms" is unclear in the literature. Sheri Berman suggests that a key distinction is tenacity: "While an idea can have a fleeting hold over political actors, it seems nonsensical to talk about norms or culture that do not have staying power. Indeed, norms and culture should be thought of as ideas or beliefs that are institutionalized, persist over time, and, at least in the case of culture, are associated with particular communities." Sheri Berman, "Review: Ideas, Norms, and Culture in Political Analysis," *Comparative Politics* 33, no. 2 (2001): 231–250. Given that racial ideas always have some normative dimension, I use the terms "ideas" and "norms" interchangeably throughout the text.

8 Barbara Fields, "Slavery, Race and Ideology in the United States of America," *New Left Review* 181, no. 1 (1990): 95–118.

9 Omi and Winant, *Racial Formation*; Ange-Marie Hancock, "When Multiplication Doesn't Equal Quick Addition: Examining Intersectionality as a Research Paradigm," *Perspectives on Politics* 5, no. 1 (2007): 63–79; Sumi Cho, Kimberlé Williams Crenshaw, and Leslie McCall, "Toward a Field of Intersectionality Studies: Theory, Applications, and Praxis," *Signs* 38, no. 4 (2013): 785–810.

a person's racial identity, including (but certainly not limited to) bodily appearance, ancestry, self-awareness of ancestry, public awareness of ancestry, culture, experience, subjective identification, and transgressiveness.[10] Racial ideas can be animated through practices that are geographic (global, hemispheric, continental, national, regional, local), relational (diasporic, national, cultural, ethnic, communal, familial), and/or ontological (semantic, discursive, symbolic, textual, visual, programmatic, experiential) in nature.

My analysis emphasizes the ways that racial ideas exist transnationally – within, through, and beyond the nation-state. Race was born in the transnational realm and bred to be central to discourses and realities of nation-building, empire, and the evolution of the global capitalist system. These processes resulted in the creation of a world racial system, in which various geographical, relational, and ontological patterns of racial signification and structure are immersed.[11] A focus on the *roots* of racial ideas, however, is only part of the story. We must also consider, in Paul Gilroy's formulation, the *routes* though which encounters among individuals, ideas, and institutions shift, realign, constitute, and recreate race across space and time.[12] Aiwah Ong writes that the *trans* in transnational denotes "moving through space or across lines, as well as changing the nature of something. Besides suggesting new relations between nation-states and capital, transnationality also alludes to the *trans*versal, the *trans*actional, the *trans*lational, and the *trans*gressive aspects of contemporary behavior and imagination that are incited, enabled, and regulated by the changing logics of states and capitalism."[13] Transnational lenses zoom in on interactions, exchanges, constructions, and translations across borders as well as the significance of different national experiences of the same global phenomenon.[14]

[10] Charles W. Mills, *Blackness Visible: Essays on Philosophy and Race* (Ithaca: Cornell University Press, 1998), 41–66.

[11] Howard Winant, *The New Politics of Race: Globalism, Difference, Justice* (Minneapolis: University of Minnesota Press, 2004).

[12] Paul Gilroy, *The Black Atlantic: Modernity and Double Consciousness* (London and New York: Verso, 1993). See also Iain Chambers and Lidia Curti, eds., *The Post-Colonial Question: Common Skies, Divided Horizons* (London and New York: Routledge, 1996), and Jacqueline Nassy Brown, *Dropping Anchor, Setting Sail: Geographies of Race in Black Liverpool* (Princeton: Princeton University Press, 2005).

[13] Aiwah Ong, *Flexible Citizenship: the Cultural Logics of Transnationality* (Durham: Duke University Press, 1999), 4.

[14] David Thelen, "The Nation and Beyond: Transnational Perspectives on United States History," *Journal of American History* 86, no. 3(1999): 965–975; Nikhil Pal Singh, *Black is a Country: Race and the Unfinished Struggle for Democracy* (Cambridge, MA:

The emphasis here on transnationalism is not meant to be a negation of the nation-state, but is instead the displacement of its assumed primacy. After all, this is a book centrally concerned with examining the role of the state in designing race-based classification systems in comparative context. At their core, censuses are quantitative containers of a national populace and racial taxonomies are designed to abide by domestic specifications. And yet, while racial politics inevitably reflect national circumstances, *the idea of race itself* – whether it is understood as a biological truth or social construct, whether different races should be hierarchically ordered or governed for egalitarian ends – is not bound by national borders. To argue that race is a global phenomenon is simply to highlight one set of practices of social signification (among many others) that have a particularly transnational origin, existence, activation, and effect. Drawing from scholarship on the causal role of ideas in comparative politics and constructivist international relations (IR),[15] I focus on two types of racial ideas that meet these criteria.

First, macro-level racial worldviews cut across a number of substantive policy areas and reside in the taken-for-granted background of political and policy debates. Scholars associated with the "Stanford School" of sociology, for example, argue that cultural scripts that support and legitimate social behaviors are substantially organized on a worldwide basis and nation-states are deeply embedded within this distinct global culture.[16]

Harvard University Press, 2004); Ian Tyrrell, *Transnational Nation: United States History in Global Perspective since 1789* (New York: Palgrave Macmillan, 2007); Micol Seigel, *Uneven Encounters: Making Race and Nation in Brazil and the United States* (Durham and London: Duke University Press, 2009); Gurminder Bhambra, "Historical Sociology, International Relations and Connected Histories," *Cambridge Review of International Affairs* 23, no. 1 (2010): 127–143.

15 Peter A. Hall, ed., *The Political Power of Economic Ideas: Keynesianism across Nations* (Princeton: Princeton University Press, 1989); Jeffrey Checkel, "The Constructivist Turn in International Relations Theory," *World Politics* 50, no. 2(1998): 324–348; Martha Finnemore and Kathryn Sikkink, "International Norm Dynamics and Political Change," *International Organization* 52, no. 4 (1998): 887–917; Sheri Berman, "Review"; Robert C. Lieberman, "Ideas, Institutions, and Political Order: Explaining Political Change," *American Political Science Review* 96, no. 4 (2002): 697–712; Vivien A. Schmidt, "Discursive Institutionalism: The Explanatory Power of Ideas and Discourse," *Annual Review of Political Science* 11(2008): 303–326; Daniel Béland and Robert Henry Cox, eds., *Ideas and Politics in Social Science Research* (Oxford: Oxford University Press, 2011).

16 For overviews, see Martha Finnemore, "Norms, Culture, and World Politics: Insights from Sociology's Institutionalism," *International Organization* 50, no. 2 (1996): 325–347; and John Meyer, John Boli, George M. Thomas, and Francisco O. Ramirez, "World Society and the Nation-State," *American Journal of Sociology* 103, no. 1 (1997): 144–181.

Worldviews about the meaning of race and the nature of racial difference exist rather ubiquitously and can change over time, but can also be made more finite through their internalization in international organizations and processes. Second, worldviews breed meso-level programmatic beliefs, which are considered more systematic, coordinated, and policy-specific ideas that guide programs of action. These ideas are often discussed within and transmitted through international organizations, epistemic communities, and networks of state actors.[17] Racial worldviews inform the legitimate ends of race policies, while programmatic beliefs inform the appropriate means of achieving those ends. Together, these transnational ideas work as a global-level cultural code, providing a range of acceptable options that actors can draw from when making decisions.[18]

Each chapter of this book examines the origins, impacts, and reconstitution of four major shifts in these two types of transnational racial ideas. Chapter 3 considers the nineteenth and early twentieth century debates of the international scientific community, which legitimated – and in some cases challenged – the central tenets of biological racialism that arose from and enabled domestic and international racial projects such as imperialism, colonialism, slavery, and segregation. At the same time, epistemic communities of statisticians advanced the idea that moral statistics could be used to solve pressing social issues and largely agreed that counting by race served compelling state interests. In Chapter 4 I explore the demise of the biological concept of race in the post-war era, which was spurred by a tidal wave of exogenous global events – the Holocaust, decolonization, the burgeoning norm of human rights, the foreign policy debates of the Cold War, and so on. The post-war era was a transnational moment: a brief period of transition, both temporal and temporary, when the normative context surrounding the previously dominant conceptualization of race as irrefutably biological, determinative, and hierarchically ordered fundamentally shifted. Perceptions of democratic legitimacy in the Anglophone West now depended in part on an adherence – at least, officially – to the principles of racial equality. The invalidation of biological racialism raised important pragmatic questions in the newly formed International Statistical Commission of the

[17] Peter M. Haas, "Introduction: Epistemic Communities and International Policy Coordination," *International Organization* 46, no. 1 (1992): 1–35; Anne-Marie Slaughter, *A New World Order* (Princeton: Princeton University Press, 2005).

[18] Thanks to Phil Triadafilopoulos for this insight. See Triadafilos Triadafilopoulos, *Becoming Multicultural: Immigration and the Politics of Membership in Canada and Germany* (Vancouver: University of British Columbia Press, 2012).

United Nations: if race was no longer considered legitimate, were census questions that differentiated among racial groups appropriate? Given the use of racial statistics in service of the sinister state – to locate and transport Jews in Europe to concentration camps, to intern Japanese Americans and Canadians on the west coast of North America – should the enterprise be abandoned?

The transnational ideational shift in Chapter 5 was not of the same magnitude as in previous incarnations. The internationalization of race as a social construction could not be undone, nor could states be as unabashedly white supremacist as they had in the not-so-distant past. Reactions to minority movements of the 1960s and 1970s catalyzed a shift in the *framing* of race rather than its meaning: a change in understandings of "race and" – race and liberalism, race and equality, race and democracy. The "multicultural moment" of the 1980s and 1990s gave credence to the idea that diversity could be a positive and governable attribute of the nation – a community that had most often been associated, at least in the Anglophone West, with racial hegemony. Given technological innovations in the execution of censuses, especially the adoption of self-enumeration and the recognized need for accurate racial data to properly implement anti-discrimination legislation, international epistemic communities of statisticians reconsidered the appropriateness of census questions about race. This time the United Nations Statistical Commission approved the validity of questions on racial or ethnic identity and provided principles and guidelines on how to ask questions, gather accurate data, and tabulate appropriate responses. A few years later, the proceedings of an international conference in 1992 provided the opportunity for transnational networks of state actors to work together to identify, address, and learn from the shared challenges of counting racial identities, which were perceived as increasingly complicated. Finally, in Chapter 6, I call the most recent transnational shift in the framing of race "multiracial multiculturalism," signifying the extent to which mixed-race identities, once considered a problem for census-takers, have become a progressive characteristic of the multicultural nation and a (perhaps misleading) sign of the forthcoming post-racial era.

By envisioning race as a set of ideas or norms, I build on several important studies in political science that explore the role of racial ideologies, themselves often embedded in policy paradigms and institutional orders, in producing political outcomes, most notably in the work of Rogers Smith, Desmond King, Erik Bleich, and Robert

Lieberman.[19] In these accounts, ideological traditions such as white supremacy, illiberalism, ascriptive Americanism, egalitarianism, color-blindness, and race-consciousness, as well as their constitutively embedded expression in racial institutional orders, *include* dominant ideas about the nature of race and racial difference, but are not *reducible* to them. King and Smith define racial institutional orders, which embody white supremacist and/or transformative egalitarian patterns of behavior, as coalitions of state institutions and other political actors/organizations that seek to secure and

> exercise governing power in ways that predictably shape people's statuses, resources, and opportunities by their placement in "racial" categories. The orders rarely originate such categories. But their proponents often modify inherited racial conceptions to attract new supporters while retaining old ones and stigmatizing opponents. ... The shifting ways in which actors in racial orders institutionalize these categories partly constitute persons' senses of racial identity.[20]

Focusing on racial worldviews and transnational programmatic ideas about racial statistics rather than nationally constituted and specified racial ideologies allows us to think through the formulation and reconstitution of *global* racial orders as well as the ways that national racial orders may be compared. Racial ideas – essentially the "racial conceptions" that King and Smith mention in the quotation above – spill over, seep through, defy, extend, challenge, and negate national boundaries. The similarities and differences revealed through structured comparison can thus be complemented by examining the transnational connectivity among the United States, Great Britain, and Canada, which have long and sordid histories of interactions predicated, directly and indirectly, on racial politics.[21] Thinking both through and outside the container of nation and state also highlights important, but often obscured, strands

19 Smith, *Civic Ideals*; Desmond S. King, *In the Name of Liberalism: Illiberal Social Policy in the USA and Britain* (Oxford and New York: Oxford University Press, 1999); Lieberman, "Ideas, Institutions, and Political Order"; Erik Bleich, *Race Politics in Britain and France: Ideas and Policymaking since the 1960s* (New York: Cambridge University Press, 2003); Desmond S. King and Rogers M. Smith, "Racial Orders in American Political Development," *American Political Science Review* 99, no. 1 (2005): 75–92.

20 King and Smith, "Racial Orders," 78–79.

21 Gilroy, *The Black Atlantic*; Sarah-Jane Mathieu, *North of the Color Line: Migration and Black Resistance in Canada, 1870–1955* (Chapel Hill: University of North Carolina Press, 2010); Srdjan Vucetic, *The Anglosphere: A Genealogy of Racialized Identity in International Relations* (Stanford: Stanford University Press, 2011).

within racial orders: national racial categories are created not only by reference to other social categories such as gender, class, ethnicity, and religion, but also from modes of racial categorization in other national contexts; ideas about different racial groups – the hypersexualized black male, the yellow peril, model minorities – are eerily similar across national settings; white supremacy and racial hierarchies exist in plural rather than singular, and resistance to unequal relations of racial power has always found strength in global numbers; and American exceptionalism in race relations – a particularly powerful and consequential idea in both Canada and Britain – is, tragically, not particularly exceptional.

RACIAL PROJECTS AND POLITICAL INSTITUTIONS

Benedict Anderson's *Imagined Communities*, James Scott's *Seeing Like a State*, and Michel Foucault's essay on governmentality theorize that the census is a political institution indispensable to modern statecraft. These totalizing classificatory grids, they argue, are driven by the political motives of appropriation, control, and manipulation and ultimately create populations with the standardized characteristics that can be most easily monitored, counted, assessed, and managed.[22] But why do the lines of the grid change over time? Racial categories on the American census fluctuated considerably throughout the nineteenth century, only stabilizing after 1930. Canada also changed its classification rules for mixed white/non-white people in 1951, though this created inconsistencies in the population counts. After putting its first ethnic question on the census in 1991, the statistical agency in Great Britain undertook a review of its classification schema, making several important changes for the next iteration in 2001. Interestingly, these shifts occurred in a policy area that is innately predisposed toward the status quo.[23] To get comparable data over time, it is necessary to have comparable census categories from one census to the next. Against this backdrop, the particular racial schematics

[22] Benedict Anderson, *Imagined Communities: Reflections on the Origins and Spread of Nationalism*, 2nd edn (London and New York: Verso, 1991), 163–170; Michel Foucault, "Governmentality," in *The Foucault Effect: Studies in Governmentality*, eds. Graham Burchell, Colin Gordon, and Peter Miller (Chicago: University of Chicago Press, 1991), 87–104; Scott, *Seeing Like a State*, 81–82.

[23] Stanley Lieberson, "The Enumeration of Ethnic and Racial Groups in the Census: Some Devilish Principles," in *Challenges of Measuring an Ethnic World: Science, Politics and Reality*, Proceedings of the Joint Canada-United States Conference on the Measurement of Ethnicity, April 1–3, 1992 (Washington D.C.: U.S. Government Printing Office, 1993), 26–27.

of each census in the United States, Canada, and Great Britain are even more peculiar.

These circumstances raise empirical questions about change, stability, and choice: where do racial taxonomies on a particular census come from, and why are some racial categories included while others are not? Racial ideas provide the context and motive for change over time, but do not, on their own, explain the substantive content of shifting racial schematics within a given period of time. The literature on race and the census provides fragmented answers, though all scholars agree with former Census Bureau Director Kenneth Prewitt's postulation that "the categories made explicit in classifications are never politically neutral."[24] In their detailed studies of the race question on the American census, Melissa Nobles, Kim Williams, Alice Robbin, and others suggest that civil rights legislation of the 1960s and 1970s created incentives for racial minorities to be counted and, as a result, census policy outcomes have been shaped by a push-and-pull politics of negotiation and accommodation between state and societal interests.[25] However, Canada and Great Britain effectively aligned their census practices with the United States in the 1990s, decades after passing civil rights legislation and without social mobilization devoted to the cause. In fact, minority and majority factions in these countries have at times been highly suspicious of the state's intentions in its proposal to count by race. Moreover, not all groups that mobilize succeed in attaining official recognition through the census. The Cornish lobby, for example, petitioned unsuccessfully throughout the 1980s and 1990s to be included as an ethnic group on the British census. Nor can social mobilization-centered explanations explain change *in* or *over* time: racial categories in America were unstable long before civil

[24] Kenneth Prewitt, "The U.S. Decennial Census: Politics and Political Science," *Annual Review of Political Science* 13 (2013): 239.

[25] Rainier Spencer, *Spurious Issues: Race and Multiracial Identity Politics in the United States* (Boulder, Colorado: Westview Press, 1999); Nobles, *Shades of Citizenship*; Alice Robbin, "Classifying Racial and Ethnic Group Data in the United States: The Politics of Negotiation and Accommodation," *Journal of Government Information* 27 (2000): 139–156; G. Reginald Daniel, *More than Black? Multiracial Identity and the New Racial Order* (Philadelphia: Temple University Press, 2002); Kimberly McClain DaCosta, "Multiracial Identity: From Personal Problem to Public Issue," in *New Faces in a Changing America: Multiracial Identity in the 21st Century*, eds. Loretta I. Winters and Herman L. DeBose (Thousand Oaks: Sage Publications, 2003), 68–84; Reynolds Farley, "Identifying with Multiple Races: A Social Movement that Succeeded but Failed?" in *The Changing Terrain of Race and Ethnicity*, eds. Maria Krysan and Amanda E. Lewis (New York: Russell Sage Foundation, 2004); Kim Williams, *Mark One or More: Civil Rights in Multiracial America* (Ann Arbor: University of Michigan Press, 2006).

rights incentives, when the "locus of power" over the creation of racial identity categories rested far more with the state than with groups subject to classification.[26]

Explanations that hold in comparative context and over time must take political institutions seriously. The field of American Political Development (APD) does exactly this, contending that political change is not a direct, instrumental, or functional response to social interests, but, rather, occurs within the context of pre-existing institutions and orders. To explain political development, defined as durable shifts in governing authority, APD examines the ways that the entrenchment of institutional arrangements at specific historical moments foreclose otherwise viable alternatives while still paying attention to how those acting within state institutions and in the name of the state make, enforce, and interpret public policy.[27] Jennifer Hochschild and Brenna Marea Powell's analysis of racial categorizations in the American census between 1850 and 1930, for example, demonstrates that officials' choices of categories were driven by three sets of motivations, which interacted in a specific historical context of extraordinary transformations in America's population: contestation between Congress and the bureaucracy over political control of counting; officials' commitments to maintaining the scientific integrity of the census; and ideological beliefs about race held by those with decision-making power.[28] An APD approach reveals a deep and constitutive connection between the development of state-based institutions such as census questions and categories, the evolution of racial ideas and ideologies, and, consequently, the allocation of power and privilege.

Two sets of evolving institutional arrangements have been highly influential in shaping racial categorizations in the three countries under study here. First, racial projects provide the institutional incentives for including or avoiding racial questions and/or specific categories on the census. In their ground-breaking work on racial formation in the United States, Omi and Winant define racial projects as "*simultaneously an interpretation, representation or explanation of racial dynamics, and an effort to*

[26] Kertzer and Arel, "Censuses, Identity Formation, and the Struggle for Political Power."

[27] Karen Orren and Stephen Skowronek, *The Search for American Political Development* (New York: Cambridge University Press, 2004); Joseph E. Lowndes, Julie Novkov, and Dorian Warren, eds., *Race and American Political Development* (New York: Routledge, 2008).

[28] Jennifer L. Hochschild and Brenna Marea Powell, "Racial Reorganization and the United States Census 1850–1930: Mulattoes, Half-Breeds, Mixed Parentage, Hindoos and the Mexican Race," *Studies in American Political Development* 22, no. 1 (2008): 59–96.

reorganize and redistribute resources along particular racial lines."[29] Racial projects link particular discursive meanings of race with ideas about or attempts to organize institutions, policies, and other social structures in accordance with these racial ideas. Conflicts between various racial projects that combine representational/discursive elements with structural/institutional ones result in continuing articulations of the meaning of race on multiple analytical planes, from the individual to the global.[30]

The census itself is a racial project. It codifies ideas about the nature of race and helps solidify the boundaries that encase racial categories, ultimately allowing for the organization of society along racial lines. But it is also informed by other historically situated racial projects, which have their own drivers and dynamics. The racial projects most likely to capture the attention and concern of census officials are, first, the most *predominant* racial projects of a given era and socio-political context. Some projects are so entrenched and pervasive that their effects spill over national borders and continue to shape political outcomes well after the institution itself has met its demise. Influential racial projects will also *create specific institutional, legal, or political incentives* to count by race or to avoid doing so. Not all racial projects are state-driven, but because the mandate of the census is to serve the interests of the government first and foremost, those that are sanctioned and authorized by state power can compel questions on race and specific racial categories. Conversely, racial projects can provide disincentives to count by race, especially when doing so would create institutional conflict. Finally, racial projects that *advocate unique racial schematics* will catch the eye (and sometimes ire) of census officials. Alternative modes of classification, especially those that contradict the official racial schematic endorsed by the census, can tarnish its perceived accuracy and authority.

Racial projects constrain and enable the development of racial census taxonomies by determining the political stakes of racial enumeration. In the era of biological racialism, political elites and census officials drew from three evolving racial projects – slavery and its aftermath, the colonization of indigenous peoples, and race-based immigration restrictions – in their formulation of census classifications. The institution of slavery, undoubtedly the ascendant racial project of the time, made the distinction between black and white the most brightly drawn line the world had ever seen. Counting

[29] Omi and Winant, *Racial Formation*, 56, emphasis in original.

[30] Howard Winant, "Race and Race Theory," *Annual Review of Sociology* 26 (2000): 182.

"Indians not taxed" measured rates of genocidal extermination and paternalistic assimilation, devastating precursors to the appropriation of indigenous lands. As nativist sentiments sparked eugenicist anxiety in the early twentieth century, racial taxonomies normatively and numerically defined the difference between desired and undesired immigrants. In white settler societies such as Canada and the United States, counting, then, was a tool of racial domination. Great Britain, by contrast, was an imperial power and further removed – at least, geographically – from the political consequences of slavery, colonialism, and immigration; while there were certainly racial projects in place during the same period, none incentivized the creation and promotion of racial schematics in the same manner as in the other two cases.

The predominant racial project of the post-war era was the large-scale reformulation of discriminatory laws and policies. In a relatively short time span, racial statistics in the United States became weapons in the struggle for civil rights, first demonstrating the detrimental effects of segregation and then becoming the quantitative cornerstone of the Voting Rights Act and affirmative action programming. Governments in Britain and Canada formulated unique anti-discrimination regimes throughout the 1950s and 1960s as well, but these legislative initiatives did not mandate the collection of racial statistics. By the last two decades of the twentieth century the most consequential racial projects fell under the rubric of diversity governance. Multiculturalism, a widely accepted liberal framework in the Anglophone West, encompasses a range of laws, policies, and discourses designed to provide some level of public recognition, support, or accommodation to minority ethnic, racial, or cultural groups, both "new" (that is, immigrants and refugees) or "old" (national minorities and indigenous peoples).[31] This politics of recognition,[32] combined with evolving protections against racial discrimination that made the need for accurate data more acute, created stronger institutional incentives for Great Britain and Canada to create a direct question on race on their national censuses. As demographic trajectories from new immigration patterns, increased rates of interracial marriage, and a growing awareness of multiracial populations challenged established racial

[31] Will Kymlicka, *Multicultural Odysseys: Navigating the New International Politics of Diversity* (Oxford: Oxford University Press, 2007).

[32] Charles Taylor, "The Politics of Recognition," in *Multiculturalism: Examining the Politics of Recognition*, ed. Amy Gutmann (Princeton: Princeton University Press, 1994), 25–73.

schematics, multicultural paradigms in these cases shifted to incorporate mixed-race identities as a positive, rather than problematic, attribute of diverse societies. At the same time, the belief that we now live in a post-racial era has been used, ironically enough, to insulate systemic racial disparities from criticism or condemnation.

The second set of institutional arrangements structure the relationship between the state and society in the census policy sphere. Degrees of centralization and autonomy, as well as the protocols of census administration, largely determine the structure of the policy network and participants in the policy process.[33] These arrangements have changed substantially over time – census bureaus did not spring, fully formed, from the depths of state-building. The rise of statistical science, spearheaded in the mid-nineteenth century by Adolphe Quetelet of Belgium and William Farr of England, diffused globally and catalyzed the development of state institutions with the specific purpose of collecting and analyzing statistical data. It was decades, however, before statistical agencies were made permanent and could break free of political interference over issues of representation. Over time, the vertical and horizontal organization of statistical systems were arranged and rearranged and lines of accountability drawn and redrawn. Moreover, clear guidelines for conducting censuses did not emerge in the international arena until after the Second World War, and to this day the international community cannot compel standardization in census questions or classifications. Each chapter of this book, therefore, identifies and analyzes the dynamism of institutions alongside the ways they constrain and enable political action at different points in time.

The centralization of authority refers to the concentration or dispersal of decision-making power within a statistical system. The Canadian statistical system is highly centralized. Control rests within the central

[33] I use Marsh and Smith's "dialectical approach" to analyzing policy networks to emphasize the interactive relationships between variables, which occur through processes of strategic learning and compounded causality. David Marsh and Martin Smith, "Understanding Policy Networks: Towards a Dialectical Approach," *Political Studies* 48, no. 1 (2000): 4–21. On policy networks more generally, see also Frank R. Baumgartner and Bryan D. Jones, "Agenda Dynamics and Policy Subsystems," *Journal of Politics* 53, no. 4 (1991): 1044–1074; David Marsh and R.A.W. Rhodes, eds., *Policy Networks in British Government* (Oxford: Clarendon Press, 1992); Paul A. Sabatier, and Hank C. Jenkins-Smith, eds., *Policy Change and Learning: An Advocacy-Coalition Approach* (Boulder: Westview Press, 1993); Grace Skogstad, "Policy Networks and Policy Communities: Conceptualizing State-Societal Relationships in the Policy Process," in *The Comparative Turn in Canadian Political Science*, eds. Linda White, Richard Simeon, Robert Vipond, and Jennifer Wallner (Vancouver: UBC Press, 2008).

statistical office, Statistics Canada (formerly the Dominion Bureau of Statistics), which is governed by a single piece of legislation and is responsible for producing statistics and data for all levels of government. The United States, in contrast, has developed a highly decentralized statistical system, with statistical activities in approximately 129 different agencies in the 2012 fiscal year, fourteen of which have the collection, analysis, and dissemination of statistics as their primary mission.[34] In the 1970s, a small group in the Statistical Policy Branch of the Office of Management and Budget (OMB) was tasked with coordinating this system by establishing standards, classifications, and other guidelines for the administration and operation of statistical activities. Great Britain has a history of decentralized statistical activities that has slowly moved toward a more centralized, but devolved, statistical system. Jurisdiction over the census in England and Wales has moved from the Central Statistical Office, created in 1941 to collect and publish economic statistics related to the war effort, to the Office of Population Censuses and Surveys (OPCS), created in 1970 to manage the censuses and other surveys aimed at individuals and households, and finally to the Office for National Statistics, which merged OPCS and the Central Statistical Office in 1996.[35] In 1998, devolution enabled the Northern Ireland Statistics and Research Agency and the General Register Office for Scotland (now merged with the National Archives of Scotland and renamed the National Records of Scotland in 2011) to create unique racial taxonomies for the censuses of Northern Ireland and Scotland, respectively. Further, as a unitary state, Britain's local authorities are now key participants in census policy decisions because they are often the bodies responsible for delivering government programming. Conversely, in the federalist systems of the United States and Canada, responsibility for the census is a reserved federal power mandated by the constitution,[36] with little state

[34] Janet L. Norwood, *Organizing to Count: Change in the Federal Statistical System* (Washington D.C.: Urban Institute Press, 1995); National Research Council, *Principles and Practices for a Federal Statistical Agency*, 5th edn, eds. Constance F. Citro and Miron L. Straf (Washington D.C.: The National Academies Press, 2013).

[35] John Pullinger, "The Creation of the Office for National Statistics," *International Statistical Review* 65, no. 3(1997): 291–308; Karen Dunnell, "Evolution of the United Kingdom Statistical System," Country Papers on the Evolution of National Statistical Systems, United Nations Statistics Division, 2007, accessed August 15, 2013, http://unstats.un.org/unsd/statcom/statcom_seminar/UK%20paper%20for%20UNSC%20final.pdf

[36] Article 1, section 2 of the American constitution states that "The actual enumeration shall be made within three years after the first meeting of the Congress of the United States, and within every subsequent ten years, in such manner as they shall by law direct." Section 8

or provincial involvement other than through normal consultative channels. This federal-level control helps secure the capacity of the state in these contexts, enabling it to be, paradoxically, a forceful agent of racist repression *and* an anti-discrimination enforcer.[37]

These institutions also have varying degrees of autonomy, defined as the ability of statistical agencies to operate independently of political or other external influences. Impartiality in the development, production, and analysis of statistical data is widely recognized as a fundamental principle of official statistics, key to providing credible, objective, reliable, and accurate information.[38] Of course, statistical agencies can never be wholly independent – as governmental organizations, they are subject to executive and legislative authority, budgetary processes, statutory mandates, and judicial review. Moreover, statistical agencies must adhere to established lines of accountability, largely determined by the system of government. The parliamentary systems of Britain and Canada are executive-dominated with cohesion-inspiring party discipline and a highly secretive state led by elected Ministers and high-level civil servants that are part of the professional, non-partisan public service. The Chief Statistician of Canada is a senior civil servant who holds the rank of Deputy Minister and serves at the pleasure of the executive branch, but is traditionally retained through changes in government.[39] The Chief Statistician reports to the Minister of Industry, but unlike other Deputy Ministers defends Statistics Canada's budget before Parliament and cannot be overruled by the Minister of Industry on issues of confidentiality.[40] In Great Britain the Registrar General, a senior civil servant, directed the execution of the census through numerous changes in institutional venue. The position of an independent National Statistician of the United Kingdom was created in 2000, and

of Canada's Constitution Act of 1867 likewise mandates that a census occur in 1871 and every ten years thereafter. Beginning in 1906, a separate census of agriculture was conducted in the Prairie Provinces every five years, and the tradition of quinquennial national censuses has been in place since 1956.

37 Thanks to an anonymous reviewer for this point.

38 National Research Council, *Principles and Practices*, p. 35–42; United Nations Statistics Division, *Fundamental Principles of Official Statistics*; European Statistical System Committee, *European Statistics Code of Practice for the National and Community Statistical Authorities* (Luxembourg: Eurostat, 2012).

39 For example, Robert H. Coats served as Dominion Statistician from 1918 to 1942, Walter E. Duffett from 1957 to 1972, and Dr. Ivan Fellegi held the position of Chief Statistician from 1985 to 2008 – all through numerous changes in government.

40 United States General Accounting Office, *Statistical Agencies: A Comparison of the United States and Canadian Statistical Systems*, Report to Congressional Requesters, GAO/GGD-96–142 (Washington D.C.: U.S. GAO, 1996), 22.

responsibility for the leadership of ONS was delegated to a new Director-General in 2009 to enhance lines of accountability and safeguard the oversight function of the National Statistician.

In contrast, the presidential system of the United States fragments power between the executive, legislative, and judicial branches, and the weakness of party discipline facilitates pressure group politics. While the Chief Statistician of the OMB is a career civil servant, the Director of the Census Bureau is a presidential appointee who served at the pleasure of the president until 2012; the Director now serves a fixed term of five years, a move that secures more independence from partisan politics. The Director reports to the Secretary of Commerce, another presidential appointee. The Bureau's position within the Department of Commerce and the application of congressional oversight pose problems for its autonomy. Former Director Barbara Bryant complained that as more cities began to sue the federal government over census adjustments in the 1980s and 1990s, the Department of Commerce precipitated a "take over" of the Bureau, which ultimately diminished the Bureau's autonomy.[41] Congressional oversight of the census is mandated by the constitution and there are several examples throughout American history when the census became the target of partisan animosities, especially in the legislature when apportionment formulas were still in flux and census questions had to first be approved by Congress, and later in congressional committees, especially after the 1994 election when polarization reached new heights and debates over census adjustments took a decidedly partisan tenor.[42] In sum, the American presidential system has more veto points and players, which enables more conflict in the design and execution of census policy but also makes the policymaking process more public, potentially transparent, and subject to greater lobby pressure from societal interests. The centralized power of the executive in the parliamentary systems of Canada and Britain creates clearer lines of accountability, but hidden sites of veto power ultimately constrain interest group access to decision-makers and make safeguards of bureaucratic autonomy, especially against the presidential-like power of the executive branch, all the more necessary.

[41] Barbara Bryant and William Dunn, *Moving Power and Money: The Politics of Census Taking* (New York: New York Strategist Publications, 1995), 158–159.

[42] Anderson and Fienberg, *Who Counts?*; Skerry, *Counting on the Census?*; D. Sunshine Hillygus, Norman H. Nie, Kenneth Prewitt, and Heili Pals, *The Hard Count: The Political and Social Challenges of Census Mobilization* (New York: Russell Sage Foundation, 2006).

Finally, protocols of census administration and the feedback effects arising from traditions of racial enumeration can be highly consequential for both the design and execution of the census. Protocols of census administration are the institutional rules, objectives, precedents, and procedures that determine how a census is to be conducted. International epistemic communities such as the International Statistical Commission of the United Nations, Eurostat, and the International Statistical Institute have set forth guidelines for conducting national censuses, which promote the core values of legitimacy and credibility of statistical systems. National-level committees comprised of professional statisticians and other stakeholders also perform important advisory functions, though their purpose and pull vary. By and large, one of the most significant developments in census administration was the shift from government-employed enumerators to self-enumeration in the 1970s, which personalized and politicized the census questions on race as never before. Response burden and other survey-related issues such as response order bias became quite important. Further, as APD research on path dependency and policy feedback has demonstrated, initial institutional choices at particular historical junctures can decisively influence subsequent developmental trajectories.[43] Decisions to include particular stakeholders in the design of census content, for example, cannot be easily reversed. Thus, while minority group representation is institutionalized through a number of advisory committees in the United States, when Britain sought stakeholder input into the design of its ethnic question in the 1990s it could create a policy network of the state's choosing almost from scratch. Particular policy outcomes can also become institutions as they constrain the viability and feasibility of future courses of action. For example, because multiple responses to the ethnic origins question had been accepted on Canadian censuses since 1981, bureaucrats in Statistics Canada understood that demanding a single response to the race question was politically and socially unpalatable.

This focus on the institutional incentives emanating from racial projects and contours of political institutions demonstrates that census policy outcomes are much more than the sum of countervailing pressure from organized groups. Social mobilization is the dominant narrative explaining

[43] Paul Pierson, "Path Dependency, Increasing Returns, and the Study of Politics," *American Political Science Review* 94, no. 2 (2000): 251–267; Paul Pierson, *Politics in Time: History, Institutions, and Social Analysis* (Princeton: Princeton University Press, 2004); B. Guy Peters, Jon Pierre, and Desmond S. King, "The Politics of Path Dependency: Political Conflict in Historical Institutionalism," *Journal of Politics* 67, no. 4 (2005): 1275–1300.

American census politics because of the institutional incentives for racial minorities to be counted and the nature of decentralization and autonomy in the statistical system provide multiple policy venues and access points through which interest groups can influence the policymaking process. Racial projects and institutional arrangements compound to create distinct sets of interests and politics that ultimately motivate individual behavior and political outcomes.

SCHEMATIC CIRCULATION

So far, I have identified two broad sets of factors that contribute to the convergent and divergent outcomes in census politics in the United States, Canada, and Great Britain over time and space: transnational worldviews about the nature of race and programmatic beliefs about the appropriateness of racial statistics as a policy instrument, and domestic-level racial projects that constitute and are constituted by racial concepts and institutions, which determine the participants and structures in the policymaking process. Three larger questions still remain. First, what is the relationship between these factors and how do they interact? What are the mechanisms and processes by which ideas spread and transnational norms affect domestic spheres? Second, what of agency? How do ideas and institutions enable and constrain the behavior, choices, and decisions of political actors? And finally, what happens after ideas and institutions collide? What are the consequences of political decisions in census politics in particular and the politics of race more broadly?

I argue that the state actively mediates between transnational ideas and domestic institutions. Transnational ideas about race operate in the same ways as other "principled ideas," such as human rights, women's suffrage, Keynesianism, environmentalism, and so on. A "first wave" of constructivist IR scholars focused largely on the spread of these kinds of norms and their influence on state behavior in the world system.[44] But transnational norms are not always adopted in domestic contexts. The International Covenant on Economic, Social, and Cultural Rights, for example, has

[44] Andrew P. Cortell and James W. Davis, "How Do International Institutions Matter? The Domestic Impact of International Rules and Norms," *International Studies Quarterly* 40, no. 4 (2000): 451–478; Amitav Acharya, "How Ideas Spread: Whose Norms Matter? Norm Localization and Institutional Change in Asian Regionalism," *International Organization* 58, no. 2 (2004): 239–275. Examples of this "first wave" include Finnemore, "Norms, Culture, and World Politics," and Finnemore and Sikkink, "International Norm Dynamics."

been signed and ratified by most of the world's nations, but the domestic institutionalization of the right to an adequate standard of living, universal health care, and education is more unlikely now than it was in 1966 when the treaty was signed by the United Nations General Assembly. When domestic actors do draw from transnational ideas, outputs are rarely emulated blindly and completely. Norms are often modified to fit with existing social orders. As a "second wave" of scholars interested in policy diffusion argues, domestic circumstances affect whether, when, and how governments accept ideational transfers from abroad.[45] By "actively mediates," then, I mean that the state is a primary, though not exclusive, medium through which transnational racial ideas and programmatic beliefs are transferred to domestic spheres.

Racial ideas are mediated, filtered, obstructed, or refracted through two interpretive processes. Cultural translation is the process through which actors create congruence between transnational and domestic norms. Checkel argues that a norm's "cultural match" is the degree to which international norms resonate with domestic norms; if in place, this will make norm diffusion more rapid.[46] The process of creating cultural congruence is an interpretive exercise – actors can make norms appear congruent by discursively aligning transnational racial ideas and "national cultural repertoires," which frame the ways that citizens and policymakers in each country conceptualize and comprehend race as a political category and conceive of rational solutions to problems of racial conflict and inequality.[47] Institutional translation is the process through which actors localize programmatic beliefs by incorporating them into domestic institutional orders. Acharya argues that localization is not simply a matter of changing institutional practices and behaviors to make them consistent with external ideas;[48] rather, it is a process through which local agents use their power and position to adapt programmatic beliefs of international epistemic communities to meet and mesh with local institutional practices. In either form of translation, domestic-level actors learn from the experiences and experiments of policymakers in other countries, rationally rejecting wholesale policy emulation and

[45] David Marsh and J.C. Sharman, "Policy Diffusion and Policy Transfer," *Policy Studies* 30, no. 3 (2009): 279; Kelly Kollman, "Same Sex Unions: The Globalization of an Idea," *International Studies Quarterly* 51 (2007): 329–357.

[46] Jeffrey Checkel, "Norms, Institutions and National Identity in Contemporary Europe," *International Studies Quarterly* 43, no. 1 (1999): 84–114.

[47] Lieberman, "Ideas, Institutions, and Political Order," 156.

[48] Acharya, "How Ideas Spread," 251.

instead excluding certain elements of transnational ideas that might harm the existing social or political order and adapting other aspects that may be more effective in specific national contexts.[49] Given that the conceptual and political terrain of race politics is full of landmines, these translative processes do not inevitably lead to policy change. Formidable obstacles may exist; even with support from powerful actors, ideas constantly run the risk of blockage as they traverse political arenas.

The success of cultural translation depends in part on the characteristics of the norm itself. Not all transnational ideas about race readily resonate with domestic racial ideas. In particular, where there are strong racial norms in the domestic sphere that directly contradict a transnational norm, norm displacement – when a foreign or transnational norm replaces a local norm whose moral claim or functional adequacy has already been challenged by domestic actors[50] – will probably fail. France's ardent republicanism once again makes a striking example of a strong identity norm that is not easily displaced. Though norms can be altered to be made more palatable to domestic audiences, transnational norms must at least have the *potential* to be localized. For example, the histories of slavery, the mass transfer of indigenous populations and programs of aboriginal assimilation, and the status of white settler societies in North America helped create aspects of the transnational norm of biological racialism and therefore made the process of adapting the norm to suit domestic ideational orders less arduous. Though race-making is an inherently contentious process – localization is far more easily written about than done – the ideational distance separating transnational conceptualizations of race and domestic racial projects matters. Similar racial impetuses can create coherency and therefore enable transnational norms to augment, alter, or justify domestic practices; ideational conflict can have the opposite effect.

The success of institutional translation depends on the venues in which the norm operates. Programmatic beliefs incubated in international epistemic communities are more likely to be influential when there are fewer veto points in domestic institutional settings. The institutional positions of local agents that seek to adopt, adapt, or obstruct these programmatic ideas, also determined by the degrees of institutional autonomy and centralization as well as the administrative protocols of census design and execution, can enhance or constrain their credibility in so doing. The debate in the international epistemic community of statisticians in

[49] Ibid., 245.
[50] Ibid., 247.

the aftermath of the Second World War that questioned the appropriateness of collecting racial statistics were, for example, far more influential in Canada than the United States because of important institutional factors: Canada's Dominion Bureau of Statistics was centralized and the Dominion Statistician, Herbert Marshall, held a great deal of sway with political elites when it came to decisions about the census; the statistical system of the United States was far more decentralized and comparatively less autonomous; a stronger civil rights regime in the United States also mandated the continued collection of racial data. And, as Britain's bureaucrats discovered when they were blocked from collecting racial data in the late 1960s by political elites, institutional translation is only possible when the policy options derived from programmatic beliefs are a politically and administratively viable course of action.[51]

Policy trajectories can appear more (or less) viable depending on how transnational ideas are framed by local actors during the processes of institutional and cultural translation. By framing a transnational norm in more local terms, actors can construct linkages that may not otherwise be immediately apparent, or dislodge selected elements from a larger norm in order to specify which lessons are to be drawn and which should be discarded. Just as anti-apartheid campaigners in America used the discourse of the civil rights movement to draw linkages between these different struggles for racial equality,[52] civil rights organizations referenced South Africa's decimated apartheid regime to illustrate the dangers of institutionalizing a mixed-race category in the 2000 American census. Framing can be a means of providing coherency to an unstable norm or its fluctuating elements. In Great Britain, political elites changed their tune about the political difficulties of counting by race in the mid-1980s, instead framing the proposed addition of a census question as a positive development that would make Britain's anti-discrimination regime more robust. Of course, not all translations find a receptive audience. Policymakers are the key transmitters and translators of these ideas, but are situated within policy networks and other institutional structures that can facilitate or constrain strategic action. Even after the Canadian parliament passed the Employment Equity Act in 1986, which required more accurate racial data to be effectively implemented, an influential interdepartmental working group of bureaucrats still could not persuade political elites to add

[51] Peter Hall, "Conclusion," in *The Political Power of Economic Ideas: Keynesianism Across Nations*, ed. Peter Hall (Princeton: Princeton University Press, 1989), 369–375.

[52] Klotz, *Norms in International Relations*.

a question on race. When internal protocols of census administration created unexpected policy contingencies that necessitated the question be added, the Chief Statistician went to great lengths to disassociate the "population group" question from the terminology of race, which conflicted with the race-free ideal of Canadian multiculturalism.

This approach bridges the literatures on norm diffusion and policy learning over the terrain of the comparative and longitudinal empirics of census politics, illuminating both the underscored role of agency and the range of possible outcomes that lie between the acceptance and rejection of norms. New and different ideas drive policy change as policymakers look to their peers to diminish uncertainty surrounding the effectiveness or legitimacy of a particular course of action. Change cannot occur without ideational entrepreneurs,[53] who operate in a dialectical relationship with the structures that provide the context these agents must act within. Through their actions, agents interpret and change the structures themselves. In an iterative, spiral-like process,[54] these new structures provide the altered context in which agents again must act. If their efforts are successful, the subsequent policies are more often mimicked than mirrored; through deliberation, bargaining, and persuasion, actors frame racial worldviews and statistical programmatic beliefs to suit their interests and navigate their national contexts. The diffusion of transnational norms and the lessons drawn from abroad are partial and not always positive. Whereas the literature on policy diffusion focuses largely on cases in which it is possible to trace policy emulation and learning,[55] the political development of racial questions and categories on national censuses over time and space provides examples of both policy convergence and divergence, lessons drawn as exemplary and heeded as warnings. There is no one master process of policy diffusion. What is clear, however, is that the characteristically uncoordinated national policy choices in different places are formulated through interdependent – rather than independent or isolated – processes.[56]

[53] Peters, Pierre, and King, "The Politics of Path Dependency," 1284.

[54] Rogers M. Smith, *Political Peoplehood: The Roles of Values, Interests, and Identities* (Chicago: University of Chicago Press, 2015).

[55] Christoph Knill, "Introduction: Cross-National Policy Convergence: Concepts, Approaches and Explanatory Factors," *Journal of European Public Policy* 12, no. 5 (2005): 764–774; Marsh and Sharman, "Policy Diffusion and Policy Transfer."

[56] David P. Dolowitz and David Marsh, "Learning from Abroad: The Role of Policy Transfer in Contemporary Policy-Making," *Governance* 13, no. 1 (2000): 5–24; Beth A.

This interdependent relationship between transnational and domestic arenas does not simply cease once racial ideas are made legible. In standard accounts of norm diffusion and policy learning, the life-cycle of a norm ends after its internalization in domestic politics when it attains a taken-for-granted quality.[57] An institutionalized norm is assumed to become immortal, synonymous with common sense, unless it erodes because of a lack of central enforcement authority or punishment of non-compliance when the norm is violated,[58] or it simply dies quietly when alternative norms are championed by new entrepreneurs in another iteration of this process. The effects of a localized norm are presumed to stay local over time,[59] unless these circumstances themselves become the subject that other actors apply to their own domestic situations through policy learning or emulation. In either case, local norms are assumed to be static when they are "repatriated" back to the global world.[60]

Racial ideas, however, are anything but static. The translation and modification of transnational racial ideas in domestic policy reverberate not just in other domestic contexts as policymakers learn from the choices of others, but also develop a renaissance – literally, a rebirth – of the very concept of race in the global realm. Global ideas about race are tenacious but dynamic, changing over time precisely because of their translations in domestic racial projects. The demand for new norms when old rules are questioned, or when a normative contagion spreads, can occur at both domestic and global levels. In this part of the process, local agents are powerful as they actively appropriate, interpret, and adapt racial worldviews and programmatic beliefs, and domestic outcomes are influential as their effects diffuse *upwards*.

Simmons and Zachary Elkins, "The Globalization of Liberalization: Policy Diffusion in the International Political Economy," *American Political Science Review* 98, no. 1 (2004): 171–189; Beth A. Simmons, Frank Dobbin, and Geoffrey Garrett, "Introduction: The International Diffusion of Liberalism," *International Organization* 60 (2006): 781–810; Frank Dobbin, Beth A. Simmons, and Geoffrey Garrett, "The Global Diffusion of Public Policies: Social Construction, Coercion, Competition, or Learning?" *Annual Review of Sociology* 33 (2007): 449–472; Charles R. Shipan and Craig Volden, "The Mechanisms of Policy Diffusion," *American Journal of Political Science* 52, no. 4 (2008): 840–857.

[57] Finnemore and Sikkink, "International Norm Dynamics."

[58] Diana Panke and Ulrich Petersohn, "Why International Norms Disappear Sometimes," *European Journal of International Relations* 18, no. 4 (2012): 719–742.

[59] Acharya, "How Ideas Spread," 253.

[60] Arjun Appadurai, *Modernity at Large: Cultural Dimensions of Globalization* (Minneapolis: University of Minnesota Press, 1996).

The relative influence of domestic developments is geographically "lumpy,"[61] and temporally tendrillar. The biological construction of race endured for several centuries before being shattered beyond repair or salvation in a comparatively short time frame. The development of multicultural discourse and the fallaciously heralded absolution of the post-racial era quickly followed, though each period substantially overlaps with its predecessor and successor. The weight of race is not borne equally across the globe, and therefore the effects of racial projects are geopolitically uneven. In models of policy learning, psychological and cultural proximity can be powerful triggers of learning and emulation, because "countries that see themselves as members of subglobal groupings based on history, culture, language, level of development, or geography may copy one another's policies because they infer that what works for a peer will work for them."[62] This logic applies to the cases of this study during the process of active mediation, as policymakers and social actors often turned to their counterparts in other countries to observe how their peer group (re)acted given similar situations or policy goals.

The process of transforming of global racial ideas is disproportionately dispersed and far less discernible. The United States is a hegemonic exemplar of race relations, for better and for worse. As Goldberg writes, "racial americanization projects itself as *the* model, the one to be emulated, the failure of which bears more significant costs than in each of the other, if related, instances."[63] The American civil rights movement demonstrated both the explosive dangers of racial segregation once an oppressed group begins to challenge established racial orders and the promise that anti-discrimination policy was politically and pragmatically viable – even in a deeply segregated society. In census politics, political elites in Great Britain and Canada cautiously bore witness to these events and concluded that an institutional emphasis on race in a forum such as the census would negatively affect social cohesion, ultimately choosing to avoid counting by race to reduce the political salience of a concept they felt was overly divisive. Other circumstances have simply caught and held the world's attention because of extraordinary events, leaders, politics, tragedies, or timing – as I write this orientation the world continues to mourn Nelson Mandela, who unrepentantly fought to end apartheid in South Africa.

[61] Frederick Cooper, "What Is the Concept of Globalization Good For? An African Historian's Perspective," *African Affairs* 100 (2001): 189–213.

[62] Dobbin, Simmons, and Garrett, "The Global Diffusion of Public Policies," 462.

[63] Goldberg, *The Threat of Race*, 68.

While domestic social movements have thus been important (though not causally parsimonious) in the development of American racial taxonomies in the late twentieth and early twenty-first centuries, Canada and Great Britain did not need social movements to push for racial questions or multiracial categories – *the conceptual work had already been done, leaving an altered transnational racial norm in its wake.*

Racial ideas reflect and reconstitute local, regional, and national conditions as well as globally textured forms of domination in the world racial system, modes of resistance, and flows of diasporic consciousness. Forged through interactions that are simultaneously local and global, racial worldviews travel across time and space, changing in the process of their circumnavigation.

3

Transnational Biological Racialism

In 1844, census enumerators set out to count the population of the two newly united provinces of the Dominion of Canada. It was a logistical nightmare. With no centralized authority to oversee the execution of the census, responsibility fell to localities. Municipal assessors were given the census schedules in the dead of winter and were to deliver two sworn copies of their returns to the warden or mayor, who was in turn to pass the results on to the governor – though there was no set time limit on the assessors' duties. Rural areas of present-day Quebec lacked the municipal administrative machinery to appoint and pay assessors, and many viewed the census as a mechanism of taxation that further exploited those already burdened by dîme and seigneurial rents. Even more confusing were the ambiguous columns on the schedule itself, labeled "persons of colour" ("*personnes de couleur*"). For whites, the space was to be left blank; that much was clear. Blacks could also be counted by using the letter "b" – an important distinction, particularly in keeping track of Canada's former slave population, which had been freed just ten years earlier, and the increasing influx of black American refugees. One census commissioner complained that the census form failed to differentiate between "full-blooded blacks" and "mulattoes" – yet another important demarcation. In a continent defined by a black–white dualism, it was also unclear on which side of the dividing line aboriginals fell. The commissioner went on to lament: "and as for the poor savages, the primitive children of the earth, we have great difficulty in knowing what to do with them. What corner shall we put them in? This is a prickly question. Shall we blacken their faces and line them up in the 39th and 40th columns, among 'people of colour'?"[1]

That different races existed was a matter of common sense. The precise meaning of "race," however, was a different story.[2] During the nineteenth century an entire body of scientific thought arose to explain the nature of racial differences and develop the most accurate classification system of the human species.[3] Importantly, biology was perceived to be determinative – though it was always unclear how, exactly, somatic differences such as skin color, eye shape, and hair texture worked to dictate human nature. F. James Davis argues that the ideology of biological racialism consists of five key beliefs, all of which scientists now generally agree to be false: (1) some races are physically superior to others and can be ranked from strongest to weakest based on differences in longevity and rates of selected diseases; (2) some races are mentally superior to others and can be ranked from most to least intelligent; (3) race causes culture, to the extent that each race's distinct culture is genetically transmitted along with physical traits; (4) race determines temperamental dispositions and behaviors of individuals within racial groups; and (5) racial mixing lowers the biological quality of all.[4]

This chapter explores the ways that these composite racial ideas were embedded in national imaginaries by and through the census. Racial worldviews of the nineteenth and early twentieth century were incredibly complex, encompassing beliefs in immutable biological differences among races alongside conceptualizations of the nature of civilization, democracy, capitalism, morality, and the natural social order, all masked by a language that equated scientific rationalism with truth. The scientific revolution was also a catalyst in the international rise of statistics and an emerging broader interest in the "science of society" throughout the

1 Bruce Curtis, *The Politics of Population: State Formation, Statistics, and the Census of Canada, 1840–1875* (Toronto: University of Toronto Press, 2001), 55–64, quotation on p. 60.

2 There is some debate as to when, exactly, the concept of race came into being. George Fredrickson argues that the modern concept of race was not invented until the eighteenth century. In contrast, Bruce Baum's history of the Caucasian race suggests that the basic idea of racial differences was fairly well established by the late seventeenth century. Fredrickson, *Racism*; Baum, *Rise and Fall.*

3 See Stanton, *The Leopard's Spots*; Jordan, *White over Black*; Fredrickson, *The Black Image*; Gould, *The Mismeasure of Man*; Stepan, *The Idea of Race*; Barkan, *The Retreat of Scientific Racism*; Young, *Colonial Desire*; Gossett, *Race*; Hirschman, "The Origins and Demise"; Baum, *Rise and Fall*; Smedley, *Race in North America.*

4 F. James Davis, *Who Is Black? One Nation's Definition* (University Park: Pennsylvania State University Press, 1991), 23–25.

nineteenth century. The transnational trend began with European imperial powers – France, Belgium, England – and soon extended throughout Europe, its colonies, and North America. Statistical societies sprung up at both national and international levels. Census administrators had access to new ideas, drew lessons from elsewhere and in turn saw their innovations molded to fit other contexts.[5] State institutions with the specific purpose of collecting and analyzing statistical data consolidated, and these data began to be used to formulate public policy and to shape national imaginaries. Importantly, statistics also proved useful to study pressing social problems – disease, public health, deviancy, crime, education, poverty, and particularly in North America, racial difference.[6]

It is no coincidence that biological racialism, the institutionalization of a routinized census, and the development and internationalization of statistical science occurred simultaneously. All were central to the building of the nation and the state. By the middle of the nineteenth century, the purpose of the census had transformed from an instrument of representation to an instrument of knowledge.[7] Therein, *racial knowledge* was both given and taken. Race figured predominately in the sectarian and federal politics of representation and the politics of re-presentation, a glossing of individuals into aggregate form through the articulation of supposedly inalienable social divisions. Note, too, that all were part of wider global trends, with origins and reverberations beyond any one nation-state. For

[5] For example, Patriarca examines how the traditions of German academic statistics and the experiences of the governments established during the French occupation of Italy during the Napoleonic war provided important models for the development of Italian state statistics in the first half of the nineteenth century. Silvana Patriarca, *Numbers and Nationhood: Writing Statistics in Nineteenth-Century Italy* (Cambridge: Cambridge University Press, 1996).

[6] On the history of statistics and the rise of statistical knowledge, see Patricia Cline Cohen, *A Calculating People: The Spread of Numeracy in Early America* (Chicago: University of Chicago Press, 1982); Theodore M. Porter, *The Rise of Statistical Thinking, 1820–1900* (Princeton: Princeton University Press, 1986); Stephen M. Stigler, *The History of Statistics: The Measurement of Uncertainty before 1900* (Cambridge: Harvard University Press, 1986); Paul Starr, "The Sociology of Official Statistics," in *The Politics of Numbers*, eds. William Alonso and Paul Starr (New York: Russell Sage Foundation, 1987): 7–58; Stuart Woolf, "Statistics and the Modern State," *Comparative Studies in Society and History* 31, no. 3 (1989): 588–604; Ian Hacking, *The Taming of Chance* (Cambridge: Cambridge University Press, 1990); and Libby Schweber, *Disciplining Statistics: Demography and Vital Statistics in France and England, 1830–1885* (Durham and London: Duke University Press, 2006).

[7] Richard Saumarez Smith, "Rule-by-Records and Rule-by-Reports: Complementary Aspects of the British Imperial Rule of Law," *Contributions to Indian Sociology* 19 (1985): 166.

much of this transnational history, the state dictated racial classifications and invoked race in its policies and laws in order to dominate, banish, manage, control, expunge, segregate, eliminate, and exclude non-white populations from the social fabric of Western societies. In census politics, this amounts to the first of Rallu, Piché, and Simon's four governmental approaches to racial enumeration, whereby counting by race is used to dominate and maintain control over racialized populations.[8]

These wider global trends led to several important similarities in the nineteenth- and early-twentieth-century censuses of Canada and the United States. First, the census was an effort on behalf of the state to police whiteness, racial boundaries, and biological racialism with classification schemas designed to maintain racial hierarchies. Second, this effort coincided with and was compounded by racial projects of the state housed in other areas of law and policy; as such, the classifications used in the census were closely related to debates surrounding slavery, reconstruction, colonialism, nation-building, eugenics, progressivism, and the like. Third, in the racial project of the census and its counterparts, mixed-race was perceived as problematic, necessitating even further management above and beyond that provided for "pure" races. Finally, these multiple racial projects were not a coherent or rational policy regime, but were instead messy, contradictory, and extraordinarily regulated aspects of the many different moving parts of the evolving schematic state.

However, there are also striking differences. The tradition of counting the British population in a census also dates back over two hundred years, but Britain did not include a question on race until the late twentieth century.[9] Why did Britain not use its census to manage and control, as the other cases did? And why did racial categories and classification rules vary not simply between countries, but also from census to census within a particular country? I argue that these differences are the result of the collisions of transnational biological racialism, the institutional evolution of statistical agencies, and the racial projects of the schematic state put in place alongside the census. Among the most important are: debates over slavery and the politics of representation; the colonial project and the international rise of statistical science; and immigration and the quest for bureaucratic autonomy.

[8] Rallu et al., "Démographie et Ethnicité."

[9] Between 1841 and 1961 (excluding 1941, in which Great Britain did not conduct a decennial census) the census included a question on nationality. In 1841 this question pertained only to persons born in Scotland or Ireland, while the years between 1851 and 1891 contained a question as to whether or not the respondent was a British subject.

SLAVERY AND REPRESENTATION

The creation of the modern ideology of race did not coincide perfectly with the emergence of the transatlantic slave trade; it took far longer to become systematic.[10] As slavery became exclusively black, white majoritarian societies began to develop their own peculiar formulations of racial ideology, thereby shaping the contours of transnational biological racialism and providing a means of explaining, rationalizing, and justifying transatlantic slavery and European imperialism. By the middle of the nineteenth century, race was a hotly contested topic of debate among scientists around the world. Conflict reigned over consensus. Monogenists such as the French physician François Bernier and naturalist Georges Buffon, Britain's Johann Blumenbach and James Pritchard, and America's Samuel Stanhope Smith argued that all races of man were the same species, had a common historical ancestry, and differences in skin color, anatomy, temperament, intelligence, and morality could be attributed to different physical and social environments. Conversely, polygenists such as Sir William Lawrence and George Gliddon in Great Britain, Georges Cuvier and Joseph Arthur de Gobineau in France, and Samuel Morton, Louis Agassiz, and Josiah Nott in the United States believed that the various races were, in fact, different species, racial hierarchies were natural, and racial hybrids degenerate.[11] Of course, these scientific debates did not occur in an ideational vacuum. Scientists' interest in race and racial classification was informed by the political, cultural and social discourses of their time, just as their theories were often transported into political debates over conquest, colonization, slavery, and citizenship. For example, in his 1839 study *Crania Americana*,

[10] Fields, "Slavery, Race, and Ideology," 106.

[11] Samuel Morton, *Crania Americana; Or, a Comparative View of the Skulls of Various Aboriginal Nations of North and South America: To which is Prefixed an Essay on the Varieties of the Human Species* (Philadelphia: J. Dobson, 1839); Josiah C. Nott, "Diversity of the Human Race," *Debow's Review* 10, no. 2 (1851): 113–132; Louis Agassiz, "Sketch of the Natural Provinces of the Animal World and Their Relation to the Different Types of Man," in *Types of Mankind: Or, Ethnological Researches, Based upon the Ancient Monuments, Paintings, Sculptures, and Crania of Races, and upon their Natural, Geographical, Philological, and Biblical History*, eds. J. Nott and G. Gliddon (Philadelphia: Lippincott, Grambo, 1854); Josiah C. Nott and G.R. Gliddon, *Types of Mankind: or, Ethnological Researches, Based upon the Ancient Monuments, Paintings, Sculptures, and Crania of Races, and upon Their Natural, Geographical, Philological, and Biblical History* (Philadelphia: Lippincott, Grambo, 1854); Joseph Arthur de Gobineau, *The Moral and Intellectual Diversity of Races, with Particular Reference to Their Respective Influence in the Civil and Political History of Mankind* (Philadelphia: J.B. Lippincott, 1856).

Samuel Morton introduced how quantitative measurement could be used to estimate the average "cranial capacity" or "ingenuity" of different races by measuring the volume of skulls – a technique he used to demonstrate the natural inferiority of blacks. His research, along with Nott and Gliddon's *Types of Mankind*, provided the South with a scientific theory that was respectable, transportable, and could be used to rationalize slavery. Even among abolitionists, references to the science of race supported the view that those of African descent were essentially inferior to whites.[12]

The transatlantic slave trade and slavery in North America put issues of personhood and the limits of democratic citizenship squarely on the table. How could burgeoning democracies reconcile slavery with the rule of law and the natural rights? Racial ideology provided a means of justifying slavery within republics founded on doctrines of liberty, becoming a more systematic and more powerful explanation once the distinction between those who were free and those who were not became clearer after the demise of indentured servitude.[13] Put quite simply, "Euro-Americans resolved the contradiction between slavery and liberty by defining Afro-Americans as a race."[14] Slavery also had to be reconciled with other modicums of democratic rule, including whether slaves should be included for purposes of taxation, trade, defense, and, importantly, representation. Political contention over these issues complicated the early attempts to administer censuses in the nineteenth century, which were programmatically haphazard and logistically difficult. Though the data were often faulty, census classifications and tabulations were integral to the institutional edifice of slavery, disenfranchisement and segregation, identifying, labelling, binding, and constituting the categorical bases for biological racialism within and between racial states.

United States

Biological racialism, representation, and the census were uniquely intertwined in the United States, not because of the existence of slavery – many of the northern states abolished slavery well before Canada, which only did so along with the rest of the British Empire in 1833 – but, rather, because

[12] Mason I. Lowance, Jr., *A House Divided: The Antebellum Slavery Debates in America, 1776–1865* (Princeton and Oxford: Princeton University Press, 2003).

[13] Fields, "Slavery, Race, and Ideology," 114.

[14] Ibid. See also Barnor Hesse, "Escaping Liberty: Western Hegemony, Black Fugitivity," *Political Theory* 42, no. 3 (2014): 288–313.

representation was institutionally linked to slavery in the American constitution. Census categories between 1790 and 1840 were largely concerned with distinguishing free persons (including free colored persons and all other free persons except Indians not taxed) and slaves because of the infamous "three-fifths compromise." The compromise was an agreement reached at the Constitutional Convention of 1787, which stipulated that for purposes of the apportionment of congressional seats, each slave would be counted as three-fifths of a person. James Madison noted at the time that the inherent contradiction of the compromise was that slaves were considered to be property in some contexts but as persons in others: "[T]he Federal Constitution therefore, decides with great propriety on the case of our slaves, when it views them in the mixt character of persons and property. This is in fact their true character."[15] According to the 1790 Census, there were 694,280 slaves in the United States, nearly 18 percent of the entire population.

In these early first decades of the census, the task of counting the population and filing census returns fell to the marshals, who followed the instructions provided by the Secretary of State after Congress determined the content of the questionnaire each decade. By the time of the fourth decennial census in 1820, it was possible to derive patterns of population growth by comparing the results of one census to another. This was of particular interest to Congress because westward expansion disrupted the relative equilibrium between northern and southern states – free and slave states – as more states joined the union. Congress asked the Secretary of State, John Quincy Adams, to collect more information, and in 1820 the census required the sex and age of the slave and free black populations as well as occupational and social details on the unnaturalized foreign population.[16] The question on race, however, was not legally required. Whether one was free or slave was salient for congressional apportionment, and though slavery was increasingly linked to race by the early nineteenth century,[17] counting by race in the census was not mandated by the same constitutional logic. Melissa Nobles contends that

[15] Quoted in Jordan, *White Over Black*, 323.

[16] Margo J. Anderson, *The American Census: A Social History* (New Haven: Yale University Press, 1988), 23.

[17] The labor pool in British colonies of North America was originally comprised of both slaves imported from Africa and white indentured servants, often from Great Britain. The long process by which slavery became exclusively black is explored in Jordan, *White over Black*; Gossett, *Race*; Fredrickson, *The Black Image*; Smith, *Civic Ideals*; and Smedley, *Race in North America*.

the census contained racial distinctions because race was a salient political and social category. Further, racial identification mattered because citizenship status often depended on it – to be free and white and to be free and black were two entirely different political experiences.[18]

In accordance with global programmatic beliefs about census-taking at the time, the 1840 Census marked "the beginning of a concerted effort to make the decennial enumeration the instrument for ascertaining something beyond the mere number of persons of each sex and of various ages constituting each of the three great divisions of the population."[19] Yet, efforts to expand the scope of the census were not entirely successful. In 1843, the American Statistical Association filed a report before Congress that "various and gross errors" had been found.[20] Many of these inconsistencies highlighted popular conceptions about the contentious relationship between freedom and race. For example, when the results of the 1840 Census showed that there was a higher rate of insanity among free blacks than those who were enslaved, Southern representatives in Congress used this information to speak of the clear benefits of slavery. The criticisms of the American Statistical Association, physicians, and politicians, however, revealed that on some census returns the number of insane black people equaled the number of townspeople, and in other cases insane black people were counted in towns where no black people lived. Controversy ensued and, despite several attempts led by John Quincy Adams of Massachusetts to determine the validity of the census, the results stood.[21]

After the fiasco of the 1840 Census, a small group of intellectuals, including American Statistical Association President Edward Jarvis, pressed for the institutional reform of census administration. Between 1790 and 1840 the census was carried out by temporary organizations that were disbanded shortly after the tabulations were complete; it was Congress that determined the question content of the schedules. The distribution of seats in the House was also allocated *after* census data were published, with obvious consequences. Those who stood to lose their seats argued for an apportionment formula that would better suit their interests. The institutional apparatus was strengthened

[18] Nobles, *Shades of Citizenship*, 26–28; see also Smith, *Civic Ideals*.

[19] Carroll D. Wright and William O. Hunt, *The History and Growth of the United States Census* (Washington D.C.: Government Printing Office, 1900), 36.

[20] House Reports, Twenty-Eighth Congress, first session, Vol. III no. 580.

[21] Nobles, *Shades of Citizenship*, 33–35.

in March 1849 when Congress created a Census Board comprised of the Secretaries of State and Interior and the Postmaster General. The amended census bill made the census a permanent and automatic enterprise – future censuses would occur as scheduled unless Congress legislated otherwise – and the apportionment method and House size were to be set before the census was conducted.[22] The first superintendent of the Census Office, Joseph C.G. Kennedy, was a patronage appointment of Whig President Zachery Taylor. Kennedy took his position seriously and was intrigued by the conceptualization of "moral statistics" being developed throughout Europe. He conversed with social statistics pioneer Adolphe Quetelet at the World's Exhibition in London in 1851 and helped to organize the first International Statistical Congress, held in Brussels in 1853, bringing back the lessons he learned from this growing international statistical community to the United States.[23] The problems associated with the 1840 Census made political elites more amenable to allowing outside opinions on the inner machinery of census administration, and for the first time statistics experts were consulted on the census design process. The scope of the 1850 Census was much larger than for previous censuses and included six separate schedules on the free population, slave population, mortality, agriculture, manufacturing, and social statistics. A special enumeration of all Native Americans (and not simply "Indians Taxed") was included. This was also the first census where the individual, rather than the household, was the unit of analysis.

By the middle of the nineteenth century, both pro-slavery advocates and abolitionists were interested in what potential census data held for bolstering their opposing positions and maneuvered accordingly when debating the questions that were proposed for the slave schedule. Northerners sought more information about the slave population, but did so in order to support their arguments about the evils of slavery and the necessity of abolition. Southerners wanted to eliminate several proposed questions for the 1850 Census that would make slaves seem more human – recording names, children, family ties, and place of birth. Defenders of the census bill pointed out that the polygenist expert Josiah Nott had recommended these new questions because the data were

[22] Anderson, *American Census*, 41–42.

[23] See Kennedy's address to the American Geographical and Statistical Society in 1860, in which he justifies the need for moral statistics and puts the collection of American statistics in an international context; Joseph Camp Griffith Kennedy, "The Origin and Progress of Statistics," *Journal of American Geographical and Statistical Society* 2 (1860): 92–120.

important for determining the relative longevity of white and black races.[24] Politics won over scientific curiosity, and these particular clauses were deleted from the final schedule.

The 1850 Census was the first to enumerate mulattoes as a separate racial category. Historians have assumed that this inclusion is because the Census Office desired to better measure racial intermixture and demographic composition.[25] However, Nobles argues that "the mulatto category was added and other race queries debated because of the lobbying efforts of race scientists and the willingness of certain legislators to do their bidding. The mulatto category signaled the ascendance of race science."[26] Indeed, the first draft schedule of the census contained an inquiry on the respondent's degree of removal from pure white and black races. After the census bill debate in the Senate on April 9, 1850, degenerated into an exchange about the virtues and vice of slavery, Joseph Underwood, the Senator from Kentucky, explained that the rationale for the proposed question on the "degree of removal from pure race" was scientific; he "never dreamed" it would lead to such a debate over the institution of slavery itself:

> The gentleman [Nott] in conversation with me said that he believed that a certain class of colored people had fewer children than a certain other class; and he believed the average duration of the lives of the darker class was longer than that of the lighter colored class, or mixed. And it was for the purpose of ascertaining that physiological fact, that he wanted the inquiry made ... it was to illustrate the truth or falsity of the theory on this subject.[27]

The final version of the census did not include the specific question about purity of blood, though the mulatto category was included. The 1850 Census recorded 159,095 free mulattoes and 246,656 enslaved, representing 36.6 percent of the free colored population and 7.7 percent of the slave population.

[24] Anderson, *American Census*, 40.

[25] Joel Williamson, *New People: Miscegenation and Mulattoes in the United States* (New York: The Free Press, 1980).

[26] Nobles, *Shades of Citizenship*, 36. Though enumerators were to count the mulatto population, they were not given any instructions as to how to determine who, exactly, was a mulatto. Forbes contends that at this conjecture the word "mulatto" implicated all people of any mixed background, not just those of black/white origins; Jack D. Forbes, *Africans and Native Americans: The Language of Race and the Evolution of Red-Black Peoples*, 2nd edn (Urbana: University of Illinois Press, 1993).

[27] *The Congressional Globe, Debates and Proceedings*, Senate, 31st Congress, 1st session, April 19, 1850, p. 676. Nobles, *Shades of Citizenship*, 38–42, and Anderson, *American Census*, 40, both agree that Underwood is referring to Nott.

The 1860 Census was similarly informed by slavery in that the Civil War, abolition, and the future of freed slaves figured prominently in the interpretation of census data. Statistics were used to assess military strength, finance combat efforts, and procure taxes. The census also provided stark numerical reality for numerous policy problems surrounding emancipation. President Lincoln's scheme of state-sponsored black colonization to Haiti or Liberia, for example, had to be reconfigured (and eventually abandoned) after data showed approximately four million slaves in the South. These debates continued to be informed by transnational racial ideas. Superintendent Kennedy, for one, still believed that extinction was a viable outcome of the competition between races: "[T]he colored population in America, where ever, either free or slave, it must in number and condition be greatly subordinate to the white race, is doomed to comparatively rapid absorption or extinction."[28] His views were supported by the racial experts called upon to comment on the political consequences of emancipation. For example, Samuel Howe, a member of the Freedman's Inquiry Commission appointed by President Lincoln in 1863, consulted with Harvard biologist Louis Agassiz on the nature of mulattoes. Agassiz emphasized that mulattoes were a sterile, short-lived population that would quickly disappear once amalgamation with whites ceased: "By a natural consequence of unconquerable affinities, the colored people in whom the negro nature prevails will tend toward the South, while the weaker and lighter ones will remain and die out among us."[29] Racial lessons that supported these conclusions were also drawn freely from the global context. In Howe's 1864 report, *The Refugees from Slavery in Canada West, Report to the Freedmen's Inquiry Commission*, he argued that the black population of Canada was a representative sample of blacks in North America, especially since many were mulattoes who had escaped slavery in the South. At a time when miscegenation laws were repealed by Republican governments in the South (only to have more severe versions reinstated at the end of Reconstruction), he pointed out that intermarriage in Canada was rare, writing that "With freedom and protection of their legal rights; with open field for industry, and opportunities for mental and moral culture, colored people will not seek

[28] United States Census Office, *Population of the United States in 1860: Compiled from the Original Returns of the Eighth Census* (Washington D.C.: GPO, 1864), xii.

[29] Elizabeth Cary Agassiz, ed., *Louis Agassiz: His Life and Correspondence* (London: Macmillan and Company, 1885), 600.

relationship with whites, but will follow their natural affinity, and marry among themselves."[30]

Policymakers believed that, with the right questions and classifications, the census could predict whether blacks would be absorbed or extinguished. The Census Office, which was still a temporary organization in spite of efforts by James Garfield to centralize and reorganize its functions, solicited outside advice from Edward Jarvis of the American Statistical Association. He suggested the census continue to distinguish between blacks and mulattoes to ascertain if the lower biological quality of the mixed-race population would hasten an end to what Gunnar Myrdal would eventually call "the Negro problem."[31]

Canada

There was no institutional mandate to count slaves in Canada, but not because they did not exist. The institution of slavery first took hold in New France in the late seventeenth century and followed the *Code Noir*, a French legal document of 1685 that governed slave colonies, offered protection to slaves, and outlined a slave owner's obligations to his property.[32] After the British Conquest in 1760, the newly formed colonial government legally strengthened the system of slavery, assuring French slave owners that they would be permitted to keep their slaves.[33] Toward the end of the century, even as the British offered and gave freedom to slaves who fought against the American revolutionaries and approximately 3,500 black Loyalists joined the flight northward to Nova Scotia, the institution persisted in what is now modern-day Ontario, Quebec, and Eastern Canada.[34] The legal protections for slave owners residing in British North America, imperial protections for emigrants to import slaves along with other belongings, and the influx of post-revolutionary

30 Samuel G. Howe, *The Refugees from Slavery in Canada West: Report to the Freedmen's Inquiry Commission* (Boston: Wright and Potter Printers, 1864), 18; see also Matthew Furrow, "Samuel Gridley Howe, the Black Population of Canada West, and the Racial Ideology of the 'Blueprint for Radical Reconstruction'," *Journal of American History* 97, no. 2 (2010): 344–370.

31 Gerald N. Grob, *Edward Jarvis and the Medical World of Nineteenth Century America* (Knoxville: University of Tennessee Press, 1978), 196.

32 Maureen G. Elgersman, *Unyielding Spirits: Black Women and Slavery in Early Canada and Jamaica* (New York: Garland Publishing, 1999), 14–15.

33 Ibid., 22–23.

34 James W. St G. Walker, *Black Loyalists: The Search for a Promised Land in Nova Scotia and Sierra Leone, 1783–1870* (Toronto: University of Toronto Press, 1992).

Loyalists caused a rapid expansion of the total number of slaves in Canada.[35] Since the governance of these various regions of British North America was far from democratic, issues of representation did not factor into the decision to include a means of counting by race on the early censuses as it did in the United States. For example, in 1767 both Nova Scotia and Prince Edward Island (then called St. John Island) provided origin choices of English, Irish, Scotch, American, German, Acadian, and "not given," while a race question provided three options: White, Indian, or Negro.[36] The next pre-Confederation census, held in New Brunswick, classified the population only according to race, using the options "White" or "Coloured."

Slavery was gradually dismantled in British North America and abolished altogether throughout the entire British Empire in 1833. A few years later the first semblance of self-government was granted to the colony when the 1840 Act of Union created a united Dominion with two distinct components – Canada East (now Quebec) and Canada West (now Ontario) – governed by a single Legislative Assembly. Each section had the same number of seats in the legislature, and a two-thirds majority was required to pass laws. The principle of equal representation was initially promoted by the Anglophone minority, while Francophones preferred representation by population, each group attempting to maximize its legislative power. These respective positions would completely reverse when increased Anglophone immigration created new settlement patterns that dwarfed the Quebecois population. Much like in America, the "losers" of representation by population often claimed that census results upon which the apportionment formula was based were faulty once the political implications of the data were made clear.

Both groups had good reason to question the accuracy of census data. In spite of the dramatic transformation and centralization of political power and administrative capacity after the Act of Union, the mid-nineteenth century colonial censuses of Canada East and Canada West were poorly administered and highly unreliable. The 1841 Census Act, one of the first legislative measures of the United Canadas, called for a quinquennial household enumeration of residents and their occupations, religious affiliations, agricultural and industrial production, rents, public institutions, and number of "coloured" people. The lack of

[35] Robin Winks, *The Blacks in Canada: A History*, 2nd edn (Montreal and Kingston: McGill-Queen's University Press, 1997).

[36] Census of Nova Scotia (1767), Census of St. John Island (P.E.I.) (1767).

administrative machinery, however, alongside local resistance to what was perceived as simply a "taxation machine," led to numerous census failures in the mid-nineteenth century – 1842, 1848, and 1850, and an aborted census in 1847.[37]

Pressures from the British Parliament for a system of regular and accurate statistical reporting and rising sectarian demands for a colony-wide census led to the 1847 Census and Statistics Act, which created a Board of Registration and Statistics to oversee general statistical matters. Its first Secretary, Walter Cavendish Crofton, was a patronage appointee who was an incompetent administrator and did little to advance Canada's statistical system beyond the status quo. Against the recommendations of the international statistical community, census administration depended on the cooperation of local government, which caused many problems in terms of consistency.[38] Enumerators delivered their returns to municipal clerks, who then checked for errors and reported to the Board. In comparative terms, the American system of using marshals for census administration was far more centralized.

The 1852 Census of Canada East and Canada West was the first attempt to exert more government control over census administration. After so many earlier failed attempts, this next iteration was coerced by imperial will and informed by international trends. The Colonial Office, dreaming of an empire-wide census, urged the colonies to synchronize their census dates with the 1851 British enumeration. The instructions provided to the colonies requested that the race of respondents be recorded, indicating that its inclusion in the census was a "sufficiently obvious" matter that required no further elaboration.[39] In other words, counting by race was simply common sense. At the same time, Quetelet and Farr developed international standards of census-taking that required enumeration by name, so as to minimize counting fallacies. Census-taking procedures from the United States, which used the *de jure* technique of enumeration to record a person's habitual place of residence and gathered economic and social information well beyond a simple headcount, was a workable model that was deliberately emulated in Canada.[40]

Counting by race in the Canadian censuses was an obvious, self-evidently rational exercise, informed partially and tangentially by the

[37] Curtis, *The Politics of Population*, 46–91. [38] Ibid. [39] Ibid., 94.

[40] David A. Worton, *The Dominion Bureau of Statistics: A History of Canada's Central Statistical Office and Its Antecedents, 1841–1972* (Montreal and Kingston: McGill-Queen's University Press, 1998), 17.

transnational ripple effects of American slavery. The United States Fugitive Slave Act of 1850 strengthened the provisions of the Fugitive Slave Act of 1793 by requiring marshals and other federal officials to arrest anyone suspected of being a runaway slave. "All good citizens" were "commanded to aid and assist in the prompt and efficient execution" of the law, and anyone found providing food or shelter to escaped slaves risked six months imprisonment and a thousand dollar fine.[41] The Northern states were no longer safe for free blacks and escaped slaves alike and many fled to Canada, where the British government recognized that "every man is free who reaches British ground" in spite of American proposals for extradition.[42] The 1852 and 1861 censuses of the Canadas used a combination of birthplace and origin data to identify the population, publishing more than twenty-five countries, regions, and origins. Enumerators were to identify any "persons of colour – negroes" ("personnes de couleur, ou nègres") and "Indians." Though blacks were granted refuge from chattel slavery under the British flag, they were still subject to residential segregation, widespread unemployment, white ideas and attitudes about their inherent biological, cultural, and social inferiority, and racially segregated public schools.[43] For example, Barrington Walker documents the history of blacks who appeared before Ontario criminal courts between 1858 and 1958, arguing that formal legal equality offered little protection against pervasive patterns of social, legal, and attitudinal racial inequality.[44]

A steady increase of black American refugees entered Canada as America teetered on the brink of Civil War, drawing demand from both sides of the border for knowledge about the number of black people in Canada. In 1861 the instructions requested that colored persons be counted carefully to improve upon previous estimates of the population. The designation "persons of colour" also included mulattoes, who were to be discerned on the census schedule by an "M" after the respondent's name. The same racial ideas that caused such political contention in the

41 Wilbur H. Siebert, *The Underground Railroad: From Slavery to Freedom* (New York and London: Macmillan, 1898), 22–24.

42 Letter from Albert Gallatin, United States Minister to Great Britain to Henry Clay, United States Secretary of State, September 26, 1827, Niles' Register, p. 290, cited in Siebert, *The Underground Railroad*, 193.

43 Winks, *Blacks in Canada*, chapters 6–7; James W. St. G. Walker, *"Race," Rights and the Law in the Supreme Court of Canada: Historical Case Studies* (Waterloo: Wilfred Laurier University Press, 1997).

44 Barrington Walker, *Race on Trial: Black Defendants in Ontario's Criminal Courts, 1858–1958* (Toronto: University of Toronto Press, 2010).

United States were equally present in Canada, though without a national context of slavery they failed to stir the same controversy. Though the census was becoming more accurate with each decade, the precise number of blacks in Ontario in the 1850s and 1860s is unclear. The Anti-Slavery Society assumed in 1852 that the black population was approximately 30,000. In his report to the Freedmen's Inquiry Commission in 1864, Samuel Howe concluded in that there were no more than 15,000 to 20,000 blacks living in the province, though he admitted that most contemporaries thought the figure to be much higher. The 1861 Census Report gave a population of 11,223, but census rolls include entries on 17,053 blacks in Canada West. A decade later, the 1871 Census recorded a black population of approximately 13,500.[45] Inadequate as census data may have been at the time, it is clear that the total number of black people in Canada declined sharply after 1865, when many former slaves returned to the United States to fight for the Union army or settle permanently in the land from which they once absconded.[46]

In contrast to the efforts to count blacks and mulattoes in 1861, the inclusion of "Indians" in the pre-Confederation censuses served a specifically Canadian political purpose. Bruce Curtis writes that at the time, "most politicians and intellectuals were convinced of the inevitability of Aboriginal assimilation – or extinction, but counting them in the interim would increase the number reported as the colonial population, something in which the board was interested – while perhaps satisfying imperial government demands for information about the magnitude of its treaty obligation."[47] These same themes – the concern with the burden of Indian administration, the status of Aboriginal assimilation, and the equation of colonial progress with population growth – would be continually rearticulated in subsequent Canadian censuses.

COLONIAL PROJECTS AND THE RISE OF INTERNATIONAL STATISTICAL SCIENCE

Like transatlantic slavery, European imperialism was a modern race-making institution. Colonialism, an initial project of imperialism, is most often associated with European powers' attempts to exploit and

[45] See Michael Wayne, "The Black Population of Canada West on the Eve of the American Civil War: A Reassessment Based on the Manuscript Census of 1861," *Histoire sociale/Social History* 28, no. 56(1995): 465–485.

[46] Winks, *Blacks in Canada*, 484–496.

[47] Curtis, *Politics of Population*, 109.

appropriate the resources and manage the populations and economies of their colonies in Asia, South America, the Caribbean, and Africa, using the capital from these endeavors to develop industry in the metropole. Biological conceptions of race and racial difference were fundamental to the means and mechanisms by which Europe instituted colonial rule. The age of empire demanded and enabled the international rise of statistics. European imperialism required a specific kind of state knowledge; knowledge that could institute order in a world of chaos, bringing light to what Joseph Conrad called the Heart of Darkness and creating the vast systems of documentation required to measure wealth and maintain rule over foreign lands. The spread of numeracy and the rising popularity of statistics toward the latter half of the nineteenth century led to the creation of national and international institutions to gather, analyze, and disseminate this information. Founder of international statistics Adolphe Quetelet, British scholars and statisticians Thomas Malthus, William Farr, and Charles Babbage, American bureaucrat Joseph C.G. Kennedy, and Canadian Civil Secretary Rawson W. Rawson frequently corresponded through and beyond the international bodies they created, which included the Statistical Society of London, the International Statistical Congress, and its successor, the International Statistical Institute.[48] The increasingly popular use of "rational moral science" in France, England, and elsewhere provided an avalanche of statistical analysis on deviancy, crime, pauperism, mental and physical "defects," and education.

The racial dynamics of these social problems did not go unnoticed in North America, where white settler societies such as Canada and the United States faced an intractable "Indian problem." Both governments recognized the Indian population in treaties and their respective censuses. Both also incorporated similar programs of assimilation during the last four decades of the nineteenth century, based on the premise that Indians could be "civilized." Natives were not threatening in the same way as other non-white races, which were often depicted in rhetoric of peril or pestilence. Rather, they were considered wards of the state in need of government protection. At its core, the discourse of North American conquest "regards tribal peoples as normatively deficient and culturally, politically, and morally inferior."[49] Policymakers used education to

[48] Walter F. Willcox, "Development of International Statistics," *The Milbank Memorial Fund Quarterly* 27, no. 2 (1949): 143–153.

[49] Robert A. Williams, *The American Indian in Western Legal Thought: Discourses of Conquest* (New York: Oxford University Press, 1990), 326.

isolate young people from their cultures, allowed churches and missionaries a large role in acculturation efforts, demanded that Indians become farmers or ranchers, refused to accept communal land use patterns, and generally assumed that Indians had to integrate into the social and economic systems of each respective country, but simultaneously believed that Indians would likely die out or assimilate.[50] Political elites of the newly born Canadian state also hoped their program of assimilation would avoid the expensive and disastrous "Indian Wars" that plagued the American frontier. Constructing Natives as dependent and primitive served this purpose well.

Great Britain

Britain was a leader in the development of statistical science. It was also an imperial power, not an immigrant-receiving country. The British state thus saw no need to count by race on its national census, though the same does not hold true for its colonies. The same European powers (France, Britain, Belgium) that wholly rejected the proposition to enumerate their populations according to "cultural nationalism" in sessions of the International Statistical Congress as their counterparts in Eastern Europe were already doing[51] acted without hesitation in using the census and other administrative means to categorize their colonial subjects.

The census was an important though imperfect means through which British imperial identity and power were extended. In practical terms, tabulations provided London with a sense of the empire's resources, wealth, territory, and population. In 1817 the Parliamentary Select Committee on Finance asked for more information on the financial returns of the colonies, and in 1822 each colonial governor was sent a "Blue Book" in which they were to fill in details relating to taxes, income and expenditures, military requirements, birth, marriages, deaths, and other statistics.[52] Numerous attempts were also made at a census of the

[50] Roger L. Nichols, *Indians in the United States and Canada: A Comparative History* (Lincoln: University of Nebraska Press, 1998), 207–8.

[51] Kertzer and Arel, "Censuses, Identity Formation, and the Struggle for Political Power," 9. For example, on the colonial governance and enumeration of nineteenth-century Netherland Indies, see Ann Laura Stoler, *Along the Archival Grain: Epistemic Anxieties and Colonial Common Sense* (Princeton: Princeton University Press, 2009).

[52] Bruce Curtis, "The Canada 'Blue Books' and the Administrative Capacity of the Canadian State, 1822–67," *Canadian Historical Review* 74, no. 4 (1993): 535–565, and Sarah Preston, *The Colonial Blue Books: A Major Resource in the Royal Commonwealth Society Library*, Reproduced from the Bulletin of the Friends of Cambridge University

entire British Empire for over one hundred years between 1840 and 1940, though success was limited by the lack of a centralized administrative statistical system and poor colonial responses.[53] In more ideological terms, the systematic counting of bodies in the colonies was, as Arjun Appadurai argues, not just an extension of the same preoccupation with numeracy sweeping across Europe, but also worked to create a sense of imperial control and define what was controllable. Thus, while the census of the British metropole was largely tied to the politics of representation, its most invasive investigations for those labeled as deviant – the poor, the promiscuous, the lunatic, the criminal – were extended to entire populations abroad.[54]

Though the racial classification principles of the colonies varied widely, racial counts were explicitly requested by the Colonial Office. The first Blue Books contained a three-fold distinction between white, free colored, and slave populations. Once slavery was abolished in 1833 a white–colored dualism replicated from the American system formed the basis for the majority of classification systems throughout the empire. Initial proposals for taking a census of all British colonies in the mid-nineteenth century, advocated by Superintendent of Statistics William Farr and Lord Stanley, the Secretary of State for War and Colonies, specifically required that a question on race be included.[55] In India, for example, the British Colonial Office institutionalized caste distinctions,

Library Number 26–27 (2006), accessed March 11, 2014, www.lib.cam.ac.uk/deptserv/rcs/rcs_op_project/FriendsofCULibraryarticle.htm

53 Anthony J. Christopher, "The Quest for a Census of the British Empire, c. 1840–1940," *Journal of Historical Geography* 34, no. 2 (2008): 268–285.

54 Arjun Appadurai, "Number in the Colonial Imagination," in *Orientalism and the Postcolonial Predicament*, eds. Carol A Breckenridge and Peter van der Veer (Philadelphia: University of Pennsylvania Press, 1993), 117–118. See also Frederick Cooper and Ann Laura Stoler, "Between Metropole and Colony: Rethinking a Research Agenda," in *Tensions of Empire: Colonial Cultures in a Bourgeois World*, ed. Frederick Cooper and Ann Laura Stoler (Berkley: University of California Press, 1997): 1–56; Catherine Hall, *Civilising Subjects: Metropole and Colony in the English Imagination, 1830–1867* (Chicago and London: University of Chicago Press, 2002).

55 Christopher, "Quest for a Census of the British Empire," 274; see also Anthony J. Christopher, "Race and the Census in the Commonwealth," *Population, Space and Place* 11, no. 2 (2005): 103–118. The attempts at an empire-wide census were largely unsuccessful. However, the final Report on the Census of the British Empire 1901 noted that "there appears to be no standard classification of the varieties of the human species, but some information under the heading in the Colonial Census Reports possesses considerable interest," and estimated the broad racial numbers of the empire at 398 million "Coloured" and 54 million "White." Christopher, "Race and the Census," 278–279.

which in turn created the conditions for emergent social patterns, systems of stratification, and electoral politics.[56]

As white settler societies, the United States and Canada did not share Britain's concern for its paramount racial project: maintaining colonial distinctions and imperial stability. These settler societies were, however, preoccupied with maintaining a colonial relationship with their indigenous populations and gaining underlying title to the land. This imperative was taken to such an extreme in Australia that the colonial administration ignored the urgings of the British House of Commons Select Committee on Aborigines to count the indigenous population in 1837. Historian Rob Watts' analysis of the birth of the census in Australia demonstrates that the census-making and -taking practices rendered the territory as *terra nullius* and confirmed white territorial sovereignty and legal authority. By not counting Aborigines in the census, the colonial administration effectively dispossessed and disregarded the indigenous population, "blanking out" previous modes of black occupation and governance even as it specifically included other causes of racial anxiety, counting "Chinamen, Malays, Polynesians and other foreigners," while purposefully excluding "native blacks."[57] Occluding indigenous populations from the censuses of the United States and Canada, however, was not an option.

Canada

In the years following the Civil War and leading up to Confederation, political elites in both countries began to realize that an institutionalized system of statistics was the most effective way of measuring the nation's

[56] On the census in India, see Smith, "Rule-by-Records"; Bernard Cohn, "The Census, Social Structure and Objectification in South Asia," in *An Anthropologist Among the Historians and Other Essays* (Delhi: Oxford University Press, 1987): 224–254; Rashmi Pant, "The Cognitive Status of Caste in Colonial Ethnography: A Review of Some Literature on the North West Provinces and Oudh," *Indian Economic and Social History Review* 24 (1987): 145–162; Appadurai, "Number in the Colonial Imagination"; Norbert Peabody, "Cents, Sense, Census: Human Inventories in Late Precolonial and Early Colonial India," *Comparative Studies in Society and History* 43, no. 4 (2001): 819–850.

[57] Rob Watts, "Making Numbers Count: The Birth of the Census and Racial Government in Victoria, 1835–1870," *Australian Historical Studies* 34, no. 121 (2003): 26–47. On the divergent Maori enumeration strategies in New Zealand, see Tahu Kukutai, "Building Ethnic Boundaries in New Zealand: Representations of Maori Identity in the Census," in *Indigenous Peoples and Demography: the Complex Relation between Identity and Statistics*, eds. Per Axelsson and Peter Sköld (Oxford: Berghahn Books, 2011), 33–54.

wealth, progress, and resources. Canadian politician D'Arcy McGee was so impressed by the Dutch delegates to the 1860 Statistical Congress that he sought to model Canada's statistical system after their example. McGee institutionalized statistical work within the Department of Agriculture and appointed Joseph-Charles Taché as the Deputy Minister in 1864. Taché's first task was to give the Board more administrative autonomy, with a permanent staff, and create an interdepartmental statistical commission.[58]

Confederation in 1867 resolved the Canadian contestation over representation by population by instituting a bicameral legislature with a lower house elected according to population and an appointed upper house to ensure regional representation. Section 91(6) of the British North America Act identified "the census and statistics" as being under the sole jurisdiction of the federal government. Shortly thereafter, the Census Act of 1870 provided the legislative basis for the first official census of Canada to occur in 1871 in order to "ascertain and show, with the utmost accuracy possible ... all statistical information which can conveniently be obtained and stated in tabular form touching [the] population and the classification thereof, as regards age, sex, social condition, religion, education, race, occupation, and otherwise."[59] The first post-Confederation censuses of 1871 and 1881 largely followed the established practice of the pre-Confederation censuses of gathering origin data, though the 1891 Census broke with tradition and omitted the origin question, instead asking a question on the French Canadian population.

Biological conceptions of race and racial difference were fundamental to the crafting and implementation of Canada's colonial project and the mechanisms of surveillance used to control the indigenous population.[60]

[58] Curtis, *The Politics of Population*, 247.

[59] Canada, Dominion Bureau of Statistics, *Eighth Census of Canada, 1941: Administrative Report of the Dominion Statistician* (Ottawa: King's Printer, 1941), 10. Canadian censuses are held on the first year of every decade as a lagging echo of imperial pressure. The 1860 Statistical Congress endorsed a common census date throughout the British Empire and the enumeration schedule after 1861 was adjusted to match the Empire's wishes. This tradition continues to this day.

[60] Scholars refer to the historical and contemporary relationship between indigenous people and the Canadian state as one of "internal colonialism," whereby colonization is considered to be an ongoing exploitative relationship that consists of the physical occupation of indigenous lands, the appropriation of traditional power structures, political authority and forms of governance, and the negation of Aboriginal cultural self-determination, economic capacity, and strategic location. See James Tully, "Indigenous Peoples Struggles for and of Freedom," in *Political Theory and the Rights of Indigenous Peoples*, eds. Duncan Ivison et al. (Cambridge: Cambridge

Aboriginal–government relations have largely been defined by the Indian Act, one of the most all-encompassing colonial instruments at the disposal of the Canadian state.[61] Designed to manage Indian lives literally from cradle (determining who was and who was not a status Indian) to grave (governing inheritance rights), the purpose of the Indian Act was to remove Indian status. This was not an attempt by the state to ensure the equal treatment of Aboriginal people in Canadian society. Rather, the federal government was compelled by legal precedent, constitutional convention, and colonial legacy to administer "Indians and land reserved for Indians," as per section 91(24) of the constitution. The legal category of status Indian, after all, "is the only category to whom a historic nation-to-nation relationship between the Canadian and Indigenous people is recognized."[62] The removal of Indian status, therefore, was a two-fold strategy: it removed the constitutional Indian status of individuals, thereby diminishing their collective claims of underlying Aboriginal title to the land, and simultaneously alleviated the burden of Indian administration on the Crown. The loss or retention of Indian status was also highly gendered. Under what would become the infamous section 12.1(b) of the 1876 Act, Indian women who married non-Indian men would lose status, as would their offspring. Indian men who married non-Indian women, however, would not only retain status for himself and his progeny, but his wife would gain status as well.[63]

In 1901 enumerators were required to write the names of the tribes (for example, Chippewa and Cree) and were instructed to carefully record white/Indian "mixes." The instructions read:

> persons of mixed white and red blood – commonly known as "breeds" will be described by the initial letters "f.b" for French breed, "e.b." for English breed, "s.b"

University Press, 2000), 36–59; Taiaiake Alfred, *Wasa'se: Indigenous Pathways of Action and Freedom* (Peterborough: Broadview Press, 2005); Joyce Green, *Making Space for Indigenous Feminism* (Black Point: Fernwood Pub, 2007); and Glen Coulthard, *Red Skin, White Masks: Rejecting the Colonial Politics of Recognition* (Minneapolis: University of Minnesota Press, 2014).

61 See John Leslie and Ron Maguire, *The Historical Development of the Indian Act* (Ottawa: Department of Indian Affairs, 1978); Canada, *The Indian Act, Past and Present: A Manual on Registration and Entitlement Legislation* (Ottawa: Indian Registration and Band Lists Directorate, 1991).

62 Bonita Lawrence, "Gender, Race, and the Regulation of Native Identity in Canada and the United States: An Overview," *Hypatia* 18, no. 2 (2003): 6.

63 Ibid., 8–9. See also Debra Thompson, "Racial Ideas and Gendered Intimacies: The Regulation of Interracial Relationships in North America," *Social and Legal Studies* 18, no. 3 (2009): 353–371.

for Scotch breed, and "i.b" for Irish breed. For example: "Cree f.b." denotes that the person is racially a mixture of Cree and French; and "Chippewa s.b." denotes that the person is Chippewa and Scotch. Other mixtures of Indians besides the four above specified are rare, and may be described by the letters "o.b." for other breed. If several races are combined with the red, such as English and Scotch, Irish and French, or any others, they should also be described by the initials "o.b."[64]

The Canadian state was interested in two distinct sets of information gathered by the act of recognizing and recording such an elaborate taxonomy of Aboriginal and French, English, Scotch, or Irish offspring. First, the specific details about the composition of these racial amalgamations is related to the history of disputes and violent clashes between the Canadian government and the Métis population of the prairie provinces during the Red River Rebellion of 1869–1870 and the Battle of Batoche in 1885. Legally designated as "half-breeds" by the federal government, these descendants of Aboriginal women and French fur traders were never seriously considered by the state to be either within the definition of Indian or a distinct segment of the indigenous population.[65] To acknowledge either of these scenarios would contradict the purpose of the Indian Act regime, which was to remove all legal distinctions between the Native population and other Canadians while maintaining hierarchical race relations and social stratification. The census provided a means of counting the Métis; though the census is a type of legal recognition, it does not confer rights or responsibilities. This complex enumeration of Métis and other mixed-race people with Aboriginal heritage enabled the government to keep tabs on a population which, in its view, threatened the security of the still unstable, still largely unsettled, western provinces.

Second, counting the number of persons with indigenous ancestry was necessary in order for the government to determine the progress of the assimilative goals of the Indian Act, which used intermarriage as a means of reducing the legal ability of Aboriginal people to claim Indian status. In accordance with global racial ideas of the era, many believed that the population would eventually die out. A 1915 Bureau of Statistics memorandum on the issue states:

In taking a census of an aboriginal race, the anthropological and ethnological point of view must be considered. Hints on the subject are to be found in the 35 questions

[64] Canada, *Fourth Census of Canada, 1901. Instructions to Chief Officers, Commissioners and Enumerators* (Ottawa: Government Printing Bureau, 1901), 14.

[65] Chris Andersen, *"Métis": Race, Recognition, and the Struggle for Indigenous Peoplehood* (Vancouver: University of British Columbia Press, 2014).

proposed by the International Statistical Institute for territories peopled by native races without censuses. The views of experts, however, would be necessary for a final decision. As the Indian population is small, and is decreasing it is doubtful if the expenditure which such an inquiry would entail would be warranted with any other than a scientific end in view. The United States in 1911 took a census of Indians of this nature, but has announced that it will not repeat the inquiry.[66]

The number of "half-breeds" was correlated to the success of reducing "the Indian problem" – that is, the simultaneous existence of a non-white, "uncivilized," "inassimilable" population with legal claims to Canadian land and the Crown's fiduciary obligations toward Aboriginal peoples.

United States

Issues of race and representation stabilized in the post-Civil War/ Confederation era. The United States Congress passed the Fourteenth and Fifteenth Amendments and made the three-fifths compromise inapplicable, though the size of the black population remained a pressing policy concern during Reconstruction and beyond. Though African Americans had consistently been included in the census from its first iteration, the exemption of "Indians not taxed" from census counts was a standard instruction to marshals and their assistants throughout the first half of the nineteenth century. The first attempts to count the indigenous population of America through the census were many and varied, particularly after 1860 as the "Indian problem" emerged as a political concern. Francis Walker, who served as the Superintendent of the Census Office during the 1870 and 1880 censuses, argued in his report to the Secretary of the Interior in 1872 that:

the fact that the Constitution excludes from the basis of representation Indians not taxed affords no possible reason why, in a census which is on its face taken with equal reference to statistical as to political interests, such persons should be excluded from the population of the country. They should, of course, appear separately, so the provisions of the Constitution ... may be carried out; but they should appear, nevertheless, as a constituent part of the population of the country viewed in light of all social, economical, and moral principles. An Indian not taxed should, to put it on the lowest possible grounds, be reported in the census just as truly as the vagabond or pauper of the white or colored race. The fact that he sustains a vague political relation is no reason why he should not be recognized as

66 NAC RG31 vol. 1417, Records of the Assistant Dominion Statistician, Census Material 1891–1940. Memorandum for the Honourable Minister of Trade and Commerce – the Northwest Census of Population and Agriculture, 1916, and Cognate Subjects. September 16, 1915.

a human being in a census which counts even the cattle and horses of the country.[67]

Walker's rationale for counting the indigenous population rests on his belief – far from isolated at the time – that though Indians were part of the common family of humanity and thus should be counted in a census of the population, they were also a problem similar to the morally and productively corrupt vagabond or pauper. Indians, Walker argued in 1874, were once "proud and mean alike beyond compare; superior to torture and the presence of certain death, yet, by the standards of all other peoples, a coward in battle," but now, "broken down by the military power of the whites, thrown out of his familiar relations, his stupendous conceit with its glamour of savage pomp and glory rudely dispelled, his occupation gone, himself a beggar, the red man becomes the most commonplace person imaginable, of very simple nature, limited aspirations, and enormous appetites."[68] The ambiguous political status of untaxed Indians, Walker believed, was no reason why they should not be counted in the decennial census. Indeed, this ambiguity may have provided even more of an incentive for their enumeration. For Walker, the "Indian question" was two-fold, united by the demographic anxiety over territorial control: "What shall be done with the Indian as an obstacle to the national progress? What shall be done with him when, and so far as, he ceases to oppose or obstruct the railways and the settlements?"[69]

Since the census schedule no longer needed to differentiate between free and enslaved segments of the population, the additional categories of "Indian" and "Chinese" were included under the inquiry respecting color on the 1870 Census. For the first time, the enumeration instructions on how to categorize mixed-race people were included, though not all mixes were classified in the same way. While enumerators were told that mulatto included "quadroons, octoroons, and all persons having any perceptible trace of African blood," the classification of Indian "half-breeds" required more detail:

Where persons reported as "half-breeds" are found residing with whites, adopting their habits of life and methods of industry, such persons are to be treated as

[67] U.S. Census Office, *The Statistics of the Population of the United States* (Washington D.C.: US Government Printing Office, 1872), xvi–xvii.

[68] Francis A. Walker, "The Indian Question," *North American Review* 116, no. 239 (1873): 336–337.

[69] Ibid., 337.

belonging to the white population. Where, on the other hand, they are found in communities composed wholly, or mainly of Indians, the opposite construction is taken. In a word, in the equilibrium produced by the equal division of blood, the habits, tastes, and associations of the half-breed are allowed to determine his gravitation to the one class or the other.[70]

Instructions to enumerators in the previous census in 1860 placed Indians who had renounced tribal rule under the heading "Color," along with whites (the space was to be left blank), blacks, and mulattoes. Mixed-race Indians and blacks, however, were clearly subject to different classification rules. Similar to the discussion of Aboriginal classifications in Canada, racial ideas about the Native American population focused on territorial possession, way of life, and other "habits and customs" – the markers of civilization.

In 1876 Walker used his experience as the former Commissioner for Indian Affairs to carry out an enumeration of mixed- and full-blooded Indians. Four years later the 1880 Census, strengthened by 1879 legislation that gave the Census Office more control over enumeration processes by replacing marshals with census field supervisors, included a special census of untaxed Indians. Enumerators were required to specify the fraction of blood from black or white ancestry and to record whether black, mulatto, or white people had been adopted by a tribe.[71] More clarity on who was considered an Indian was required by the 1887 Dawes Act, which functioned similarly to Canada's Indian Act by granting citizenship to "civilized" Indians through mechanisms of forced assimilation. The 1890 Census was an important innovation used to achieve this goal, featuring a series of publications on taxed and untaxed Indians. In 1900, with the west effectively "won," the distinction between taxed and untaxed Indians was dropped from census classifications.[72] Yet, the schematic state's management of the Indian population continued: just over a decade later Indians with one half or more "white blood" were

[70] U.S. Census Office, *Statistics of the Population of the United States*, xiii.

[71] Note, however, that the government "continued to discourage racial intermarriage on or near Indian reservations, for the sake of civilizing the Indians ... by encouraging mixed individuals to give up their tribal status and be separated from their tribes." Thomas N. Ingersoll, *To Intermix with Our White Brothers: Indian Mixed Bloods in the United States from the Earliest Times to the Indian Removals* (Albuquerque: University of New Mexico Press, 2005), 243–244.

[72] William Seltzer, "Excluding Indians Not Taxed: Federal Censuses and Native-Americans in the 19th Century," Paper presented at the 1999 Joint Statistical Meetings, Baltimore MD, 1999.

forced off tribal rolls established under the Dawes Act, becoming both territorially dispossessed and subject to federal taxes.[73]

IMMIGRATION, NATION-BUILDING, AND BUREAUCRATIC AUTONOMY

White settler societies were more than a matter of demographic composition. They required purposeful state action in order to create and maintain a specific, racialized conceptualization of nationalism, identity, and manifest destiny. Nation-building efforts intensified during the rapid surge in globalizing forces in the late nineteenth and early twentieth centuries – the development of transcontinental railways and transoceanic steam ships, the rise of competition in the transportation industry and the associated reduction in travel costs, mass literacy, and the creation of industrialized urban centers, to name but a few – and spurred unprecedented levels of transnational migration. Immigrant-receiving countries sought, for the first time, to make immigration racially exclusive by curbing migrant settlement from non-white countries while permitting, and in some cases encouraging, emigration from Western Europe. Making distinctions between "desirable" and "undesirable" immigrants was a pressing policy issue, especially on the west coast where Asian indentured servitude had replaced the slave trade as the primary means of cheap labor.[74]

By the turn of the century, racial ideas had morphed. The terminology of race was used to differentiate among what we would now consider to be white ethnic groups; British, for example, was more than a nationality, but was considered a race and civilization apart. These were the decades of lynching and segregation, but also of the white man's burden, fear of the yellow peril, and what Bruce Baum calls the "fall of the Caucasian race," when national variants of whiteness took on new meanings and the rise of the global eugenics movement solidified nationalistic discourses of racial

[73] Hochschild and Powell, "Racial Reorganization," 79.

[74] See Desmond S. King, *Making Americans: Immigration, Race, and the Origins of Diverse Democracy* (Cambridge: Harvard University Press, 2000); Najia Aarim-Heriot, *Chinese Immigrants, African Americans, and Racial Anxiety in the United States, 1848–82* (Urbana and Chicago: University of Illinois Press, 2003); Mae M. Ngai, *Impossible Subjects: Illegal Aliens and the Making of Modern America* (Princeton: Princeton University Press, 2004); Triadafilos Triadafilopoulos, "Building Walls, Bounding Nations: Migration and Exclusion in Canada and Germany, 1870–1939," *Journal of Historical Sociology* 17, no. 4 (2004): 385–427.

superiority and inferiority.[75] Though the most violent and coercive implementation of eugenicist policies occurred in Nazi Germany preceding and during the Second World War, it was first a transnational movement with international conferences organized by the British Eugenics Education Society and the United States Department of State held in London in 1912, and New York in 1921 and 1932. In the early twentieth century varying eugenic policies could be found in Canada, the United States, Sweden, Australia, China, the Soviet Union, Latin America, Germany, Australia, Norway, France, Finland, Denmark, Japan, Iceland, and Switzerland.[76]

At the same time, important institutional developments shaped the trajectory of census politics. The United States and Canada initiated parallel efforts to consolidate and centralize responsibility for the census and free statistical agencies from political influence. Both later adopted a stance of statistical decentralization – provinces and states were left alone to gather their own data and within the national government statistics were departmentalized. As censuses became more complicated, asking more questions and requiring more detail on aspects of economic

[75] Baum, Rise and Fall; see also David Roediger, *The Wages of Whiteness: Race and the Making of the American Working Class* (New York: Verso, 1991), and Matthew Frye Jacobson, *Whiteness of a Different Color: European Immigrants and the Alchemy of Race* (Cambridge: Harvard University Press, 1998).

[76] The creators and carriers of these pseudo-scientific ideas were not necessarily the main consumers of them. Larson's analysis of eugenics in the Deep South demonstrates that though the region was not the home to scientists or research centers that contributed to the discourse of eugenics, decision-makers were nevertheless eager proponents of sterilization programs. Nor were ideas blindly emulated: as Nancy Stepan's research on eugenics in Latin America suggests, a body of social knowledge about scientific racism developed in reference to both the global discourse and the peculiar political, cultural, and historical dynamics of the region. Edward John Larson, *Sex, Race, and Science: Eugenics in the Deep South* (Baltimore: Johns Hopkins University Press, 1995); Nancy Stepan, *The Hour of Eugenics: Race, Gender, and Nation in Latin America* (Ithaca: Cornell University Press, 1991). See also Mark B. Adams, ed., *The Wellborn Science: Eugenics in Germany, France, Brazil and Russia* (New York: Oxford University Press, 1990); Angus McLaren, *Our Own Master Race: Eugenics in Canada, 1885–1945* (Toronto: Oxford University Press, 1990); Frank Dikötter, *The Discourse of Race in Modern China* (London: Hurst, 1992); Daniel J. Kevles, *In the Name of Eugenics: Genetics and the Uses of Human Heredity*, rev. edn (Cambridge: Harvard University Press, 1995); Alberto Spektorowski, "The Eugenic Temptation in Socialism: Sweden, Germany, and the Soviet Union," *Comparative Studies in History and Society* 46, no. 1 (2004): 84–106; Alison Bashford and Phillippa Levine, eds., *The Oxford Handbook of the History of Eugenics* (Oxford and New York: Oxford University Press, 2010); and Randall Hansen and Desmond King, *Sterilized by the State: Eugenics, Race, and the Population Scare in Twentieth-Century North America* (New York: Cambridge University Press, 2013).

and social life well beyond a demographic headcount, both made the move toward a centralized and permanent census bureau. These long processes – arguably part of a larger trend of the institutionalization of bureaucratic autonomy[77] – were only finalized when the offices responsible for the census in the United States and Canada were made permanent in 1902 and 1905, respectively.[78]

United States

The 1870 American census was the first to enumerate the Chinese population. The category was added under the "Color" heading, as the Census Report of 1870 states, "so as to throw some light on the grave questions which the arrival of the Celestials among us has raised."[79] Racial taxonomy again expanded in 1890 with the inclusion of the categories "white," "black," "mulatto," "quadroon," "octoroon," "Chinese," "Japanese," and "Indian." Anti-Asian sentiment prevailed in this era of increasingly restrictive immigration policies: a failed 1890 proposal in Congress even went so far as to require that the Census Office issue identification cards that would be proof of legal residency in the United States; any Chinese person found without a card was to be deported.[80]

How people of African ancestry were to be classified in the 1890 American census involved quite specific fractionalizations: "black" described those with three-fourths or more black blood; "mulatto" those with three-eighths to five-eighths; "quadroon" one-fourth; and "octoroon" those who had one-eighth or any trace of black blood. The historical record is unclear why the categories "quadroon" and "octoroon" were added. However, Commissioner of Labor Caroll D. Wright argued at the time that "comprehensive information relating

[77] See Ken Rasmussen, "Administrative Reform and the Quest for Bureaucratic Autonomy, 1867–1919," *Journal of Canadian Studies* 29, no. 3 (1994): 45–62, and Daniel P. Carpenter, *The Forging of Bureaucratic Autonomy: Reputation, Networks, and Policy Innovation in Executive Agencies, 1862–1928* (Princeton: Princeton University Press, 2001).

[78] In 1905 Sydney Fisher, the Minister of Agriculture, made the Census Office permanent; the Dominion Bureau of Statistics would not become its own government agency until 1918.

[79] United States Congress, *Report of the Ninth Census*, U.S. House of Representatives, 41st Congress, 2nd session (Washington D.C.: Government Printing Office, 1870), 51.

[80] United States Congress, *Enumeration of the Chinese Population of the United States*, U.S. House of Representatives, 51st Congress, 1st session (Washington D.C.: Government Printing Office, 1890). The bill failed in the Senate.

to the negro is absolutely demanded by the present condition of affairs."[81] The size and growth of the black population was indeed critical to how individual states justified their policies toward African Americans. If the black population was outgrowing the white, or reverting back to its "dominant form" (namely, if mulattoes were dying out), then white southerners who would soon be outnumbered by blacks could justify their repressive laws. If, however, the data demonstrated that black population growth was declining, then such measures could be challenged as unnecessary.[82] Lee suggests that the preoccupation with defining the black and partially black population can be explained against the prevailing racial climate of the United States, particularly in the South.[83] Rather than entrenching mixed-race as distinct from parent racial groups, these regulations worked to reinforce a hierarchy in which mixed-race status was encompassed within the same racialized social status as non-white groups.

Against the backdrop of increased non-white immigration and new forms of and barriers to whiteness, palpable nativist sentiment necessitated a complex racial classification system to legitimate the belief in distinct races. This was achieved in the United States through a consolidated, but not easily accessed, "white" racial category. The establishment of a permanent Census Bureau in 1902 made the enumeration of race a more administrative process, out of the reach of Congress and those who could lobby its representatives. This watershed institutional development did not come easily.[84] Under Superintendent Robert Porter in 1890 the Census Office was a temporary agency in the Department of the Interior. In 1893 it was moved back to the Department of Labor, where it had resided between 1885 and 1890. In institutional terms, the many examples of schematic indecisiveness in racial classifications were threads of a much larger and longer patchwork struggle for autonomy. In particular, congressional involvement in the design of the race question had disrupted the Census Office's attempt to maintain scientific rigor. Porter wrote in 1894 that the race question on an "ideal population schedule" would include just five classifications: white, black, Chinese, Japanese, and Indian.[85] When no instructions from

[81] Congressional Record 1889, p. 2246. [82] Nobles, *Shades of Citizenship*, 57.

[83] Sharon M. Lee, "Racial Classifications in the U.S. Census: 1890–1990," *Ethnic and Racial Studies* 16, no. 1 (1993): 77.

[84] See Walter F. Willcox, "The Development of the American Census Office since 1890," *Political Science Quarterly* 29, no. 3 (1914): 438–459.

[85] Robert Porter, "The Eleventh United States Census," *Journal of the Royal Statistical Society* 57, no. 4 (1894): 643–677.

Congress were given on racial classifications in 1900, the Census Office dropped the categories mulatto, quadroon, and octoroon.[86]

According to census historian Margo Anderson, a number of changes led to a permanent census office at the turn of the century: (1) there was Republican control over Congress and the Presidency after 1896; (2) advocates coordinated a systemic lobbying effort that combined the efforts of important expert groups such as the National Board of Trade, the American Economic Association and the American Statistical Association, and institutional insiders such as Caroll Wright and other Republican leaders; (3) the growing interest in social and economic statistics – especially of the cotton market – suggested the potential for additional surveys between decennial censuses; and (4) census administration had become routinized with regard to congressional apportionment and decoupled from the tax system.[87] To these I would add a fifth trend, transnational in scope – the centralizing of statistical agencies throughout the Western world.[88] The United States recognized at least forty years earlier that it was lagging behind in the production of reliable official statistics. A Report of the Secretary of the Interior in 1861 pleaded that "[a]ll enlightened foreign governments and several of the States sustain statistical bureaus, while the United States ... has yet to institute such an agency."[89] The establishment of a permanent Census Bureau aligned the United States with developments in census administration elsewhere.

This newly won administrative autonomy did not, however, make the Bureau immune to the social and political climate of the time. In the first few decades of the twentieth century, Congress took legislative initiatives to ensure the racial purity of America's national character. In 1911, Dillingham's Immigration Commission made claims of Nordic superiority, echoed five years later by Madison Grant's best-selling book, *The Passing of the Great Race*. Census data became the centerpiece of exclusionary immigration policies designed to keep all those designated

[86] Hochschild and Powell, "Racial Reorganization," 70.

[87] Anderson, *American Census*.

[88] Other countries in Europe and beyond followed similar trajectories: centralization took place in Germany in 1872, Norway in 1875, Hungary in 1897, the Netherlands in 1899, and Australia in 1906, and attempts to create a centralized imperial statistical office for the British Empire were made in the early twentieth century. A. Ross Eckler, *The Bureau of the Census* (New York: Praeger, 1972), 7; Jean-Pierre Beaud and Jean-Guy Prévost, "Statistics as the Science of Government: the Stillborn British Empire Statistical Bureau, 1918–20," *Journal of Imperial and Commonwealth History* 33, no. 3 (2005): 369–391.

[89] Quoted in Eckler, *Bureau of the Census*, 8.

with racial labels other than white – a shifting, unstable marker at the time – outside American borders. The 1921 Emergency Quota Act restricted immigration to 3 percent of foreign-born persons of each nationality resident in the United States according to 1910 census data. The National Origins Act of 1924 increased the restriction to 2 percent (based on the Census of 1890), and after June 30, 1927, limited total immigration from all countries to 150,000 based upon national origins of inhabitants according to census data from 1920. These provisions applied only to white would-be immigrants, since the 1924 Immigration Act also excluded all immigration from Asia.

Given the anxiety over immigration generally, and non-white immigration in particular, the state's need to control both the external boundaries of the nation and the internal population manifested through the expansion of census categories, which included "Filipino," "Hindu," "Korean," and "Other" (with a write-in space) in 1920. Hochschild and Powell note that census officials never did explain why these groups were based on nationality or religion rather than some amalgamated racial category such as "Asiatic" or "Mongolian."[90] This disaggregation is also particularly curious, given that other levels of the schematic state did not hesitate to paint these broad racial strokes. For example, interracial marriage with "Mongolians" was prohibited by a number of miscegenation laws during the same time period.[91] As Rogers Smith points out in his seminal book on the history of American citizenship, while congressional signals on questions of race, ethnicity, and access to citizenship were confused during the Progressive Era, the exclusionary thrust was clear.[92]

The mulatto category was again included in 1910 and 1920 before disappearing completely from the list of enumerated racial categories.

[90] Hochschild and Powell, "Racial Reorganization," 72.

[91] On the history of miscegenation laws in the United States, see Williamson, *New People*; David Fowler, *Northern Attitudes Towards Interracial Marriage: Legislation and Public Opinion in the Middle Atlantic and the States of the Old Northwest, 1780–1930* (New York and London: Garland Publishing, Inc., 1987); Davis, *Who is Black?*; Martha Hodes, *White Women, Black Men: Illicit Sex in the Nineteenth Century South* (New Haven: Yale University Press, 1997); Rachel Moran, *Interracial Intimacy: The Regulation of Race and Romance* (Chicago and London: University of Chicago Press, 2001); Peter Wallenstein, *Tell the Court I Love my Wife: Race, Marriage, and Law: An American History* (New York: Palgrave Macmillan, 2002); Julie L. Novkov, *Racial Union: Law, Intimacy, and the White State in Alabama, 1865–1954* (Ann Arbor: University of Michigan Press, 2008); Peggy Pascoe, *What Comes Naturally: Miscegenation Law and the Making of Race in America* (Oxford: Oxford University Press, 2009).

[92] Smith, *Civic Ideals*, 446–448.

During these last two appearances, "mulatto" was defined as all persons with any perceptible trace of Negro blood. Official reports of the Census Bureau imply that the validity of the data gathered in previous censuses was increasingly questioned. In a 1918 report, the Census Bureau admitted "It is probably true that a much greater population than 20.9 per cent of the Negro population in 1910 were of mixed parentage. The proportion more or less affected by the dissemination has been estimated as high as three-fourths, and although no adequate data are available to substantiate such an estimate, the estimate itself is not in itself improbable."[93] The Census Bureau attributed the variation in the proportion of respondents counted as mulatto to the employment of black enumerators in 1910 and white enumerators in 1920; the former tended to assign more people to the mulatto category than the latter.[94]

The contraction of the black category was a reflection of the changing social, political, and legal definitions of race in early twentieth century America – and, indeed, throughout the Western world. Not only did racial and scientific thought settle into a set of ideas that would dominate for nearly forty years, but racial segregation, sanctioned by the Supreme Court in the 1896 case of *Plessy v. Ferguson*,[95] hardened as the South accepted and actively promoted the policy of the one-drop rule. From the point of view of black nationalists, this development was not necessarily a bad thing. W.E.B. Du Bois, for example, was commissioned by Chief Statistician Walter Willcox to write a special population study to address policy issues pertaining to the African American population, and argued therein that all those of African ancestry should be classified together on the census.[96] Discussions of the nature of race were not monopolized by the international scientific community; it was also a sincere topic of discussion at conferences where the resistance to biological racialism took an international form. Both Franz Boas and W.E.B. Du Bois contributed to the 1911 Universal Races Congress in London. The Pan-African Congresses of 1919, 1921, 1923, and 1927 are also a testament to the early transnational linkages among communities of color around the world. Du Bois in particular emphasized the shared experience of

[93] United States Bureau of the Census, *Negro Population 1790–1915* (Washington D.C.: U.S. Government Printing Office, 1918), 209.

[94] Paul Schor, "Mobilising for Pure Prestige? Challenging Federal Census Ethnic Categories in the USA (1850–1940)," *International Social Science Journal* 57, no. 183 (2005): 91.

[95] *Plessy v. Ferguson* [1896] 163 U.S. 537.

[96] W.E.B. Du Bois, "The Twelfth Census and the Negro Problems," *The Southern Workman* 29, no. 5 (1900): 305–309.

exploitation entrenched by the global color line and used articulations of transnational blackness to promote international unity and racial pride.[97]

The extraordinary degree of variation in the racial taxonomies of the census between 1850 and 1930 was followed by relatively stable classification schema.[98] This trajectory was enabled by a 1929 Act of Congress that gave control over question content to the Census Bureau, finally providing an unprecedented level of institutional autonomy to America's statistical agency.[99] Racial ideas about impermeable racial boundaries remained an important factor that shaped classification schemas. After the elimination of the mulatto category, mixed-race people of various ancestries were classified in accordance with rather complicated equations:

- black + white = Negro ("no matter how small the percentage of Negro blood")
- black + Indian = Negro (in most cases – unless the person was regarded as an Indian in the community)
- white + Indian = Indian (in 1930; the 1940 Census reverted back to the "full-blood/mixed-blood" dichotomy of classifying Indian identity and in 1950 blood quantum was reintroduced with "full blood," "half to full" "quarter to half," and "less than one quarter" options)
- white + non-white = non-white
- non-white + non-white = race of the father

American institutions and racial projects continued to be important in terms of molding broader transnational racial ideas to the domestic context. Take the inclusion of a Mexican category in 1930 as an example. The category was dropped in 1936 following mass mobilization in opposition of Mexicans being classified separately from the white category. The Bureau, before agreeing to reclassify all Mexicans as white under intense political pressure, attempted to convince prominent Mexicans to participate because, officials argued, the census would engender greater visibility, which in turn would be a source of pride for Mexican-Americans.

[97] Julia E. Liss, "Diasporic Identities: The Science and Politics of Race in the Work of Franz Boas and W.E.B. Du Bois, 1894–1919," *Cultural Anthropology*, 13, no. 2 (1998): 146–51.

[98] Hochschild and Powell ("Racial Reorganization") argue that during this anomalous period of instability between 1850 and 1930, racial taxonomies in the census were driven by three motivations: a) the political desire for partisan advantage and the desire of one institution (Congress or the Census Bureau) to control or be autonomous of the other; b) the scientific efforts of agency analysts to produce results acceptable to their professional peers; and c) the ideological push for the census to reinforce or act upon normative beliefs about the racial order of American society.

[99] Eckler, *Bureau of the Census*.

However, Mexicans were concerned over the risk of being categorized as "colored" and subsumed under Jim Crow segregation and protested the change.[100] While it is true that immigration concerns extended to Hispanics and white ethnicities (Irish, Italian, Greek) as well, it is telling that only non-white categories were considered separate "races" in the census, at times in spite of relatively small populations. As Ian Haney Lopez has demonstrated, whiteness in the United States has long been defined by a process of negation – that is, by defining what whiteness is not, rather than what it is.[101]

Canada

The nineteenth century was a time of open Canadian borders. For example, between 1867 and 1896 Canada used promotional activities to attract its ideal immigrant: of British, American, or northern European "stock" and with agricultural experience.[102] Both the promotional activities and incentives for emigration at the time exhibited strong racial preferences, though an official immigration hierarchy had not yet been formalized in law. Origin information proved useful to track the influx of an estimated 15,000 Chinese laborers to the west coast in the 1880s, a situation that was advocated by political and business elites as necessary, and, importantly, temporary. As Prime Minister John A. MacDonald assured the House of Commons in 1882, once the Canadian Pacific Railroad was completed he would "join to a reasonable extent in preventing a permanent settlement in this country of Mongolian or Chinese immigrants."[103] The definition of desirable immigrants was expanded after 1896, when Sir Wilfred Laurier's Minister of the Interior, Clifford Sifton, committed to the rapid settlement of the West. His recruitment

[100] See Clara E. Rodriguez, *Changing Race: Latinos, the Census, and the History of Ethnicity in the United States* (New York: New York University Press, 2000), and Hochschild and Powell, "Racial Reorganization."

[101] Ian Haney Lopez, *White by Law: The Legal Construction of Race* (New York: New York University Press, 1996).

[102] On the history of immigration policy in Canada, see Freda Hawkins, *Critical Years in Immigration: Canada and Australia Compared* (Kingston and Montreal: McGill-Queen's University Press, 1989); Valerie Knowles, *Strangers at our Gates: Canadian Immigration and Immigration Policy, 1540–1990* (Toronto: Dundurn Press, 1992); Ninette Kelley and Michael Trebilcock, *The Making of the Mosaic: A History of Canadian Immigration Policy*, 2nd edn (Toronto: University of Toronto Press, 2010); Triadafilopoulos, *Becoming Multicultural.*

[103] House of Commons, *Debates*, May 12, 1882, 1477.

policy originally preferred and actively recruited immigrants from Britain, the United States, Germany, and other northern European countries. When these numbers proved insufficient the range of preferred source countries was enlarged to include Central and Eastern Europeans. In particular, Sifton sought those with farming experience or those who were willing to work the land.

State strategies for preventing non-white immigration to Canada became increasingly stringent over time, aided and abetted by informal mechanisms of controlling the activities and movement of non-white populations already inside the country.[104] Formal policies of the state – such as the Chinese head tax of 1885, the 1910 Immigration Act's "continuous journey" clause, and the total exclusion of Chinese immigration in 1923 – were compounded by regulatory policies, such as the 1919 amendment to section 38(c) of the 1910 Immigration Act, which allowed Canada to prohibit the entry of any immigrant belonging to any race or nationality deemed unsuitable to the climate, industrial, social, educational, labor, or other conditions of the country or deemed undesirable due to their peculiar customs, habits, modes of life, and methods of holding property, or because of the likelihood such immigrants would be inassimilable.[105] Census policy was designed in collaboration with immigration officials, and census data were useful for determining the success of these initiatives.[106]

[104] On racial segregation in Canada, see Peter S. Li, *The Chinese in Canada* (Toronto: Oxford University Press, 1988); Agnes Calliste, "Race, Gender and Canadian Immigration Policy: Blacks from the Caribbean, 1900–1932," *Journal of Canadian Studies* 28, no. 4 (1993): 131–148; Constance Backhouse, *Colour-Coded: A Legal History of Racism in Canada: 1900–1950* (Toronto: University of Toronto Press, 1999); Walker, *"Race," Rights and the Law*; Sarah-Jane (Saje) Mathieu, "North of the Colour Line: Sleeping Car Porters and the Battle against Jim Crow on Canadian Rails, 1880–1920," *Labour/Le Travail* 47 (2001): 9–42.

[105] Hawkins, *Critical Years in Immigration*, 17. Informal mechanisms proved particularly useful for excluding potential non-white immigrants, including African Americans that were deemed inadmissible by immigration officials because the Canadian climate was "too cold for Negroes." See Harold Martin Troper, "The Creek-Negroes of Oklahoma and Canadian Immigration, 1909–11," *The Canadian Historical Review* 53, no. 3 (1972), 287.

[106] NAC RG31 Accession 1989–90/133, box 29, file 7267, "Nationality, Orientals and Others," memorandum for Mr. Macphail, Chief, Division of Census and Vital Statistics, Re: Chinese Population [n.d.]. Though the bureaucracy faced pressure that "Every Oriental in Canada should be ear-marked" from White Canada organizations such as the Maple Leaf Association and the White Canada Association, R.H. Coats replied that "the information collected in the Census cannot be used for any other than purely statistical purposes." Letter from Coats to Chas E. Hope. Secretary, White Canada Association, January 12, 1931.

In contrast to the all-encompassing "white" category on the American census, the Canadian census conceptualized white ethnicities as different races largely because of the paramount and contentious relationship between English and French Canada. From Lord Durham's 1839 report, which identified Canada as "two nations warring within the bosom of a single state" and recommended increased immigration from Britain to aid in the assimilation of (the purportedly inferior) French culture, to the Confederation debates and beyond, the major cleavage throughout Canadian history and society has been the ethnic, cultural, and linguistic differences between its French- and English-speaking elements. The assimilation of the French was an overt policy goal before 1867, and the increase of the Anglophone population was progress toward that goal. This changed with Confederation when the Quebecois morphed into a "founding race."[107] In 1871 and 1881, census enumerators were instructed to enter information on origin "scrupulously," using the words "English, Irish, Scotch, African, Indian, German, French and so forth."[108] Sympathetic to Francophone nationalism, Deputy Minister Joseph-Charles Taché tweaked the underlying schematic of the 1871 Census, splitting the British origins into English, Scottish, Welsh, and Irish while homogenizing French Canadian identity, though, as Bruce Curtis astutely points out, France was an unstable entity at the time. The same outcome arose from asymmetrically applied rules of patrilineal descent. Origin was traced through the father; however, if a person's mother *or* father was born in Quebec, the respondent became "census French." This practice, a schematic state strategy of Francophone protectionism, was only followed in Quebec but effectively made "French" the largest group in Canada.[109]

By 1905, the Census and Statistics Office was established as a permanent, separate entity within the Department of Agriculture. Institutionalization came before centralization and neither emerged without help from abroad.

[107] The language of race was also used to characterize the English–French conflict, most notably in Siegfried's 1907 treatise, *The Race Question in Canada*. See also Henri Bourassa (1913) "Le langue française et l'avenir de notre race" (the French language and the future of our race) and even the much-later 1968 autobiography of Pierre Vallières, "Nègres blanc d'amérique, autobiographie précode d'un 'terroriste' québécois" (White Niggers of America: the Precocious Autobiography of a Quebec "Terrorist"). See Corrie Scott, "How French Canadians Became White Folks, or Doing Things with Race in Quebec," *Ethnic and Racial Studies* 39, no. 7 (2016): 1280–1297.

[108] Canada, Department of Agriculture, *Census of Canada, 1870–71* (Ottawa: I.B. Taylor, 1871).

[109] Curtis, *The Politics of Population*, 285–286.

On the heels of the Boer War in 1911, the Dominions Royal Commission was struck to determine the natural resources, manufacturing capabilities, status of international trade, and fiscal policy of each part of the British Empire. Canada's representative was George Foster, who was also the newly appointed Minister of Trade and Commerce. One of the first things the Commission uncovered was the abysmal state of statistics. Foster made several important decisions to rectify the situation, moving the Census and Statistics Office to the Ministry of Trade and Commerce and appointing a departmental commission on official statistics. This commission was heavily influenced by A.L. Bowley, a British expert on statistics who viewed a central statistical office as a "central thinking office." In 1914 the Dominions Commission drew again from Bowley and the Australian experience and made the same recommendation for the creation of a centralized office that would manage the production of Canadian statistics. Its proposal certainly was not an order from the Crown to revamp Canada's statistical system. It did, however, send a strong signal and provide a positive incentive for Canada to align with developments in the statistical systems of other countries. In 1916 the government created the position of Dominion Statistician and appointed Robert Hamilton Coats to it; he would serve in this position for over twenty-five years, until 1942. Coats immediately submitted to Cabinet a paper entitled "A National System of Statistics for Canada – Centralization, Reorganization and Enlargement of Canadian Statistics." Following these recommendations, the Dominion Bureau of Statistics was created in 1918.[110]

In spite of substantial institutional innovation and centralization between 1901 and 1941, the racial origin question remained insidiously consistent though the racial categories within the schematic state were sometimes contradictory. Canadian census-taking began the dawn of a new century by explicitly focusing on racial origins, rather than the previously used label of simply "origins." The census guide defined "race" as "a subgroup of the human species related by ties of physical kinship. Scientists have attempted to divide and subdivide the human species into groups on the basis of biological traits, such as the shape of head, stature, colour of skin, etc."[111] Policymakers in the Dominion Bureau of Statistics

[110] This history draws from Coats' recollection, documented in Robert Hamilton Coats, "Beginnings in Canadian Statistics," 27, no. 2 (1946): 109–130, and Worton's (*The Dominion Bureau of Statistics*, 59–80) analysis.

[111] Canada, Dominion Bureau of Statistics, *Sixth Census of Canada, 1921. Instructions to Commissioners and Enumerators* (Ottawa: Government Printing Bureau, 1921). Similar to the United States, these racial ideas were fueled by a growing discourse on eugenics.

drew from the ways in which American policy had modified the global idea of race, using, for example, the United States Immigration Commission's 1911 *Dictionary of Races or Peoples* for census grouping purposes.[112]

Census monographs and instructions to enumerators provide examples of different races, including English, Scotch, Irish, Welsh, French, German, Italian, Danish, Swedish, Norwegian, Bohemian, Ruthenian, Bukovinian, Galician, Bulgarian, Chinese, Japanese, Polish, and Jewish. Some races that did not readily align with the global color line needed further clarification; for example, in 1911 enumerators were instructed that if a respondent was born in Turkey, "the enumerator should ask whether European Turkey or Asiatic Turkey, and write Turkey (E.) or Turkey (A.) accordingly."[113] The census also warns that the terms "American" and "Canadian" should not be used as racial origins, as "there are no races of men so called." As early as in the 1920s, census officials noted public agitation to record "Canadian" as a racial origin. This was, however, hard to fit into the racial schematic and maligned with global definitions of race. In 1926, a memorandum to the Dominion Statistician quipped,

> One cannot change the shape of one's skull or one's physical characteristics by Act of Parliament nor would it be possible for us to insert the term "Canadian" in our racial origin classification without exposing ourselves to the ridicule of the scientific ethnologists throughout the world. It would be a step which, with all their spread-eaglism, the Americans have never taken, and they have succeeded as we all recognize in working up a very high degree of national sentiment without it.[114]

This was not the last of these debates. The status of "Canadian" – whether it was an origin or a nationality – would return to plague census officials after the Second World War and again in the 1990s.

As in America, however, the idea of a "Caucasian race" that was unified against races on the other side of the color line persisted.[115] French Canadians, along with continental and Eastern Europeans, faced

See McLaren, *Our Own Master Race*, and Mariana Valverde, *The Age of Light, Soap and Water: Moral Reform in English Canada, 1885–1925* (Toronto: University of Toronto Press, 1991).

[112] NAC RG31 Accession 1989–90/133, box 29, file 7267, "Nationality, Orientals and Others," Letter from R.H. Coats, Dominion Statistician, to Dr. Helen R.Y. Reid, Chairman, Division on Immigration, Canadian National Committee for Mental Hygiene. December 10, 1930.

[113] Canada, *Fifth Census of Canada, 1911. Instructions to Officers, Commissioners and Enumerators* (Ottawa: Government Printing Bureau, 1911), 27.

[114] NAC RG31, vol. 1417, Records of the Assistant Dominion Statistician, Racial Origin. Memorandum for Mr. Coats, from Chief, General Statistics Branch. May 12, 1926.

[115] Baum, *Rise and Fall.*

prejudice and discrimination during this time period and were racialized in particular ways by reference to a shifting set of factors that defined whiteness. But these groups have also had access to white privilege – the right to vote and retain legal counsel in Canada and the avoidance of Jim Crow in the United States, for example – in ways that non-white populations have not.[116] And while two classic studies of origin statistics in Canada deny the relevance of the white/non-white divide, contending that the question was "clearly cultural rather than biological in intent,"[117] each country's invocation of some variant of the one-drop rule in its classification of mixed-race identities tells a different story about the pervasiveness of transnational biological racialism.

That is to say, while white respondents were classified by patrilineal descent, Canada adopted its own version of the one-drop rule to classify white/non-white progeny. For those of Aboriginal descent, beginning in 1911 the census required that the names of "tribes" be recorded and that racial origin be traced through the mother's side. This requirement of matrilineal descent is particularly interesting given that the progeny of Aboriginal women and non-Aboriginal men would be considered to be "Indian" in the census and yet would be denied Indian status by the Indian Act. Why this inconsistency? On the one hand, a long process of institutional development may have prevented schematic standardization. During its formative years the Dominion Bureau of Statistics was likely not overly concerned with promoting a standardized racial classification system throughout the federal government. The fact that two distinct arms of the state would categorize the same population in different ways is simply another example of the contradictory rationality of the schematic state apparatus. The Indian Act, whose unabashed goal was to, as Duncan Campbell Scott, Deputy Superintendent for the Department of Indian Affairs, put it, "get rid of the Indian problem ... to continue until there is not a single Indian in Canada that has not be absorbed into the body politic and there is no

116 On this point in the American context, see Noel Ignatiev, *How the Irish Became White* (New York: Routledge, 1995) and David Roediger, *Working toward Whiteness: How American's Immigrants Became White; The Strange Journey from Ellis Island to the Suburbs* (New York: Basic Books, 2005).

117 N.B. Ryder, "The Interpretation of Origin Statistics," *The Canadian Journal of Economics and Political Science* 21, no. 4 (1955): 478; John Kralt, "Ethnic Origins in the Canadian Census, 1871–1986," in *Ethnic Demography: Canadian Immigrant, Ethnic and Cultural Variations*, eds. Shiva S. Halli, Frank Trovato, and Leo Driedger (Montreal and Kingston: McGill-Queen's University Press, 1990), 13–29.

Indian department,"[118] had a different function and purpose – and therefore, different political consequences – than the census.

On the other hand, however, both the census and the Indian Act were historically, and remain today, legal instruments through which racial categories are made and manipulated. They do not simply reflect racial reality, but are fundamental to its existence. As such, discourses of race and gender collide through the state's schematizing impetus: there were legal sanctions for Aboriginal women who married non-Aboriginals through the Indian Act regime, once again affirming the stereotype that Aboriginal women were far more likely to "marry out" than the unfathomable circumstance that white women would "marry in."[119] At the same time, the rationale of the census required Aboriginal ancestry be traced through matrilineal descent since women were perceived as the vessels of (un)civilization, culture, and morality,[120] juxtaposed with the patrilineal tracing of white descent, since men were the conveyors of property and citizenship rights.

Patrilineal or matrilineal descent mattered not for mixed white/non-white progeny, as "the children begotten of marriages between white and black or yellow races will be classed as Negro or Mongolian (Chinese or Japanese) as the case may be."[121] In the 1931 and 1941 censuses, eugenicist language permeated the wording of the question, referring to "the distant coloured stocks ... involving differences in colour (i.e. the black, red, yellow, or brown races)."[122] In other words, any mixed-race person whose parental or ancestral lineage was comprised of European and non-white components would legally be counted by the census as non-white. This concern about the classification of mixed-race offspring reflects eugenicist anxiety not simply about non-white immigration to Canada, but also regarding the reproduction of "degenerates" and the so-called

[118] Quoted in E. Brian Titley, *A Narrow Vision: Duncan Campbell Scott and the Administration of Indian Affairs in Canada* (Vancouver: University of British Columbia Press, 1986).

[119] Sylva Van Kirk, "From 'Marrying-In' to 'Marrying-Out': Changing Patterns of Aboriginal/Non-Aboriginal Marriage in Colonial Canada," *Frontiers: A Journal of Women Studies* 23, no. 3 (2002): 1–11.

[120] Valverde, *The Age of Light, Soap and Water;* Dorothy Roberts, *Killing the Black Body: Race, Reproduction, and the Meaning of Liberty* (New York: Vintage, 1997).

[121] Canada, *Sixth Census of Canada,* 1921.

[122] Canada, Dominion Bureau of Statistics, *Seventh Census of Canada, 1931. Instructions to Commissioners and Enumerators* (Ottawa: King's Printer, 1931); Canada, Dominion Bureau of Statistics, *Eighth Census of Canada, 1941. Instructions to Commissioners and Enumerators* (Ottawa: King's Printer, 1941).

"unfit" already in the country. According to these beliefs, mixed-race people were contaminants to the nation, their contribution to society questionable. For example, a 1941 article in the *Journal of Negro Education* attempts to determine the intelligence of "negroes of mixed blood in Canada," by testing the relationship between standardized test scores and Negro groups comprising "full bloods," "3/4 bloods," "1/2 bloods," and "1/4 bloods" – in the author's words, "the correlation between intelligence and degree of White blood."[123] These views were also promoted by political elites. In 1922 Prime Minister William Lyon Mackenzie King argued in the House of Commons that Gresham's Law of Precious metals applied to the races of men; just as base metals tended to overwhelm finer metals, King cautioned that the presence of "lower" races in Canada would lead to the dilution of the Anglo-Saxon population.[124] Those with such inherently degenerate characteristics could never be considered potential members of the dominant race; in the words of Ann Laura Stoler, white is a color that is easily stained.[125] Hence, white/non-white mixes were classified as non-white on the census.

CONCLUSION

During the nineteenth and early twentieth centuries the census was an evolving racial project, shaping and being shaped by dominant global ideas of race and racial difference of the time. Racial ideas evolved via the debates and discussions of international epistemic communities of scientists, anthropologists, and ethnologists and were mediated by state-level political institutions and national political contexts. National imperatives sometimes augmented larger global debates about racial difference and in other circumstances prevented an explicit emulation of the ways that race was institutionalized elsewhere. At the same time, the development of administrative machinery to support and guide census-taking was informed by larger global trends in statistical science. Political institutions were initially weak and census administration haphazard, providing more incentive for political elites and bureaucrats to seek successful models that could be adapted to North American contexts. Over time, statistical systems

[123] H.A. Tanser, "Intelligence of Negroes of Mixed Blood in Canada," *The Journal of Negro Education* 10, no. 4 (1941): 650–652. The results of the test were inconclusive.

[124] Canada, House of Commons, *Debates*, May 8, 1922, 1555.

[125] Ann Laura Stoler, *Carnal Knowledge and Imperial Power: Race and the Intimate in Colonial Rule* (Berkley: University of California Press, 2002), 15.

became more centralized. The participants in census policy decisions during this time period foreshadow the key agents in each country. In America, the office that eventually became the Census Bureau consulted with experts and often struggled for autonomy under congressional oversight (and sometimes congressional overstep). In contrast, the statistical office of Canada was firmly entrenched within a centralized Westminster structure and the involvement of political elites was limited once the representation by population issue was settled by Confederation. The Dominion Bureau of Statistics was also less prone to consulting experts and innovation was driven by senior-level civil servants, especially the Dominion Statistician.

The schematic state interpreted global ideas of biological racialism and deployed changing grids on a society that constantly defied these best-laid plans of elites and bureaucrats. Racial discourses were complex and constantly changing as they were adopted in national contexts. New racial categories were added each decade, while others were discarded, disaggregated, or modified. The schematic state possessed significant autonomy over racial definitions in all areas of law and policy, shared among its legislative, bureaucratic, and judicial branches, which often offered competing definitions of whiteness, blackness, foreignness, and who should count as what. These boundary-making practices helped to shape the meaning of racial difference; though there was clearly a normative exclusionary thrust and a desire to protect the boundaries of whiteness, different racial groups invoked peculiar strands of a larger racial ideology. Aboriginals had to be civilized and territorially dispossessed; blacks were exploited as property before they were condemned as a dehumanized people; Asians were a global migratory threat; ethnic whites were undesired, but could be assimilated into whiteness if necessary; and mixed-race was problematic for the totalizing racial schematic, which depended on cordoned-off impermeable spaces, not blurred lines. These ideas did not influence census outcomes directly, but, rather, were mediated through political institutions. This means that institutional structures, path dependencies, and national politics all mattered a great deal in the formulation of the classificatory content. However, these cases held in common state-directed efforts to make the population legible by solidifying racial discourse and imposing a hierarchical racial order.

4

The Death and Resurrection of Race

The Second World War began a transnational moment – a brief period of transition, both temporal and temporary – when the normative context surrounding previously dominant conceptions of race as irrefutably biological, determinative, and hierarchically ordered fundamentally shifted. The Holocaust and the demise of Nazi Germany shook the foundations of the biological construction of race to its core. During the war the Allies drew ideological distinctions between "us" and "them," and by underscoring the connection between the wickedness of racism and the evilness of the enemy created a normative standard by which they too could be judged. As the Cold War enveloped the world shortly thereafter, Canada, Great Britain, and the United States found themselves in positions where their legitimacy on the international stage and to their citizens, as well as their claims about the virtues of democracy in the global struggle between ideological systems, depended in part on how they addressed the tension between these shifting transnational norms and racism in their domestic spheres of influence.

This chapter begins by examining a number of key factors that animated racial discourse during this transitory moment, many of which were located beyond the control or purview of any one nation-state. These international developments coalesced with changes in domestic racial projects, together forming transnational impulses that shaped the legitimacy of state action and inaction with regards to racial discrimination. American developments were particularly important, holding implications for a number of political arenas, including the census. British, Canadian, and American governments drew upon these transitioning norms when reforming their approaches to racial enumeration.

This macro-level change in the idea of race did not compel states to abide by the terms of the global normative context, nor were the ways racial ideas were put into practice in different societies perfectly emulated. In fact, as decision-makers in the United States turned to racial data in the census to formulate and monitor civil rights regimes, political elites in Canada and Britain sought to simultaneously avoid American-style racial tension and create anti-discrimination regimes to suit their national circumstances. Both countries translated worldviews and programmatic beliefs in several ways that obstructed any impetus to create a census question on race that could be used to monitor the effectiveness of their newly instituted civil rights legislation. First, an important institutional driver of counting by race was missing: civil rights legislation that specifically mandated the use of racial census data. Second, the cultural translations of the changing racial worldview in Canada and Britain prevented racial enumeration. The concerns of the international statistical community and the low policy stakes associated with the census led policymakers in Canada to abandon the *terminology* of race, though not the origin question itself. In Great Britain, where the post-war immigration of colonial subjects made race a salient domestic issue, elites worried about the "offensive" nature of a question on race and about the ways that racial data could be used by anti-immigration agitators. In general, public officials in both countries viewed race as being overly divisive and the nature of Canadian and British census-making institutions privileged their arguments and obstructed the potential for policy change. At least part of the cause of racial tension and violence in the United States, elites in these countries assumed, was the continuing salience of and institutional emphasis on the very concept of race.

THE TRANSNATIONAL DEMISE OF BIOLOGICAL RACIALISM

The edifice of biological racialism began to crumble in the wake of the Second World War, spurring a change not simply in the operation of racial politics or the way that race was invoked therein, though these changes did eventually occur in, for example, the delegitimizing of race as a criterion for exclusion in immigration policies.[1] Rather, *there was also a fundamental shift in the transnational idea of race itself*. Thus, while

[1] Daniel J. Tichenor, *Dividing Lines: The Politics of Immigration Control in America* (Princeton: Princeton University Press, 2002) and Christian Joppke, *Selecting by Origin: Ethnic Migration in the Liberal State* (Cambridge: Harvard University Press, 2005).

the substantive stakes of domestic racial politics did not immediately shift, the world-historical racial project destabilized when the support structure of biological racialism was challenged. More concretely, the practical consequences of warfare catalyzed change, especially in America's color line. Philip Klinkner and Rogers Smith demonstrate that during the Second World War, "the interaction of pressing requirements of national security, the service and heroism of blacks in uniform, protest by black civilians, and the need to set America apart from its undemocratic and racist opponents put great strain on the nation's Jim Crow system."[2] As Eleanor Roosevelt openly expressed, "the nation cannot expect colored people to feel that the United States is worth defending if the Negro continues to be treated as he is now."[3] The phrase "Double V" – victory over enemies abroad, and victory over discrimination at home – became a popular wartime slogan for many African Americans.

In the academy, the biological construction of race – and the naturalized racial hierarchies the concept relied upon – was already under siege. Anthropologist Franz Boas' 1911 work, *The Mind of Primitive Man*, disputed the notion of hereditary racial purity and argued that races are not immutable entities but, rather, are influenced by environmental and other factors. His students, including Ruth Benedict, Melville Herskovits, and Margaret Mead, also redefined understandings of race and social difference. In contrast to the epistemic communities of scientists that helped to create and reify biological racialism, in the post-war era egalitarian views of race from the social sciences were important, cumulatively forming a transnational, interdisciplinary response to Nazism from 1933 to 1940.[4] These efforts compounded the much earlier, but often ignored work of African American scholars, including W.E.B. Du Bois and the "Howard School" of international relations.[5] Cracks turned to chasms in

[2] Philip A. Klinkner and Rogers M. Smith, *The Unsteady March: The Rise and Decline of Racial Equality in America* (Chicago: University of Chicago Press, 1999), 162.

[3] Quoted in Paul Gordon Lauren, *Power and Prejudice: The Politics and Diplomacy of Racial Discrimination*, 2nd edn (Boulder: Westview Press, 1996), 149.

[4] Barkan, *The Retreat of Scientific Racism*, 302–306; see, for example, Julian Huxley and Alfred Haddon, *We Europeans: A Survey of "Racial" Problems* (New York and London: Harper, 1935); Ruth Benedict, *Race: Science and Politics* (New York: Modern Age Books, 1940); and Ashley Montagu, *Man's Most Dangerous Myth: The Fallacy of Race* (Walnut Creek: AltaMira Press, 1942).

[5] Aldon Morris, *The Scholar Denied: W.E.B. Du Bois and the Birth of Modern Sociology* (Oakland: University of California Press, 2015); Robert Vitalis, *White World Order, Black Power Politics: The Birth of American International Relations* (Ithaca: Cornell University Press, 2015).

many academic disciplines, which were increasingly divided in their support of biological racialism before the Second World War and which now challenged some of its basic operating principles.[6]

These developments helped spur an emerging global discourse of human rights, solidified by important declarations of international organizations in the 1950s and 1960s. The United Nations and its 1948 Universal Declaration of Human Rights enshrined inalienable rights for all members of the human family and made it clear that racial discrimination was morally indefensible. In December 1949, UNESCO, under the direction of British anthropologist Julian Huxley, invited prominent anthropologists and sociologists of the day to form an expert committee on the concept of race. The committee, which included Claude Levi-Strauss, Ashley Montagu, and Gunnar Mydral, published *The Race Question* in 1950. The statement distinguishes between the biological and social constructions of race, condemns the human and social damage done by the myth of race, and suggests dropping references to the term "race" altogether in favor of the phrase "ethnic groups."[7] The idea that race was more myth than biological reality prompted criticism from the scientific community and a second statement was published in 1951. Written by prominent physical anthropologists and geneticists, *The Race Concept: Results of an Inquiry* retained the concept of race, but noted there was no evidence to support doctrines of racial superiority and inferiority.[8] In 1964 another international group of experts convened. In *Proposals on the Biological Aspects of Race*, the group agreed with the principle of racialism (that humans could be divided into subgroups for classification purposes), but concluded that "the biological data given above stand in open contradiction to the tenets of racism. Racist theories can in no way pretend to have any scientific foundation."[9] UNESCO's 1967 *Statement on Race and Racial Prejudice* was a further effort to identify and address the social causes of racism. Article 26 of the 1966 International Covenant on Civil and Political Rights also required states to guarantee equal and effective protection against discrimination, and the International Declaration on the Elimination of All Forms of Racial Discrimination of 1963 led to an international legal treaty in 1965.[10]

[6] See Dorothy Ross, *The Origins of American Social Science* (Cambridge: Cambridge University Press, 1991).

[7] UNESCO, *The Race Question* (Paris: UNESCO, 1950).

[8] UNESCO, *The Race Concept: Results of an Inquiry* (Paris: UNESCO, 1952).

[9] UNESCO, *Proposals on the Biological Aspects of Race* (Paris: UNESCO, 1964).

[10] See Michael Banton, *The International Politics of Race* (Oxford and Malden: Blackwell Publishers, 2002).

Cumulatively, these efforts were a powerful international condemnation of biological racialism and state efforts to maintain racial hierarchies.

Decolonization in Asia and Africa similarly shifted the transnational normative context surrounding both international and domestic race relations. In the post-war period there was a growing global consensus that conflicts of the future would be racial in character.[11] For example, Frank Füredi writes that officials in the Anglo-American world took exception to their deliberate exclusion from the Bandung Conference of 1955, which brought together the leaders of twenty-nine nations in Africa, the Middle East, and Asia, but were more concerned that the "colored nations" of the world would unite together against white global dominance.[12] By the time the UN General Assembly adopted the Declaration on the Granting of Independence to Colonial Countries and Peoples in 1960, African member states had already begun to increase their presence in the international arena.[13] The significance of these newly sovereign states lies in Cold War tactics for maintaining the stalemate between the world's two superpowers. As both the Soviets and Americans pushed these nations to adopt one ideological system or the other, many former colonies sought to create a neutral, non-aligned "Third World."[14]

Equally important were the ways in which the norm of human rights changed the international cultural standard of moral legitimacy,[15] thereby shaping the terms and conditions of the global struggle over ideological systems. Soviet propaganda highlighted the tension between American ideals of democracy and its reality of racial discrimination, turning domestic race relations crises into global performances for a watchful world audience.[16] For example, when Arkansas Governor Orval Faubus declared a state of emergency and called in the Arkansas National

[11] Frank Füredi, *The Silent War: Imperialism and the Changing Perception of Race* (New Brunswick: Rutgers University Press, 1998), 18, 183. See also Lauren, *Power and Prejudice*, and Penny M. Von Eschen, *Race against Empire: Black Americans and Anti-Colonialism, 1937–1957* (Ithaca: Cornell University Press, 1997).

[12] Ibid., 206. See also Seng Tan and Amitav Acharya, eds., *Bandung Revisited: The Legacy of the 1955 Asian-African Conference for the International Order* (Singapore: National University of Singapore Press, 2008).

[13] At the end of the 1950s, 11 African states were UN members; 10 years later they represented 41 of the 128 member states.

[14] Lauren, *Power and Prejudice*, 210–250.

[15] See Yasemin Nuhoğlu Soysal, *Limits of Citizenship: Migrants and Postnational Membership in Europe* (Chicago: University of Chicago Press, 1994).

[16] John David Skrentny, "The Effect of the Cold War on African-American Civil Rights: America and the World Audience, 1945–1968." *Theory and Society* 27, no. 2 (1998): 262. On the relationship between the Cold War and the advancement of civil rights in the

Guard to prevent the enrolment of nine African American students at Central High School in Little Rock on September 4, 1957, there was extensive international media coverage of the event and its aftermath – so much so that American newspapers viewed the international coverage itself as newsworthy.[17] America's international image was on President Dwight Eisenhower's mind when he sent federal troops to Little Rock. In a radio and television address to the American public on September 24, 1957, he explained:

> At a time when we face grave situations abroad because of the hatred that Communism bears toward a system of government based on human rights, it would be difficult to exaggerate the harm that is being done to the prestige and influence, and indeed to the safety of our nation and the world. Our enemies are gloating over this incident and using it everywhere to misrepresent our whole nation. We are portrayed as a violator of those standards of conduct which the peoples of the world united to proclaim in the Charter of the United Nations.[18]

The United States claimed a superior system of governance based on principles of liberalism and equality and yet, as Gunnar Mydral argued in *An American Dilemma*, there was a stunning disconnect between the "American creed" and African Americans' social reality.[19] In order to

United States, see Derrick Bell, "Brown v. Board of Education and the Interest-Convergence Dilemma," *Harvard Law Review* 93 (1980): 518–533; Gerald Horne, *Black and Red: W.E. B Du Bois and the Afro-American Response to the Cold War, 1944–1963* (Albany: State University of New York Press, 1986); Mary L. Dudziak, "Desegregation as a Cold War Imperative," *Stanford Law Review* 41, no. 1 (1988): 61–120; Klinkner and Smith, *Unsteady March*; Mary L. Dudziak, *Cold War Civil Rights: Race and the Image of American Democracy* (Princeton: Princeton University Press, 2000); Thomas Borstelmann, *The Cold War and the Color Line: American Race Relations in the Global Arena* (Cambridge: Harvard University Press, 2002); and Alvin B. Tillery, *Between Homeland and Motherland: Africa, U.S. Foreign Policy, and Black Leadership in America* (Ithaca: Cornell University Press, 2011). For a more theoretical take along similar lines, see Doug McAdam, "On the International Origins of Domestic Political Opportunities," in *Social Movements and American Political Institutions*, eds. Anne N. Costain and Andrew S. McFarland (Oxford and New York: Rowman and Littlefield Publishers, 1998), 251–267.

[17] Mary L. Dudziak, "The Little Rock Crisis and Foreign Affairs: Race, Resistance and the Image of American Democracy," *Southern California Law Review* 70, no. 6 (1997): 1664–1679. See also Azza Salama Layton, "International Pressure and the U.S. Government's Response to Little Rock," *The Arkansas Historical Quarterly* 56, no. 3 (1997): 257–272.

[18] Quoted in Dudziak, "Little Rock Crisis," 1681–1682.

[19] Gunnar Myrdal, *An American Dilemma: The Negro Problem and Modern Democracy*, 20th anniversary edn (New York: Harper and Row, 1962).

gain strategic leverage in Cold War politics, America was forced to confront its own hypocrisy.[20]

Civil rights activists, well aware of these concerns, used international criticisms to leverage their positions. In 1947 the NAACP filed a petition to the United Nations Commission on Human Rights, entitled *An Appeal to the World: A Statement on the Denial of Human Rights to Minorities in the Case of Citizens of Negro Descent in the United States of America and An Appeal to the United Nations for Redress*. The fact that the Soviet Union introduced the petition to the Commission complicated the intentions of NAACP's Du Bois and Walter White. During a time when activists and their social change agendas were often red-baited as subversive, civil rights leaders wanted to present their organizations as being helpful to American foreign relations.[21] Du Bois and White also knew the power of the UN to address domestic racism was limited. Though the UN did not act on the petition, the worldwide publicity it received negatively affected America's global legitimacy and helped catalyze action at home.[22] Years later, Martin Luther King's Nobel Peace Prize in 1964 cemented his appeal to the world audience and provided the civil rights movement with more strategies for using the global stage.[23] From a jail cell in Selma, Alabama, King wrote an ad for the *New York Times* asking for support, decrying:

> When the King of Norway participated in awarding the Nobel Peace Prize to me he surely did not think that in less than sixty days I would be in jail. He, and almost all world opinion will be shocked because they are little aware of the unfinished business in the South. By jailing hundreds of Negroes, the city of Selma, Alabama, has revealed the persisting ugliness of segregation to the nation and the world.[24]

[20] Importantly, as John Skrentny ("The Effect of the Cold War") points out, not all branches of the United States government were equally concerned with the damage American race relations did to its image abroad. Sub-national governments – especially of the southern states intent on retaining, as Governor of Alabama George Wallace famously said in his 1963 inaugural address, "segregation now, segregation tomorrow, segregation forever" – were far less concerned with the world audience than other arms of the state, especially the Presidency and State Department.

[21] Mary L. Dudziak, "Brown as a Cold War Case," *Journal of American History* 91, no. 1 (2004): 36. While the Cold War created an environment that provided the civil rights movement with political opportunities that could then be used to advance racial equality, it came with a serious cost to many individual African-Americans. The FBI, for example, put many civil rights leaders under surveillance to ascertain Communist infiltration.

[22] Skrentny, "Effect of the Cold War," 257.

[23] John D. Skrentny, *The Minority Rights Revolution* (Cambridge: Harvard University Press, 2002), 36.

[24] Quoted in Skrentny, "Effect of the Cold War," 259.

Ripples of diasporic awareness were awakened by the civil rights movement and the struggle for human rights throughout the world. Racial minorities in Britain, Canada, and elsewhere identified with the civil rights movement, though their targets differed and were tempered by their own political circumstances. On-the-ground challenges to state-based discrimination were abetted – for neither the first nor the last time – by transnational popular culture, music, hero-worship, folklore, promise, potential, and symbolism that imagined racial communities as interconnected and struggling together in multiple places at once. For example, in 1969 black Canadian newspapers in Toronto and Montreal spread the message that "we are all Black," making explicit the linkages between the plights of black Canadians, other racialized populations in Canada, and the transnational contexts of the African diaspora, the American Black Power movement, anti-colonialism in Africa, and the first years of Caribbean independence.[25] Ideas and identities from the civil rights movement and other anti-racist and anti-colonial movements once again reframed racial struggles in a global context.

By the time of the Convention of the Elimination of All Forms of Racial Discrimination, adopted by the United Nations in 1966 and ratified in 1969, the idea of universal human rights was indisputable. American developments were undoubtedly important; civil rights abuses made headlines around the world and victories, such as the *Brown* decision, were used by Americans as Cold War propaganda that racism was diminishing.[26] This period was one of rapid change. Before the Second World War, beliefs in a natural racial hierarchy were dominant throughout Europe and North America. In contrast, the post-war era witnessed a clear shift in normative contexts from both domestic and international events, whose effects were fundamentally transnational.[27] This is not to

[25] Dorothy Williams, *The Road to Now: A History of Blacks in Montreal* (Montreal: Vehicule Press, 1997); Jonathan Thompson, *"We Are All Black": Contrast, Uhuru and the African-Canadian Press, 1969–1970*, Unpublished M.A. Thesis (Kingston: Queen's University, 2008); Mathieu, *North of the Color Line;* Sean Mills, *The Empire Within: Postcolonial Thought and Political Activism in Sixties Montreal* (Montreal and Kingston: McGill-Queen's University Press, 2010).

[26] Dudziak, "Brown as a Cold War Case," 38–39.

[27] Kathryn Sikkink, "The Power of Principled Ideas: Human Rights Policies in the United States and Western Europe," in *Ideas and Foreign Policy: Beliefs, Institutions and Political Change*, eds. Judith Goldstein and Robert O. Keohane (Ithaca: Cornell University Press, 1993), 139–170; Thomas Risse, Stephen C. Ropp, and Kathryn Sikkink, eds., *The Power of Human Rights: International Norms and Domestic Change* (New York: Cambridge University Press, 1999); Lake and Reynolds, *Drawing the Global Colour Line;*

say that (scientific) racism was dead. However, for the first time a new tension existed between domestic-level racial discrimination and international norms, language, and discourse. This tension was most obvious in the United States, where the civil rights movement had captured the world's attention.

CIVIL RIGHTS AND CENSUS COUNTS IN THE UNITED STATES

In 1950s and 1960s America, grassroots mobilization, the legal strategies of civil rights organizations, and the policy legacies of civil rights victories were unequivocally consequential for subsequent legislative gains.[28] Against "a rising tide of discontent" that characterized the violent turn of civil rights protests, President Kennedy sent a civil rights bill to Congress in 1963 – it would later become the Civil Rights Act of 1964, a legislative success owed in part to Kennedy's assassination. When Johnson assumed the presidency, his first speech to the nation affirmed that "no memorial oration or eulogy could more eloquently honor President Kennedy's memory than the earliest possible passage of the civil rights bill for which he fought so long ... There could be no greater source of strength to this Nation both at home and abroad."[29] Johnson spearheaded a number of civil rights developments during his tenure, including the 1965 Hart-Cellar Act, which reformed America's immigration policy regime by abolishing the national origins formula that had been in place for over forty years; the Voting Rights Act (VRA), which prohibited discriminatory disenfranchisement practices; and the 1968 Civil Rights Act, also called the Fair Housing Act. These were followed by the Equal Opportunity Act (1972) and the Equal Educational Opportunities Act (1974). When the equal opportunity discourse of the 1960s had little effect on alleviating entrenched patterns of discrimination, President Nixon instituted the use of numerical quotas in construction industry hiring practices as part of the Philadelphia Plan. This protocol was

Triadafilopoulos, *Becoming Multicultural*; and Jack Donnelly, *Universal Human Rights in Theory and Practice*, 3rd edn (Ithaca: Cornell University Press, 2013).

[28] Doug McAdam, *Political Process and the Development of Black Insurgency, 1930–1970* (Chicago: University of Chicago Press, 1982); Hugh Davis Graham, *The Civil Rights Era: Origins and Development of National Policy 1960–1972* (New York: Oxford University Press, 1990); Charles Epp, *The Rights Revolution: Lawyers, Activists and Supreme Courts in Comparative Perspective* (Chicago: University of Chicago Press, 1998); Skrentny, *Minority Rights Revolution*.

[29] Quoted in Klinkner and Smith, *Unsteady March*, 272–273.

emulated throughout the 1970s in regulations that applied to all private contractors and evolved into minority "set-aside" programs that required government contractors to allocate funds to minority firms.[30]

The legal developments of the 1960s and 1970s were a watershed for the politics of the census. Race data were critical to the implementation of these policies and the census became the main source for statistical information on the labor force availability, used to determine the rate of minority underemployment. The statistical requirements of the VRA are particularly important. The Act legally requires the Census Bureau to report the demographic distribution of racial populations. It also:

(1) prohibits "tests or devices" that had been used in the past to disenfranchise racial minorities – for example, literacy tests, education requirements, tests of good character, racial gerrymandering, and English-only elections in jurisdictions in which a single linguistic minority constitutes more than 5 percent of the voting-age population;
(2) makes clear that if the effect of a practice is discriminatory, it is unlawful, regardless of the intent of its originator; and
(3) requires that "covered" jurisdictions gain federal permission to implement any changes in electoral laws or procedures to assure that such changes are not "retrogressive," i.e. do not make it more difficult for protected minorities to elect representatives of their choice.[31]

Importantly, the VRA is the only domain that legally requires census data on race and (Hispanic) ethnicity. The principle of non-discriminatory results in congressional redistricting is assessed, according to the Supreme Court, by "the extent to which members of the minority group have been elected to public office in the jurisdiction"[32] and the potential existence of a significant discrepancy between the African American and

[30] Daniel Sabbagh and Ann Morning, *Comparative Study on the Collection of Data to Measure the Extent and Impact of Discrimination in a Selection of Countries: Final Report on the United States* (Lyon: European Commission, Employment and Social Affairs DG, 2004), 5; see also John D. Skrentny, *Ironies of Affirmative Action: Politics, Culture and Justice in America* (Chicago: University of Chicago Press, 1996).

[31] Paula D. McClain and Joseph Stewart Jr., *Can We All Get Along? Racial and Ethnic Minorities in American Politics*, 5th edn (Boulder: Westview Press, 2010), 58–59. This "pre-clearance" provision was struck down by a divided U.S. Supreme Court in *Shelby County v. Holder*, 570 U.S. ___ (2013), effectively freeing nine states (Alabama, Alaska, Arizona, Georgia, Louisiana, Mississippi, South Carolina, Texas, and Virginia) to change their electoral laws without the advance approval of the federal government.

[32] *Thornburg v. Gingles*, 478 U.S. 30 (1986), at 36–37.

Hispanic proportions of a district's population and their percentage among elected representatives.[33] The Supreme Court extended its logic of "one person, one vote," that voting power must be proportional to population size, to situations in which racial gerrymandering and the unnecessary concentration or fragmentation of racial minorities created an unequal opportunity for minority or white voters to elect their preferred candidate. Census data are critical to these assessments as well as the determination of vote dilution, defined as "the impairment of the equal opportunity of minority voters to participate in the political process and to elect candidates of their choice."[34]

The institutional connection between racial census data and voting rights raised the ante of racial enumeration and the classifications employed in the census. As Eugene Ericksen, a sociologist who served as an advisor to the Secretary of Commerce on the issue of census adjustment, observed during his congressional testimony on the 1990 Census, "were it not for the civil rights aspects of this issue, it would not be something we would be focusing on so much."[35] The more important outcome for the comparative politics of the census is that the *purpose* of the question on race in the American census was fundamentally altered – though some argue that the census remains an instrument of government control, the use of racial data to combat discrimination gave the census a powerful new role. These new laws also provided minority groups with more incentives for being officially counted, raising the stakes of racial enumeration.

These changing stakes had important implications for the administration of the census. The American statistical system was highly decentralized; this was a legacy of the many attempts at centralizing statistical functions in the federal government, which were thwarted in the 1930s. However, a 1937 report by the American Statistical Association, the Committee on Government Statistics and Information Services, and the Central Statistical Board recommended a coordinating agency to oversee the decentralized statistical activities of the different departments and agencies. The original Census Statistical Board was transferred to the Bureau of the Budget in 1939. Reorganized as the Office of Management and Budget by the Nixon

[33] Sabbagh and Morning, *Comparative Study on the Collection of Data*, 21.

[34] Laughlin McDonald and John A. Powell, *The Rights of Racial Minorities: The Basic ACLU Guide to Racial Minority Rights*, rev. edn (Carbondale: Southern Illinois University Press, 1993), 27.

[35] Quoted in Skerry, *Counting on the Census*, 4.

administration in 1970, officials within this agency are tasked with coordinating the statistical system.[36]

Census-taking procedures also underwent their own revolution of sorts due to technological advances in sampling procedures and the introduction of mail-in questionnaires, used for the first time in 1960 and expanded in each subsequent census until it was used throughout the United States by 1980.[37] Self-enumeration was a cost-effective and widely diffused method of census-taking throughout Western societies at this point, and also heightened public awareness of racial categories in the census in unexpected ways. Though there had always been a question on race on American censuses, in previous decades trained enumerators could record a respondent's race based on visual inspection, asking questions of clarification only in cases when race was not corporeally obvious. Allowing respondents to peruse their racial choices and pick among them personalized the census and led to demands that census categories reflect an increasingly racially diverse demographic reality.

THE REVERBERATIONS OF RIGHTS

Civil rights developments in the United States had global ripple effects that were pervasive for a number of reasons: America's position in the Cold War as a global leader and the intensity of its propaganda war with the Soviet Union; the perceived exceptionalism of American race relations; the sheer moral pull of civil rights mobilization, the proliferation of civil rights organizations, and the rhetoric of inspiring black leaders such as Martin Luther King and Malcolm X. The transnational normative imperative of human rights was also important, working in conjunction with American concessions to redefine the legitimate ends of race policies and appropriate means of addressing circumstances of racial inequality in two ways. First, racial politics in the United States made acute to other nations the need to avoid American-style racial conflict and violence. British and Canadian governments viewed these

[36] Eckler, *Bureau of the Census*, 17–22; Margo Anderson, "The Census and the Federal Statistical System: Historical Perspectives," *ANNALS of the American Academy of Political and Social Science* 631 (2010): 152–162.

[37] Nampeo R. McKenney and Arthur R. Cresce, "Measurement of Ethnicity in the United States: Experiences of the U.S. Census Bureau," in *Challenges of Measuring an Ethnic World: Science, Politics and Reality*. Proceedings of the Joint Canada-United States Conference on the Measurement of Ethnicity, April 1–3, 1992 (Washington D.C.: U.S. Government Printing Office, 1993), 200.

circumstances as uniquely American; deteriorating race relations in the United States were, however, enough to give both pause. The perceived cause of racial tension and hence the lessons that could be drawn from the American experience were interpreted differently in each country. The British state viewed the presence of a non-white populace that faced circumstances of racial discrimination as the spark for potential conflict similar to the United States and implemented a "package-deal" of immigration control and integration measures. Meanwhile, Canadian elites and bureaucrats viewed racialism as the culprit and eradicated references to race in a number of policy areas before passing laws that cemented a commitment to broader conceptions of *human* rights and *cultural* equality. Second, the civil rights movement and the American state's concessions opened the possibility for similar types of legislation in other countries that prohibited racial discrimination in public interactions, though none went so far as to mandate the collection of racial data.

Great Britain

The 1960s were a turbulent time, with coverage of urban unrest in the United States splattered across newspapers around the world. In spring 1961 black and white Freedom Riders crossed the South in buses in an attempt to integrate interstate transportation facilities and were attacked by angry mobs of whites in Alabama as the local police stood by. In September 1962 President Kennedy was forced to send troops to restore order to the University of Mississippi, where James Meredith had just become the first African American student to enroll. Public Safety Commissioner Eugene "Bull" Connor's use of mass arrests, tear gas, attack dogs, and fire hoses against demonstrators in Birmingham, Alabama, shocked the world, as did the racially motivated bombings of black churches, homes, and establishments by white extremists.[38] According to journalist Theodore White, in the ten weeks following Birmingham, the Department of Justice counted 758 demonstrations across the nation and 13,786 arrests of demonstrators in just 75 cities of the 11 Southern states alone.[39] Doug McAdam demonstrates that the number of hostile outbursts grew after 1963, from 8 cities with 12 outbursts to 106 cities with 155 outbursts in 1968, also becoming

[38] Klinkner and Smith, *Unsteady March*, 258–265.
[39] Quoted in Klinkner and Smith, *Unsteady March*, 267.

increasingly violent.[40] These events often made international headlines. For example, during the Birmingham campaign headlines in the *London Times* reported the "rising tide of Negro unrest in Alabama," and warned that "the American Negro giant awakes."[41]

The warning bells rang loud and clear in Britain, where race was a central element to debates over immigration. When race riots broke out in Notting Hill and Nottingham in late August and early September of 1958, the primary cause of racial violence was attributed to the very presence of non-white people.[42] As Cyril Osborne, a Conservative MP, said during the 1958 riots, Britain was "sowing the seeds of another 'Little Rock' and it is tragic. To bring the problem into this country with our eyes open is doing the gravest disservice to our grandchildren, who will curse us for our lack of courage. I regard the Nottingham incident as a red light to us all." He went on to argue that in the next Queen's Speech, he would like to see "the complete prohibition on Commonwealth and colonial immigration for 12 months," warning that if these measures were not enacted, "there will be trouble. It will be black against white."[43] In October 1961 the Conservative government announced its intention to introduce legislation to control immigration from other parts of the Commonwealth. The Labour opposition accused the resulting 1962 Commonwealth Immigrants Act of being an "anti-colour" measure, particularly because it exempted the Irish from immigration control though they were one of the largest migrant groups in Britain at the time (see Table 4.1).

By the time Labour gained its slim two-seat majority in 1964, party elites acknowledged that immigration control was "indispensable."[44] As Randall Hansen and Erik Bleich have each demonstrated, immigration control and anti-discrimination measures were part of a "package deal" that the Labour government constructed in order to appease supporters who believed immigration restrictions were normatively and politically

[40] McAdam, *Political Process*, table 8.7, p. 222. See also Bryan T. Downes, "A Critical Reexamination of Social and Political Characteristics of Riot Cities," *Social Science Quarterly* 51, no. 2 (1970): 349–360.

[41] "Rising Tide of Negro Unrest in Alabama," *The Times*, May 4, 1963, p. 9; "Negro Leader Talks of U.S. 'Revolt'," *The Times*, June 1, 1963, p. 7; "The American Negro Giant Awakes," *The Times*, June 10, 1963, p. 13.

[42] In his study of the riots, Robert Miles concludes that West Indian immigrants were primarily the victims of attacks by British-born residents. Robert Miles, "The Riots of 1958: Notes on the Ideological Construction of 'Race Relations' as a Political Issue in Britain," *Immigrants and Minorities* 3, no. 3 (1984): 255.

[43] "Renewed Call for Changes in Immigration Law," *The Times*, August 28, 1958, p. 4.

[44] Bleich, *Race Politics*, 46.

TABLE 4.1: *Estimates of selected immigrant populations in England and Wales, 1951, 1961, and 1966*

Area of origin	1951	1961	1966
India	30,800	81,400	163,600
Pakistan	5,000	24,900	67,700
Ceylon	5,800	24,900	67,700
West Indies	15,300	171,800	267,900
West Africa	5,600	19,800	36,000
Far East	12,000	29,600	47,000
Total Coloured	74,500	336,500	595,100
Cyprus and Malta	24,700	66,600	90,800
Total Commonwealth	336,400	659,800	942,300
Irish Republic	472,100	644,400	674,600
Total population	43,758,000	46,105,000	47,135,500
Coloured persons per 1,000	1.70	7.30	12.6

Source: Eliot Joseph Benn Rose et al., *Colour and Citizenship: A Report on British Race Relations* (London: Printed for the Institute of Race Relations by Oxford University Press, 1969), table 10.1, 97.

unpalatable, but who also desperately wanted to prevent the troublesome race relations plaguing North America.[45] As Labour MP Roy Hattersley famously said, "Integration without control is impossible, but control without integration is indefensible."[46] The introduction of the concept of integration was wrought with an air of prevention. At the time, elites believed that without political institutions to address the social problems

[45] Randall Hansen, *Citizenship and Immigration in Post-War Britain: The Institutional Origins of a Multicultural Nation* (Oxford: Oxford University Press, 2000) and Bleich, *Race Politics.* On the history of British immigration control, see also Kathleen Paul, *Whitewashing Britain: Race and Citizenship in the Postwar Era* (Ithaca: Cornell University Press, 1997); Ian R.G. Spencer, *British Immigration Policy since 1939: The Making of Multi-Racial Britain* (London: Routledge, 1997); and Joppke, *Immigration and the Nation-State.* Though the British government did not restrict immigration by legislative action until the Commonwealth Immigrants Act of 1962, a study by Carter et al. concluded that between 1948 and 1962 the state was involved in a complex political and ideological racialization of British immigration policy, in which covert and sometimes illegal administrative measures were implemented by both Labour and Conservative governments to discourage black immigration. Bob C. Carter, Clive Harris and Shirley Joshi, "The 1951–1955 Conservative Government and the Racialisation of Black Immigration," *Immigrants and Minorities* 6, no. 3 (1987): 335–347.

[46] Quoted in Robert Miles and Annie Phizacklea, *White Man's Country: Racism in British Politics* (London: Pluto Press, 1984), 57.

of immigrants, Britain would soon be facing the prospect of American-style violence.[47] Home Secretary Frank Soskice made this much clear during the introduction of the 1965 Race Relations Act when he said, "it is far better to put this Bill on the Statute Book now, before social stresses and ill-will have the change of corrupting and distorting our relationships."[48] At the same time, the adoption of a British anti-discrimination law was not inevitable. Race relations were a particularly volatile issue and British law was seen as "the quintessence of colour blindness."[49] For example, freedom of contract and property were important elements of British law, upheld by the courts above any abstract principles of nondiscrimination in the late 1950s when a British court ruled that the "colour bar" in a Wolverhampton ballroom could be legally maintained because it was in the interests of the business to do so.[50] By committing to legislate against racial discrimination in the Queen's Speech in November 1964, the Labour government sought to diffuse the "ticking bomb" by settling the race issue through bipartisan parliamentary consensus over a relatively weak anti-discrimination law.[51]

The resulting Race Relations Act of 1965 prohibited expressed racism with the intent to incite hatred and discrimination in public places such as hotels and pubs. Substantial parts of the legal and institutional framework of British race relations were, as Stephen Small writes, "begged, borrowed, or stolen from the United States."[52] During the development of the bill in 1965, a group of prominent Labour lawyers advocated for the creation of an administrative machinery based on Canadian and

[47] John Solomos, *Race and Racism in Britain*, 3rd edn (New York: Palgrave Macmillan, 2003), 81.

[48] *Hansard*, House of Commons, 3 May 1965, vol. 711, col. 942.

[49] Eliot Joseph Benn Rose et al., *Colour and Citizenship: A Report on British Race Relations* (London: Printed for the Institute of Race Relations by Oxford University Press, 1969), 200.

[50] Anthony Lester and Geoffrey Bindman, *Race and Law* (London: Longman, 1972), 53.

[51] Bleich, *Race Politics*, 49. The initial Race Relations bill proposed the use of criminal law to punish "access racism," or the denial of entry or access to public services on the grounds of race. In the final version, the criminal provisions were replaced with a process that relied on administrative procedures backed by civil court enforcement, a result of bipartisan negotiation, concession, and accommodation. Ibid., 52–59.

[52] Stephen Small, *Racialised Barriers: The Black Experience in the United States and England in the 1980s* (London and New York: Routledge, 1994); see also Nathan Glazer and Ken Young, eds., *Ethnic Pluralism and Public Policy: Achieving Equality in the United States and Britain* (Lexington: Lexington Books, 1983) and Michael Banton, *Racial and Ethnic Competition* (Cambridge: Cambridge University Press, 1983).

American models that would use conciliation rather than criminal proceedings to punish racial discrimination.[53] Key actors in the Labour party, such as Shirley Williams, Anthony Lester, and Jeffrey Jowell, also spent time in the United States during the 1960s and brought ideas based on the American experience into debates about the institutional form British race relations should take.[54]

By 1965, there was an implicit agreement among the parties of the necessity of depoliticizing race.[55] However, the violent turn of events in the United States formed the backdrop of discussions about race relations in Great Britain. As Bleich observes, virtually every actor or observer of this era made frequent and explicit references to America's racial problems in media as wide-ranging as newspaper editorials, parliamentary debates, and memos by Home Office bureaucrats who visited North America, using the comparison to draw lessons about what Britain must avoid.[56] For example, the Race Relations Board wrote in its 1967 annual report that

> our own experience of legislation against discrimination is supplemented by what we have learned of such legislation in the United States and Canada. There, despite initial doubts, the law is now regarded as essential to the success of other government policies and is a powerful stimulus to voluntary action. A combination of all of these, to ensure equal opportunities for all, is the only sound basis for successful action against discrimination.[57]

The 1967 Street Report on anti-discrimination laws used the legislative experience in North America to affirm that "the law is an acceptable and appropriate instrument for handling the problem."[58] Driven by a coalition of "race bureaucrats" and a key cabinet minister, Home Secretary Roy Jenkins, and backed by the support of minority communities, the 1968 Race Relations Act created additional protections against racial

[53] Keith Hindell, "The Genesis of the Race Relations Bill," *Political Quarterly* 36, no. 4 (1965): 395; Lester and Bindman, *Race and Law*, 110–111.

[54] Bleich, *Race Politics*, 54–61.

[55] Ira Katznelson, *Black Men, White Cities: Race, Politics, and Migration in the United States 1900–30 and Great Britain 1948–68* (Chicago: University of Chicago Press, 1976); Anthony M. Messina, *Race and Party Competition in Britain* (Oxford: Oxford University Press, 1989).

[56] Bleich, *Race Politics*, 73. See also Race Relations Board, *Report of the Race Relations Board for 1966–67* (London: HMSO, 1967); Rose et al., *Colour and Citizenship*; Lester and Bindman, *Race and Law*.

[57] Race Relations Board, *Report*, 21.

[58] Harry Street, Geoffrey Howe, and Geoffrey Bindman, *Anti-Discrimination Legislation: The Street Report* (London: Political and Economic Planning, 1967), 62.

discrimination in employment, housing, and in the provision of other goods and services.[59] The 1976 version, which introduced the legal concept of indirect discrimination, was similarly inspired by the American experience of affirmative action against institutionalized forms of racism.[60]

Canada

The Canadian state also sought to promote racial integration, but viewed the very notion of race as the instigator of social distress. The Canadian strategy was to implement incremental policy shifts while keeping the substantive policy stakes firmly intact. In policy areas with high political and legal consequences, such as conferring equal economic and social rights to racial minorities or implementing a non-discriminatory immigration policy, the decades following the Second World War provided little change. For example, Prime Minister Mackenzie King's Liberal government repealed the ban on Chinese immigration in 1947 but retained limits on both family reunification and the immigration of Chinese nationals.[61] In 1951, Parliament repealed the sections of the Indian Act prohibiting traditional activities such as the potlatch and making it illegal for Aboriginals to hire lawyers, but was unwilling to address the discriminatory provisions of section 12.1(b) – even after the United Nations ruled it in contravention of the human rights of Aboriginal women – until 1985. Though there was no castle to smash with regards to legal segregation, Ontario closed its last racially segregated school a decade after *Brown v. Board of Education* in 1965, around the same time that British Columbia grudgingly opened up the franchise to Chinese, Japanese, and South Asians.[62] As we shall see below, unlike human rights law there was

[59] Bleich, *Race Politics*, 70–80.

[60] Joppke, *Immigration and the Nation-State*, 225; Solomos, *Race and Racism*, 84.

[61] Race-based immigration restrictions were not removed until the Immigration Act of 1962 and were eventually replaced by a new "points system" in 1967. However, Satzewich demonstrates that even after the deracialization of Canadian immigration policy the Department of Manpower and Immigration was reluctant to open visa offices in the Caribbean. In fact, by 1970, three years after the points system was introduced, there were more visa offices in the United Kingdom than in the whole of Asia and the Caribbean combined. See Vic Satzewich, "Racism and Canadian Immigration Policy: The Government's View of Caribbean Migration, 1962–66," *Canadian Ethnic Studies*, 21, no. 1 (1989): 77–97, and Freda Hawkins, *Canada and Immigration: Public Policy and Public Concern* (Montreal: McGill-Queens University Press, 1972), 379–382.

[62] Robin W. Winks, "Negro School Segregation in Ontario and Nova Scotia," *Canadian Historical Review* 50, no. 2 (1969): 164–191 and Frances Henry and Carol Tator,

little at stake by changing the discursive content of the origin question on the census.

Nevertheless, these incremental policy shifts were promising developments, soon joined by the introduction of additional legal protections against racial discrimination. Tarnopolsky writes that two events with international dimensions shook the nation and caused increased concern about the protection of civil liberties. The first is related to the treatment of Japanese-Canadians, who had their property seized and were forced into internment camps during the Second World War. Once the war ended and a policy of dispersal and deportation was adopted, "the inhumanity of the measures taken brought a sense of shame and a resolution to prevent them in the future."[63] The second event was the exposure of Soviet espionage in Canada and the criticism of the methods used to deal with suspected members of the spy ring, which though pursuant to an Order in Council still contradicted the legal sensibilities of the right to *habeas corpus*, the right to retain legal counsel, and protection against self-incrimination.[64] In the immediate post-war period, innovation in Canadian provinces began the legal alignment with the global normative context of human rights, as they each adopted provincial bills of rights and fair employment legislation in quick succession.[65]

At the federal level, change was much slower. The UN Declaration catalyzed a number of developments as the specter of human rights "dominate[d] Ottawa's concern with the human rights issue and ... threatened to undermine the Liberal government's position that a rights guarantee at home was unnecessary."[66] Importantly, as MacLennan notes, the international environment provided Canadian civil liberties organizations with new arguments and ideas they could use to advance

The Colour of Democracy: Racism in Canadian Society, 4th edn (Toronto: Harcourt Brace, 2010), 57–64.

[63] Walter Tarnopolsky, *The Canadian Bill of Rights*, 2nd rev. edn (Toronto: McClelland and Stewart, 1975), 4.

[64] Ibid. See also Christopher MacLennan, *Toward the Charter: Canadians and the Demand for a National Bill of Rights, 1929–1960* (Montreal and Kingston: McGill-Queen's University Press, 2003), 34–43.

[65] Walter Tarnopolsky, *Discrimination and the Law in Canada* (Toronto: R. De Boo, 1982); Carmela Patrias and Ruth Frager, "'This is Our Country, These are Our Rights': Minorities and the Origins of Ontario's Human Rights Campaigns," *Canadian Historical Review* 82, no. 1 (2001): 1–35; Carmela Patrias, "Socialists, Jews, and the 1947 Saskatchewan Bill of Rights," *Canadian Historical Review* 87, no. 2 (2006): 265–292; and Dominique Clément, *Canada's Rights Revolution: Social Movements and Social Change, 1937–1982* (Vancouver: University of British Columbia Press, 2008).

[66] MacLennan, *Toward the Charter*, 59.

their cause.[67] However, the Liberals under Prime Minister Mackenzie King and his successor Louis St. Laurent remained recalcitrant. Having been in power for most of the interwar years and the post-war era,[68] the Liberals had little reason to give up their parliamentary authority by creating a bill of rights that would bind their political decisions, were wary of overstepping the bounds of federalism into provincial jurisdiction, and generally believed that a bill of rights would be an undesirable break from British legal tradition.[69] For example, in 1949 the Liberal Minister of Justice, Stuart Garson, argued that lynching in the United States and the "wholesale denial" of black enfranchisement in the South clearly demonstrated that the constitutional guarantees of the American Bill of Rights were less protective than the principle of parliamentary supremacy operating in Canada.[70] The issue lay dormant until John Diefenbaker's Conservative government won a strong majority in 1958. Diefenbaker believed that a federal bill of rights would create a unified Canada and pushed through the legislation in 1960. In retrospect, the Canadian Bill of Rights was both a symbolic victory for human rights and an abysmal failure in ensuring their protection.

Problematically, some of the more explicit racial lessons drawn from America were taken to the liberal extreme. In 1969, the Liberal government under Prime Minister Pierre Elliott Trudeau introduced a White Paper on Canadian Indian policy, which proposed the repeal of the Indian Act and the removal of all legal distinctions between Aboriginal and non-Aboriginal Canadians. As Weaver argues, this radical departure in 1969 was the culmination of changes that had occurred in the definition of the "Indian problem" throughout the 1960s, driven by three factors: (1) centennial celebrations created a "national curiosity" about Canada's past, including the treatment of the Native population; (2) the strengthening of Canadian identity at the same time as news of the American civil rights movement dominated the press, allowing liberal-minded people to develop a concern for minority groups and their rights to linguistic and cultural expression; and (3) the dominance of discussions of national unity.[71] The language of

[67] Ibid.

[68] There were two brief interruptions during the Conservative governments of Arthur Meighan (1926) and R.B. Bennett (1930–1935).

[69] MacLennan, *Toward the Charter*, 56–57. French Canada was also hesitant to support a bill that could result in a derogation of provincial powers. Clément, *Canada's Rights Revolution*, 22.

[70] MacLennan, *Toward the Charter*, 91.

[71] Sally M. Weaver, *Making Canadian Indian Policy: The Hidden Agenda, 1968–1970*, (Toronto: University of Toronto Press, 1981), 13.

the White Paper at certain parts even mirrors the logic and phrasing of the United States Supreme Court's decision in *Brown*:

> For many Indian people, one road does exist, the only road that has existed since Confederation and before, the road of different status, a road which has led to a blind alley of deprivation and frustration. This road, because it is a separate road, cannot lead to full participation, to equality in practice as well as in theory. In the pages which follow, the Government has outlined a number of measures and a policy which it is convinced will offer another road for Indians, a road that would lead gradually away from different status to full social, economic and political participation in Canadian life. This is the choice.[72]

In proposing to eliminate the Indian Act, the Crown also proposed to absolve itself of its historic fiduciary relationship with Aboriginal peoples and its responsibility for providing social services on reserve. When indigenous groups angrily responded through mass mobilization – a premonition of a "Red Power" movement in Canada that drew inspiration from social mobilization of racial minorities in the United States – the government quickly withdrew its proposal.

INSTITUTIONAL TRANSLATION AND RACIAL APPREHENSION

The international context was changing and being changed by ideas about the saliency of human rights, the normative ideal of racial equality, and what steps ought to be taken to address racial discrimination. These norms helped alter perceptions of legitimacy, both in terms of international legitimacy of democracies accused of hypocrisy in the Cold War and what domestic publics – including minorities with diasporic connections and white majorities sympathetic to civil rights struggles – would view as meaningful and necessary state action in addressing racism. Circumstances in the United States also served as a negative exemplar for other diverse societies, showcasing the worst-case scenario of race relations. America became the tell-tale heart under the floorboards of other nations, making clear the explosive potential should discrimination go unaddressed. Influences across national borders – including impressions and images from the civil rights movement transferred worldwide, political elites and bureaucrats that deliberately sought anti-discrimination models from the other two countries;

[72] Canada, Department of Indian Affairs and Northern Development, *Statement of the Government of Canada on Indian Policy (The White Paper)* (Ottawa: Queen's Printer, 1969).

systemic evidence gathered by institutions such as the Commission for Racial Equality, which sent representatives on exchange to the United States with the purpose of learning from American institutions; and academics who drew their theories and concepts concerning race relations from the growing body of literature in the United States – contributed to reformulations of the meaning of race and perceptions of legitimate ways to address racial discrimination that were domestic in application but transnational in scope. Most importantly, American circumstances demonstrated to policymakers in other countries how census data could serve as a critical tool to monitor and combat racial discrimination – however, neither Great Britain nor Canada would follow this course of action.

Great Britain

In Great Britain, policymakers recognized that the census was the most obvious vehicle to gather information on both the extent of racial discrimination and the effectiveness of the new race-relations legislation, but considered it infeasible to ask a question on race or ethnic identity in preparation for the 1971 Census. Bureaucrats discussed the possibility of including a question on ethnic origin in the census as early as 1966.[73] When the plans for the 1971 Census took more definitive shape in 1967, policymakers in the Ministry of Health suggested there be a question on ethnic origin. The Home Office did not initially agree to support this proposal because of the "considerable political implications" of asking the question, even in the context of a test survey. However, the need for racial data was acknowledged by senior Home Office bureaucrat Jack Howard-Drake, who wrote in an internal government memo that his initial concerns surrounded "the impossibility of defining immigrant or colour in precise terms," but that he was "now not so sure this view is correct," noting that "[with] the emergence of the second generation it will become increasingly important for us to have as much statistical information as we can about the coloured minority in the United Kingdom."[74] In early 1968 the matter was referred to the Statistical Policy Committee for Cabinet Ministers to decide. Therein, the majority of the Committee was clearly in favor of collecting information about

[73] PRO HO 376/175, Letter by J.T.A. Howard-Drake to Miss Hornsby, November 14, 1966.

[74] PRO HO 376/175, Minute by J.T.A Howard-Drake, November 17, 1967.

racial origin and decided to make the suggestion at the upcoming Home Affairs Committee meeting.[75] At the meeting, the Minister of Health Kenneth Robinson proposed that a question on ethnic origin be included on the census, but an archived report on the meeting notes that Home Secretary James Callaghan recorded his concern about the "political difficulties" that would result.[76] The decision to include a question on parents' country of origin rather than a direct question on race was made by Cabinet Ministers,[77] though elites acknowledged that using this proxy would not provide accurate information on ethnic origin.[78]

Several "political difficulties" played prominent roles in the decision-making process at the Ministerial level. First, British bureaucrats and members of Cabinet alike felt that it was impossible to define race or color in the precise terms required for a statistical exercise such as the census. The biological construction of race had destabilized, but policy-makers were not yet sure what to put in its place. As noted in a 1969 draft memorandum from the Home Office to the Select Committee on Race Relations and Immigration, "the impracticability stems from the impossibility of defining what is meant by 'colour' in the instructions which would have to go out to those making returns." The classification of mixed-race people was especially troublesome:

> No doubt many people could be identified by inspection as broadly falling within the definition of white or coloured, but this is a different matter from providing precise guidance on how any doubts should be resolved (persons of mixed blood would be an obvious example) and it would be necessary to rely on subjective judgments which would obviously vary – as would the willingness of people completing the questionnaire to identify.[79]

[75] PRO HO 376/175, letter from J.T.A Howard-Drake to Mr. Weiler, January 19, 1968. There were also substantial discussions at the meetings of the Select Committee on Race Relations and Immigration in 1968 and 1969, but these took place after the decision to not include a direct question on ethnicity had already been made (PRO HO 376/123).

[76] PRO HO 376/175, Note on the Home Affairs Committee meeting, n.a., February 6, 1968.

[77] PRO HO 376/123, Memorandum on the Collection of Racial Statistics, Cabinet Committee on Immigration and Community Relations, March 19, 1969.

[78] PRO HO 376/124, Cabinet document dated February 6, 1968. The original wording of the question on parents' country of origin stated: "Was your father/mother of African, Asian or West Indian origin? If 'yes' state the country (for example, Pakistan, Nigeria, Jamaica, etc.)." This was later changed to a more generic question about parents' country of origin because this original version was too explicit in its focus on the non-white population (PRO HO 376/175, Paper to Statistical Policy Committee, January 1968).

[79] PRO HO 376/123, Memorandum submitted by the Home Office to the Select Committee on Race Relations and Immigration, April 23, 1969.

Neither bureaucrats nor political elites knew how to make the subjectivity of race practical and the categorization of mixed-race pragmatic. In 1966, classifying those of mixed-race was described as a "technical difficulty" and contributed to the Home Office's initial skepticism on the topic.[80] Later, when the Statistical Policy Committee endorsed the proposal in 1968, Ministers again acknowledged that "a question specifically about 'race' would be difficult for persons of mixed-race to answer."[81]

Second, political elites were worried that asking a direct question on race or color would be perceived as offensive to both "coloured" and white respondents. The proposal to instead ask the country of origin of the respondent's parents was more familiar, and thus less controversial, since the 1961 Census queried country of birth with the intention of identifying immigrants to the United Kingdom. According to Rose et al.'s analysis of the census data, between 1951 and 1966 the "Commonwealth population" grew from 336,000 to 942,300. By asking a question on parents' country of origin, the 1971 question was not the extreme break from tradition that a direct question on race represented.

Third, the government could not ignore the political implications that arose from its own policies. The Race Relations Act of 1968 was on the table at the same time that these discussions about the census were taking place. Given that the Labour government had "acknowledged as accepted policy" the task of promoting the integration of the immigrant population, a memo to Prime Minister Harold Wilson stated that it was "undeniably important that the Departments concerned should have the particulars [of the immigrant population's] numbers, whereabouts, employment, housing circumstances, education and so forth."[82] Cabinet Ministers knew that the American experience in using racial data to combat racial discrimination could be emulated in Britain. Counting by race in the American census was viewed as a success story: "are Ministers prepared to see racial questions included in the census? The American experience, which began by thinking it would be discriminatory to keep records of race, has come to see that discrimination can be combated more effectively if reliable data is available. For this reason you may find it possible to agree to the inclusion of racial questions."[83] The memo also

[80] PRO HO 376/175, memo by Miss M. Hornsby, November 11, 1966.
[81] PRO HO 376/175, Statistical Policy Committee, 3rd Meeting Minutes, January 30, 1968.
[82] PRO PREM 13/2703, Memo to Prime Minister, subsection "Country of origin of the respondent's parents," February 5, 1968.
[83] Ibid.

notes that a failure to collect this information, or, as it was put at the time, to "take the opportunity of obtaining it," would open the government to criticism about the seriousness of its commitment to alleviating racial discrimination in Great Britain.[84]

Finally, the politics of numbers were a paramount concern. As James Hampshire argues in his book *Citizenship and Belonging*, British immigration policy in post-war Britain was a tool of "demographic governance" that heavily relied on insidious racial ideas, incorporating them into policymaking ventures. Negative attitudes toward immigration that framed the influx of black and Asian populations as a problem to be controlled and associated immigrants with social disorder and malady structured the terms of political debate, though Britain simultaneously sought to avoid charges of explicit racism given the shifting international context that deplored racial discrimination.[85] During this time of restricted immigration policy, anti-immigrant agitators used the politics of numbers to claim that the actual size of the black population in Britain was considerably larger than official estimates.[86] For example, in 1964 Conservative MP Peter Griffiths ran in the general election in the constituency of Smethwick under the infamous anti-immigration slogan "If you want a nigger for a neighbour, vote Liberal or Labour" – and won. The most prominent spokesman for the anti-immigrant crusade, Conservative MP Enoch Powell, claimed the size of the non-white population was a public concern. In 1971, coinciding with the decision to avoid a direct question on race in the census, Powell spoke to the West Midlands Conservative Political Center in Birmingham, declaring Britons "must be mad, literally mad, as a nation to be permitting the annual inflow of some 50,000 dependents who are for the most part the material of the future growth of the immigrant-descended population. It is like watching a nation busily engaged in heaping up its own funeral pyre." Drawing a comparison between Great Britain and the United States, Powell continued:

> That tragic and intractable phenomenon which we watch with horror on the other side of the Atlantic but which there is interwoven with the history and existence of the States itself, is coming upon us here by our own volition and our own neglect.

[84] Ibid.

[85] James Hampshire, *Citizenship and Belonging: Immigration and the Politics of Demographic Governance in Postwar Britain* (New York: Palgrave Macmillan, 2005).

[86] Martin Bulmer, "A Controversial Census Topic: Race and Ethnicity in the British Census," *Journal of Official Statistics* 2, no. 4 (1986): 472.

Indeed, it has all but come. In numerical terms, it will be of American proportions long before the end of the century.[87]

Any statistics concerning the actual size of the non-white population of Britain could serve multiple political purposes. The forthcoming census data could be used, as bureaucrats hoped, to establish the true facts and "disprove wild estimates of the future coloured population."[88] However, Conservatives sought the same facts to call for more restrictive immigration policies. For example, between 1967 and 1972 Enoch Powell made frequent speeches in the House of Commons and elsewhere on the subject of the number of colored immigrants in the United Kingdom, often using a 1967 statistical prediction (invalidated shortly thereafter) that the non-white population of Great Britain would reach 3.5 million by 1986.[89] The seminal study of race in Britain in the 1960s, *Colour and Citizenship*, noted that fears of being "swamped" by the incoming "flood" of immigrants – an image later invoked by Margaret Thatcher in her 1979 election campaign – was a key element to the formation of racist attitudes and that these fears were largely derived from exaggerated notions about the size of the colored population, which, the study contends, were compounded by the absence of reliable statistics on the subject.[90] The connection between immigration and race relations was as political as numerical: would the natural increase of the second and third generations of non-white Britons make immigration restrictions less salient, or would it give further reason to restrict the flow?

These political considerations inhibited the government's willingness to directly enumerate race. As such, the 1971 Census collected information on both the respondent's country of birth (as in the 1961 Census) and his or her parents' country of birth in order to gauge the approximate size of the racial population. It was acknowledged at the time – and indeed, throughout the policymaking process – that this method would be inaccurate to enumerate those white Britons who happened to be born in colonies overseas, pockets of the historic black British population, in, for example, Cardiff and Liverpool, and people of mixed-race. Generated indirectly using country of birth, parents' country of birth, nationality, and surnames, the subsequent census data were flawed and

[87] Full text of the speech is available at www.telegraph.co.uk/comment/3643823/Enoch-Powells-Rivers-of-Blood-speech.html, accessed March 14, 2015.

[88] PRO HO 376/175, memo by Miss M. Hornsby, November 11, 1966.

[89] PRO RG 26/436, Brief – Statistics of the Immigrant Population, June 24, 1975.

[90] Rose et al., *Colour and Citizenship*, 551–605.

inaccurate,[91] but nevertheless estimated that 36.5 percent of the non-white British population was born in the United Kingdom.[92]

Canada

As Britain pondered and ultimately rejected the possibility of adding a direct question on race, Canada found itself in a different position. The censuses of the nineteenth and twentieth centuries, until this point, waded in racial waters without hesitation. The new transnational normative context in the post-war era now poked and prodded at the racial project of the census. International epistemic communities of statisticians at the Population Commission and the Statistical Commission of the United Nations and elsewhere extensively discussed "the nature of the questions which may be appropriately asked in a nation-wide census [more so] than in any previous census."[93] These concerns were influential in Canadian census politics, in part because of the structure of political institutions. The Dominion Bureau of Statistics was increasingly centralized, had earned an admirable international reputation for its statistical analysis of resources and labor trends during the Second World War, and was well on its way to becoming an independent agency, which occurred in 1971. More importantly, these international discussions were influential because the Dominion Statistician, Herbert Marshall, took them seriously. Marshall, who held the position of Dominion Statistician from 1945 to 1956, was also the Chair of the UN Statistical Commission from 1947–1948 and was highly involved in these debates. In turn, political elites often deferred to Marshall's expertise, and decisions about the census were largely left in the hands of the bureaucracy.

When some in the Dominion Bureau of Statistics suggested abandoning the racial origin question altogether because of the issues raised in international statistical communities, Marshall wrote that "the question cannot be omitted from the Census if for no other reason than the demand of

91 Ken Sillitoe and Philip H. White, "Ethnic Group and the British Census: The Search for a Question," *Journal of the Royal Statistical Society, Series A (Statistics in Society)* 155, no. 1 (1992): 142; Roger Ballard, "Negotiating Race and Ethnicity: Exploring the Implications of the 1991 Census," *Patterns of Prejudice* 30, no. 3 (1996): 10.

92 Office of Population Censuses and Survey, "Country of Birth and Colour," *Population Trends* 2 (1975): 2–8.

93 NAC RG2 vol. 148 file D-25-3-C, Privy Council Office of Canada, Department of Trade and Commerce, Dominion Bureau of Statistics, Census, 1951. Memorandum Re: Population Card, Cabinet Document No 139–50, May 6, 1950.

important groups that it be included." It was far more practical, from Marshall's point of view, to simply change the label of the question rather than its content. The Bureau recommended that the column on the census card simply be called "origin," because "'[r]acial' has some odious implications, stresses the biological aspect and is thoroughly unscientific. 'Ethnic' includes more to the cultural aspects, which is what we want, but it has been criticized as being too academic a term to be easily understood."[94] Unlike human rights laws or immigration policies, which the government changed only in halting increments, there was little at stake by changing the phrasing of the origin question in the census.

The term "race" was dropped from the census, with the question in 1951 now requesting details on the "origin" of the population. The instructions to census enumerators relayed the importance of carefully distinguishing between citizenship/nationality and origin, admonishing that "[o]rigin refers to the cultural group, *sometimes erroneously called 'racial' group*, from which the person is descended; citizenship (nationality) refers to the country to which the person owes allegiance."[95] Instead of assigning mixed-race offspring of white/non-white relationships to a non-white designation as occurred during the first half of the twentieth century, these people were now classified according to the same principles of patrilineal descent as other white ethnic mixes. This change in classification rules had statistical consequences, partially accounting for the decline in the Chinese and Japanese populations and largely explaining the large drop in the black population, from 22,174 in 1941 to 18,020 in 1951.[96] The social construction of race certainly did not appear overnight, nor was the idea of race as biological fully abandoned in the social foundations of the census. The introduction to the origin question in the 1951 Census refers to the data as "partly cultural, partly biological, and partly geographical" in nature.[97]

The state also maintained its interest in the precise categorization of people of Aboriginal descent. Enumerators were instructed that those

[94] NAC RG31 vol. 1517 file 123, Records of the Assistant Dominion Statistician (Walter Duffet) 1961 Census – Origin or Ethnic Question. Letter from Herbert Marshall, Dominion Statistician to M.W. Mackenzie, Deputy Minister, Department of Trade and Commerce, March 10, 1950.

[95] Canada, *Census of Canada, 1951. Instructions to Commissioners and Enumerators* (Ottawa: King's Printer, 1951), emphasis added.

[96] Canada, *Ninth Census of Canada, 1951, Volume X, General Review and Summary Tables* (Ottawa: Queen's Printer, 1956), 138.

[97] Ibid.

living on Indian reserves were to be recorded as "Native Indian," while the origin of those not living on reserve would be traced through the line of the father. This change from a designation of "half-breed" in the 1941 Census to a complex interplay between place of residence and state-imposed labels is significant. The administrative distinction found in the census between those identified as "Native Indian" based on whether or not respondents lived on a reserve and regardless of parentage and those who lived off-reserve carries consequences for the rights and privileges assigned to each. The Canadian state's constitutional responsibility for "Indians and lands reserved for Indians" has often been interpreted by the government as a fiduciary duty for *only* Indians *on* lands reserved for Indians.

The 1951 Census also made the linkage between ethnic origin and language more explicit. Instructions to enumerators read: "you will first attempt to establish a person's origin by asking the language spoken by the person (if he is an immigrant), or by his paternal ancestor when he first came to this continent."[98] However, in some cases the focus on language was insufficient to garner the information the census was actually after. If origin could not be established via linguistic difference, enumerators were instructed to ask, "Is your origin in the male line English, Scottish, Ukrainian, Jewish, Norwegian, North American Indian, Negro, etc.?" Though the General Review of the 1951 Census notes that at varying times throughout previous censuses the origin question had been qualified by racial or ethnic attributes, the purpose of the inquiry remained the same: "Fundamentally, it is an attempt to distinguish groups in the population having similar cultural characteristics, based on a common heritage."[99]

Yet, some wondered whether the question itself did more harm than good. Conservative MP John Diefenbaker claimed that the emphasis on the origins of the white population was "the one thing that has caused more difficulty than any other in attaining Canadian unity." In the 1946 debates surrounding the proposed Citizenship Act, Diefenbaker claimed the census was a "back door" that simply accentuated ethnic divisions.[100] After becoming Prime Minister in 1958, Diefenbaker continued his criticism of this practice because "regardless of the number of generations that have elapsed or the admixtures of nationality that have taken place during the 40, 50, 75 or 125 years, so long as persons must register under the nationality of their paternal ancestor, there will never be that Canadianism which

[98] Canada, *Census of Canada*, 1951, 44. [99] Canada, *Ninth Census of Canada*, 131.
[100] House of Commons, Debates, April 30, 1946, 1043–1046.

we wish to establish."[101] In a 1959 Cabinet meeting, Diefenbaker confessed that he would prefer to see the question omitted altogether.[102] If a question had to appear on the 1961 Census, he reasoned, "Canadian" should be included as a marked position on the census form.[103]

However, this proposal proved infeasible and was withdrawn for three reasons. First, the question was still necessary in order to identify the non-white population. Political elites understood that this was a relevant use of the census in the United States, and so too it could be used for similar purposes in Canada.[104] Second, Marshall's successor as Dominion Statistician, Walter Duffett, leveraged his institutional position and power to convince political elites that because the origin question was immediately preceded by a question on citizenship, a "Canadian" origin entry would confuse both enumerators and respondents.[105] Further, Duffett and other senior-level bureaucrats had long recognized that the inclusion of a Canadian entry would lead to so many people identifying as Canadian that the value and comparability of the origins data would be adversely affected.[106] Though the executive branch could have made a unilateral decision on this topic, the strong reputation of the Dominion Bureau of Statistics gave the Prime Minister and his Cabinet good reason to take the recommendations of these senior civil servants very seriously. Third, Diefenbaker's suggestion was met with opposition in Quebec. An article on the topic in *L'Action Nationale* argued that French Canadians "are led to sacrifice their interests once more before altar of national unity ... In other words, the interests of the authentic founders of the nation will be sacrificed so as to conform to the wish of certain Neo-Canadians in hiding their origin, to the clapping of those who want but 'Canadians,'

101 House of Commons, Debates, May 25, 1959, 3975–3976. See also January 20, 1961, 1280–1289; January 23, 1961, 1301–1302; January 24, 1961, 1356–1357; May 4, 1961, 4352–4354.

102 NAC RG2 vol. 2744, Cabinet Conclusions, 1959. January 6, 1959, No. 2–59.

103 Though "Canadian" was an acceptable answer to the origin question on the 1951 Census, only those respondents who insisted on the designation to enumerators were counted in this way. Prior to 1951 neither "Canadian" nor "American" were considered acceptable racial origins.

104 House of Commons, Debates, April 30, 1946, 1043–1046

105 NAC RG31 vol. 1517 file 123, Records of the Assistant Dominion Statistician (Walter Duffet) 1961 Census – Origin or Ethnic Question. Queries about the Census Origin Question, April 28, 1961.

106 NAC RG2 vol. 148 file D-25-3-C, Privy Council Office of Canada, Department of Trade and Commerce, Dominion Bureau of Statistics, Census, 1951. Letter from C.D. Howe, Minister of Trade and Commerce, to Louis St-Laurent, Prime Minister, May 6, 1950.

period."[107] The Liberals also appeared to be building a strong campaign in the province against the inclusion of a "Canadian" option and Diefenbaker could not afford to further antagonize the growing resentment of French Canadians.

As Britain and the United States entered into the second rounds of antidiscrimination legislation in the 1970s, Canada became embroiled in national circumstances that hid problems of racial discrimination and disadvantage. The largely ineffectual 1960 Bill of Rights, the October Crisis of 1970, Trudeau's 1971 multiculturalism statement, the volatile nature of language politics after the Quiet Revolution in Quebec, a Supreme Court still reluctant to recognize aboriginal rights, and slow-changing immigration practices (and therefore demographic patterns) all worked to keep race off the country's radar.[108] In particular, the friction between the rise of the sovereignty movement in Quebec and the purposeful introduction of multiculturalism as a more pluralistic alternative to the compact thesis – that Canada was made of two founding nations – was important. According to Ken McRoberts, Trudeau's liberal vision of a pluralistic Canada whereby language was an individual (rather than collective or cultural) right was institutionalized in his many reforms, including multiculturalism, official bilingualism, and the repatriated constitution in 1982. These reforms resonated with English Canada, which would soon become more unwilling to recognize a dualist understanding of the Canadian compact.[109] The original multiculturalism policy was far more symbolic than substantive. It was not until the early 1980s that the policy shifted from an emphasis on ethnocultural artistic expression to incorporate greater support for anti-racist strategies.

Alone, the census has been at the forefront of the shift to the social construction of race, changing its language well in advance of other policy spheres and dominant social norms. In tandem with other policy and legal arenas, the evolution of the origin question on the census demonstrates the willingness of the Canadian state to change its use of racial discourse and language at the same time it proved hesitant to make

[107] François-Albert Angers, "Between Ourselves," *L'Action Nationale*, vol. XLVII, no. 9–10, Montreal, May–June 1959 [translated].

[108] See Sunera Thobani, *Exalted Subjects: Studies in the Making of Race and Nation in Canada* (Toronto: University of Toronto Press, 2007) and Eve Haque, *Multiculturalism within a Bilingual Framework: Language, Race, and Belonging in Canada* (Toronto: University of Toronto Press, 2012).

[109] Kenneth McRoberts, *Misconceiving Canada: The Struggle for National Unity* (Toronto: Oxford University Press, 1997).

substantive legal or policy change in other political realms, such as immigration law or Aboriginal affairs, that featured virulent and rampant racial discrimination.

CONCLUSION

Comparatively speaking, while the United States shifted from its previous approach of counting to manage and control racial populations to counting to justify positive action, Canada abandoned the terminology of race in the census and Great Britain considered, but decided against counting by race. All three cases had legislation that prohibits discriminatory state action and condemns racial discrimination in housing, employment, and other areas of social life. These pieces of legislation, however ineffectively designed or implemented, each had the goal of alleviating or eradicating racial disadvantage in social, political, and economic life. Here, a major point of departure among the cases is the institutional mandate arising from civil rights legislation and its relationship to census data. The comparison of Canada, the United States, and Great Britain suggests that unless provisions for ethnic monitoring are expressly stated in legislation, or are absolutely necessitated for the implementation of the legislation (as is the case with the VRA in the United States), an institutional mandate does not necessarily lead to the implementation of a direct census question on race. If simply the existence of civil rights legislation mattered, then both Britain and Canada would have seen the emergence of a direct question on race far sooner than they did. Civil rights legislation is likely a necessary and certainly important, but insufficient cause for the collection of racial data.

Some commonalities between the circumstances in Canada and Great Britain are worth noting. In spite of their commitments to racial equality and civil rights legislation, there was still a general discomfort around the very notion of race in Britain and Canada. In the upper echelons of government, this translated into the concern that counting by race would negatively affect national and social cohesion. However, the aversion to race is specific to census counts and is not necessarily an opposition to race-consciousness, which may feature predominately in other political commitments to racial equality. In short, these states do not wholly or explicitly adhere to the republican principle of color-blindness, and therefore not counting by race in the census is not because the state ignores race in all avenues.[110] And finally, at least in Britain, this refusal to count occurred in spite of calls for the collection of racial data or an acknowledged need for racial statistics from within the state bureaucracy. In these circumstances, institutional and cultural translations of transnational racial norms of the post-war era worked to prevent a policy shift to counting by race.

[110] This is a crucial distinction between two of Rallu, Piché, and Simon's approaches to racial enumeration: not counting in the name of multiculturalism, and not counting in the name of national integration, the latter of which occurs when race or ethnicity is rejected by reference to attempts to integrate a diverse political community, as is presently the case in many African nations, or in the name of the republican principle of national unity, as occurs in Western Europe. Rallu, Piché, and Simon, "Démographie et Ethnicité," 536.

5

The Multicultural Moment

As windows of opportunity for policy change firmly closed in the 1970s, the ramifications of (and backlash against) the implementation of civil rights regimes contributed to another transnational shift in the last decades of twentieth century. This multicultural moment, spurred by the various bottom-up nationalized reactions to its predecessor, is a rearticulation of racial formation in the Anglophone West. It is also a moment we have yet to exit. The meaning of race has not changed in the same way or magnitude as occurred in the post-war era, when the global normative context invalidated biological racialism and ejected it from political and vernacular discourse. The racial reactions to the minority movements of the 1960s, which grew and developed in the 1970s and matured in the 1980s, catalyzed changes to the *framing* of race rather than its meaning; in ideational terms, there was a discernable shift in understandings of "race and": race and equality, race and social justice, race and liberalism, race and democracy.

These reformulations of race manifest in the racial project of liberal multiculturalism, defined by Christian Joppke as a pervasive but controversial intellectual and political movement in Western democracies that seeks equal rights and public recognition for ethnic, racial, religious, or sexually defined groups.[1] Gaining traction in increasingly diverse societies

[1] Christian Joppke, "Multiculturalism and Immigration: A Comparison of the United States, Germany, and Great Britain," *Theory and Society* 25, no. 4 (1996): 449. See also Iris Marion Young, *Justice and the Politics of Difference* (Princeton: Princeton University Press, 1990); Taylor, "The Politics of Recognition"; Hollinger, *Postethnic America*; Will Kymlicka, *Multicultural Citizenship: A Liberal Theory of Minority Rights* (Oxford and New York: Clarendon Press, 1995); Bhikhu Parekh, *Rethinking Multiculturalism:*

in the 1970s and 1980s, multiculturalism has descriptive, institutional, and normative dimensions. As a description, multiculturalism refers to the fact of racial, ethnic, and religious diversity. The liberalization of explicitly discriminatory provisions in immigration policies led to new, more ethnically and racially diverse immigration and demographic patterns throughout the Western world. Between 1970 and 1990, the percentage of the American population that identified as white dropped from 87.5 percent to 80.3 percent, while African American, American Indian, Asian, and especially Hispanic population shares all grew.[2] In Canada approximately 31 percent of the population reported ethnic backgrounds other than English or French in 1991, an increase from 25 percent just five years earlier in 1986. The largest gains came from those reporting Asian origins (including South, East, and South East Asian ethnic origins), which increased from 3.5 percent of the population to 5.1 percent.[3] Britain's Labour Force Survey estimated in 1982 that the black population was around 700,000.[4] The first ethnic question on the census in 1991 revealed that the non-white population was just over 3 million people, or 5.5 percent of the population.[5] Both pragmatically and conceptually, the demographic fact of multicultural societies is a direct challenge to the nation-state, which is premised on the nation as an imagined, but still homogenous, primary, and singular cultural community.

Institutionally, multiculturalism refers to a broad range of legislation, policy, and programs that manage racial and ethnic diversity, often seeking to prevent, reduce, or punish discrimination based on racial, ethnic, or religious grounds in public and private spheres. Though multicultural institutions provide a means by which historically disadvantaged groups seek to achieve public recognition and legitimation of their identities and/or compensatory treatment for historical and continuing

Cultural Diversity and Political Theory (Cambridge: Harvard University Press, 2000); Ayelet Shachar, *Multicultural Jurisdictions: Cultural Differences and Women's Rights* (Cambridge: Cambridge University Press, 2001); Tariq Modood, *Multicultural Politics: Racism, Ethnicity, and Muslims in Britain* (Minneapolis: University of Minnesota Press, 2005); Kymlicka, *Multicultural Odysseys*.

2 United States Census Bureau, *Historical Census Statistics on Population Totals by Race, 1790 to 1990, and by Hispanic Origin, 1970 to 1990, for the United States, Regions, Divisions, and States*, Working Paper Series No. 56 (Washington D.C.: United States Census Bureau, 2002), Table 1.

3 Statistics Canada, *1991 Census Highlights* (Ottawa: Statistics Canada, 1994), 53.

4 Small, *Racialised Barriers*, 61.

5 Office of Population Censuses and Surveys, *Ethnicity in the 1991 Census: Volume One: Demographic Characteristics of the Ethnic Minority Populations* (London: HMSO, 1996).

discrimination, not all groups are necessarily provided the same form of or access to the so-called politics of recognition.[6] Will Kymlicka, a prominent theorist of multiculturalism, draws a distinction between two types of minority groups: whereas national minorities, such as indigenous peoples, can claim historical homeland rights that predate the political community, ethnic or immigrant groups are understood as having voluntarily entered into a receiving society. Both should be afforded certain group-specific rights that are consistent with liberal ideology, such as special group representation rights (for example, affirmative action) and polyethnic rights (for example, religious accommodation), though only national minorities, he argues, should have the right of self-government. A special status is reserved for African Americans (though not necessarily all descendants of slaves in other polities), who were subject to coercive migration and thus claims to public recognition can be extended to further include compensatory action for overt and systematic oppression.[7] Though Kymlicka was perhaps too eager when he declared in 1999 that "multiculturalists have won the day,"[8] multicultural protections in the international arena, such as the United Nations Declaration on the Rights of Persons Belonging to National or Ethnic, Religious, and Linguistic Minorities in 1992, as well as a wide array of multicultural policies varying from country to country in scope, breadth, and application proliferated in the last two decades of the twentieth century.[9]

Finally, in a normative sense multiculturalism is a social ideal – an ideological stance about how individuals and groups across racial, ethnic, and religious lines can coexist and together work toward the creation of more just and equitable societies. This dimension of multiculturalism generates the greatest level of debate and there is no consensus about the best way to balance identity politics and minority rights with majoritarian

[6] Taylor, "The Politics of Recognition."

[7] Hollinger, *Postethnic America*; Will Kymlicka, "American Multiculturalism and the 'Nations Within'," in *Political Theory and the Rights of Indigenous Peoples*, eds. Duncan Ivison, Paul Patton, and Will Sanders (New York and Cambridge: Cambridge University Press, 2000), 216–236.

[8] Will Kymlicka, "Comments on Shachar and Spinner-Halev: An Update from the Multicultural Wars," in *Multicultural Questions*, eds. Christian Joppke and Steven Lukes (Oxford: Oxford University Press, 1999), 113; see also Nathan Glazer, *We Are All Multiculturalists Now* (Cambridge, MA: Harvard University Press, 1998).

[9] Michael Banton, *International Action against Racial Discrimination* (Oxford: Oxford University Press, 1996); Christine Inglis, "Multiculturalism: New Policy Responses to Diversity," Policy Paper No. 4, UNESCO Management of Social Transformation, accessed April 15, 2014, www.unesco.org/most/pp4.htm

culture. For example, Brian Barry offers a liberal critique of multiculturalism in his book *Culture and Equality*, in which he contends that cultural conflict should be left to the private sphere.[10] In contrast, Ayelet Shachar is more concerned with the "paradox of multicultural vulnerability," which she defines as situations in which individual rights such as women's rights inside a particular cultural group are violated by the very policies that accommodate the cultural difference of the group itself.[11] Critical race theorists have also challenged multiculturalism, acknowledging that though the multicultural agenda is an ideological inheritance of the anti-colonial struggle, which fundamentally challenges the assumed universality and superiority of Western culture,[12] the extent to which multicultural policies actually make a difference in eradicating racism and systemic discrimination remains in question. For example, criticizing the discursive impact of multiculturalism on women of color in Canada, Himani Bannerji argues that the mere public recognition of identities "speaks to nothing like class formation or class struggle, the existence of active and deep racism, or of a social organization entailing racialized class productions of gender." Discourses of multiculturalism and diversity, she argues, simultaneously hide and enshrine the power relations that actively sustain racial and gender hierarchies.[13]

This last criticism highlights the major normative and conceptual tension that multiculturalism both seeks and embraces, but ultimately fails, to overcome – the conflict between color-blindness and race-consciousness. Multiculturalism is a concerted shift away from older models of diversity governance that sought assimilation over integration. In emphasizing the importance of the public recognition of identities, race-consciousness is built into the architecture of multiculturalism. However, the normative consensus of racially conscious multicultural paradigms has never been a fait accompli. Color-blindness, referred to by some scholars as neo-racism,[14] rests on the idea that the civil rights movement was successful

[10] Brian Barry, *Culture and Equality: An Egalitarian Critique of Multiculturalism* (Cambridge: Polity Press, 2001).

[11] Shachar, *Multicultural Jurisdictions*.

[12] Joppke, "Multiculturalism and Immigration," 452–453.

[13] Himani Bannerji, "The Paradox of Diversity: The Construction of a Multicultural Canada and 'Women of Color'," *Women's Studies International Forum* 23 (2000): 554–555.

[14] Etienne Balibar, "Is There a Neo-Racism?" in *Race, Nation, Class: Ambiguous Identities*, by Etienne Balibar and Immanuel Wallerstein (New York and London: Verso, 1991). See also Omi and Winant, *Racial Formation*; Philomena Essed, *Understanding Everyday Racism: An Interdisciplinary Theory* (Newbury Park: Sage Publications, 1991); Amy

and racism no longer exists (in the United States), had only ever existed in the United States (in Canada), or is of little consequence, especially when compared to prevalent social cleavages based on class (in Great Britain). Color-blind positions view race as little more than skin color, divorced from structural and institutional power dynamics. Racism is therefore understood as any and all invocations of race. Ian Haney Lopez writes that colorblindness conceives of racism in individualistic and symmetrical terms: "individual in that racism harms the person classified by race, and symmetrical in that nothing distinguishes the group positions of whites and nonwhites."[15] Based on liberal values of individualism, state non-intervention, and market-based opportunity, this framing rejects racialism or state policies that engage in "race thinking"; race-conscious policies such as affirmative action not only continue an unwarranted emphasis on the saliency of race, but also can be likened to "reverse discrimination."[16] The propagation of race thinking is believed to be caused by militants who have a vested interest in maintaining racial difference and hence the saliency of race.[17]

This chapter explores these varied reframings of race and their influence on census politics. As with its ideational predecessors, the multicultural moment has clear temporal and geographic limitations. Widely employed as an organizational framework in Anglo-American democracies, the uptake of multiculturalism as fact, institution, and social ideal was far more ephemeral in Europe and the Global South and faced retrenchment everywhere after the events of September 11, 2001 – points I return to in Chapter 7. In the United States, Canada, and Great Britain,

Elizabeth Ansell, *New Right, New Racism: Race and Reaction in the United States and Britain* (New York: New York University Press, 1997); Lawrence D. Bobo and Ryan A. Smith, "From Jim Crow to Laissez-Faire Racism: The Transformation of Racial Attitudes," in *Beyond Pluralism: The Conception of Groups and Identities in America*, eds. Wendy F. Katkin, Ned Landsman, and Andrea Tyree (Urbana: University of Illinois Press, 1998), 182–220; Michael K. Brown et al., *Whitewashing Race: The Myth of a Color-Blind Society* (Berkley: University of California Press, 2003); Eduardo Bonilla-Silva, *Racism without Racists: Color-Blind Racism and Racial Inequality in Contemporary America*, 3rd edn (New York: Rowman and Littlefield Publishers, 2010).

15 Ian F. Haney Lopez, "Is the 'Post' in Post-Racial the 'Blind' in Colorblind?" *Cardozo Law Review* 32, no. 3 (2011): 824.

16 As Nathan Glazer argues, "[Affirmative action] has meant that we abandon the first principle of a liberal society, that the individual's interests and good and welfare are the test of a good society, for we now attach benefits and penalties to individuals simply on the basis of their race, color and national origins." Glazer, *Affirmative Discrimination: Ethnic Inequality and Public Policy* (New York: Basic Books, 1975), 220.

17 Brown et al., *Whitewashing Race*.

however, liberal multiculturalism was more pervasive, clashing with in some ways, and subsuming in others, the racial schemes of the state. At the beginning of the multicultural moment, each state employed a different method of counting race. In the 1970s and 1980s, the direct question on race in the United States was unique. Canada's parallel question pertained to ethnic origins, which Statistics Canada used alongside proximate indicators such as birthplace and language to derive statistical data on race. Similarly, Britain relied on the parents' country of origin question to estimate the size of the non-white population. In both countries, these indirect methods of racial enumeration were neither accurate nor sustainable.

The development of different models of diversity governance in Canada, the United States, and Great Britain bled into the transnational sphere, where liberal multiculturalism was gaining traction. An increasing number of states ratified the United Nations' International Convention on the Elimination of All Forms of Racial Discrimination: from 41 states in 1970, to 107 in 1980, 129 in 1990, and 143 in 1995.[18] The recognition and institutionalization of indirect discrimination in North America and Great Britain, a concept that necessitates the collection of accurate racial statistics, was paralleled in the European Union directives on equal treatment: the Racial Equality Directive (2000/43/EC) and the Employment Equality Directive (2000/78/EC).[19] Multicultural norms were further augmented in census politics throughout the 1980s by programmatic beliefs that gave primacy to racial self-declaration and recognized racial statistics as an acceptable policy instrument. International bodies tasked with monitoring human rights collect data on racism and discrimination, analyze these global statistics, and disseminate standards for the creation of global indicators such as the Racial Equality Index and the Fundamental Rights Index.[20] States also must collect data in order to submit reports to international treaty monitoring bodies. For example, the Convention on the Elimination of All Forms of Racial Discrimination was adopted by the General Assembly of the United Nations in 1965 and is considered to be the international community's only tool for combatting

[18] Banton, *International Action*, 99.

[19] Timo Makkonen, *Measuring Discrimination: Data Collection and EU Equality Law* (Luxembourg: Office for Official Publications of the European Communities, 2007); Julie Ringelheim, "Collecting Racial or Ethnic Data for Antidiscrimination Policies: A U.S.-Europe Comparison," *Rutgers Race and the Law Review* 10, no. 1 (2009): 39–142.

[20] Patrick Simon, "The Measurement of Racial Discrimination: The Policy Use of Statistics," *International Journal of Social Science* no. 183 (2005): 9–25.

racial discrimination.[21] The UN Committee responsible for monitoring the Convention adopted revised guidelines for reporting in 1993, which stated:

> The ethnic characteristics of the country are of particular importance with the International Convention on the Elimination of All Forms of Racial Discrimination. Many States consider that, when conducting a census, they should not draw attention to factors like race lest this reinforce divisions they wish to overcome. If progress in eliminating discrimination based on race, colour, descent, national and ethnic origin is to be monitored, some indication is needed of the number of persons who could be treated less favourably on the basis of these characteristics.[22]

Reporting guidelines for this Convention, which had been ratified or acceded to by 148 states by September 1996, require that states include information about the demographic composition of their populations, including statistics on mother tongue, race, color, descent, and national and ethnic origins.[23] State actors drew lessons from these programmatic beliefs and one another, with global conversations culminating at an international conference on the measurement of race and ethnicity held in Ottawa, Canada, in 1992. Less than a decade later, the Durban Declaration and Plan of Action, adopted by the United Nations World Conference against Racism in 2001, urged states to "collect, compile, analyse, disseminate and publish reliable statistical data at the national and local levels and undertake all other related measures which are necessary to assess regularly the situation of individuals and groups of individuals who are victims of ... racial discrimination,"[24] thereby solidifying a worldwide change of tide regarding the necessity, viability, and feasibility of collecting racial statistics.

As lobbies in the United States formed to capitalize on the material and political incentives to being counted and the reality of a decentralized statistical system led the Office of Management and Budget (OMB) to standardize the federal classification of race, groups of bureaucrats and elites in Canada and Great Britain – often working in agencies, commissions, or committees not directly responsible for the census – highlighted an institutional need for more accurate racial data. However, it was only when elite-level support was combined with unexpected policy

21 United Nations, *Manual on Human Rights Reporting under Six Major International Human Rights Instruments* (Geneva: United Nations, 1997), 267.

22 Ibid., 270. 23 Ibid.

24 United Nations, *World Conference Against Racism, Racial Discrimination, Xenophobia, and Related Intolerance, Declaration* (Geneva: United Nations, 2002), 37.

contingencies arising from protocols of census administration that statistical agencies decided to change the status quo and adopt an approach to racial enumeration whereby counting was used to justify positive action toward reducing racial discrimination.

These elements – the relative influence of minority lobbies, the drive for standardization, the support of political elites, and policy feedback effects – were mediated by the structure and membership of each respective census policy network. In all three cases, census policy networks expanded significantly beyond bureaucrats, elites and experts when self-administered census forms replaced trained enumerators in the 1970s. Because census bureaus needed to ensure that questions were understandable to the public, focus groups and extensive census field tests became part of the institutional business of census administration. But not all consultative exercises are created equal. The multiple veto points of the decentralized statistical system enabled minority groups to seek and win institutionalized roles in census administration in the United States, providing them with the opportunity to be involved in the decision-making process during its formative stages. The relatively closed structure of the policy network in the Westminster systems, in which members of Cabinet held ultimate decision-making power, combined with an already conservative (in the institutional sense) statistical system to prevent the emergence of new ideas that would radically alter existing policy trajectories. Consultations occurred only after question designs had already been decided and minority groups were granted comparatively less access to the policymaking process.[25] But the members of the policy network are also important. The unitary system of Great Britain provided local authorities with both a unique perspective as the level of government largely responsible for program delivery and a seat at the table where representatives advocated for a direct question on race that would aid their administrative data needs. In contrast, the federal-level jurisdictional power in Canada protected the autonomy and control of Statistics Canada.

In contrast to the causal influence of minority lobbies in America, then, developments in census politics in Canada and Great Britain were driven by the decisions of bureaucrats and political elites. Importantly, the

[25] This is not to assume that minority groups will mobilize around census politics if given the chance. However, it has been argued that the multiracial movement in the United States was "a movement in search of bodies," mobilizing for the sole purpose of participation in debates surrounding the 2000 Census and dissipating soon after census policy decisions were formalized. See Nobles, *Shades of Citizenship*; Farley, "Identifying with Multiple Races."

feedback effects from previous census policy trajectories often forced the government's hand. The British state did not foresee mass opposition to its proposed ethnic question in 1979, when racial minorities believed that Thatcher's Conservative government was only counting by race to keep tabs on the non-white population and to, one day, mandate repatriation to the far-flung edges of the British Empire; the Canadian state could not predict that the "Count me Canadian!" campaign, a neoconservative backlash against multiculturalism and hyphenated identities, would corrupt the ethnic origin data derived from the 1991 Census so much that the bureaucracy would be unable to tell which Canadians were racial minorities and which were not. In different ways, these circumstances made both the need for racial data more acute and the proposal for a direct question on race more politically and administratively viable.

PARTICIPATION AND STANDARDIZATION IN THE UNITED STATES

Nowhere is the normative tension between competing race-conscious and color-blind frames clearer than in racial politics in the United States at the end of the twentieth century. As Desmond King and Rogers Smith contend in their recent book, *Still a House Divided: Race and Politics in Obama's America*, battles between the pro-segregation forces and the racial egalitarian policy alliances of the 1960s transformed over the following decade. Instead of debating segregation or integration, issues centered on whether policymaking should be blind to racial differences, or whether policies needed to pay heed to race or initiate some form of positive action. Both the race-conscious and color-blind sides of the debate, they note, tie moral claims to policy preferences, each representing themselves as the true heirs of the civil rights movement.[26]

For example, the maturation of the Reagan Revolution in the 1980s gave neoconservative framings of race a permanent place in the American political landscape. Michael Omi and Howard Winant argue that the emergence of the New Right in the United States was not simply a backlash against the civil rights gains of the 1960s, but was also an innovative political project of authoritarian populism, in which the Reagan administration consistently opposed civil rights measures both proposed and

[26] Desmond S. King and Rogers M. Smith, *Still a House Divided: Race and Politics in Obama's America* (Princeton and Oxford: Princeton University Press, 2011), 9.

already in place.[27] Validating and utilizing a number of key tenets of the transnational color-blind racial ideology,[28] Reagan and his administration denounced affirmative action as "reverse racism," undermined federal enforcement efforts, slowed the pace of school desegregation, and eliminated many social welfare programs which disproportionately supported the non-white underclass.[29] Even the courts, the branch of government most insulated from political and popular opposition to affirmative action, issued rulings in 1989 that undermined the policy. In *Ward's Cove Packing v. Antonio*, the Supreme Court ruled that in job discrimination cases it is insufficient for plaintiffs to only demonstrate a statistical disparity in minority employment; they must also connect the disparity to the specific employment practices alleged to have caused the discrimination. In *Richmond v. Croson*, the Court ruled that a city's "set-aside" contracts for minority-owned firms must be narrowly defined, temporary, and linked to established prior discrimination. Both of these cases feature a greater burden of proof on the plaintiffs to prove the extent of racial discrimination beyond statistical evidence.[30]

And yet, race-consciousness continued to be important both in the practice of politics and in the politics of the everyday. After the unity of the civil rights movement eroded in the mid-1960s, anti-racist advocates continued to emphasize the centrality of race in the construction of American culture and society,[31] arguing that the elimination of *de jure* racial segregation and the endorsement of positive state action to end racial discrimination failed to substantively alter circumstances of racial inequality. Moreover, race was not simply going to *go away*. Unlike Canada and Great Britain, whose histories of the avoidance of racial

[27] Omi and Winant, *Racial Formation*, 123. The Reagan administration tried to eliminate racial record-keeping in the Department of Housing and Urban Affairs and the Veterans Administration. Jerry McMurray, staff director for the housing subcommittee of the House Banking Committee, said the Reagan administration "would rather not know" the racial composition of its programs so it could not be challenged on its civil rights record. Omi and Winant, *Racial Formation*, 209, fn 73; see also Steven A. Shull, *A Kinder, Gentler Racism?: The Reagan-Bush Civil Rights Legacy* (Armonk: M.E. Sharpe, 1993).

[28] See Glazer, *Affirmative Discrimination;* Dinesh D'Souza, *The End of Racism: Principles for a Multiracial Society* (New York: the Free Press, 1995); Stephen Thernstrom and Abigail Thernstrom, *America in Black and White: One Nation, Indivisible* (New York: Simon and Schuster, 1997).

[29] Ansell, *New Right, New Racism*, 195.

[30] McClain and Stewart, *Can We All Get Along*, 182.

[31] Howard Winant, *The World Is a Ghetto: Race and Democracy Since World War Two* (New York: Basic Books, 2001), 166–167.

enumeration demonstrate a national discomfort with the language of race, American politics and society have always produced and reified race as a meaningful social, legal, and political category. Importantly, race-consciousness and color-blindness, seemingly contradictory though they may be, exist in the same time and place. The various institutions of the state have at times eroded race-consciousness in favor of color-blind approaches in some areas of law and policy – particularly the judiciary's ongoing interpretation of the constitutionality of affirmative action – while simultaneously continuing with the use of racial categories in the census.

After the legislative gains of the civil rights movement changed the stakes of racial enumeration, minority groups began to lobby for additions or changes to the American racial classification system. For example, the lobby efforts to include a means of enumerating America's Hispanic population began while the census form was being printed in 1968 and lasted until the Census Advisory Committee on the Spanish Origin Population was successful in getting a specific question on Hispanic identity on the 1980 Census.[32] These efforts were met with significant resistance on the part of the Census Bureau, which initially did not want to allow minority populations to participate in the decision-making process. The eventual formalization of minority census advisory committees throughout the 1970s occurred because of sustained political action, increased lawsuits over the significant undercounts of racial minority populations, and congressional hearings in which the Census Bureau was continually put on the defensive, which cumulatively created a situation that necessitated that the Bureau find some means of increasing its public legitimacy.[33] The newly formed census advisory committees became an institutionalized part of the census policy network, significantly altering political discourse between the state and minority interest groups precisely when the census itself transformed from an instrument for managing race to a tool for monitoring racial disadvantage and promoting a national discourse of diversity and integration.

[32] Harvey M. Choldin, "Statistics and Politics: The 'Hispanic Issue' in the 1980 Census," *Demography* 23, no. 3 (1986): 403–418.

[33] Alice Robbin, "The Politics of Representation in the US National Statistical System: Origins of Minority Population Interest Group Participation," *Journal of Government Information*, 27, no. 4 (2000): 444. These minority advisory committees were chartered by the U.S. Department of Commerce for the black population in 1974, the Spanish-origin population in 1975, and Asian and Pacific American population in 1976. The American Indian advisory committee was not created until the late 1980s in spite of requests throughout the 1970s. Ibid., en. 84.

Around the same time, one of the most significant developments to shape the politics of census-taking in the United States came to pass: the implementation of Statistical Directive 15 in 1977. The origins of the Directive are from the recommendations of the Federal Interagency Committee on Education (FICE) Subcommittee on Minority Education 1973 report, *Higher Education for Chicanos, Puerto Ricans, and American Indians*,[34] which deplored the lack of useful data on racial and ethnic groups. The need for standardization was due in part to the decentralized nature of the American statistical system. Each of the more than thirty federal government agencies that comprised FICE was responsible for developing, implementing, or monitoring civil rights policies and programming. Working independently, different agencies developed categories that suited their specific institutional needs, a practice that hampered data sharing and systematization.[35] To address these issues, the report's second recommendation suggested that the government "coordinate development of common definitions for racial and ethnic groups."[36] The Secretary of the Department of Health, Education, and Welfare, Caspar Weinberger, endorsed this recommendation and appointed an ad hoc committee within FICE, chaired by Charles E. Johnson Jr., the assistant chief of the Population Division of the Census Bureau, to develop these racial and ethnic definitions. The 1975 report recommended that four racial categories (American Indian or Alaskan Native, Asian or Pacific Islander, Black/ Negro, and Caucasian/White) and one ethnic category (Hispanic) be created.[37]

Statistical Directive 15 also had institutional origins. In October 1977, President Jimmy Carter issued Executive Order 12013, transferring responsibility for statistical policy from OMB to the Department of Commerce. The Secretary of Commerce then established the Office of

[34] This report was never published, but is referenced in the preface and background of the United States Federal Interagency Committee on Education, *Report of the Ad Hoc Committee on Racial and Ethnic Definitions* (Washington D.C.: U.S. Department of Health, Education, and Welfare, National Institute of Education, 1975).

[35] Spencer, *Spurious Issues*, 65. On the political development of Statistical Directive 15, see also Office of Management and Budget, "Standards for the Classification of Federal Data on Race and Ethnicity," *Federal Register* 60, no. 166 (1994): 44674–44693; Victoria Hattam, *In the Shadow of Race: Jews, Latinos, and Immigrant Politics in the United States* (Chicago and London: University of Chicago Press, 2007), 111–121; and Kenneth Prewitt, *What Is Your Race?: The Census and Our Flawed Efforts to Classify Americans* (Princeton and Oxford: Princeton University Press, 2013), 99–104.

[36] Federal Interagency Committee on Education, *Report of the Ad Hoc Committee*, 8.

[37] Ibid., 9–13.

Federal Statistical Policy and Standards. As a result of the administrative change, the Secretary of Commerce issued the *Statistical Policy Handbook*, which included federal standards for the collection of data, also called Statistical Directives.[38] The fifteenth of these directives mandated the use of four standardized racial categories in the official reporting of all statistical data pertaining to race by the federal government. The categories are:

- *American Indian or Alaskan Native*: a person having origins in any of the original peoples of North America and who maintains cultural identification through tribal affiliations or community recognition.
- *Asian or Pacific Islander*: a person having origins in any of the original peoples of the Far East, Southeast Asia, the Indian Subcontinent, or the Pacific Islands. This area includes, for example, China, India, Japan, Korea, the Philippine Islands, and Samoa.
- *Black*: a person having origins in any of the black racial groups of Africa.
- *Hispanic*: a person of Mexican, Puerto Rican, Cuban, Central or South American, or other Spanish culture or origin regardless of race.[39]
- *White*: a person having origins in any of the original peoples of Europe, North Africa, or the Middle East.

The resulting classificatory framework is what David Hollinger refers to as "the ethno-racial pentagon," extended to all federal agencies.[40] The Directive specifically noted that the mandated categories were not scientific or anthropological in nature, but, rather, were necessary in order to ascertain statistical counts of the population. The Directive recommended, but did not require, that self-identification be the preferred manner of data collection, although it had been standard operating practice for agencies to assign racial and ethnic group identity by observation rather than by respondent self-declaration.[41] Though other agencies could

[38] Administrative control again changed hands in 1980 because of the Paperwork Reduction Act, which assigned OMB responsibility for overseeing and coordinating the federal statistical system.

[39] Note that Hispanic is considered an ethnic category, not a racial category. In 1976 Congress passed Public Law 94–311, which required all federal agencies to provide separate counts of the Hispanic population, a development largely attributed to the lobby efforts of Hispanic organizations. See Choldin, "Statistics and Politics," Rodriguez, *Changing Race*, and Victoria Hattam, "Ethnicity and the Boundaries of Race: rereading Directive 15," *Daedalus* 134, no. 11 (2005): 61–69.

[40] Hollinger, *Postethnic America*.

[41] Robbin, "Classifying Racial and Ethnic Group Data," 134.

collect information on ethnic subgroups, this information had to be aggregated into the main categories outlined in the Directive. This configuration of race and ethnicity was magnified and spread throughout the government and society as the standard classification scheme for state and local agencies, the private sector, and the academic research community.[42] Reflecting dominant racial ideas of the time, the Directive acknowledged the existence of mixed-race but instructed that multiracial respondents select one category "which most closely reflects the individual's recognition in his community."[43] In the shift from counting to control racial boundaries to (standardized) counting to justify positive action, the schematic state continued to make the population legible in the only way it knew how – via discrete racial categories.

RACIAL APPREHENSION REVISITED

Canada

In contrast to America's innovations, neither Canada nor Great Britain counted race directly on their 1971 or 1981 censuses. Canada's question on ethnic ancestry in 1971 followed the pattern used in 1961, which listed more than thirty ethnic groups, including "Czech," "Greek," and "Negro," in alphabetical order. Only single responses were accepted in data capture procedures. If multiple ethnic origins were reported in the mark-in spaces, the darkest mark was retained and other responses dropped. If a respondent filled in a mark-in space and wrote a response in the free-text field, only the write-in was retained.[44]

Dissatisfaction with the quality of data in 1971 led to a review of the ethnic concepts proposed for the 1981 Census. Statistics Canada then made four important modifications to the administration of the ethnic question. First, Statistics Canada's experiment with self-enumeration was a success, but nevertheless posed problems in terms of data quality. There was an estimated undercount of about 10 percent between the number of Band or Treaty Indians enumerated in the 1971 Census when compared with the number of Band Indians recorded in the Indian Register.[45] John Kralt, an employee of Statistics Canada at the time, notes that the Canadian government was interested obtaining an official estimate of

[42] Sabbagh and Morning, *Comparative Study on the Collection of Data*, 3.

[43] OMB, "Race and Ethnic Standards for Federal Statistics and Administrative Reporting," Statistical Directive No. 15, 1977.

[44] Kralt, "Ethnic Origins in the Canadian Census," 17. [45] Ibid., 18.

the number of Métis and non-status Indians. This is undoubtedly a result of the proposal to recognize aboriginal and treaty rights in the Canadian constitution; under what would eventually become section 35 of the Constitution Act, 1982 the legal designation "Aboriginal" includes Indians, Métis, and Inuit. Policymakers were also aware that section 12.1(b) of the Indian Act could not withstand judicial review given the gender equity provisions in the proposed Charter of Rights. Unofficial estimates of these populations toward the end of the 1970s varied anywhere from 350,000 to 1.5 million persons.[46] If Indian status was to be reinstated for the women who fell victim to the discriminatory provisions of the Indian Act, the government needed to know how large a population would suddenly shift from non-status to status designations.

The 1981 Census provided Aboriginal respondents with four choices on the ethnic question under the heading "Native Peoples": Inuit, status or registered Indian, non-status Indian, or Métis (Figure 5.1). The conceptual implications of including these categories on the census and, importantly, implying that all were equally *Aboriginal*, are significant. Chris Andersen points out that the categorical instability used by instruments of governance – of which the census is but one example – to define, manage, and control the Métis population over the course of Canadian history has often worked to ensure the Métis were not recognized as a cultural or legal indigenous group.[47] In this sense, the administrative recognition of the Métis and non-status Indians as Aboriginal in the 1981 Census had important feedback effects in the struggles of these groups for solidarity, legal recognition in constitutional debates, political activism, and court challenges. The increased political awareness and activism within First Nations communities between the 1971 and 1981 censuses also posed a problem for Statistics Canada: a small number of First Nations bands refused to cooperate with the 1981 Census.[48] In particular, the bands were offended by the use of the phrase "on coming to this continent" in the wording of the ethnic origin question. Again, this activism is likely linked

[46] Ibid., 19.

[47] Chris Andersen, "From Nation to Population: the Racialisation of 'Métis' in the Canadian Census," *Nations and Nationalisms* 14, no. 2 (2008): 347–368; Chris Andersen, "Underdeveloped Identities: The Misrecognition of Aboriginality in the Canadian Census," *Economy and Society* 42, no. 4 (2013): 626–650.

[48] In response, Statistics Canada arbitrarily assigned data for all records. For example, all respondents from the Kahnewake reserve in Montreal were assigned Iroquois as mother tongue, Quebec as place of birth, and status Indian as ethnic origin. Kralt, "Ethnic Origins in the Canadian Census," 23.

26. To which ethnic or cultural group did you or your ancestors belong on first coming to this continent?
(See Guide for further information.)

25 ☐ French
26 ☐ English
27 ☐ Irish
28 ☐ Scottish
29 ☐ German
30 ☐ Italian
31 ☐ Ukrainian
32 ☐ Dutch (Netherlands)
33 ☐ Polish
34 ☐ Jewish
35 ☐ Chinese
36 ☐ Other (specify)

Native Peoples
37 ☐ Inuit
38 ☐ Status or registered Indian
39 ☐ Non-status Indian
40 ☐ Métis

FIGURE 5.1: Census of Canada, 1981

to the constitutional debates occurring during the same time period. Though the census both is and is not connected to other areas of law and policy, it remains an apparatus of state power. It is one means (among others) of suturing meanings of race to state-endorsed mechanisms of imposing racial legibility. As such, targeted protest against the connotation in the census that Canadians are all immigrants served an important symbolic purpose in reaffirming Aboriginal claims as *First* Peoples.

The second major change in 1981 – one with significant discursive and statistical consequences – was the wording of the question. Instead of asking for the respondent's lineage on the male side, the question was now ambilineal: "To which ethnic or cultural group did you or your ancestors belong on first coming to this continent?" More than ten years after the publication of the Royal Commission's Report on the Status of Women and during a time of increasing emphasis on women's rights, those within and outside the government viewed the insinuation that ethnic identity was inherited from the paternal ancestor as sexist.[49] This new emphasis on the ethnic origins of

[49] Pamela White, Jane Badets, and Viviane Renaud, "Measuring Ethnicity in Canadian Censuses," in *Challenges of Measuring an Ethnic World: Science, Politics and Reality*, Proceedings of the Joint Canada-United States Conference on the Measurement of

both parental ancestors had an important impact on the data, making it far more likely that Canadians would record two or more ethnic groups.

This leads to the final two changes on the 1981 Census: the ordering of ethnic groups on the census form according to population size, and the allowance of multiple responses. Because of the desire to have census categories reflect the actual origins of Canadians rather than just paternal ancestry, two new policy problems arose. First, there was an increased likelihood that respondents would report multiple responses, which would require new and potentially costly methods of tabulation. Second, census designers held a related fear that if multiple origins were not permitted a significant proportion of the population would claim to be Canadian or American, thus defeating the purpose of the question.[50] While Statistics Canada recognized that Canadian social reality had evolved to the point that mixed ethnic marriages were practically the norm and increased ethnic and racial diversity from immigration was inevitable, multiple responses were not encouraged in the wording of the question, which referred to "ethnic or cultural group" in the singular. Nonetheless, Statistics Canada accepted multiple responses and tabulated them in data-capture procedures when approximately 11 percent of the Canadian population reported an ancestry comprised of more than one ethnic group. Given that over one-tenth of the Canadian population gave multiple responses *even without prompting*, multiple responses subsequently became an integral aspect of the ethnic origin question – and, eventually, the race question.

The ordering of ethnic groups also changed. In the 1971 Census, which was the first in which the respondent could view and fill out the census form him or herself, ethnic groups were listed in alphabetical order. In 1981, census designers used the official counts produced in the 1971 Census to determine the eleven most populous ethnic groups,[51] which were then listed on the form in alphabetical order, alongside one blank mark-in space labeled "Other." The only non-white group included was "Chinese." This ordering according to population count is important because evidence has long demonstrated that the power of suggestion has a tremendous impact on responses to questions of this type.[52]

Ethnicity, April 1–3, 1992 (Washington D.C.: U.S. Government Printing Office, 1993), 233.

[50] Kralt, "Ethnic Origins in the Canadian Census," 20.

[51] The groups listed were: French, English, Irish, Scottish, German, Italian, Ukrainian, Dutch (Netherlands), Polish, Jewish, and Chinese.

[52] Karen Kelly, *Collecting Census Data on Canada's Visible Minority Population: A Historical Perspective* (Ottawa: Statistics Canada, 1995).

Respondents are far more likely to check a box listed than to take the time and effort required to fill in a free-text field.

Great Britain

Meanwhile, the 1971 Census in Great Britain relied on an even more distant proximate indicator to determine racial identity: parents' country of origin. A growing number of public bodies advocated for the collection of racial statistics in the mid-1970s, including the Race Relations Board, the Community Relations Commission, and the Parliamentary Select Committee on Race Relations and Immigration.[53] The Office of Population Censuses and Surveys (OPCS) initiated a series of field trials between 1975 and 1979 in order to develop a direct question on race that would be both acceptable to the public and would generate more reliable and accurate data than the indirect measure used in 1971. A number of alternative designs and question wordings were tested in separate field trials. In general, there were two main difficulties recorded by OPCS bureaucrat Ken Sillitoe. First, West Indians were suspicious of the motives behind data collection. Response rates were generally low, and this group was among the most likely to object to the question in principle. However, Sillitoe notes that the hostility could be avoided if they were able to design some form of category "to record that although of non-UK descent he is nevertheless a UK citizen ... because asking about ethnic origins only ... can be taken to imply that anyone who is not of UK origin continues to be in some sense different, or alien to our society, no matter how long he or his forebears have been in Britain."[54] Throughout the trials, and, indeed, the debates proceeding the 1981, 1991, and 2001 censuses, many black respondents felt that while the choice of "West Indian" on the census form

[53] Race Relations Board, *Report of the Race Relations Board for 1974* (London: HMSO, 1975); Community Relations Commission, *Review of the Race Relations Act* (London: HMSO, 1975); Her Majesty's Government, Select Committee on Race Relations and Immigration, *The Organisation of Race Relations Administration* (London: HMSO, 1975). However, the continued tension surrounding the collection of racial data was epitomized by the Home Office's White Paper on race relations, which stated that "the Government considers that a vital ingredient of equal opportunities policy is a regular system of monitoring," but failed to recommend the collection of racial data that would support these activities. Erik Bleich, "Institutional Continuity and Change: Norms, Lesson-Drawing, and the Introduction of Race-Conscious Measures in the 1976 British Race Relations Act," *Policy Studies* 27, no. 3 (2006): 228.

[54] Ken Sillitoe, *Ethnic Origins I: An Experiment in the Use of a Direct Question about Ethnicity, for the Census*. Office of Population Censuses and Surveys, Occasional Paper No. 8 (London: OPCS, 1978), 46.

may have described their ancestors' geographic origins, it failed to adequately classify the ethno-racial identity of those born and raised in Britain.

The second difficulty that arose in the field trials was the classification of mixed-race. During the first tests in June and July 1975, mixed-race respondents presented a problem to the question designers, with 20 percent providing "ambiguous" answers and 15 percent giving "no answer," likely because respondents were unsure which box to check. The second field trial in July 1976 experimented with two alternative designs: on one test version, mixed-race respondents were instructed to "tick all boxes that are applicable," and on the second version they were provided with a separate box, but without a request for actual ancestry to be described. Though, in the words of Sillitoe, neither method "proved to be very good," there was a problem with the multiple response option that may, in retrospect, have been specific to this particular test. The design also employed a "European descent" category rather than "white," and many respondents, especially among the West Indian population, checked both the "European descent" box as well as their own racial category to indicate their nationality alongside their race. This confusion led the OPCS to conclude that "to ask form fillers to indicate mixed ancestry by ticking all boxes that apply is too unreliable."[55] The third test of autumn 1977 combined the box for "Other" and "Mixed descent," effectively alleviating the problem of people being recorded as mixed-race when they were not.[56] However, in many cases mixed-race respondents continued to give either single or multiple responses rather than be counted as "Other."

These tests did not guarantee the question's implementation on the 1981 Census. The 1978 Report of the Select Committee on Race Relations and Immigration recommended including the question, and Ministers with responsibilities for social services felt that better information about ethnic minorities was required. However, some political elites and central agencies, including the Lord President of the Privy Council, Michael Foot, felt this change would be "ill-advised" given the focus of the public's attention on immigration issues in the pre-election period.[57] Specifically,

[55] Ken Sillitoe, *Ethnic Origins II: An Experiment in the Use of a Direct Question about Ethnicity, for the Census*. Office of Population Censuses and Surveys, Occasional Paper No. 9 (London: OPCS, 1978), 18.

[56] Ken Sillitoe, *Ethnic Origins III: An Experiment in the Use of a Direct Question about Ethnicity, for the Census*. Office of Population Censuses and Surveys, Occasional Paper No. 10 (London: OPCS, 1978), 9.

[57] PRO CAB 128/63/14, Conclusions of Cabinet Meeting, April 13, 1978.

the Cabinet concluded that "the category 'white' in particular would be open to sensational and damaging treatment in the popular Press."[58] Nevertheless, Cabinet Ministers agreed that a reintroduction of the 1971 question on parents' country of origin would not only be ineffective, but would also be interpreted as a sign of weakness, showing a lack of resolve to tackle the problems of racial disadvantage. The final Cabinet decision in April 1978, summed up by Prime Minister James Callaghan, recognized the need for racial data that could only be provided by a direct question on the census but stated in his final recommendation on the issue that Cabinet "rejected the form of the question proposed for the census test, in particular the inclusion of the category 'white'."[59]

OPCS heeded the Cabinet order to find an alternative schema couched exclusively in ethnic terms, and in the census test in the London borough of Haringey in 1979 the ethnic designations "English, Welsh, Scottish or Irish" were used as well as an additional category, "Other European," alongside the non-white ethno-national-geographical categories of "West Indian or Guyanese," "African," "Indian," "Pakistani," "Bangladeshi," "Arab," "Chinese," and "Any other racial or ethnic group, or if of mixed racial or ethnic descent." However, the results of this test were skewed by a local campaign which urged people not to answer the question on race or ethnicity. Approximately 25,000 pamphlets were purportedly distributed to residents, linking these questions to the proposed nationality laws that "would make nationality dependent on your parents' nationality, not where you were born . . . If we say now who is and who is not of British descent, we may one day be asked to 'go home' whether we were born here or not."[60]

This social mobilization of racial minorities against the state's proposal to count by race was shaped by the taut connection between race and immigration in the pre-election climate of 1979. William Whitelaw, the Conservative spokesman on Home Affairs who later would become the Home Secretary in Thatcher's first Cabinet, outlined the Conservative platform for "racial harmony," which included a new British Nationality Act; restrictions on the entry of parents, grandparents, and children over 18; immigration quotas; and the promise to "severely restrict the conditions under which anyone from overseas can come to work here."[61] Future Prime

[58] Ibid. [59] Ibid.

[60] Quoted in OPCS, *Census 1981: General Report, England and Wales* (London: HMSO, 1990), 9.

[61] PRO PREM 16/1689, Extract from a speech by the Rt. Hon. William Whitelaw, the Opposition Spokesman on Home Affairs, replying to the Debate on Immigration and

Minister Margaret Thatcher reinforced the politics of numbers more infamously when she responded to a question about Tory policy on immigration in a January 1979 television interview for Granada World in Action by stating:

Well, now, look, let us try and start with a few figures as far as we know them ... if we went on as we are then by the end of the century there would be four million people of the new Commonwealth or Pakistan here. Now, that is an awful lot and I think it means that people are really rather afraid that this country might be rather swamped by people with a different culture and, you know, the British character has done so much for democracy for law and done so much throughout the world that if there is any fear that it might be swamped people are going to react and be rather hostile to those coming in.[62]

Two years before the Nationality Act saw the light of day, Haringey campaigners believed that the reformed nationality law would jeopardize the status of racial minorities in Britain, and the number of people who objected in principle to the questions on ethnicity rose dramatically. Only 54 percent of households returning their census test forms and as many as 32 percent of both the West Indian and Asian respondents expressed views that they thought the inclusion of such a question was wrong. Even greater objections were expressed in regards to the parents' country of birth question.[63]

After consultations with ethnic organizations following the Haringey affair, the new Conservative government decided in November 1979 not to include a question on ethnicity in the 1981 Census. At the time, the government presented the decision as a matter of technicality; the official justification provided to the House of Commons by Patrick Jenkin, the Secretary of State for Social Services, emphasized that the high non-response rates to the ethnic question could jeopardize the census as a whole and concluded that "the census simply is not the right means for obtaining proper information about ethnic origin."[64] When reporting on this chronology of events in 1990, OPCS noted that the elimination of the ethnic origin question was because of the low response in Haringey

Race Relations at the Central Council Annual Meeting at the Centre Hotel, Leicester, April 7, 1978.

62 www.margaretthatcher.org/speeches/displaydocument.asp?docid=103485, accessed June 6, 2009. Note that the BBC transcript is slightly different than this, the Granada transcript, recording that Thatcher commented that people are afraid of being swamped by people *of* a different culture (emphasis added).

63 OPCS, *Tests of an Ethnic Question*, OPCS Monitor CEN 80/2, 1980.

64 *Hansard*, House of Commons, vol. 983, April 29, 1980, col. 1305.

and because of the lack of agreement among "various interested parties" about whether such a question should be asked and the form the question would take.[65]

Haringey was indeed a factor that led to the exclusion of the ethnic question; however, other mitigating circumstances played important and often overlooked roles in the decision-making processes of census administration. The Registrar General (the head of OPCS) took the position that a potentially offensive ethnic question would put the entire census project at risk. Conversely, it is likely that the same line departments responsible for social services that had argued for racial data since the 1960s continued to do so. Some powerful organizations, such as university departments, census users, and the Commission for Racial Equality (CRE), argued that an ethnic question was necessary to monitor and combat racial disadvantage and that the incident in Haringey was caused by inadequate public relations.[66] Others, including the British Society for Social Responsibility in Science, the Haringey Community Relations Council, and numerous ethnic organizations, opposed the inclusion of a question for a variety of reasons, ranging from the argument that the collection of racial data would indicate that non-whites – rather than institutional racism – were the problem,[67] to the uncertainty surrounding the proposed nationality law.[68] In the end, the decision to present the government's conclusion as technical was a matter of political spin. An internal memo to Home Secretary William Whitelaw and Minister of State Tim Raison suggested that this justification was the lesser of all evils:

> The least unsatisfactory course would seem to be to try to present the decision as essentially a technical one; namely, that the Haringey test has shown that the Census is not a way of getting this information and that the Government will employ other and more acceptable techniques. It will be particularly important, therefore, that any announcement of the decision should be framed in as positive a way as possible, both to emphasise the Government's continuing commitment to obtaining information designed to be used for the benefit of the ethnic minority communities and to indicate that positive steps are being taken to find alternative sources of data.[69]

[65] OPCS, *Census 1981*, 2.

[66] Commission for Racial Equality, *1981 Census: Why the Ethnic Question Is Vital – A Discussion Document* (London: Commission for Racial Equality, 1980).

[67] PRO HO 376/223, Press Release – British Society for Social Responsibility in Science, October 17, 1979.

[68] PRO HO 376/223, Haringey Community Relations Council – Response to 1981 Census Test, July 1979.

[69] PRO HO 376/223, Memo from G.I. de Deney to Raison (Minister of State) and Whitelaw (Secretary of State), November 2, 1979.

The government was aware that the exclusion of the ethnic question from the census would leave it open to criticism about its commitment to race relations. Accepting the Registrar General's concern about the ethnic question's potentially damaging effect to the census project as a whole was a convenient way to quash the initiative while minimizing the damage to the new government's credibility in the politics of race relations. Moreover, the technicality justification also permitted the government to mask the true weight that organized opposition had in determining the outcome of the Haringey test and the subsequent policy decision to drop the question, a revelation which government officials believed "could be seriously damaging to race relations."[70] It is also likely that the mobilizing power and impact of ethnic organizations were deeply troubling to government officials – it was therefore necessary to belay any public insinuations that local organizations could sway the course of racial politics in Britain.

The ideological climate of the 1970s was another mitigating factor. If Haringey had never happened, would the newly instated Conservative government have approved a direct question on race for the 1981 Census? It is likely not. Thatcherism held many ramifications for race relations that either directly related to the government's neoconservative platform or were inflamed by it. Extreme racist and nationalist political parties also rose to prominence throughout the 1970s. The National Front, for example, was quite vocal on the issue of the census; its newspaper, *Spearhead*, argued "the 1981 Census MUST ask the vital question 'What is your ethnic origin?' Only then can we get an idea of the true size of the coloured population ... Our repatriation policy demands we have accurate figures of the number of people who, sooner or later, are going home."[71]

In this political climate, a direct question asking minorities to identify their race was bound to be met with suspicion and hostility, particularly if this question was proposed by Thatcher's government. Though one Conservative Member of Parliament argued that "the truth is that in this world at this time people do not like being asked a question of that kind ... They will not like it being asked whichever Government are in power," the response rates of the pre-Haringey field trials indicate that either political climate, or who asked the questions, or both, in fact mattered a great deal. As a member of the Opposition observed, "there was legitimate anxiety among black people about the possibility of a Conservative Government dedicated to discriminating against them

[70] Ibid. [71] *Hansard*, House of Lords, vol. 408, April 22, 1980, col. 740.

taking office ... In a couple of months after the Prime Minister's speech about swamping, it was no surprise to me that many black people were anxious about the contents of the census."[72]

The question would probably not have succeeded given the political climate of the time; but would the Conservative government have included an ethnic question at all? Again, the evidence suggests that it is not likely. Prime Minister Margaret Thatcher believed that much of the information gained from the census was unnecessary because it duplicated data available elsewhere. In a testament to the principles of neoconservative thought, Thatcher was "very concerned about the intrusion into the private affairs of individuals and [felt] strongly that Government [would] lay itself open to justifiable criticism unless it can be shown that these questions are really necessary for policy analysis and decisions."[73] Upon further inspection, Thatcher found many of the questions were, in her opinion, "completely unnecessary."[74] Cost-cutting was another of Thatcher's priorities. The introductory speech on the 1980 Census Order in the House of Lords ended with the proclamation that the census budget of £44 million was a 17.5 percent decrease in the cost projected by the previous Labour administration's White Paper.[75] To be clear, the decision to drop the ethnic question from the census was made in early November 1979, over a month before Thatcher culled other "unnecessary" census questions from the final product. However, as noted by government officials at the time, "[Thatcher's] concern to avoid complexity and unnecessary intervention into privacy seems to have been likely to lead her to challenge the ethnic question on these grounds had the decision not already been taken to abandon them."[76] Haringey or not, the proposed ethnic question would likely not have resurfaced until the 1991 Census, when its implementation was unavoidable, for reasons discussed further below.

THE MULTICULTURAL TURN

Not counting by race in Canada and Great Britain was unsustainable for a number of reasons. By the 1980s, multiculturalism emerged throughout the West as a widely accepted liberal framework, encompassing a range of

[72] *Hansard*, House of Commons, vol. 983, April 29, 1980, col. 1321; col. 1317–18.

[73] PRO 376/223, Letter from Patrick Jenkin, Secretary of State for Social Services, to William Whitelaw, Secretary of State for Home Department, December 13, 1979.

[74] Ibid. [75] *Hansard*, House of Lords, vol. 408, April 22, 1980, col. 737.

[76] PRO HO 376/223, Letter from G.I. de Deney to Miss Maurice (Director of Statistics), re: 1981 Census Ethnic Question, December 12, 1979.

laws, policies, and discourses "designed to provide some level of public recognition, support or accommodation to non-dominant ethnocultural groups, whether these groups are 'new' minorities (e.g. immigrants and refugees) or 'old' minorities (e.g. historically settled national minorities and indigenous peoples)."[77] The multicultural norm is transnationally pervasive because of the global diffusion of ideas and practices surrounding diversity governance and the codification of these ideas in quasi-legal international norms, especially in United Nations declarations of minority rights. For a time, the debate in Western democracies was not on whether or not to adopt multiculturalism, but, rather, centered on which kinds of multicultural policies to adopt.[78]

Accordingly, anti-discrimination law in Britain and Canada evolved substantially in the 1970s and 1980s. In 1976 Britain passed the Race Relations Act, which sanctioned direct discrimination and introduced the concept of indirect discrimination, which "requires the investigation of the effects and consequences of an act, procedure or judgment, and not only the determination of discriminatory intent," and "cannot go without the ability to *prove the fact* which is made possible through statistical reasoning since it allows for an objective view of inequalities arising from an observable event. It is on this basis that '*adverse impact*' can be analysed."[79] Statistical data were crucial for establishing indirect discrimination.

Canada also created its own version of indirect discrimination, led by the judiciary's interpretation of the Canadian Charter of Rights and Freedoms. Section 15(1) of the Charter protects equality before the law, provides equal protection and benefit of the law, and prohibits discrimination based on race, national or ethnic origin, color, religion, gender, age, or mental or physical disabilities. In *Action Travail des Femmes v. Canadian National Railways* (1987) the Supreme Court defined systemic discrimination as:

> the form of discrimination that simply results from the enforcement of the established methods of recruitment, enrolment and promotion, neither of which being specifically designed to promote discrimination. Discrimination is then

[77] Kymlicka, *Multicultural Odysseys*, 16.

[78] Glazer, *Affirmative Discrimination;* Will Kymlicka, *Politics in the Vernacular: Nationalism, Multiculturalism and Citizenship* (Oxford: Oxford University Press, 2001); Kymlicka, *Multicultural Odysseys*.

[79] Joan Stavo-Debauge and Sue Scott, *Comparative Study on the Collection of Data to Measure the Extent and Impact of Discrimination in a Selection of Countries: Final Report on England* (Lyon, FR: European Commission, Employment and Social Affairs DG, 2004), 54 (emphasis in original).

reinforced by the very exclusion of the disadvantaged group, as exclusion promotes the belief, both inside and outside the group, that it is produced by "natural" forces, for instance that women "simply can't do the work".

The precedent set by this decision, compounded by jurisprudence that emphasized the role of statistics in establishing proof of discrimination,[80] necessitated the use of statistical evidence to demonstrate prejudicial outcomes and "adverse effects," becoming "a major piece of evidence" in cases of this type.[81] Landmark decisions by the Canadian Human Rights Tribunal in the 1990s also required statistical evidence to explain observed unequal effects, and statistics were particularly important to demonstrate the underutilization of the relevant labor force pool.[82]

In census politics, this multicultural turn was also supported by a burgeoning programmatic belief about the validity of collecting racial data, spurred by international organizations such as the UN, UNESCO, and the European Union and their enshrinement of human rights, minority rights, and the right to self-declaration in international human rights law. Over the past thirty years, these international organizations have pushed for the collection of more accurate statistical information on racial discrimination. The European Commission, the United Nations Committee on the Elimination of All Forms of Racial Discrimination, the Council of Europe Commission Against Racism and Intolerance, the Advisory Committee on the Council of Europe Framework Convention on the Protection of National Minorities, the Durban Declaration and Plan of Action adopted by the World Conference Against Racism, Racial Discrimination, Xenophobia and Related Intolerance of September 2001, and the International Labour Organisation have all urged states to collect and analyze reliable statistical data that allows for the proper assessment of the extent of racial discrimination in order to better enable states to produce effective anti-discrimination measures.[83]

80 See *O'Malley v. Simpson-Sears* [1985] 2 R.C.S 536 and *Bhinder v. National Railways* [1985] R.C.S. 561.

81 Maryse Potvin and Sophie Latraverse, *Comparative Study on the Collection of Data to Measure the Extent and Impact of Discrimination in a Selection of Countries: Final Report on Canada* (Lyon, FR: European Commission, Employment and Social Affairs DG, 2004), 8.

82 Maryse Potvin, "The Role of Statistics on Ethnic Origin and 'Race' in Canadian Anti-Discrimination Policy," *International Social Science Journal* 57, no. 163 (2005): 31–32. See *Gauthier and others v. Canadian Forces* (1995 C.H.R.R. D/90) and *National Capital Alliance on Race Relations (NCARR) v. Health Canada* (1997 28 C.H.R.R. D/179).

83 Ringelheim, "Collecting Racial or Ethnic Data," 41–42.

In more policy-relevant terms, the United Nations Statistical Commission, which produces international statistics, sets international statistical standards, and is the highest decision-making body for international statistical activities, identified the enumeration of national and/or ethnic group as a legitimate census question in its 1980, 1998, and 2008 lists of principles and recommendations for population censuses.[84] An increasing number of states incorporated some form of ethnic enumeration during this time period, helping to augment the pervasiveness of the norm. Ann Morning's global analysis of 138 national census questionnaires between 1995 and 2001 demonstrates that 87 countries, or 63 percent of the sample, employed some variety of ethnic classifications.[85] Epistemic communities of statisticians and policymakers began to recognize their shared challenges to enumerating race and ethnicity, and at a 1990 Population Association meeting in Toronto, Canada, Edward Pryor of Statistics Canada suggested an international conference on the topic be organized.

The resulting 1992 conference, "Challenges of Measuring an Ethnic World," was a joint effort on the part of Statistics Canada and the United States Bureau of the Census. It brought together policymakers, statisticians, researchers, and data users from the United States, Canada, the United Kingdom, Australia, Malaysia, and the former Soviet Union for a three-day discussion on national experiences, the meaning and dimensions of ethnicity,[86] the impact of data needs, the socio-political context of data collection and use, and future challenges to measuring ethnicity. A main theme of the conference was whether or not the census was an appropriate vehicle to collect data on ethnicity. Participants responded with a unanimous and resounding yes, noting that for numerically small groups and small geographic areas the census is the only instrument that can provide reliable data. The majority of conference participants, and, indeed, each of the six countries that presented their national experiences

[84] United Nations, *Principles and Recommendations for Population and Housing Censuses*, Statistical Paper M/67 (New York: United Nations, 1980); United Nations, *Principles and Recommendations for Population and Housing Censuses*, Statistical Paper M/67/Rev. 1 (New York: United Nations, 1998); United Nations, *Principles and Recommendations for Population and Housing Censuses*, Statistical Paper M/67/Rev. 2 (New York: United Nations, 2008).

[85] Ann Morning, "Ethnic Classification in Global Perspective: A Cross-National Survey of the 2000 Census Round," *Population Research and Policy Review* 27, no. 2 (2000): 245.

[86] Here, as well as in the UN's principles, "ethnicity" is understood as including aspects such as race, origin, ancestry, language, and religion. United Nations, *Principles and Recommendations*.

in the conference program, also agreed that self-identification is the most appropriate method of obtaining ethnic data.[87] In short, racial statistics were internationally recognized as an acceptable policy instrument and self-declaration became the endorsed method of obtaining this data. These transnational developments were influential in Great Britain and Canada insofar as they augmented arguments for the collection of racial data from influential actors within the government.

The diffusion of programmatic beliefs was particularly important because in contrast to institutionalized minority participation in the United States, census policy networks in Britain and Canada were far more difficult for social groups to access. In both circumstances state institutions involved in the administration of the census remained fairly autonomous, retaining the power to determine when and how the network was formed, what issues were on the table for discussion, and who held final decision-making power. In effect, tight policy networks reduce minority group participation to the more traditional channels of access created by the state, for the state's established purposes. In these cases, Statistics Canada and OPCS monopolized the policymaking process. In Britain, this meant that the government could pursue its plans to include a direct question on race; in Canada, the government could continue to avoid it.

Canada

Throughout the 1980s the Canadian government – regardless of the party in power – began to acknowledge and seek policy avenues to address circumstances of racial disadvantage and discrimination in more proactive ways. Though a Minister of State for Multiculturalism and a Multiculturalism Directorate were established in the Secretary of State Department in 1972 as a result of the formal multiculturalism policy of 1971, it was not until a decade later that the federal government announced a national program to combat racism. In 1981 the Race Relations Unit within the Multiculturalism Directorate was established and undertook a number of initiatives, which ultimately led to the formation of the House of Common's Special Committee on the Participation of Visible

[87] Statistics Canada and United States Bureau of the Census, *Challenges of Measuring an Ethnic World: Science, Politics, and Reality*. Proceedings of the Joint Canada-United States Conference on the Measurement of Ethnicity, April 1–3, 1992 (Washington D.C.: U.S. Government Printing Office, 1992).

Minorities in Canadian Society in 1983.[88] Submissions to the Committee by non-governmental organizations, including the Canadian Ethnocultural Council, the Centre for Research-Action on Race Relations, and provincial Human Rights Commissions, emphasized the under-representation of racial minorities in virtually all major public institutions.

In its 1984 report, the Committee recommended that the government pursue affirmative action programs, but was "struck by the absence of hard data or official statistics on the work force profile of visible minorities" – data that were necessary in order to determine reasonable goals and the size of the potential pool of qualified workers. Noting that "the importance of compiling such data should not be minimized," and that several of the groups representing racial minorities who testified in Committee hearings had already given their public support for the collection of racial statistics, the Committee recommended that Statistics Canada include the "requisite additional questions to elicit accurate data on visible minorities" in the 1986 mini-census and the 1991 decennial census.[89] Calls for more accurate statistical data on racial minorities were echoed by Judge Rosalie Abella in the Royal Commission on Equality in Employment.[90] Her report outlined the substantial statistical data required to determine the situation of visible minorities, Aboriginal peoples, women, and persons with disabilities in the working environment, including longitudinal studies to measure progress over time.[91] In 1986 the Employment Equity Act aligned Canada with the United States and Great Britain in terms of "positive action" legislation. Circumstances of systemic discrimination in Canada were clearly a driver, though the incentives to engage in this policymaking enterprise were also transnational as Canadian state drew lessons from abroad. For example, the Royal Commission recommended the use of the term "employment equity" because of the negative reaction to "affirmative action," the phraseology dominant in the United States.

[88] Canada, *Equality Now! Report of the Special Committee on Visible Minorities in Canadian Society* (Ottawa: Supply and Services Canada, 1984), 3. According to the Employment Equity Act (1995), visible minorities are "persons, other than aboriginal peoples, who are non-Caucasian in race and non-white in colour." Aboriginal peoples are not included in this definition, as they are defined separately in both the census and for employment equity purposes.

[89] Canada, *Equality Now!*, 54.

[90] Canada, *Royal Commission on Equality in Employment* (Ottawa: Supply and Services Canada, 1984).

[91] Ibid.

In short, there was a recognized lack of data on the situations of racial minorities in Canada, and government commissions and committees agreed the best way to elicit better data was through the census. Statistics Canada also confirmed the multiple and substantial problems with using the ethnic origin question to enumerate racial minorities. These issues are laid out by Wally Boxhill, an employee of Statistics Canada at the time, in his 1984 report *Limitations to the Use of Ethnic Origin Data to Quantify Visible Minorities in Canada*. First, the 1981 question on ethnic origin was simply not designed to capture data on race. The references to language and cultural group in the ethnic origin question and instructions may have actually discouraged respondents from reporting their race. Second, ethnicity and race do not necessarily line up: Haitians may give their ethnic origin as French, while many persons born in Jamaica may have theirs as British. Third, while place of birth can often provide clues as to a respondent's racial identity, there is no way of knowing, for example, how many of the immigrants from the United States or Great Britain are of non-European descent. Fourth, there were issues regarding how to enumerate mixed-race people. When 181,565 people recorded multiple responses to the ethnic question involving a European and non-European origin, Statistics Canada was concerned that "attempts to make them 'visible' in a statistical sense are tantamount to the ascription of visible or of quasi-racial characteristics which may be non-existent."[92] Self-identification as a racial minority was replaced by complex data capture procedures that assigned racial identity based on deduction and conjecture.

In the 1986 Census,[93] however, the ethnic question appeared once again, with fifteen groups and three write-in spaces provided. The major change was that the question now asked "to which ethnic or cultural group(s) do you or did your ancestors belong?" dropping the reference "on first coming to this continent" because of protests by indigenous groups, and instructing that respondents "mark or specify as many as applicable."[94] The Aboriginal designations "Inuit," "North American Indian," and "Métis" were included at the bottom of the list of choices.[95] A list of

[92] Walton O. Boxhill, *Limitations to the Use of Ethnic Origin Data to Quantify Visible Minorities in Canada* (Ottawa: Statistics Canada, 1984), 17–18.

[93] The 1986 Census was originally cancelled by the Conservative government due to fiscal constraints and was later reinstated because of constitutional provisions dating back to when the prairie provinces joined Confederation that require a mid-decade census occur.

[94] Statistics Canada, *Census of the Population, 1986* (Ottawa: Statistics Canada, 1986).

[95] The use of "status Indian" and "non-status Indian" in the 1981 Census led to misreporting by persons born in India or with origins in the Indian sub-continent, who thought that

non-European ethnic groups was provided as examples of potential entries for the write-in space, including "Indian (India)," "Filipino," "Japanese," and "Vietnamese." Two non-European groups were shown on the list of fifteen: "Chinese" and "Black." "Chinese" had appeared on the list in 1981 because the categories are listed on the basis of population counts from previous censuses. The category of "Black," however, was specifically added to improve reporting of that population and to meet the need for data to implement the Employment Equity Act.[96] Rather than adding a direct question on race as recommended by political elites and other interested parties, policymakers incrementally adjusted their existing approach. Estimates of the non-white population were derived from indirect measures such as ethnicity, language, and place of birth, though it was understood that the use of these racial proxies would be inadequate and would not meet the acute need for accurate racial statistics in order to properly implement and monitor the 1986 Employment Equity Act.

The interdepartmental employment equity working group, which arose after the Abella Report, was a strong contingent within the Canadian bureaucracy that felt that a direct question on race should be included on subsequent censuses, and that this proposal would be supported by a majority of government departments.[97] The working group, comprised of representatives from the Departments of Immigration and Citizenship, Statistics Canada, Human Resources and Development, the Public Service Commission, the Human Rights Commission, and the Treasury Board Secretariat,[98] was tasked with deciding which groups would count as visible minorities, which would not, and how to count mixed-race people for the purposes of employment equity policies. The working group discussed the possibility of including an explicit question on race in the 1991 Census and set the ball in motion. Advisory committees to Statistics Canada, such as the National Statistics Council, the Advisory Committee on Demography, and the Advisory Committee on Social Conditions, were asked to consider possible wording for a question on race. Between 1987

the term "status" referred to whether or not they were permanent residents or citizens of Canada. In 1986 the reference to status was replaced by "North American Indian." Kelly, *Collecting Census Data*, 24.

96 White et al., "Measuring Ethnicity," 230; Potvin, "The Role of Statistics," 35. This strategy was successful. According to census data, Canada's black population increased from 30,975 in 1981 to 260,335 in 1986; Kelly, *Collecting Census Data*, 37. While some of this increase is a result of immigration, the majority can be attributed to adding "Black" as a choice on the census form.

97 Interview with Statistics Canada representative, October 2009.

98 Interview with Statistics Canada representative, October 2009.

and 1989, Statistics Canada conducted extensive public consultations, a major departure from consultations done for previous censuses, which had focused primarily on major data users in the government and private sector.[99] The majority of the 169 oral and written submissions on the "visible minority issue" and the sixty-two comments on the "race issue" were in favor of including a direct question on race and the government consultation report recommended this course of action.[100] The policymaking process was bureaucratic in origin and implementation – as one Statistics Canada employee put it, "We drive the process, though, that has to be quite clear. We don't react to – I don't even think there is an official lobby in this country, but we don't react to that."[101]

Statistics Canada also undertook testing in a number of forums. In the 1986 Census over-coverage study, respondents were asked "Do you consider yourself to belong to Canada's visible or racial minority population?" The analysis of responses indicated that there was considerable confusion pertaining to the term "visible minorities." In 1988, two National Census Tests (in preparation for the 1991 Census) asked respondents to indicate which pre-coded category best described their race or color. There was a low level of non-response and few backlash or nonsense responses[102] – in effect, the question tested well. In spite of these positive results, a direct question on race did not appear on the 1991 Census; instead, the 1991 ethnic question mirrored its 1986 predecessor.

Why was the question excluded? Pamela White, a senior bureaucrat at Statistics Canada at the time, argues that though a direct question on race was tested in time for the 1991 Census, it was dropped from the final version because of fiscal constraints.[103] A number of civil servants at Statistics Canada confirmed during interviews that the exclusion of the question was likely linked to money; in one's words, "adding

[99] Edward T. Pryor, Gustave J. Goldmann, Michael Sheridan, and Pamela White, "Measuring Ethnicity: Is 'Canadian' an Evolving Indigenous Category?" *Ethnic and Racial Studies* 15, no. 2 (1992): 222.

[100] Statistics Canada, *1991 Census Consultation Report* (Ottawa: Statistics Canada, 1988).

[101] Interview with Statistics Canada representative, October 2009.

[102] Walton O. Boxhill, *Making Tough Choices in Using Census Data to Count Visible Minorities in Canada* (Ottawa: Statistics Canada, 1990); Pamela White, "Challenges in Measuring Canada's Ethnic Diversity," in *Twenty Years of Multiculturalism: Successes and Failures*, ed. Stella Hryniuk (Winnipeg: St. John's College Press, 1992), 170; Monica Boyd, Gustave Goldmann, and Pamela White, "Race in the Canadian Census," in *Race and Racism: Canada's Challenge*, eds. Leo Driedger and Shiva Halli (Montreal: Queens-McGill University Press, 2000), table 3.3.

[103] White, "Challenges in Measuring Canada's Ethnic Diversity."

a question to the census could cost, literally, a million dollars."[104] Reusing the same question from census to census keeps the data produced comparable, and is also low-cost. Statistics Canada representatives also emphasized the longevity of the census-making process. When asked why the question failed to appear in 1991, one civil servant relayed, "there's no conspiracy theory, you know. These things just take time."[105] However, in contrast to these explanations, a different civil servant argued that the upper echelons of Statistics Canada "never wanted to have a question on race," and when the deed was finally cemented in 1995, "they went kicking and screaming the entire way."[106] The recognized need for more accurate racial data than the ethnic question could provide from within the state apparatus, this interviewee suggested, was tempered by a risk-averse bureaucracy:

> I think that there was no real driver from them to put [the question] in in 1991. Because by then, and using the algorithm we had invented, we were getting numbers that were robust enough to pass the test. So Fellegi [the Chief Statistician] didn't want to "jeopardize" the census by having a race-like question.[107]

It is difficult to confirm either interpretation directly with the available evidence. Census tests alone indicate a willingness to consider putting a question on race on the census, but do not prove a clear intention to do so. When asked if a question on race had been proposed to the Cabinet, which has the final approval on changes to census content, several interviewees noted that they could not divulge that information because of the provisions of Canada's Security of Information Act (formerly, and tellingly, known as the Official Secrets Act).[108]

Nevertheless, circumstantial evidence indicates a continuing discomfort with the public recognition of race, which played out during the constitutional politics and national identity crises of the early 1990s. For example, in 1992 the federal and provincial governments collaborated on a series of proposed constitutional amendments, packaged together as the Charlottetown Accord. Charlottetown, which followed the defeat of its elite-driven predecessor, the Meech Lake Accord, proposed a "Canada Clause" as a response to Meech Lake's "Quebec Clause"; instead of only recognizing Quebec as a distinct society, as Meech Lake had done, the

[104] Interview with Statistics Canada representative, October 2009.
[105] Interview with Statistics Canada representative, October 2009.
[106] Interview with Statistics Canada representative, October 2009.
[107] Interview with Statistics Canada representative, October 2009.
[108] Interview with Statistics Canada representative, October 2009.

Charlottetown Accord provided recognition to Quebec's distinctiveness, the Aboriginal right to self-government, and Canadian values of egalitarianism and diversity. Even before a slim majority (54.3 percent) of Canadians voted against adopting the Accord in 1992, these constitutional debates were marked by overt and unprecedented opposition to multiculturalism. For example, a Decima research poll in late 1993 found that three of every four Canadians rejected the notion of cultural diversity and felt that racial minorities should try harder to fit into mainstream society. It also found that: 54 percent of respondents felt that Canada's immigration policy allowed "too many people of difference races and cultures" into the country; 50 percent agreed with the statement "I am sick and tired of some groups complaining about racism being directed at them"; and 41 percent agreed that they were "sick and tired of ethnic minorities being given special treatment." Ironically, perhaps, the same survey also found that two-thirds of respondents believed one of the best things about Canada is its acceptance of people from different races and ethnic backgrounds.[109]

In the report of the Citizens' Forum on Canada's Future (the Spicer Commission) of June 1991, the Commission argued that "federal government funding for multiculturalism activities other than those serving immigrant orientation, reduction of racial discrimination and the promotion of equality should be eliminated, and the public funds saved applied to these areas."[110] Vocal opposition to the policy and symbolism of multiculturalism led to shifts in state policy that reduced the emphasis on multiculturalism and focused instead on principles of immigrant "self-sufficiency" and "integration" into Canadian society.[111] The Department of Multiculturalism and Citizenship was disbanded in 1993 by the outgoing Conservative government, and responsibility for multicultural policies and programming became subsumed under the Department of Canadian Heritage while citizenship was housed together with immigration in a separate department.

[109] *Ottawa Citizen*, December 31, 1993: B1; *Maclean's*, December 27, 1993: 42.

[110] Canada, *Citizens' Forum on Canada's Future, Report to the People and Government of Canada* (Ottawa: Minister of Supply and Services Canada, 1991).

[111] Yasmeen Abu-Laban and Daiva Stasiulis, "Ethnic Pluralism under Siege: Popular and Partisan Opposition to Multiculturalism," *Canadian Public Policy* 18, no. 4 (1992): 365–386; Yasmeen Abu-Laban, "Welcome/STAY OUT: The Contradiction of Canadian Integration and Immigration Policies at the Millennium," *Canadian Ethnic Studies* 30, no. 3 (1998): 190–211.

Given the initial phase of the retreat from the multicultural ideal,[112] one would expect the state to be even more reluctant to reinforce racial or ethnic divisions through the census. Yet, these contradictory impulses were held together the same multicultural rubric – in this case, the erosion of multiculturalism policies and principles in certain policy spheres were in some ways isolated from the trajectory of the census, which one former employee of Statistics Canada described as being on a "collision course" with race.

In 1991 the political circumstances surrounding the ethnic question were unprecedented. Shortly before census day, media outlets in Toronto and its surrounding areas, including the *Toronto Sun*, began a campaign entitled "Count me Canadian!"[113] Strongly related to the national identity crisis that followed the failure of the Meech Lake Accord, campaigners and their allies in the Reform Party of Canada decried the lack of a Canadian category on the ethnic origin question and urged followers to declare themselves "Canadian" on their census forms using the mark-in space. Facing a disastrous situation in which the ethnic origin question could produce useless information on Canada's racial and ethnic diversity, Statistics Canada included instructions on the census form that read: "While most people of Canada view themselves as Canadian, information about their ancestral origins has been collected since the 1901 Census to reflect the changing composition of the Canadian population and is needed to ensure that everyone, regardless of his/her ethnic or cultural background, has equal opportunity to share fully in the economic, cultural, and political life of Canada."[114] After the 1991 Census, however, "Canadian" became the fastest growing ethnic group. Whereas only 130,000 people gave "Canadian" responses in 1986, that number jumped to just over 1 million in 1991. Canadian became the fourth largest single-response answer, following French, British, and German.

112 Through a comparison of multiculturalism in Britain, Australia, and the Netherlands, Joppke argues that there has been a retreat from official multiculturalism policies in many Western societies, which are now being replaced (in Europe, at least) by centrist policies of civic integration. Christian Joppke, "The Retreat of Multiculturalism in the Liberal State: Theory and Policy," *The British Journal of Sociology* 55, no. 2 (2004): 237–257.

113 See "We're Canadian, Eh?" *Toronto Sun*, May 26, 1991, p. 4; "Really Count Yourself In," editorial, *Toronto Sun*, May 26, 1991, Comment 1; "This Time, REALLY Count Yourself In: Say Count Me Canadian," *Toronto Sun*, June 2, 1991, Comment 16; "Let's Count on Canadians," *Toronto Sun*, June 4, 1991, p. 2.

114 Statistics Canada, *1991 Census, Content of the Questionnaire* (Ottawa: Statistics Canada, 1991).

The substantial responses of "Canadian" to the ethnic origin question had path-dependent implications not only for the 1991 census data but also for the future of the question itself. As Monica Boyd points out, because of the internal protocol at Statistics Canada to rank-order ethnic categories in terms of representative population size, "Canadian" would appear as one of the listed choices in the 1996 Census. This would automatically stimulate increased responses because respondents are more likely to check the box next to one of the listed options than write in their own response in the free-text field, and would also lead to increased responses because the French translation of "Canadian" is "*Canadien*," which has a historic and symbolic importance in French Canada.[115] More importantly, the increased responses of "Canadian" on the 1991 Census made it impossible for Statistics Canada to determine who was and was not a racial minority using its standard approach of cross-tabulating racial proxies. This development, ironically spurred by a backlash to multiculturalism and hyphenated Canadianism, made the need for a direct question on race all the more acute.

Because of these unexpected policy contingencies, there was continued governmental interest in eliciting more accurate data on racial minorities, and, in turn, renewed support for a direct question on race during the planning stages of the 1996 Census.[116] Much of the conceptual work was done by the interdepartmental working group on employment equity. The centralized structure of the Canadian statistical system enabled categories created in one political forum to be transferred into others. As one member of the working group recalled:

> To a large extent, we were really looking at the legislation for employment equity. That was the driving force. So which categories we had there, which categories we included, was very much based on the Act. And on the Abella Commission ... The Act itself was not very specific about which groups to be included as such but the understanding was that they were the groups from Abella. Abella had identified most of those groups. And from Abella, when I worked at Employment and Immigration, we had used those ten groups and gathered the data from ethnic origin. So there was no desire, no reason to go back and say well these groups aren't any good – it was very much from the legislation and what we called operationalizing the legislation.[117]

[115] Monica Boyd, "Canadian, Eh? Ethnic Origins Shifts in the Canadian Census," *Canadian Ethnic Studies* 31, no. 3 (1999): 1–24.

[116] Boyd et al., "Race in the Canadian Census," 51.

[117] Interview with Statistics Canada representative, October 2009.

Statistics Canada repeated the consultation efforts that had been undertaken prior to the 1991 Census, though cross-country town hall meetings were not conducted because only limited content change was expected for the 1996 Census.[118] These consultations included stakeholders both within and outside the government. However, no lobbying took place; much like the development of the ethnic question in Britain, targeted public consultations and focus groups were used to test the understandability of the question terminology. A number of government committees provided input, including intergovernmental committees with representatives from the provinces and the advisory committee for social statistics, consisting of academics, non-governmental organizations, other data users, and experts.[119] Government departments were consulted on the issue of adding a direct question on race and, according to the 1996 Census Consultation Report, five departments supported the question and two were against its inclusion. Which departments stood in opposition to the addition of the question is not known, though the government departments responsible for implementing policies and programs pertaining to employment equity – Human Resources Development Canada and Citizenship and Immigration Canada – were strongly in support of the proposal and went so far as to suggest a "direct question on race."[120] For further information on the enumeration of race Statistics Canada looked to the international arena and analyzed the experiences of census designs in Britain, the United States, and elsewhere.[121]

Statistics Canada provided three rationales for including a direct question on race: low levels of non-response, high-quality data generated from the question, and the legislative requirement to provide data on racial minorities.[122] The government announced its intention to include

[118] Statistics Canada, *1996 Census Consultation Report* (Ottawa: Statistics Canada, 1996), 3. According to the *1996 Census Consultation Report,* measures included conferences and public meetings held in Toronto, Winnipeg, Regina, and Edmonton at the request of regional offices. In addition, Statistics Canada received more than 1,500 comments from more than 990 organizations, about 15 percent of which were made as a result of the public meetings. Not all comments, of course, concerned the ethnic origin or proposed visible minority question; only slightly more than 50 of the 226 comments received on the ethno-cultural questions pertained to the topic of race, with the vast majority of comments concerning the ethnic origins question.

[119] Interview with Statistics Canada representative, October 2009.

[120] Statistics Canada, *Content of the Questionnaire, the 1996 Population Census* (Ottawa: Statistics Canada, 1996), 50.

[121] Pryor et al., "Measuring Ethnicity," 172; Statistics Canada and United States Bureau of the Census, *Challenges of Measuring an Ethnic World.*

[122] Boyd et al., "Race in the Canadian Census," 52.

a question on race in the summer of 1995 and a public debate over the nature and effectiveness of Canada's multiculturalism and employment equity policies ensued. Some argued that the inclusion of the question was "a step backward," based on ideas from the nineteenth century.[123] In response to these debates, Canada's Chief Statistician, Dr. Ivan Fellegi, published a statement on the Statistics Canada website and in major newspapers throughout the country, explaining that the question was designed to elicit information necessary for the implementation and evaluation of the Employment Equity Act. At the same time, Fellegi fervently disassociated the question from the notion of race, stating that "this question is not designed to provide information on race or racial origins of the population of Canada."[124]

In previous censuses race was avoided because of its controversial nature, the threat it posed to data quality, and its potential for further fractiousness in an era of rampant identity politics. This time, the justification for its inclusion in 1996 relied on established normative principles of equality and social justice. The rationale provided on the census form relayed to Canadians that the information would support programs that promote "equal opportunity for everyone to share in the social, cultural, and economic life of Canada." Similarly noting that "much of the criticism of Question 19 appears to be directed more at the idea of employment equity than at the collection of statistics," the Chief Statistician encouraged Canadians to accept that "employment-equity legislation has been the law of the land since 1986," and recognize the value in using the census to collect these data, as "the census is the only possible source of the objective information which is needed to administer the act and to evaluate its impact." Invoking the necessity of fair and informed debate on these issues, Fellegi argued that "it is in everyone's interest that the debate on issues related to employment equity, and the many other issues illuminated by census data on the composition and characteristics of our population, be supported by objective, impartial and reliable data, rather than by impressions, unfounded opinion or stereotypes."[125] Canadians may not have liked employment equity, and were still uncomfortable with a question that

[123] Richard Gywn, "Census Focus on Race a Step Backward," *Toronto Star*, May 19, 1996: F3.

[124] Ivan P. Fellegi, "Chief Statistician: Why the Census Is Counting Visible Minorities," *Globe and Mail*, April 26, 1996: A21.

[125] Ibid.

walked and talked like race, but the invocation of these principles – equality, fairness, and full participation in Canada's social, economic, and cultural life – were at least familiar.

The final version of Question 19 on the 1996 Census provided ten options, in order of demographic prevalence as determined from the 1991 Census: White, Chinese, South Asian (e.g. East Indian, Pakistani, Punjabi, Sri Lankan), Black (e.g. African, Jamaican, Haitian, Somali), Arab/ West Asian (e.g. Armenian, Egyptian, Iranian, Lebanese, Moroccan), Filipino, South East Asian (e.g. Cambodian, Indonesian, Laotian, Vietnamese), Latin American, Japanese, and Korean (Figure 5.2). One mark-in space was provided for "Other" designations. In contrast, the ethnic question (Q.17) abandoned its pre-designated list of options and instead featured four mark-in spaces, with the instructions providing a list of examples derived from ethnic origin responses on the previous census, including Canadian. Aboriginal identities were now enumerated separately in the preceding question (Q.18), which asked "Is this person an Aboriginal person, that is, North American Indian, Métis, or Inuit (Eskimo)?" and instructed those who responded positively to specify either North American Indian, Métis, or Inuit (Eskimo) and to skip Question 19 and to go on to two additional questions (Q.20 and Q.21), which asked respondents to name the Indian Band or First Nation they belonged to and to identify whether or not they were Treaty or Registered Indians. Importantly, neither the title of Question 19 nor the explanation thereof dared use the word "race"; rather, the question referred to "population group." Much like the use of the term "visible minority," the reference to population group dodges the four-letter word, and critics charge that this avoidance of racial language is also an avoidance of issues of racism.[126] Respondents were instructed to mark as many groups as applicable; how this decision came to pass will be explored further in the next chapter.

The question was a success, with low non-response rates and high-quality data produced. In fact, the publication of data using this direct question demonstrated exactly how inadequate the use of racial proxies had been in previous censuses. For example, only 72 percent of black respondents gave compatible ethnic origins when compared to their

[126] Daiva Stasiulis, "Symbolic Representation and the Numbers Game: Tory Policies on 'Race' and Visible Minorities," in *How Ottawa Spends: The Politics of Fragmentation, 1991–92*, ed. Frances Abele (Ottawa: Carleton University Press, 1991), 229–267.

19. Is this person:

■ *Mark or specify more than one, if applicable.*

Note:
This information is collected to support programs which promote equal opportunity for everyone to share in the social, cultural and economic life of Canada.

05 ○ White
06 ○ Chinese
07 ○ South Asian *(e.g., East Indian, Pakistani, Punjabi, Sri Lankan)*
08 ○ Black *(e.g., African, Haitian, Jamaican, Somali)*
09 ○ Arab/West Asian *(e.g., Armenian, Egyptian, Iranian, Lebanese, Moroccan)*
10 ○ Filipino
11 ○ South East Asian *(e.g., Cambodian, Indonesian, Laotian, Vietnamese)*
12 ○ Latin American
13 ○ Japanese
14 ○ Korean
Other — *Specify*
15 [ ]

FIGURE 5.2: Census of Canada, 1996

response to the race question.[127] Interestingly, an unintended consequence of the success of the race question was to make the question on ethnic origins seem obsolete. Some within Statistics Canada preferred to drop the ethnic question because its free-text form meant high tabulation and coding costs that could not be justified by reference to legislation necessitating the information. The high prevalence of "Canadian" responses also made the usefulness of the data questionable. Other civil servants in the Department of Canadian Heritage fought to keep the ethnic origin question alive, arguing it was necessary in order to track the socio-economic status of third-generation white ethnic groups.[128] So far, Parliament has kept both questions, though the elimination of the census long-form in 2011 has raised serious questions about the accuracy of the data, a development explored further in Chapter 7.

[127] Potvin, "The Role of Statistics," 39.

[128] Richard Y. Bourhis, "Measuring Ethnocultural Diversity Using the Canadian Census," *Canadian Ethnic Studies* 35, no. 1 (2003): 16–17; Jack Jedwab, "Coming to our Census: The Need for Continued Inquiry into Canadians' Ethnic Origins," *Canadian Ethnic Studies* 35, no. 1 (2003): 35–50.

Great Britain

Two contextual factors in Britain served as the backdrop for the realization that racial data could be useful rather than offensive. First, the 1980s began with often-violent clashes between second-generation Black Britons and the police. The Brixton riots of April 1981 and the nationwide riots in July of that year garnered significant media and political attention. Lord Scarman's inquiry published its final report in November 1981 and concluded that while there was no institutional racism in Britain, racial disadvantage existed and was widespread.[129] The report called for increased efforts to tackle racial discrimination, though Thatcher paid little attention to the recommendations. Regardless, when the race riots of 1985 challenged the theory that the Brixton riots were an uncharacteristic blip in otherwise tolerant and peaceful race relations, urban unrest became systematically linked to race and served as a constant reminder that the fear of social disorder and the violent potential of racial disadvantage was, in Britain, a reality.

Second, there was a consistent push from anti-racism advocates and urban local governments for political movement on race relations. These organizations understood that liberal multiculturalism, which perceived racial antagonism as derived from individual prejudice or the maladjustment of racial minorities to British life, did not address more substantive issues of racism. Local authorities were particularly active on a number of fronts, with good incentives to be so. The Local Government Act of 1966 and the Local Government Grants (Social Needs) Act of 1969 gave local authorities with substantial numbers of Commonwealth immigrants the opportunity to obtain funding for special projects designed to meet the needs of minority populations. In the early 1980s a number of local authorities and city councils began to establish Race Relations Units and some adopted, quite separate from the national government, systems of racial classification based exclusively on skin color.[130] Local governments also provided a politically palatable version of anti-racism. For example, the Greater London Council led by Ken Livingston declared London an anti-racist zone in 1984. This reconfiguration of multiculturalism in urban governance was tied to the liberal discourse of equal opportunity,

[129] Leslie Scarman, *The Brixton Disorders 10–12 April 1981. Report of an Inquiry by the Rt. Hon. The Lord Scarman OBE* (London: HMSO, 1981).

[130] Ulysses Santamaria and Kristin Couper, "The Making of the Multi-Racial Society in the United Kingdom: Strategies and Perspectives," *Social Science Information* 24, no. 1 (1985): 153–154.

allowing it to be perceived as both adjunct to and autonomous from more critical and leftist anti-racist projects.[131]

At this point, the disparate arms of the state began to publicly recognize the need for racial data. As the bodies responsible for delivering government programming, local authorities were influential advocates in matters pertaining to race relations. The CRE also provided unwavering and vocal support for including an ethnic question, and several prominent governmental bodies augmented this call for change. The 1981 report of the Home Affairs Committee on Racial Disadvantage and Lord Scarman's report on the Brixton riots both suggested a direct question on ethnicity be included in the next census.[132]

The most influential call for action was from political elites in the Sub-Committee on Race Relations and Immigration.[133] The bipartisan committee began an inquiry in 1982 into whether or not an ethnic or racial question should be asked on the national census, inviting evidence from a variety of external stakeholders, including local authorities, health authorities, and minority organizations. Its members traveled to Canada and the United States to familiarize themselves with the collection of ethnic and racial data in other countries. In its parliamentary report issued in May 1983, the committee publicly regretted the decision to not include a question on ethnicity in the 1981 Census. The report reviewed the need for information on ethnic groups in order to monitor the effectiveness of anti-discrimination policy and proposed that the OPCS carry out a further series of field tests to develop an improved design of the question on race and/or ethnicity for possible inclusion in the 1991 Census. The report accepted that the racial terms "white" and "black" needed to be used and went so far as to suggest a design for the ethnic question.[134] In its reply the following year, the

[131] Ibid., 153; see also Barnor Hesse, "Introduction: Un/Settled Multiculturalisms," in *Un/Settled Multiculturalisms: Diasporas, Entanglements, Transruptions*, ed. Barnor Hesse (London and New York: Zed Books, 2000), 9; Stephen Small and John Solomos, "Race, Immigration, and Politics in Britain: Changing Policy Agendas and Conceptual Paradigms 1940s–2000s," *International Journal of Comparative Sociology* 47, nos. 3–4(2006), 245.

[132] Kenneth Leech, *A Question in Dispute: The Debate about an "Ethnic" Question in the Census* (London: Runnymede Trust, 1989), 9.

[133] The Sub-Committee was chaired by the Conservative MP John Wheeler and was comprised of one other Conservative MP (John Hunt) and two Labour MPs (Alexander Lyon and Alf Dubs). Interestingly, the members' dedication to their task transcended party lines; Leech writes that "the members of this committee were strongly committed to the question" and were often hostile to those who expressed doubts. Leech, *A Question in Dispute*, 10.

[134] Her Majesty's Government, Parliament, *Ethnic and Racial Questions in the Census, Volume I: Report Together with Proceedings of the Committee*, Second Report from the Home Affairs Committee, Session 1982–83, HC 33-I (London: HMSO, 1983).

government accepted many of these recommendations in principle, noting that further tests needed to be carried out in order to create a reliable and publicly acceptable question for the 1991 Census.[135] The decision to re-open the issue of race and the census therefore did not exactly come from the governing political party, but nor was a completely external force, such as interest group mobilization or an exogenous shock, the driver of change. Though Scarman's inquiry and the various committees of Parliament were governmental bodies, the common thread amongst these different proponents of an ethnic question was their simultaneous connection to and autonomy from state authority, which allowed greater maneuverability in the framing of such a contentious political issue.

During the next series of field tests in Great Britain, held between 1985 and 1989, respondents demanded the categories of "Black British" and "British Asian." These labels were fraught with complexities, since some members of racial minorities born in British colonies overseas considered themselves to be "British Asian," though the use of the phrase was intended to appeal to second-generation British-born Asians. When the field trials tested the reliability of data that allowed everyone to classify themselves as British, respondents found the format confusing and the data were compromised. In subsequent trials that eliminated the qualifier "British" from the racial descriptors, those of West Indian descent continued to express their desire for a Black British category or something similar. During the trial stage, OPCS abandoned its attempts to classify mixed-race people, claiming that the variety of methods used in field trials of the 1970s had little success because "the main difficulty is that many people in this situation prefer to identify with the ethnic group of one of their parents – generally the father."[136] It is unclear whether or not this statement is accurate, particularly because reported field trials throughout

[135] Her Majesty's Government, Parliament, *Ethnic and Racial Questions on the Census*, The Government Reply to the Second Report of the Home Affairs Committee Session 1982–83 HC 33-I (London: HMSO, 1984).

[136] Ken Sillitoe, *Developing Questions on Ethnicity and Related Topics for the Census*. OPCS Occasional Paper 36 (London: OPCS, 1987), 3–5. As noted in an internal OPCS memo, the racial identification of mixed-race children was often determined by the census form-filler. If mixed-race people – usually the form-filler's children – most often identify with the race of the father (who at this point in time would likely have been non-white), then it is at least a possibility the dynamics involved in this identity choice are far more complex than a matter of preference (PRO RG 40/397, Memo by Ken Sillitoe – "Notes on Alternative designs for questions on ethnicity, religion and language – for the 1991 census," May 29, 1985). See also Jacqueline Nassy Brown, "The Racial State of the Everyday and the Making of Ethnic Statistics in Britain," *Social Text* 27, no. 1 (2009): 11–36.

the 1970s and 1980s rarely provided mixed-race people the opportunity to identify differently. The suggestion that multiracial people *prefer* to identify with only one ethnic group is not supported by field trial evidence.[137] Nevertheless, in each of the tests in the 1980s, an instruction was added to the question which read, "If the person is descended from more than one group, please tick the box to which the person considers he or she belongs, or ... describe the person's ancestry in the space provided."[138]

An OPCS internal working group created in 1985 designed the questionnaire. Consultations were also part of the group's terms of reference, but the list of stakeholders the working group consulted were mainly internal, with the sole exception of the semi-autonomous CRE. The working group appears to have understood the necessity of consulting with ethnic minority organizations to prevent the disastrous Haringey results. However, the members were undecided on the crucial question of *when* to consult. The group recognized that if minorities were consulted before field trials, there was a strong possibility that they would object to the designs being tested, but if they were not consulted in advance, "there might be complaints that we are failing to take heed to the SCORRI [Sub-Committee on Race Relations and Immigration] emphasis on the need for better public relations/publicity."[139] There is little evidence that consultations with minority groups took place during the early field trials. According to the OPCS and General Register Office for Scotland (GRO(S)), the OPCS and CRE began a series of meetings with Community Relations Officers and representatives of ethnic minority organizations in England and Wales in late 1987 when a recommended question format had already been decided. The purpose of the meetings was "to try to find out what doubts or fears, if any, people might have" rather than a deliberative democratic policymaking process.[140] Consultation, in this sense, can be likened to a public relations campaign.

The 1988 Census White Paper delivered the official justification for including an ethnic question on the 1991 Census. The White Paper noted

137 Sillitoe does not provide statistics on how many respondents ticked two boxes compared with how many recorded only one race; the fact that both are mentioned as difficulties indicates that they were at least equally prevalent. Sillitoe, *Ethnic Origins III*, 19.

138 Sillitoe, *Developing Questions*, 5.

139 PRO RG 40/397, 1991 Census: Ethnic Question Project Group – terms of reference, January 7, 1985.

140 OPCS and GRO(S), "Major steps towards the 1991 Census," *1981 ... 1991 Census Newsletter*, no. 4, December 17, 1987.

that the rectification of economic disadvantage was a matter of general public welfare and was additionally important for the maintenance of favorable race relations. It also stated that the information collected on housing, employment, educational qualifications, and age-structure of each group would help the government carry out its responsibilities under the 1976 Race Relations Act and serve as benchmarks to monitor the implementation of equal opportunities policies.[141] The proposed question read: "Please tick the appropriate box. If the person is descended from more than one group, please tick the one to which the person considers he or she belongs, or tick box 7 and describe the person's ancestry in the space provided." The categories included (numbered 1–7) were: White, Black, Indian, Pakistani, Bangladeshi, Chinese, Any other ethnic group (and a free-text field).

At this stage, the government invited further comment from members of the public and from ethnic and racial organizations on whether they would answer the question. Though minorities did not participate in the policymaking process directly, their limited involvement could still affect change: black groups continued to request details on the ethnic origins of the black population, which led to the disaggregation of the original

11 Ethnic group

Please tick the appropriate box.

White ☐ 0
Black-Caribbean ☐ 1
Black-African ☐ 2
Black-Other ☐
please describe

Indian ☐ 3
Pakistani ☐ 4
Bangladeshi ☐ 5
Chinese ☐ 6
Any other ethnic group ☐
please describe

If the person is descended from more than one ethnic or racial group, please tick the group to which the person considers he/she belongs, or tick the 'Any other ethnic group' box and describe the person's ancestry in the space provided.

FIGURE 5.3: Census of England and Wales, 1991

[141] Her Majesty's Government, *1991 Census of the Population (Census White Paper)*, Cm 4412 (London: HMSO, 1988).

"Black" category into "Black-Caribbean" and "Black-African."[142] With this amendment, census test results in 1989 indicated that OPCS had created a reliable and publicly acceptable question – a feat unaccomplished in the late 1970s. This time, less than 0.5 percent of the sample refused to take part because of the ethnic question. A number of respondents voiced objections to the question when prompted, but these numbers were also very low: 1 in 5 black respondents and 1 in 20 white and Asian respondents. The answers provided by the sample were also relatively reliable, with 90 percent accuracy for whites, 86 percent for blacks, 89 percent for Asians, and 82 percent for "other and not determined."[143] Overall, the refusal rates in the 1989 census test were the lowest they had ever been.[144] At the time, OPCS's Ken Sillitoe and Philip White puzzled that "there is no obvious explanation for why the 1989 question did not give rise to the same level of objections from Blacks as other questions tested since January 1986."[145] Years later, Philip White and David Pearce suggested the reduction in refusal rates from blacks – the group most likely to object to the ethnic question – in 1989 could be attributed to broad consultations or the fact that in previous years ethnic monitoring had become much more widespread.[146]

These positive test results did not make the inaugural appearance of an ethnic question on the 1991 Census (Figure 5.3) inevitable. Rather, as Marie Ni Bhrolcháin points out, the various stages of the decision-making process were marked by extreme caution.[147] The Home Affairs Committee's report was highly critical of several departments' lack of awareness of the need for racial data and their indifference to its value. The government's reply to the Committee's report accepted the idea of

[142] Kenneth Sillitoe and Philip H. White, "Ethnic Group and the British Census: The Search for a Question," *Journal of the Royal Statistical Society, Series A (Statistics in Society)* 155, no. 1 (1992): 155.

[143] Ibid., 158–160.

[144] Ibid., 161. Refusal rates in the field tests between 1975 and 1979 (excluding Haringey) were generally low as well. In the 1975 tests, a total of 7 households (out of 450) objected to the race/ethnic origins question. In subsequent tests the refusal rate increased slightly, though Sillitoe argues that refusal rates are correlated to the length of the form. Sillitoe, *Ethnic Origins II*; Sillitoe, *Ethnic Origins III*.

[145] Sillitoe and White, "Ethnic Group and the British Census," 162.

[146] Philip H. White and David L. Pearce, "Ethnic Group and the British Census," in *Challenges of Measuring an Ethnic World: Science, Politics, and Reality*. Proceedings of the Joint Canada-United States Conference on the Measurement of Ethnicity, April 1–3, 1992 (Washington D.C.: U.S. Government Printing Office, 1992), 295.

[147] Marie Ni Bhrolcháin, "The Ethnicity Question for the 1991 Census: Background and Issues," *Ethnic and Racial Studies* 13, no. 4 (1990): 542–567.

gathering racial data in principle, but was still very cautious – whether a question would be tested was still dependent on the strength of the case put forward by users. Both the Sillitoe study of the field tests and the White Paper in 1988 did not to guarantee that a question would be included. Though a strong lobby emerged from within the government itself – the departments that had argued for an ethnic question in the 1970s continued to do so and were joined by the local authorities that were formally involved in the consultation process for the first time – a member of the local authority consultation group reported that some within the OPCS were still very hesitant.[148]

However, the transnational multicultural norm was pervasive, spurring an ideational shift during the 1980s from feelings of being "swamped" by non-whites to the recognition of the United Kingdom as a multicultural nation. Change was gradual and helped along by advocates. In census politics, this shift in discourse helped alleviate public concern over the state's reason for collecting racial data and made the ethnic question on the census less controversial. The transcripts of parliamentary debates tell a tale of the changing terms of debate: whereas the ethnic question caused substantial discussion in 1980, the 1989 Census Order passed through both Houses easily. One member of the House of Commons commented that:

> It is interesting to note how attitudes have changed over the years. Even 10 years ago, when I was Secretary of State for Social Services and was preparing for the previous census, it was difficult to reach an agreement on questions such as the ethnic question . . . It used to be the case . . . that this [ethnic question] was the most difficult one of all because of all the sensitivities.[149]

Attitudes on the part of the public and government changed – the public was less likely to refuse to answer the question on principle and the government no longer considered the ethnic question an offensive intrusion of privacy. But as a testament to the ability of the schematic state to hold contradictory impulses together, the years when the state was most willing to make strides in racial enumeration were also marked, from the 1980s until the election of New Labour and the revelations of the Macpherson Report of 1998,[150] by the disappearance of diversity models

[148] Personal communication, April 2009.

[149] Statement of Lord Ennals, *Hansard*, House of Commons, vol. 514, 21 December 1989, col. 369–79.

[150] The Macpherson Report resulted from a public inquiry into the racially motivated murder of Stephen Lawrence and a subsequent police investigation, which concluded

that stressed the need to address structural and substantive racism from British political discourse, though multiculturalism was still valorized in political rhetoric.[151]

CONCLUSION

Single-case studies of American census politics often suggest that social mobilization is a key driver. Of course, minority groups in the United States have sought to alter the racial classification schema rather than inaugurate one – quite a different situation than in Canada and Britain, where designing and implementing a race question was an entirely new policy venture. Regardless, the motive to develop a standardized racial classification system in 1977 came from political institutions and racial ideas rather than interest group lobby activities.

Mobilization occurred in the British and Canadian contexts, but they were different from one another and from the lobbies seeking amendments to the American racial typology. The British case illustrates that racial minorities have not always welcomed enumeration with open arms. Non-whites were highly suspicious of the uses to which racial data would be put. While these fears were unfounded, it is little wonder that racial minorities, those who have most often felt the brunt force of state power, had their doubts about the government's intentions. Given that British national identity continues to be strongly raced and classed,[152] this skepticism is understandable, particularly when racial minorities are not consulted beforehand, the rationale for data collection is unpublicized, and any emphasis on difference – even something as superficially neutral as counting those who are racially different from the white majority – is a reminder of who does and does not really belong in Britain.

the London Metropolitan Police Force was institutionally racist. The Report catalyzed profound changes to the law and policing in Britain.

151 Hesse, "Introduction," 9–10.

152 Paul Gilroy, *"There Ain't No Black in the Union Jack": The Cultural Politics of Race and Nation* (London: Hutchinson, 1987); Bhikhu Parekh, *Rethinking Multiculturalism*; Sarah Neal, "The Scarman Report, the Macpherson Report, and the Media: How Newspapers Respond to Race-Centred Social Policy Interventions," *Journal of Social Policy* 32, no. 1 (2003): 55–74; Solomos, *Race and Racism*; Paul Gilroy, *Postcolonial Melancholia* (New York: Columbia University Press, 2005); Claire Worley, "'It's not About Race. It's About the Community': New Labour and 'Community Cohesion'," *Critical Social Policy* 25, no. 4 (2005): 483–496; Tariq Modood, *Multiculturalism: A Civic Idea* (Cambridge: Polity Press, 2007); Nasar Meer and Tariq Modood, "The Multicultural State We're In: Muslims, 'Multiculture' and the 'Civic-Rebalancing' of British Multiculturalism," *Political Studies* 57, no. 3 (2009): 473–497.

In contrast, the white majority in Canada mobilized against racial enumeration. Here, the push for "Canadian" responses was tied to the perception that an emphasis on racial or ethnic identities was divisive. The elite agitators, the Reform Party, also championed a political platform of color-blindness, in which the party stood firmly against, for example, selective immigration based on racial criteria, but simultaneously argued that immigration should not "be explicitly designed to radically or suddenly alter the ethnic makeup of Canada, as it increasingly seems to be."[153] The success of "count me Canadian" was not because all those who responded "Canadian" on the 1991 Census necessarily agreed with the Reform Party's neoconservative stance on race relations. The campaign and its resounding success do, however, speak to the proliferation and legitimization of normative claims about the creation of a Canadian identity above and beyond racial distinctions during a time when identity politics were prominent in society writ large. On the one hand, this could be an anti-racist goal: a call to move beyond arbitrary racial distinctions and develop a multiracial and multicultural Canadian identity. On the other hand, Canadians' tendency to avoid issues of race and racism, combined with the country's linguistic, multicultural, identity, and constitutional politics of the day, suggest that promoting a Canadian identity came at the cost of abandoning the hyphenated Canadianism at the heart of metaphors about the Canadian mosaic.

This chapter presented an alternative way to explain developments in census politics by examining the schematic state as both an actor and an arena. As an actor, schematic states drew from the transnational normative backdrop of liberal multiculturalism. Globally, the multicultural moment gave credence to the idea that racial diversity could be a positive attribute of the nation, opening the possibility for a new racial politics premised on integration and recognition rather than assimilation or marginalization. In the 1980s and 1990s, many Western democracies adopted a wide range of policies to assist the integration of immigrant groups, prevent and redress discrimination against racial minorities, acknowledge the territorial or language rights of national minorities, and recognize the self-government rights of indigenous populations. Of course, not all countries chose to adopt multicultural norms, and

153 Cited in Della Kirkham, "The Reform Party of Canada: A Discourse on Race, Ethnicity and Equality," in *Racism and Social Inequality in Canada: Concepts, Controversies, and Strategies of Resistance*, ed. Vic Satzewich (Toronto: Thompson Education Publishing, 1998), 250.

many argue that these same democracies that were once at the forefront of the "multicultural turn" have long since abandoned it in both principle and practice.[154] However, the preliminary findings of Keith Banting and Will Kymlicka's Multiculturalism Policy Index, a project that monitors the evolution of multiculturalism policies in twenty-one Western democracies, indicate that multicultural policies have persisted and, in many cases, expanded.[155] In 1980, only Australia, Canada, Sweden, and the United States scored above 3.0 on the index, as "moderate" and "strong" regimes; by 2000, three of the four had strengthened their multicultural policies (the United States retained the status quo) and were joined by four more "moderate to strong" states: Belgium, the Netherlands, the United Kingdom, and New Zealand. Ten years later, in 2010, the proverbial scales tipped in favor of a multicultural (developed) world: Norway, Portugal, Spain, and Ireland joined the moderate category while Finland leapfrogged into the strong category.[156]

The framework of liberal multiculturalism prompted states to take more proactive measures to combat racial discrimination, but simultaneously permitted tides of color-blind backlash against civil rights achievements and race-based policies. At times, political elites in Great Britain and Canada employed multicultural principles to deliberately *avoid* racial themes because of their fear that national fragmentation would follow in the wake of race-consciousness. In the 1970s and early 1980s in Great Britain and the 1980s and 1990s in Canada, elites declared that race was too controversial and too divisive to be put in the census. At the same time, however, programmatic beliefs about the necessity of racial enumeration circulated through international epistemic communities of statisticians and policymakers. These meso-level ideas were especially potent for civil servants working for the statistical agencies of Canada, Britain, and the United States, as they began to have prolonged international conversations about shared challenges and approaches to counting by race. Their appeals to the idea that statistics were an appropriate means of achieving egalitarian ends resonated with the domestic norms already in place and enabled an alignment between transnational ideas and national cultural repertoires.

[154] Joppke, "The Retreat of Multiculturalism."
[155] Keith Banting and Will Kymlicka, "Multicultural Policy Index," accessed May 1, 2014, www.queensu.ca/mcp/home
[156] Ibid.

In the arena of the schematic state, institutional structures provided incentives to standardize the American statistical system, but also gave elites in Westminster systems the final say on census issues. The bureaucratic coalitions that supported change were sometimes stymied by hesitant elites. As the transnational norm became more pervasive, elites were more open to the idea of racial enumeration, particularly once policymakers adapted these ideas to local institutional orders. The unexpected policy contingencies that arose from various forms of social mobilization and institutional protocols of census administration made the option of including a direct question on race more viable, ultimately making policy change possible.

6

The Multiracial Moment

"I think when historians write about Census 2000 in 70 or 80 years," former Census Bureau Director Ken Prewitt reflected in June 2001, "the sampling debate will be a footnote, the improved coverage will be noticed, but the books will be about the multiple race item."[1] And true enough, the shift to a "mark one or more" approach on the American census was monumental. But the United States was not alone in its reconfiguration of census classifications. This chapter explores why the United States, as well as Great Britain and Canada, made unprecedented efforts to count mixed-race at the end of the twentieth century.

As in other time periods, the interplay of transnational and domestic factors led to this convergence in approaches to racial enumeration. Still mired in the transnational multicultural moment, by the end of the twentieth century the census became an instrument of diversity governance,[2] used by the schematic state and its inhabitants to promote multiculturalism as a positive national value. This use of the census is particularly potent when combined with anti-discrimination laws and policies, sending signals within the state and to the public-at-large that equality and diversity are important national priorities. Shadowing earlier valorizations of diversity in Latin America,[3] in the Anglophone West the

[1] Population Reference Bureau, "Former U.S. Census Bureau Director Ken Prewitt Ponders Census 2000," accessed June 15, 2013, www.prb.org/Articles/2001/FormerUSCensusBureauDirectorKenPrewittPondersCensus2000.aspx

[2] Rallu, Piché, and Simon, "Démographie et Ethnicité," 481–515.

[3] Stanley Bailey and Edward Telles, "Multicultural versus Collective Black Categories: Examining Census Classification Debates in Brazil," *Ethnicities* 6, no. 1 (2006): 74–101; Juliet Hooker, "Indigenous Inclusion/Black Exclusion: Race, Ethnicity, and Multicultural

phenomena of multiraciality and mixed-race people were increasingly recognized as elements of this multiculturalism, and, in some ways, evidence of the success of the multicultural experiment. International epistemic communities of statisticians, concerned with the technocratic demands of census administration, discussed the inevitable implications of respondent self-identification during the international conference on ethnic and racial enumeration in 1992, including the mounting pressure to account for multiple responses.

Bringing this knowledge to their national statistical agencies, census designers made efforts to develop questions that would be publicly acceptable and would garner high response rates and high-quality data, but also paid heed to the symbolic issues at play in the determination of census categories and classification schemes. Precipitating a shift in transnational programmatic ideas about the underlying principles of counting by race, policymakers were very concerned with providing options that allowed respondents to identify as what they "really are" and were willing to adjust census classifications – even ones that had previously been successful at attaining high-quality data – in order to accommodate these issues of identity and recognition. When bureaucrats in Britain, Canada, and the United States set out to find a way to count their mixed-race populations, all expressed concern about giving multiracial respondents the opportunity to identify *as mixed-race* if they so desired. This shift – the recognition of mixed-race as a worthy identification in and of itself – stands in stark contrast to previous modes of racial classification in which the multiracial population could identify with one and only one race, or was reassigned as the minority designation by the census office's tabulation procedures. The difference between the census politics of this era and its predecessors, therefore, is not the mixed-race population itself, but, rather, is the recognition of multiraciality as a viable identity choice after decades of unchallenged belief in discrete racial categories and a governmental willingness to inhabit the gray zone between the administrative requirements that drive racial classifications and the more ubiquitous, symbol-driven politics of recognition. These circumstances add another dimension to the descriptive, institutional, and normative elements of multiculturalism explored in Chapter 5. In each of these cases, increasingly unsettled

Citizenship in Latin America," *Journal of Latin American Studies* 37, no. 2 (2005): 285–310; Mara Loveman, "Whiteness in Latin America: Measurement and Meaning in National Censuses (1850–1950)," *Journal de la Société des Américanistes* 95, no. 2 (2009): 207–234.

perceptions about discrete racial categories enabled mixed-race to be promoted, at times strategically, as a corollary of multicultural discourse – a phenomenon I have termed *multiracial multiculturalism*.

Though all three countries made efforts to count mixed-race as never before, each employed different methods for doing so. Why did Canada and the United States adopt a "mark one or more" approach while the census of England and Wales featured three stand-alone mixed-race categories? Each country's particular approach to multiracial multiculturalism was mediated by the institutional and cultural translations of transnational racial worldviews and programmatic beliefs. More specifically, the structure, participants, and interactions of the census policy network and path dependencies arising from traditions of enumerating race and ethnicity, civil rights legislation, and other racial projects of the state constrained viable alternatives for counting multiracials. The open nature of the American federal review process in the 1990s necessitated that political actors form coalitions and bargain for their preferred outcome, while the relatively closed structure and comparatively unconstrained nature of the policy network in Britain made the choice of stand-alone multiracial categories uncontroversial. In Canada, the only case to simultaneously inaugurate a question on race and incorporate a means of counting mixed-race, normative concerns about the primacy of racial self-declaration combined with the path dependencies arising from protocols of census administration – especially the policy of allowing multiple responses to the question on ethnic ancestry – led policymakers to adopt the "mark one or more" approach.

REVISING RACE IN THE UNITED STATES

Throughout the twenty-five years Statistical Directive 15 was in effect, there was opposition to the standardized racial classifications from both within and outside the government. The many government agencies involved in data collection, analysis, or monitoring were not unified in their data requirements or conceptions of how race should be enumerated. Within the federal government, even the principle of data collection by respondent self-identification was strongly opposed by various unidentified agencies.[4] Following the implementation of Statistical Directive 15, and within the context of an increasingly diverse America, the altered stakes of racial enumeration made counting by race more personalized and politicized,

[4] Robbin, "Classifying Racial and Ethnic Group Data," 135.

heightening incentives for minority groups to mobilize constituents around their racial identities. Interest groups also lobbied the government to add, alter, or maintain racial categories, with varying outcomes. Mexican American groups were successful in their lobby to add the "Hispanic origins question" to the 1980 Census, as were the Asian American organizations that mobilized for the addition of several Asian categories within the schematic. There were also failed efforts: for example, the Arab American Institute unsuccessfully sought to reassign persons of Middle Eastern origin from the "white" category to a new "Middle Eastern" category and a variety of groups called for the disaggregation the white category.[5] The meaning of race within the racial project of the census was increasingly contested by social actors; even with the input of its minority advisory committees, the Census Bureau could no longer dictate, unchallenged, how classificatory impulses of the census would unfold.

In response to concerns over the growing measurement error with racial and ethnic statistics, in 1988 the OMB issued a draft Statistical Policy Circular in the Federal Register that sought public comment on a comprehensive review of Statistical Directive 15 and proposed a catch-all "Other" category.[6] The proposal faced strong internal opposition from within the federal government. According to Sally Katzen, an administrator in the OMB, "those who opposed the change asserted that the present system provided adequate data, an issue we could discuss; that any changes would disrupt historical continuity, a very important consideration; and that the proposed changes could be expensive and potentially divisive."[7] Significantly, several chairs of congressional committees strongly opposed the proposal, and in a letter to the Chief Statistician chastised the OMB for its failure to coordinate the proposal with other government agencies.[8] In retrospect, members of the OMB's

[5] Williams, *Mark One or More*, 89.

[6] Office of Management and Budget, "Guidelines for Federal Statistical Activities," *Federal Register* 53, no. 12 (1988): 1542–1552. OMB granted the Census Bureau a special exemption from Directive 15 that permitted the collection of data using an "Other race" category in the 1980 and 1990 censuses. In the 1990 Census, over 250,000 Americans wrote in a combination of racial categories or used a term such as "Eurasian." The majority of this population is Hispanic and OMB has considered this phenomenon to be indicative of respondent confusion about the nature of the separate questions on race and ethnicity.

[7] United States, *Review of Federal Measurements of Race and Ethnicity*, Hearings before the Subcommittee on Census, Statistics and Postal Personnel of the Committee on Post Office and Civil Service, House of Representatives, 103rd Congress, first session (Washington D.C.: US Government Printing Office, 1994).

[8] Ibid.

Statistical Policy Branch said that the proposal "came out of the blue," and it was put in the Federal Register by then Chief Statistician Dorothy Tella without any prior consultation.[9] This violation of established consultation processes at OMB and the Census Bureau alienated other government agencies and congressional committees and prompted over 1,000 letters from the public concerning the proposal. The policy failure also drew the battle lines that would later characterize the review of federal classification standards in the 1990s: civil rights organizations and Congress on one side, concerned about the effect that changes to the census would have on racial counts, and multiracial organizations on the other, claiming that the mandated racial categories no longer represented American demographic reality.

Numerous census controversies of the previous two decades fanned the embers of discontent with the American racial typology. After the 1970 Census implemented a new system of administration by mail and self-identification, there were response problems from those respondents who did not speak English and a significant undercount, especially of the African American and Hispanic populations. The undercount and non-response rates continued to be high in the 1980 Census and the mayors of several large cities brought lawsuits against the Census Bureau, demanding a bureaucratic adjustment of the numbers. There was also increased pressure from experts regarding the issue of census adjustment. In 1990, a nationwide undercount of 2.1 percent was reported, but these figures were much higher for African Americans (4.8 percent), Hispanics (5.2 percent), American Indians (5 percent), and Asians (3.1 percent). A total of twenty-one suits were filed relating to the census, though the Bureau won a Supreme Court ruling stipulating that census adjustment was not mandatory.[10]

At the same time, America's "melting pot" was changing. Increased immigration from non-European source countries and disintegrating legal restrictions and social taboos surrounding interracial intimacy paved the way for a substantial increase in the number of interracial marriages.[11]

[9] Interview with OMB representatives, Washington D.C., February 2009.

[10] Harvey M. Choldin, *Looking for the Last Percent: The Controversy over Census Undercounts* (New Brunswick: Rutgers University Press, 1994), 30; Anderson and Fienberg, *Who Counts*, 53; Williams, *Mark One or More*, 19.

[11] Stanley Lieberson and Mary C. Waters, *From Many Strands: Ethnic and Racial Groups in Contemporary America* (New York: Russell Sage Foundation, 1988); Barry Edmonston, Sharon M. Lee, and Jeffrey S. Passel, "Recent Trends in Intermarriage and Immigration and Their Effects on the Future Racial Composition of the U.S. Population," in *The New*

Variations in rates of intermarriage within racial and ethnic groups exist, as do significant regional patterns in occurrences of interracial marriages. However, the rate of mixed-race partnerships has risen consistently for almost all groups.[12] Data from the 2000 Census revealed a disproportionately young multiracial population that was relatively small, but quickly growing: early estimates suggested that by 2050 as many as one in five Americans could claim to have a multiracial background.[13]

Demographic pressures, spurred by legal reforms and changing public opinions, are an important part of the resulting paradigm of multiracial multiculturalism in the United States. For example, Gallup polls document a long-term sea change in public attitudes about interracial marriage. In 1958, only 4 percent of Americans said they approved of interracial marriages between blacks and whites, and by 1983 50 percent of Americans continued to disapprove of such unions. The tides turned significantly during the last decade of the twentieth century, with approval ratings rising to 64 percent in 1997 and increasing to 73 percent by 2003.[14] However, demographic changes were only important because

Race Question: How the Census Counts Multiracial Individuals, eds. Joel Perlmann and Mary C. Waters (New York: Russell Sage Foundation, 2002), 227–255.

[12] Richard Wright, Serin Houston, Mark Ellis, Steven Holloway, and Margaret Hudson, "Crossing Racial Lines: Geographies of Mixed-Race Partnering and Multiraciality in the United States," *Progress in Human Geography* 27, no. 4 (2003): 457–474; Roland Fryer, "Guess Who's Been Coming to Dinner? Trends in Interracial Marriage over the 20th Century," *Journal of Economic Perspectives* 21, no. 2 (2007): 71–90.

[13] Jennifer Lee and Frank D. Bean, "America's Changing Color Lines: Immigration, Race/Ethnicity, and Multiracial Identification," *Annual Review of Sociology* 30 (2004): 221–242; Nicholas A. Jones, *We the People of More than One Race in the United States*, Census 2000 Special Reports (Washington D.C.: U.S. Census Bureau, 2005). Early estimates proved to be relatively conservative. According to data from the 2010 Census, people reporting multiple races (approximately nine million individuals) grew by 32 percent between 2000 and 2010. Specific multiple race combinations exhibited extraordinary growth – the white and black mixed-race population grew by 134 percent, or 1 million people, and the white and Asian mixed-race population increased by 87 percent or 750,000 people. See Nicholas A. Jones and Jungmiwha Bullock, *The Two or More Races Population: 2010*, 2010 Census Briefs (Washington D.C., U.S. Census Bureau, 2012). However, not all those who *can* identify as mixed-race will choose to do so. On this issue, see Joel Perlmann and Mary C. Waters, eds., *The New Race Question: How the Census Counts Multiracial Individuals* (New York: Russell Sage Foundation, 2002), especially Joshua R. Goldstein and Ann Morning, "Back in the Box: The Dilemma of Using Multiple-Race Data for Single-Race Laws," in *The New Race Question: How the Census Counts Multiracial Individuals*, eds. Joel Perlmann and Mary C. Waters (New York: Russell Sage Foundation, 2002), 119–136.

[14] Joseph Carroll, "Most Americans Approve of Interracial Marriages," Gallup News Service, accessed May 5, 2014, www.gallup.com/poll/28417/most-americans-approve-interracial-marriages.aspx

they occurred in an era in which diversity and multiculturalism were recognized and promoted by the state as positive values of the American imagined community. Simply put, the existence of mixed-race people is nothing new, though its construction as a relatively recent phenomenon demonstrates how deeply ingrained the rule of hypodescent is in American racial projects and formations.[15] What is different, rather than new, is the shift in dominant conceptualizations of mixed-race in the late twentieth century. From *Time Magazine*'s computer-generated image of the "new [mixed-race] face of America"[16] to Tiger Woods' 1997 declaration on the Oprah Winfrey Show that he was "Cablinasian" – that is, a mixture of Caucasian, Black, Indian, and Asian[17] – discourses of multiraciality in some ways challenged and in other ways confirmed the prominence of race in the United States during the federal review of racial classification standards in the 1990s.

Scholars generally agree that the hearings before the House Subcommittee on Census, Statistics and Postal Personnel in 1993 and the subsequent review of the directive in 1994 were a result of both lobbying by interested parties and the increasing questioning of the conceptual basis of the Directive 15 classifications, especially in the face of changing immigration and intermarriage patterns.[18] But why did the review begin in 1993 and

15 See, for example, the testimony of Congresswoman Eleanor Holmes Norton; United States, *Federal Measures of Race and Ethnicity and the Implications for the 2000 Census*, Hearings before the Subcommittee on Government Management, Information and Technology, of the House Committee on Government Reform and Oversight, 105th Congress (Washington D.C.: U.S. Government Printing Office, 1997), 514–515.

16 *Time*, November 1993.

17 An instrumental exploit of the multiracial model minority stereotype is the extent to which multiraciality has been adopted for marketing purposes. As Squires writes, "the dominant reporter's uncritical view of Tiger Woods's global popularity is partly a function of the desire of consumers to buy into diversity for personal satisfaction rather than embracing multiracial identity as a vehicle for interracial understanding and justice." Catherine R. Squires, *Dispatches from the Color Line: The Press and Multiracial America* (Albany: State University of New York Press, 2007), 136; see also Kimberly McClain DaCosta, *Making Multiracials: State, Family and Market in the Redrawing of the Color Line* (Stanford: Stanford University Press, 2007).

18 Katherine K. Wallman, "Data on Race and Ethnicity: Revising the Federal Standard," *The American Statistician* 52, no. 1 (1998): 31–33; Margo J. Anderson and Stephen E. Fienberg, *Who Counts?*; Nobles, *Shades of Citizenship*; Robbin, "Classifying Racial and Ethnic Group Data"; Hugh Davis Graham, "The Origins of Official Minority Designation," in *The New Race Question: How the Census Counts Multiracial Individuals*, eds. Joel Perlmann and Mary C. Waters (New York: Russell Sage Foundation, 2002): 288–299; Kim Williams, "From Civil Rights to the Multiracial Movement," in *New Faces in a Changing America in the 21st Century*, eds. Loretta I. Winters and Herman L. DeBose (Thousand Oaks: Sage Publications, 2003), 85–98.

not some other point in time? According to OMB representatives, constituents dissatisfied with the 1990 census categories wrote letters to their Members of Congress. Their concerns eventually found their way to Representative Tom Sawyer, a Democrat from Ohio, because he was the chair of the congressional subcommittee that considered issues relating the census. According to Sawyer, it was not a "wave of people" that approached him; nor was the 1990 census count any less transparent or less accurate than in previous years. Rather, Sawyer argues that the primary drivers of the congressional hearings were the massive demographic change stemming from immigration and intermarriage patterns and the shifting perceptions about the validity of Statistical Directive 15 for measuring American demographics at the dawn of the twenty-first century. A review of the directive was not, however, inevitable. Sawyer's institutional position as the chair of the subcommittee with oversight for the census and his desire to initiate a "big project" provided the leverage required to instigate the review. In his words, "I had the opportunity to deal with a big question – and so I did it."[19]

Sawyer initiated four congressional hearings on federal classification standards for race and ethnicity on April 14, June 30, July 29, and November 3, 1993, and a number of organizations appealed to participate. In addition, the OMB, Census Bureau, and some Members of Congress appeared before the committee. At the hearing on July 29, 1993, Sally Katzen of the OMB proposed a comprehensive review of Directive 15. The timing of events is important: though subsequent hearings and the OMB's review were parallel processes designed to reconsider state-driven racial classification schema, the OMB officially started its review after the hearing. The call to testify was a major motivating factor; as one OMB representative put it, "when one is called before a congressional committee, it is important to not go empty-handed."[20]

The review of the American racial schema occurred in two interrelated policy arenas, each with its own purpose, decisional bias, network structure, participants, and decision-making routines.[21] The bureaucracy-led review had a mandate and desire to reach consensus and produce a viable proposal for the congressional committee. The purpose of the

[19] Interview with Tom Sawyer, Columbus OH, February 2009.

[20] Interview with OMB representatives, Washington D.C., February 2009.

[21] See Frank R. Baumgartner and Bryan D. Jones, *Agendas and Instability in American Politics* (Chicago: University of Chicago Press, 1993).

congressional hearings was to discuss and debate – and, it could be argued, sensationalize – alternatives and the review process. These venues were not mutually exclusive. For example, the OMB designed testing programs to address concerns voiced in the hearings, and the information attained during OMB's review was used in committee deliberations.

The dual-track review at congressional and bureaucratic levels multiplied potential access points for interested parties. And indeed, multiple groups participated in the debates surrounding the classification of multiracial people, including civil rights organizations, multiracial organizations, Members of Congress, academics, and members of the public. The impact of actors' skills and resources was mitigated by the openness of the policy networks; OMB's review was equally open to everyone, whether the public's input came in the form of letters, town hall meetings, or through interest group representation. Though the state enjoyed autonomy, decision-making power was dispersed throughout the census policy subsystem between the political authority of Congress, the OMB's control over federal standards of classification, and the Census Bureau's mandate concerning the census. Centralized autonomy was also limited by the concurrent congressional hearings, which ensured the bureaucratic arm of the state could not unilaterally come to a decision, and the desire for an open, transparent process, which was particularly acute because of the policy failure of 1988. In essence, different sections of the state came together to put the underlying organizational structure of the review process into place, but the different agencies and participants had a wide variety of goals, responsibilities, and preferences. At the same time, the fact that the review process was open to participation from non-governmental actors and that various government actors and agencies participated in the forum gave the impression of a benign neutrality in the final decision. What transpired during the review process is the most telling example of how multiraciality can be strategically employed in a number of ways, with each distinct version premised on a multiracial, multicultural vision of nationhood.

At the bureaucratic level, the OMB initiated an internal multi-pronged review. First, the workshop of the Committee on National Statistics of the National Research Council was held in February 1994 and culminated in the 1996 report, *Spotlight on Heterogeneity: The Federal Standards for Racial and Ethnic Classification.* The Committee considered the four major options for change that had been proposed by OMB: eliminate the two-question format that covered the four designated racial categories and the ethnic classification of Hispanic or non-Hispanic so there would be a single question with five categories; add new race and ethnicity categories to the current set of questions for specific groups or for a multiracial identity; collect multiple responses, which would necessitate new procedures for reporting responses; or, use open-ended questions, which would similarly require new procedures for reporting.[22]

The purpose of the workshop was not to recommend the best course of action, but, rather, to determine the most important objectives of federal classification standards and the most feasible means of reaching them. To this end, the Committee emphasized the need for substantial research and testing, and workshop participants identified eight major objectives for a federal standard of racial and ethnic classifications: (1) fostering the exchange of statistical reports between agencies; (2) ensuring the availability of data for the monitoring of discrimination against minority groups; (3) designating the system for administrative and statistical records so that the data are reliable even when disaggregated by race and ethnicity; (4) ensuring that the categories are mutually exclusive and exhaustive and that the number of categories be manageable in size; (5) incorporating flexibility so that the standard can be adapted to the context of its use; (6) promoting longitudinal consistency for categories over time; (7) producing relevant and meaningful categories for federal policy purposes; and (8) producing categories that are relevant and applicable to individual respondents.[23] The Committee recognized that some of these objectives would undoubtedly conflict.

Second, the OMB established an interagency committee in 1994, cochaired by the Bureau of the Census and the Bureau of Labor Statistics and comprised of representatives from thirty government agencies, to review the racial and ethnic standards and make recommendations to OMB for any revisions. Unlike Canada, which has a centralized statistical system spearheaded by Statistics Canada, the responsibility for the collection of statistical data is dispersed among some seventy federal agencies, eleven of which have the production of statistics as their primary mission.[24] The role of the OMB within this system is to coordinate, rather than manage or control. In preparation for the National

[22] Barry Edmonston, Joshua Goldstein, and Juanita Tamayo Lott, eds., *Spotlight on Heterogeneity: The Federal Standards for Racial and Ethnic Classifications, Summary of a Workshop* (Washington D.C.: National Academy Press, 1996), 3.

[23] Edmonston et al., *Spotlight on Heterogeneity*, 49–50.

[24] United States General Accounting Office, *Statistical Agencies*, 1.

Statistical Committee's workshop, several federal agencies[25] provided information on: the use of Directive 15 for federal data collection; data collection beyond the directive's classifications; the utility and adequacy of the directive; and possible revisions of current categories. At the time, most federal agencies reported favorably on the directive, though reactions to the potential modifications of the directive were mixed: some agencies hoped for more flexibility, while others had strong reservations about the proposals.[26] The interagency committee took these concerns as well as the public input stemming from the congressional hearings and Federal Register notices into consideration when drafting the principles that would guide its work.

Data needs, technical issues of statistical analysis, and social concerns were identified as simultaneously competing and complimentary issues. Moreover, different agencies had varying priorities and preferences that influenced their participation in the interagency committee. Agencies with statutory responsibility for policy development, program evaluation, and civil rights monitoring were concerned about the historical continuity of the data in light of the proposed changes and generally opposed the implementation of a stand-alone multiracial category because the persons seeking this category were already covered within the existing framework. Data collection agencies, which use racial and ethnic data for federal programming, redistricting, and for the analysis of social, economic, and health trends of the population, were also concerned with the historical continuity of data, but felt that the categories used in Directive 15 were confusing to respondents, overly broad, and inconsistent. They too opposed a multiracial category on the grounds that it would be too heterogeneous and could affect the counts of other racial groups in unknown ways. The data collection agencies were also concerned about

[25] The complete list of federal agencies that provided information to the workshop is: Department of Agriculture, National Agricultural Statistics Service, Department of Commerce (Bureau of the Census), Commission on Civil Rights, Department of Education, Office for Civil Rights, National Center for Education Statistics, Equal Employment Opportunity Commission, Federal Reserve Board, Department of Health and Human Services, National Center for Health Statistics, Office of Minority Health, Department of Housing and Urban Development, Office of Fair Housing and Equal Opportunity, Office of Program Evaluation and Standards, Department of the Interior (Bureau of Indian Affairs), Department of Justice, Bureau of Justice Statistics, Civil Rights Division, Department of Labor, Bureau of Labor Statistics, Office of Federal Contract Compliance Programs, Office of Personnel Management, Small Business Administration, Department of Veterans Affairs (National Center for Veterans Analysis and Statistics).

[26] Edmonston et al., *Spotlight on Heterogeneity*, 10–11.

the significant technical, operational, and cost issues implicated if a "mark one or more" approach were to be adopted.[27] Though divided initially, the interagency committee had clear incentives to reach consensus on these issues by the 1997 deadline. These incentives were not simply monetary, but also professional, giving line departments the opportunity to help shape OMB policy directions.[28]

Third, OMB sought public comment through notices published in the Federal Register in 1994, 1995, and 1997 and at four public hearings held in Boston, Denver, San Francisco, and Honolulu in 1994. By the middle of 1995, OMB had received nearly 800 letters from the public responding to the 1994 Federal Register notice and had heard the testimony of ninety-four witnesses during the four public hearings.[29] While it is not uncommon for OMB to have multiple iterations of public comment, the public hearings held across the country went beyond standard consultation exercises. The OMB desired a strong outreach program and there is every indication that the agency took the public's input seriously. The requests received by OMB came in four major forms. First was the request for a specific multiracial category. Second, a number of comments sought the expansion of the minimum set of categories by adding others, such as Arabs/Middle Easterners, Cape Verdans, Creoles, European-Americans, and German-Americans. Third, some Native Hawaiians conceptualizing themselves as an indigenous group asked to be included in the same category as American Indians and Alaskan Natives, while other Native Hawaiians requested a stand-alone category. Fourth, the OMB received a number of requests for the elimination of racial categories altogether from those who argued that the collection of racial data serves to perpetuate the myth of race.[30]

Finally, and importantly, the OMB initiated a comprehensive testing program. Cognitive interviews and testing was conducted to guide the phrasing of questions. The research agenda also included several national tests. In May 1995, the Bureau of Labor Statistics added a Supplement on Race and Ethnicity to the Current Population Survey (CPS) and the Bureau of the Census tested alternative approaches to collecting data on race and ethnicity in the March 1996 National Content Survey (NCS) and

[27] Office of Management and Budget, "Standards for the Classification of Federal Data on Race and Ethnicity," *Federal Register* 60, no. 166 (1995): 44677.

[28] Interview with OMB representatives, Washington D.C., February 2009.

[29] OMB, "Standards for the Classification of Federal Data"; Suzann Evinger, "How to Record Race," *American Demographics* 18 (1996): 36–42.

[30] United States, *Federal Measures of Race and Ethnicity*, 46–47.

the June 1996 Race and Ethnic Targeted Test (RAETT), which was specifically intended to test the impact of question and category design on smaller racial and ethnic populations not captured by larger national surveys. The National Center for Education Statistics and the Office for Civil Rights conducted a survey of 1,000 public schools to determine the means and manner in which schools collect racial data. Studies were also conducted by the National Center for Health Statistics, the Office of the Assistant Secretary for Health, and the Centers for Disease Control and Prevention to evaluate the use of racial and ethnic classifications on birth and death certificates and the measurement of the health and well-being of major population groups.

In their interpretation of multiracial multiculturalism, government officials were concerned with policymaking and program delivery. The guidelines outlined by the Committee on National Statistics of the National Research Council at the beginning of the bureaucracy-led review process determined that the most important objectives of federal classification standards were largely administrative in nature, necessary to foster statistical exchange within the state apparatus, ensure data consistency, meet program and monitoring requirements, and produce categories that were meaningful and relevant for policy purposes.[31] These administrative concerns were important to the OMB and the interagency committee, though their guiding principles also warned that census categories were not scientific or anthropological in nature and that respect for individual dignity should guide the process and methods for collecting data on race and ethnicity.[32] Further, the OMB held multiple public hearings in order to ensure that the census categories would "reflect the community," partially to ensure high-quality data by producing categories that are relevant and applicable to individual respondents, but also because the legitimacy of the review process depended on societal participation, and the extent to which census categories reflected changing conceptions of race in America was crucial to the success of the policy. As one civil servant put it, "We knew that the categories of Directive 15 wouldn't last forever, they weren't intended to. Times had changed – the review was an opportunity to rethink the way we think about race in this country. We didn't know what we'd end up with when we started the process, but we had to try to adjust to the

[31] Edmonston et al., *Spotlight on Heterogeneity*, 49–50.

[32] OMB, "Standards for the Classification of Federal Data on Race and Ethnicity," *Federal Register* 59, no. 110 (1994): 29834.

changing times."[33] During the process of adjusting, however, colorblindness was not an option for policymakers who worked within the confines of an established and potent racial schematic premised on the existence of clear and well-defined racial boundaries. The legibility, transportability, and standardization of race were paramount.

In the congressional arena, subcommittee hearings were held in 1993 and 1997. The first round in 1993 was organized by Representative Thomas Sawyer (D-OH), Chair of the Subcommittee on Census, Statistics and Postal Personnel. The second round was held in May 1997 and was organized by Congressman Stephen Horn (R-CA), chair of the Subcommittee on Government Management, Information and Technology, with a final hearing held in July 1997. Though a number of issues were under consideration with regards to the federal classification of race and ethnicity, the proposed addition of a multiracial category soon rose to the front of the battle lines and a number of interest groups mobilized to compete in the political arena created by the congressional hearings.

Project RACE (Reclassify all Children Equally) and the Association of Multiethnic Americans (AMEA) advocated for multiracial inclusion in the census. Founder Susan Graham of Project RACE was highly visible in the media and claimed that the organization was national in scope. Targeting the national census proved to be a culmination of a longer strategy that involved putting pressure on states to change their racial classification schema and incorporate a multiracial category. AMEA presented itself as an umbrella organization representing numerous local multiracial organizations. The respective positions of these multiracial groups have been analyzed well by others;[34] while the positions of both groups evolved over time through coalition agreements and political decisions, the major distinction was that Project RACE was unrepentant in advocating a standalone multiracial category, whereas AMEA endorsed a multiracial category that was followed by a listing of racial and/or ethnic groups duplicated from the main classifications.

The multiracial movement was integral to bringing a politics of recognition to the forefront of discussions surrounding racial classifications in

[33] Interview with OMB representative, February 2009.

[34] Spencer, *Spurious Issues*; Nobles, *Shades of Citizenship*; Daniel, *More than Black*; DaCosta, "Multiracial Identity"; Williams, *Mark One or More*; Jennifer L. Hochschild and Vesla Weaver, "There's No One as Irish as Barack O'Bama': The Politics and Policy of Multiracialism in the United States," *Perspectives on Politics* 8, no. 3 (2010): 737–760.

the census. Previously concerned with the enforcement of civil rights legislation, funding allocations, and congressional redistricting, multiracial organizations advocated the idea that the census was a vehicle for the recognition of identities, separate from the institutional incentives associated with identifying as one race or another. Contending that appropriate labels are crucial for the positive self-development of children, Graham testified:

> When I received my 1990 census form, I realized there was no race category for my children. I called the Census Bureau. After checking with supervisors, the Bureau finally gave me their answer, the children should take the race of the mother. When I objected and asked why my children should be classified as their mother's race only, the Census Bureau representative said to me, in a very hushed voice, "Because in cases like these, we always know who the mother is and not the father". I could not make a race choice from the five basic categories when I enrolled my son in kindergarten in Georgia. The only choice I had, like most other parents of multiracial children, was to leave race blank. I later found that my child's teacher was instructed to choose for him based on her knowledge and observation of my child. Ironically, my child has been White on the United States census, Black at school and multiracial at home, all at the same time.[35]

Carlos Fernandez, the President of AMEA, testified that his organization sought "a government-wide reform to accommodate and acknowledge the particular identity of people whose racial or ethnic identification encompasses more than one of the designated classifications currently in use."[36] When asked about whether "multiracial" would or should be a protected minority category, Fernandez noted that the purpose of the proposal was about accuracy and self-esteem; they were "not asking for Congress ... to create a category where a slew of programs is going to ensue. That is certainly is not what we have in mind. We're not discounting it." Susan Graham concurred, saying "And as Carlos said, you know, we're not looking to create a new category for entitlements. That is not what we are doing at all."[37]

The mixed-race social movement summoned the norm of multiracial multiculturalism in a very different way than other network participants. Project RACE, AMEA, and the Interracial Family Circle premised their arguments on the language of recognition, arguing that the right of self-identification and recognition of what people "really are" is not just a matter of civil rights, but is something more fundamental to the ethos

[35] United States, *Review of Federal Measurements of Race and Ethnicity*, 105–106.
[36] Ibid., 128. [37] Ibid., 169–170.

of liberalism and democracy. Kim DaCosta argues that the mixed-race movement used very individualistic terms to make this point, contending that the interests of the state, schools, or other officially recognized racial groups were secondary to those of the individual checking the box.[38] Using this perspective, Nathan Douglas of Interracial Family Circle challenged the claims of civil rights advocates that a multiracial category would threaten the civil rights establishment: "how can you suggest that a group of your fellow human beings, no matter how large or small, must be denied their right to identify accurately in order to accommodate the status quo? How hypocritical. The violation of multiracials' right to self-determination should ring loud warning bells for every believer in civil rights."[39] The language of recognition was used most often and most potently to refer to the plight of mixed-race children. Susan Graham used the data collected in one school district in Georgia where students could identify as multiracial to make dual points about the 835 "real actual children, who consider themselves to be multiracial ... 835 real actual children, not government projections" and the necessity of allowing them to "embrace all of their heritage."[40] The movement also positioned multiraciality as a "unifying force" that would heal American race relations, but in doing so often expressed disapproval of all forms of racial classification and a preference for a color-blind American society.[41]

On the other side of the debate, civil rights organizations strongly opposed the addition of a multiracial category. Henry Der of the National Coalition for an Accurate Count of Asians and Pacific Islanders questioned the point of having a multiracial category, contending that

> unless there is adequate testing or sufficient evidence is provided about the experiences of biracial or multiracial persons that are unique to their being biracial or multiracial, the National Coalition asks the Census Bureau not to create a biracial or multiracial category at this time. It is not clear at this time what is the salience of knowing how many biracial or multiracial persons there are.[42]

[38] DaCosta, *Making Multiracials*, 30.

[39] United States, *Federal Measures of Race and Ethnicity*, 428–429. [40] Ibid., 283.

[41] Ibid., 127. See also a challenge to the "racial bridge" argument in Rainier Spencer, *Reproducing Race: The Paradox of Generation Mix* (Boulder and London: Lynne Rienner Publishers, 2011), ch. 9, and an analysis of the multiracial movement's color-blind discourse in Tanya Katerí Hernández, "'Multiracial' Discourse: Racial Classifications in an Era of Color-Blind Jurisprudence," *Maryland Law Review* 57, no. 1 (1998): 97–173.

[42] United States, *Review of Federal Measurements of Race and Ethnicity*, 101.

Representatives from the National Urban League, the National Congress of American Indians, and the United States Commission on Civil Rights also came out against the proposal to add a multiracial category.[43] In 1994, the Lawyers' Committee for Civil Rights Under Law, the NAACP, the National Urban League, and the Joint Center for Political and Economic Studies issued a coalition statement on the issue:

Concerned that the addition of a multiracial category may have unanticipated adverse consequences, resulting in Blacks being placed even lower in the existing American hierarchy ... [The multiracial initiative has] potential disorganizing and negative effects on Black Americans [and would] distort public understanding of their condition ... Directive 15 is appropriately viewed as part of the judicial, legislative, and administrative machinery that has been constructed over time to combat and eradicate racial discrimination. It is important to remind ourselves that this anti-discrimination capability was achieved at great cost. The sacrifices of the Civil Rights Movement ... were not in vain ... We are opposed to any action by the OMB which will result in the disaggregation of the current Black population.[44]

Civil rights organizations and their elite allies in the Democratic Party invoked a race-conscious version of multiracial multiculturalism premised on the importance of maintaining the existing racial categories in order to protect and maintain the legislative gains of the civil rights movement. In the summation of Representative Carrie Meek (D-FL):

There's no court or any legislative or legal record of discrimination against multiracials. So it's going to be, perhaps, prohibitive for multiracials to get the advantage of the discrimination which black citizens of this country have faced.

[43] The NAACP was conspicuously absent during the 1993 hearings, though the organization was scheduled to testify numerous times.

[44] AMEA and Project RACE responded angrily, again stressing the multiracial community's right to racial classification: "This statement is alarmist in tone, and implies that a multiracial category, in and of itself, has the 'power' to upset the racial/ethnic status quo ... Civil rights gains sought by any minority group in the history of the United States have never been without risk, and have been well worth changes in existing policies. The multiracial community is no less discriminated against and no less deserving of its rights than any other racial or ethnic community. The interracial community sees the rigidity of these existing categories as a means of shutting out its people from receiving the same benefits, protections, and considerations under the law as the representatives of the 'coalition' wish to retain ... [Your] stance merely perpetuates the myth that races and ethnic groups cannot mix. It encourages a continued atmosphere of antagonism, elitism, and suspicion which allowed anti-miscegenation laws to stay on record in sixteen states up until 1967 ... Let there be no doubt, this issue is as much an economic numbers game to the groups resisting the addition of a new category as it is a discussion of lofty socio-political ideals. How are the civil rights of the interracial community being properly served if you continue to ignore these families and their offspring?" Quoted in Williams, *Mark One or More*, 47–49.

Without such a record of discrimination, courts will have a hard time claiming discrimination against multiracials ... The multiracial category will just make it more difficult to identify where discrimination has taken place and where it has not taken place, because it will cloud census counts of discrete minorities who have been restricted to certain neighborhoods and, as a consequence, to certain schools. It will cloud the census count of these discrete minorities who are assigned to lower tracks in public schools, and you know that they are. It will cloud the census count of discrete minorities kept out of certain occupations or whose progress toward seniority or promotion had been skewed. The list goes on and on, Mr. Chairman, to include civil rights reporting in the arenas of lending practices and the provision of health services, and beyond.[45]

Here, the value of counting by race in the census was connected to the liberal goals of promoting racial harmony and diversity through the monitoring of circumstances of racial inequality and disadvantage. Civil rights organizations took the analogy one step further, emphasizing that attaining substantive equality would require constant vigilance; the NAACP noted its concern with the proposals to add a multiracial category stemmed from its belief that "segregation and discrimination in this country has to be battled with deeds, not just with words," inviting "all multiracial people who so identify themselves, to join us in that struggle."[46]

Within these paradigms of multiculturalism and diversity, however, were deeper indications of the nature of citizenship and belonging in the United States. In spite of its long history of discrimination based on ascriptive characteristics such as race and gender, the United States has always revered its liberal democratic values. Racial classifications in the census, though important for the achievement of liberal ideals of equality and social justice, still run counter to dominant norms of liberal democracies, which demand that the superficial morphological characteristics used to distinguish supposedly distinct races matter not. This tension was illuminated during the hearings when participants compared the American context to a regime more explicitly racialized than the United States: South Africa. Civil rights organizations cautioned that a multiracial category could have the consequence of replicating the "caste system" that had been reinforced so fervently in apartheid South Africa. The mixed-race movement's argument that individuals of racially diverse backgrounds were somehow a "new race" was also slightly too reminiscent of South Africa's "colored" category and the apartheid regime that heavily regulated racial boundaries. The extraordinary nature of racial classification under the apartheid government served as warnings

[45] United States, *Federal Measures of Race and Ethnicity*, 231.   [46] Ibid., 302–306.

to a watchful American public about giving the state the power to determine whether somebody is black, white, or multiracial.

To make this point, the representative from NAACP told an anecdote about the infamous South African "hair test," which was used to determine one's racial identity, rhetorically asking the Sub-Committee "do you really want to go there, do you really want to get involved in those kinds of determinations?"[47] Even those traditionally on the opposite end of the political spectrum found this to be an ominous comparison; Republican Stephen Horn (CA) called South Africa's racial taxonomies "a sickening commentary on the human condition," going on to state that "I do not think that we want to get into it."[48] Civil rights organizations and their elite allies strategically used race-consciousness within a multicultural paradigm to, on the one hand, emphasize the importance of maintaining the status quo to ensure the hard-fought victories of the civil rights movement remained intact, and on the other hand, to accuse the mixed-race movement of the same type of extreme race-consciousness that existed in apartheid South Africa.

The 1997 congressional hearings were influenced by three major changes in terms of institutions, participants, and information. First, the partisan politics and the political venue of census changed. Congressional oversight of the census was previously housed in the Subcommittee on Census, Statistics and Postal Personnel of the Committee on Post Office and Civil Service, an obscure subcommittee in which few strived to participate. In fact, the 1993 hearings were rarely attended even by those assigned to serve on the committee along with Sawyer.[49] Before 1997, the jurisdiction changed and the census fell under the responsibility of the Subcommittee on Government Management, Information and Technology of the Committee on Government Reform and Management. This Committee is the main investigative committee in the House of Representatives, with the power to scrutinize any program or matter with federal policy implications. This venue was undoubtedly of a higher profile and more politicized than its predecessor, altering the political playing field and stakes for those facilitating the hearings.

A related change was also institutional: Democrats won the 1996 presidential election while Republicans gained control of the House of Representatives and Senate. Congressional scrutiny of the Census Bureau increased and often took partisan form. In particular, the debate over

[47] Ibid., 302. [48] Ibid., 330.

[49] Lawrence Wright, "One Drop of Blood," *The New Yorker*, July 24, 1994.

census adjustment was drawn along partisan lines. The Congressional Black Caucus – all Democrats – took up the census as a civil rights issue, while Republicans were concerned about losing seats in congressional apportionment if the Census Bureau's proposed adjustment methodology was incorporated. Consequently, the tenacity of congressional oversight of the 2000 Census rose to unprecedented levels. The review of Statistical Directive 15 was one among seventeen formal hearings on census plans in which "Republican members challenged the bureau's sampling strategies and the Democratic members just as vigorously defended it."[50] Partisan politics reached new heights during this cycle as both parties jockeyed for advantage in census politics.

Second, the 1997 hearings featured an increase in the lobbying and coalition-building efforts of both those opposed to and in favor of the addition of a multiracial category. The NAACP and a number of members of the Black Caucus of Congress became involved and joined with other civil rights organizations to create a "Coalition of Groups Opposed to the Proposed Modification of OMB Directive No. 15." Harold McDougall, the Director of the Washington Bureau of the NAACP, told the subcommittee that the introduction of new categories had the potential for data corruption. In the NAACP's view, this danger outweighed the benefits of recognition: "we respect people's rights to make a self-identification. We just question whether the census is necessarily the best place to do that."[51] Similarly, Eric Rodriguez of the National Council of La Raza argued that "the addition of a multiracial category undermines prudent public policy, and may inadvertently subvert the Nation's ability to ensure the protection of civil rights for all groups. The drive for a new census category has on the surface been fueled almost exclusively by emotional concerns related to identity."[52] The National Asian Pacific Legal Consortium and the National Congress of American Indians also opposed a multiracial category because it would weaken the ability of civil rights agencies to effectively monitor discrimination.[53]

Between the hearings, multiracial organizations had continued to lobby at the state-level and gained important support from Republicans in Congress. This focus on making changes to state-level classification systems, though partially driven by concerns about multiracial recognition especially on school forms, was also a strategic move that took

[50] Hillygus et al., *The Hard Count*, 36–37.
[51] United States, *Federal Measures of Race and Ethnicity*, 302. [52] Ibid., 318–319.
[53] Ibid., 412–427.

advantage of the federalist system to put pressure on the center from below. As Graham stated in her testimony, "I think that part of the problem that we have at this point is that multiracial people can be multiracial people in one State and not multiracial in another State. In one State, they might be considered white or black. And if you go to different States across borders, you have that problem."[54] The creation of this problem, of course, was a result of Project RACE's state-level lobbying efforts. More broadly, the basic thrust of the multiracial movement's arguments continued to rest on the paradigm of recognition: Susan Graham's son, Ryan, testified that the fact that government forms made him choose one race made him "sad," and Ramona Douglass of the AMEA begged of the government:

> Please count us, track us, begin the process of including us in the American framework that has monitored the evolution and growth of other racial/ethnic populations throughout our history ... Asking us to endure another decade or another census unacknowledged, discounted or ignored isn't an option any of us can afford to live with any longer. If one member of our society is without freedom then none of us are truly free.[55]

The coalition forged between Project RACE and the political right further alienated the multiracial movement and undermined its legitimacy in the eyes of civil rights organizations and Democrats in Congress. Republican elites invoked a color-blind variant of multiracial multiculturalism, viewing the addition of a multiracial category on the census as a means of blurring racial distinctions. Newt Gingrich, the most prominent Republican proponent of the proposal to add a multiracial category, argued that multiracialism was a positive social and demographic development because it would inevitably lead to an American identity without race:

> I think we need to be prepared to say, the truth is we want all Americans to be, quite simply, Americans. That doesn't deprive anyone of the right to further define their heritage ... It doesn't deprive us of the right to ethnic pride, to have some sense of our origins. But it is wrong for some Americans to begin to creating subgroups to which they have a higher loyalty than to America at large.[56]

In the Republicans' interpretation, multiculturalism and diversity remain positive values that can complement American national identity and as such mixed-race people deserved to be recognized, but the racial classification systems that these notions are built upon are believed to be overly divisive. Representative Petri suggested that being on the census was

[54] Ibid., 339. [55] Ibid., 387. [56] Ibid., 659.

a marker of Americanism: "from the point of view of the individual citizen who is being asked to fill this form out, to give them the feeling either that somehow they are not fully American, and therefore they are in some other category, psychologically, I think is a mistake."[57] However, the strategic employment of multiracial multiculturalism in this way was also a clear political agenda that sought to erode civil rights legacies, which the New Right views as unwarranted, intrusive state action into the private and commercial spheres.[58]

The third and final difference between the 1993 and 1997 hearings was the information the OMB was able to access: the 1996 National Content Survey (the test for the 2000 Census) demonstrated that of the 94,500 households surveyed, approximately 1 percent of respondents identified as multiracial in versions of the race question that included such a response category.[59] The RAETT of 1996, whose findings became available during the 1997 hearings, tested the viability of two approaches to enumerating mixed-race people: the mark one more approach (the wording "mark all that apply" was also tested), and a stand-alone multiracial category. The sequence of the questions on race and ethnicity and a potential question that combined racial categories and Hispanic origin were also tested. The results demonstrated that only the Asian and Pacific Islander category would be statistically affected by the inclusion of a multiracial category – the percentage of persons reporting white, black, and American Indian/Alaskan Native remained largely the same. Of the three options tested (a stand-alone multiracial category, a question with instructions to "mark one or more," and a question with instructions to "mark all that apply"), the mark one or more approach had no effect on the total reporting of any group, including the Asian and Pacific Islander category. The RAETT concluded that "this option may be the one least likely to affect the historical continuity of data on race and ethnicity that some federal agencies use to monitor and enforce civil rights."[60]

In the congressional venue, the mark one or more approach became the endorsed course of action because of the specific ways that the structure of

57 Ibid., 241.

58 See, for example, Ward Connerly, *Creating Equal: My Fight Against Racial Preferences*, rev. edn (New York: Encounter Books, 2007).

59 U.S. Census Bureau, *Findings on Questions on Race and Hispanic Origin Tested in the 1996 National Content Survey*, Population Division Working Paper No. 16 (Washington D.C.: Bureau of the Census, 1996).

60 U.S. Census Bureau, *Results of the 1996 Race and Ethnic Targeted Test*, Population Division Working Paper No. 18 (Washington D.C.: Bureau of the Census, 1997).

the policy network shaped the interactions of the agents therein. Interest groups, politicians, and academics were vocal during the congressional hearings of 1993 and 1997. However, neither resources nor political experience could dictate who was able to present their case before the subcommittee. As Kim Williams' research reveals, the multiracial movement was relatively new, tiny, unrepresentative, and operated on shoe-string budgets.[61] Nonetheless, Project RACE and AMEA certainly held their own against long-established, better organized, and more powerful organizations such as NAACP and the National Urban League while testifying before Congress. The strategies and bargaining techniques employed by these groups were also different, with varying effects. Civil rights organizations were concerned about the tangible impact that stand-alone mixed-race categories would have on their constituent numbers and the ability of the state to adhere to its obligations under civil rights legislation. Organizations representing minority groups also had a vested interest in preserving the boundaries of their racial categories, which they had been using for decades to converse with the state. The implication is that these organizations represented *legible and recognizable constituencies*, able to parley with the state on its own terms. Though multiracial groups argued that mixed-race people faced discrimination by virtue of being mixed-race, they more often clothed their arguments in a language of recognition, contending that the absence of a census category was a denial of the validity and worth of their identities. This strategy, however, was not well aligned with the purpose of the policy, which was not about recognition but, rather, concerned the collection of accurate data in order to fulfill the state's legal obligations and justify positive action. Moreover, the mixed-race movement was fragmented even in its appearances in the congressional committee, with Project RACE and AMEA presenting different and changing proposals for Directive 15 revisions. This lack of coherence also materialized in the OMB's testing program, which demonstrated that the term "multiracial" was not well understood by respondents.

The Interagency Committee completed its work in 1997 and issued its findings in the Federal Register in July 1997. The participants of the Committee unanimously recommended that the method for enumerating the mixed-race population take the form of multiple responses to a single question and not a stand-alone multiracial category. The Committee gave a number of reasons for its decision. First, it emphasized that the mixed-

[61] Williams, *Mark One or More.*

TABLE 6.1: *Preferred label for the mixed-race population, 1995 CPS Supplement on Race and Ethnicity*

Multiracial	28.4%
No preference	27.8%
Mixed-Race	16.0%
More than one race	6.0%
Biracial	5.7%

race population was likely to grow and that adopting a means for measuring this demographic trend now would enable the government to do so more precisely and with less discontinuity in historical data series in the future. Second, though certain population groups were more likely to be affected than others by permitting multiple responses, the mark one or more approach would allow data to be recovered through tabulation procedures. Third, the proposal for a stand-alone multiracial category was problematic in several respects. One of the most pressing was the lack of consensus on the terminology to describe mixed-race, which was demonstrated in the May 1995 CPS Supplement on Race and Ethnicity (see Table 6.1).

Because respondent confusion has the potential to decrease response rates, providing a clear question is a priority in census policy. As the Interagency Committee wrote, "absent a generally accepted understanding of the term, confusion could be expected if a 'multiracial' category were to be listed among the response options. Most Americans are probably of mixed ancestry, depending on how ancestry is defined, and could confuse ancestry or ethnicity with race."[62] Other problems with a stand-alone multiracial category included the lack of legislative need for a specific count of the multiracial population, the evidence that a multiracial category would likely be misunderstood by respondents, and the cost-related concern that using a follow-up question with write-in spaces or further categories after a multiracial category would take either more space or more coding. Rather than being the lesser of all evils, the Interagency Committee clearly recognized the necessity of counting the mixed-race population and sought the most

[62] OMB, "Recommendations from the Interagency Committee for the Review of the Racial and Ethnic Standards to the Office of Management and Budget Concerning Changes to the Standards for the Classification of Federal Data on Race and Ethnicity," *Federal Register* 62, no. 131 (1997): 36906.

effective means for doing so, given its priorities involving satisfying statutory and program needs, dealing with voting rights issues, and taking into account data continuity concerns, financial costs, and public sentiment.

The report was undeniably influential. During the final congressional hearings in July 1997, the public positions of nearly all major stakeholders were altered, with federal agencies, all minority interest groups, and AMEA expressing unanimous support for the Interagency Committee's recommendations. Project RACE stood alone in its advocacy for a multiracial category, though it continued to find an ally in Speaker of the House Newt Gingrich, who testified in the July hearing that all federal forms should simply have one box with the label "American," but in the meantime, a "multiracial" box was an important step toward "transcending racial division."[63]

In October 1997 the OMB publicized its decision to allow respondents to "mark one or more," while recommending against the adoption of a singular "multiracial" category.[64] The actual implementation of the multiple response approach was left up to the Tabulation Working Group to determine. Weeks before the 2000 Census, the OMB issued guidelines that detailed how multiple-response racial data would be used for anti-discrimination policy: for the monitoring and enforcement of civil and voting rights, respondents that marked white and a non-white race would be considered members of the non-white group. A multiple response approach results in a total of 57 possible multiple-race combinations; added to the 5 single-race categories and the sixth "some other race" option, this increased the tally to 63 potential racial categories or combinations. Further, because each category could be considered in the context of Hispanic ethnicity, there are 126 total possible responses to the race/ethnic question (see Figure 6.1).

While this strategy may have practical merit, Goldstein and Morning note that there are several controversial elements to the OMB's approach: first, it is, in effect, a revival of the one-drop rule, a historical legacy that

[63] United States, *Federal Measures of Race and Ethnicity*, 662.

[64] The decision also slightly modified various other racial definitions; see OMB, "Revisions to the Standards for the Classification of Federal Data on Race and Ethnicity," *Federal Register* 62, no. 210 (1997): 58782–58790. The major change was that the OMB rejected the Interagency Committee's recommendation not to alter the category of "Asian and Pacific Islander" and instead split the categories into two – "Asian" and "Native Hawaiian and Other Pacific Islander." The official justification for the split was that the Asian population had exhibited the largest growth in the United States.

6. What is this person's race? ***Mark*** ☒ ***one or more races*** *to indicate what this person considers himself/herself to be.*

☐ White
☐ Black, African Am., or Negro
☐ American Indian or Alaska Native — *Print name of enrolled or principal tribe.*

☐ Asian Indian ☐ Japanese ☐ Native Hawaiian
☐ Chinese ☐ Korean ☐ Guamanian or Chamorro
☐ Filipino ☐ Vietnamese ☐ Samoan
☐ Other Asian — *Print race.* ☐ Other Pacific Islander — *Print race.*

☐ Some other race — *Print race.*

FIGURE 6.1: Census of the United States, 2000

necessitates persons with any traceable amount of non-white ancestry be counted – in both law and society – as non-white. While the rule of hypodescent is now used in order to redress discrimination rather than enforce segregation, it is "still open to the criticism that it repeats the mistakes of the past, further institutionalizing the divide between the white and nonwhite populations." Second, the strategy violates the principle of self-identification: "Now that many multiracial individuals are finally permitted to 'mark one or more' races, many expect to be treated as such without being put back in a single checkbox." Third, this strategy may make race-based policies more controversial than they already are. Further, there is evidence that this application of a modernized one-drop rule runs counter to how mixed-race people actually identify. Goldstein and Morning find that among people of white/American Indian background, the vast majority identify "white" as their single race and among white/Asian mixes, more than two-thirds identify as white. The one-drop rule, in effect, only properly applies to the African American/white mix, where the majority identify their single responses as black (but where nearly 40 percent of mixed-race respondents would choose white if given the opportunity).[65] Finally, mixed-race identification in the United States is highly unstable: results from a 2001 survey of census respondents revealed that 40 percent of those who had marked more than one race on their census forms in 2000 chose a single race in 2001, and there was a correspondingly large percentage that did the exact opposite.[66]

MAKING "MIXED" IN GREAT BRITAIN[67]

The inaugural appearance of the ethnic question in the 1991 Census was heralded as a resounding success. Nevertheless, the next decennial census in 2001 included several important changes to the format of the question, one of which was the inclusion of stand-alone categories to enumerate the mixed-race population. If the original format was indeed successful, why go through the cost of changing the policy content? The modifications to the ethnic question reflect two general shifts in British census politics. The first is institutional, as the census policy network expanded to include data users in a more collaborative policymaking process. The second shift is ideational. Similar to the United States and Canada, by the turn of the century Britain acknowledged rather than problematized the existence of mixed-race identities, recognized the diversity of the nation as a positive value, and sought to use the racial project of the census to promote this multiracial, multicultural schematic.

The OPCS decided to learn from and build on its experience in designing the 1991 Census by involving the main users of census data from the health sector, local authorities, academia, and the private sector alongside its renewed interdepartmental working group in an expanded policy network. The working groups did not begin their work from scratch. Prior to 1995 the OPCS, the General Register Office for Scotland (GRO(S)), and the Northern Ireland Statistics and Research Agency (NISRA) developed a substantial list of potential census

[65] Goldstein and Morning, "Back in the Box," 120–129.

[66] Claudette Bennett, *Exploring the Consistency of Race Reporting in Census 2000 and the Census Quality Survey* (San Francisco: American Statistical Association, 2003). See also Jamie Mihoko Doyle and Grace Kao, "Are Racial Identities of Multiracials Stable? Changing Self-Identification Among Single and Multiple Race Individuals," *Social Psychology Quarterly* 70, no. 4 (2007): 405–423; Jennifer Bratter, "Will 'Multiracial' Survive to the Next Generation?: The Racial Classification of Children of Multiracial Parents," *Social Forces* 86, no. 2 (2007): 821–849.

[67] In 2001 the census of England and Wales, the census of Scotland and the census of Northern Ireland featured different versions of the ethnic question. This section focuses on England and Wales, though much of the discussion pertains to Scotland as well.

topics and revisions based on the experience in 1991. This list was then considered by advisory committee representatives in the Working Group on Content, Question Testing and Classification, which pared the list down to sixty-two topics. OPCS identified the ethnic question, along with other questions concerning income and benefits, language, disability, careers, relationship within household, migration, labor market qualifications, and housing, as high priorities for testing.[68]

A subgroup on the ethnic question was then tasked in April 1995 with determining what changes should be made to the 1991 format. Chaired by Peter Aspinall of the University of Kent at Canterbury, the core membership of the ethnic question subgroup was comprised of members from all six of the main Advisory Groups, though the membership itself was not large.[69] The subgroup was required to complete a business case justifying its proposed changes to the Office for National Statistics (ONS), which amalgamated OPCS and the UK Central Statistical Office in 1996. The feasibility of proposals would be determined by four criteria set out by the Census Offices, that: a) there is a demonstrated need; b) users' requirements cannot be adequately met by information from other sources; c) a question can be devised which will produce data that are sufficiently accurate to meet users' requirements; and d) the topic is acceptable to the public and will not have an adverse effect on overall response rates.[70] The subgroup considered a number of issues: the census offices' proposal to split the ethnic group question into two separate questions about ethnic group and ethnic origin; comparability with 1991 categories; the number of ethnic groups presented on the census form; the additions of Irish and Vietnamese categories; and, most relevant for our purposes, the question of whether or not to count mixed-race.

This larger network did not include minority group representation on the advisory committees. As one working group member put it, "there was no systemic process of taking some measure of the opinion of ethnic communities."[71] He continued:

[68] OPCS and GRO(S), "Coverage in the 1991 Census," *Census Newsletter* 32, no. 3 (1995); OPCS and GRO(S), "New OPCS Area Classifications," *Census Newsletter* 33, no. 16 (1995).

[69] Other initial members included one business representative, two academic representatives, two representatives from the central government (Welsh Office and Home Office), one health representative, and two local authorities representatives.

[70] HM Government, *The 2001 Census of Population (Census White Paper)*, Cm 4253 (London: HMSO, 1999).

[71] Interview with Working Group Member, April 2009. ONS did implement this kind of process for the development of the 2011 Census.

I've always been much more sympathetic to the process in the United States by the Census Bureau, where they do these big surveys and find out what peoples preferences are, they've got the technology; and it's so important. The labels you use, which groups you represent. To my mind, Britain has always had a much more reactive process. These committees derive classifications by – quite literally by processes. By looking at the previous census, finding out who used the free text fields versus the pre-designated categories, looking at how well the data worked, and then developing new classifications and taking them for testing, and then modifying them, the process goes on for about five or six years repeatedly, designing questionnaires and taking them to the community, modifying them, redesigning them and taking them back again. In my view, the process should be much more sympathetic to building in the views of the different communities at a very early stage, through taking some measure of how people would like to be represented in terms of group labels and categories, but that doesn't happen.

In effect, even as the policy network expanded to include more participants – the main users of data – the government still maintained its autonomy in deciding which participants were to be included and in making final decision related to census content. As one civil servant said in an interview, in spite of extensive consultations and numerous advisory groups, there was never any doubt that ONS monopolized control over the process.[72]

Though limited, there are a few channels for interest group lobbies to access decision-makers: gaining support from the CRE, getting "direct roots" into Parliament by lobbying an MP, or writing directly to the ONS. Ethnic interest groups were certainly interested in the census. For example, the Cornish lobby spent nearly three decades pressuring the census offices for a separate ethnic category for the 1991, 2001, and 2011 censuses.[73] In 1999, the Secretary of State for the Home Office reported that ONS received a total of 154 submissions calling for the inclusion of additional ethnic categories on the 2001 Census: 108 from Members of Parliament and 31 from Members of European Parliament on behalf for the British Sikh Federation, the Kashmiri Workers Association, the Federation of Irish Societies, Cornwall 2000, and Cornish Solidarity, as well as 15 from individual members of the public.[74] However, in the words of an ONS representative, "one or two letters does not a category

[72] Interview with Working Group Member, April 2009.

[73] Interview with ONS representative, April 2009.

[74] *Hansard*, House of Commons, vol. 327, 15 March 1999, col. 500–501 (written response).

make."[75] Though mixed-race organizations exist in the United Kingdom,[76] these organizations did not participate in the review process.[77] Multiracial recognition on the census did not become the rallying cry as it did in the United States; in fact, there was no mixed-race lobby at all.

The subgroup's decision to consider adding mixed-race to the census was part of a larger ideational shift, which recognized mixed-race *as* mixed-race. This shift coincided with the short-lived "radical turn" in government policy on race relations, as New Labour attempted to separate itself from its Conservative predecessors by emphasizing its commitment to social justice for racial minorities. Les Back and his colleagues argue that during its first term in office, Tony Blair's New Labour embraced – or, at least, tried to manage – cultural diversity.[78] It introduced important initiatives, including the Lawrence Inquiry and the subsequent Macpherson Report, the 2000 Race Relations (Amendment) Act, and also appeared to respond (at least, initially, though perhaps not positively) to the recommendations of the independent Parekh report on *The Future of Multi-Ethnic Britain*. This shift, both discursive and institutional in nature, was reflected and compounded through census politics. When asked about what had changed between the 1991 and 2001 censuses, a subgroup member commented on the connection between social changes and the acceptability of asking a question on ethnicity:

> We made the brace that in 1991 that we included an ethnic question. We had sort of tried it out and not gone ahead with it in 1981. In 1991 it had been an undoubted success and perhaps we felt that this was now a much more acceptable – you know, it's part of society, I don't think anybody would argue now, you know, that we are a multicultural society, that we are mixed in many ways, and that this question is a very important measure of that variation. So I think it's acceptability, where as in the past – I think that's really very important, I think the acceptability of the question, I think it was probably very

[75] Interview with ONS representative, April 2009.

[76] For example, InterMix www.intermix.org.uk/homepages/homepage_default.asp and People in Harmony www.pih.org.uk/.

[77] Chamion Caballero, *"Mixed-Race Projects": Perceptions, Constructions, and Implications of Mixed-Race in the UK and USA*. Unpublished dissertation, Bristol: University of Bristol, 2004.

[78] Les Back, Michael Keith, Azra Khan, Kalbir Shukra, and John Solomos, "New Labour's White Heart: Politics, Multiculturalism and the Return of Assimilation," *The Political Quarterly* 73, no. 4 (2002): 445–454; see also Small and Solomos, "Race, Immigration and Politics in Britain"; Meer and Modood, "The Multicultural State We're In."

brave in 1991 – although I wasn't here – you know, society was very different nearly twenty years ago from the way it is today, and I think that's a very important factor to take into account ... So the acceptability, the terminology, the whole thing has changed.[79]

A different member made strikingly similar comments about the extent to which British society had changed, also drawing out the connection between legislative change and commitments to the recognition of diversity:

I think it's a change in society as well. It's a change that's reflected in the change in government. In this government we have now all these protections for different groups; very powerful legislation protecting against discrimination. I think there's much stronger movement to recognize diversity in different societies. There's been a form of identity politics if you like. Britain has been a bit slower than the United States and Canada. I think now there's just so much interest in ethnicity and race in this country; communities are organizing themselves a lot more effectively, being involved in consultations and participation and all sorts of government bodies. I think these two things are entrapped with each other. Identity politics and these new legal protections.[80]

To be clear, the impetus of enumerating by race in order to meet legislative requirements set out in the Race Relations Act was still an important factor that contributed to the initial and subsequent appearances of the ethnic question. However, several modifications to the design and content of the ethnic question speak to its reflection of, as stated above, the recognition of diversity in Britain.

First, the 2001 Census disaggregated the "white" category and provided the options of "British," "Irish," and "Any other White background" with a free-text field. These options stem from the efforts of a vocal lobby that persuaded members of the Working Group and ONS to add an Irish category. The Irish lobby used the notion of disadvantage to make its case in multiple institutional access points, targeting both the Working Group and other parts of the government, and finding a particularly powerful ally in the Department of Health.[81] This was a necessary step; as one ONS representative noted, lobby pressure from other white ethnic groups, such as the Cypriots, the Greek Cypriots, the Cornish, and the Welsh, were not persuasive because they could not

[79] Interview with ONS representative, April 2009.

[80] Interview with ethnicity question subgroup member, April 2009.

[81] Interview with ONS representative, April 2009; see also Peter J. Aspinall, *The Development of an Ethnic Group Question for the 2001 Census: The Findings of a Consultation Exercise with Members of the OPCS 2001 Census Working Subgroup* (London: United Medical and Dental Schools, 1996).

demonstrate their groups had experienced disadvantages in health, education, and the social realm.[82] When the ethnic question working group recommended the inclusion of an Irish category on the 2001 Census, the ONS was hesitant:

> ONS was reluctant to have it at all ... maybe because it wasn't driven by color. ONS didn't really have a strong appreciation of the nature and scale of the disadvantage. Although evidence was beginning to be published then ... The Irish group was a tougher sell – it was about 1997 when they came around. There was quite a lot of resistance.[83]

Though the lobby eventually achieved their goal, ONS's unease with counting Irish was partially because the category differed from the state's conceptualization of what *racial* disadvantage is and, therefore, what the ethnic question was designed to measure.

The second modification is the addition of the headings "Black or Black British" and "Asian or Asian British" in the ethnic question. The demand for a "Black British" category dates back to the early field trials of the 1970s, and its continued presence in British census politics over the decades speaks to the discursive connections between race and citizenship. As the 1980s and 1990s wore on, Great Britain experienced a more prominent disconnect between discourses of race relations and immigration, as second- and third-generation blacks and Asians lay claim to being just as British as anyone else. In previous decades, blackness was perceived by the majority population as being synonymous with immigrant,[84] but the growth of a politically active generation of British born and bred racial minorities not willing to settle as anything but full citizenship (complete with a sense of belonging as part of the nation) helped to challenge the unspoken, but dominant, paradigm that Britishness was equated with whiteness.[85]

The proposal to include the "Black British" and "Asian British" as headings rather than categories in the 2001 Census came from ONS. Working group members had struggled with the issue of retaining high-quality and comparable data that detailed ancestry while allowing

[82] Interview with ONS representative, April 2009.

[83] Interview with Working Group member, April 2009.

[84] Gilroy, *There Ain't No Black*; Roger Ballard, "The Construction of a Conceptual Vision: 'Ethnic Groups' and the 1991 UK Census," *Ethnic and Racial Studies* 20, no. 1 (1997): 182–194.

[85] See Bhikhu C. Parekh, *The Future of Multi-Ethnic Britain: Report of the Commission on the Future of Multi-Ethnic Britain* (London: Profile Books, 2000).

respondents to identify as British, since there was still such demand from the public. On this topic, one working group member commented:

> I've got to give credit to the ONS – I couldn't sort out in my head, retaining the data about Black-African or Black-Caribbean ancestry and having Black British as a tick box. Because we knew young people born in Britain, brought up in Britain, identified as Black British, they weren't fussed about ancestry from the Caribbean. Even their parents might have been born in Britain. And, you know, they just felt British. So why not give them a tick box so they can say what they are? And that appealed to a lot of us in the working group . . . but ONS wanted to know whether in ancestry terms whether people were from the Caribbean or Africa . . . ONS came up with this inspired solution of putting Black British and Asian British in the group label. Ok, you lost the facility to tick Black British as a tick box, but you got reference to national origins.[86]

The inclusion of some way of recognizing Black British or Asian British identities, according to this working group member, "had been a sticking point for a long time." This solution, which acknowledges both race and British nationality and/or citizenship, suggests a symbolic function of the census beyond the task of counting the population. The more intangible elements of census politics, where the census collides with ideas of citizenship and belonging, demand that policymakers negotiate between technical requirements and the politics of recognition.

The third major modification of the 1991 Census design concerned the enumeration of mixed-race people. In previous discussions dating back to the mid-1960s, census designers used mixed-race to illustrate the difficulty in defining race or color in terms precise enough for this kind of statistical exercise. Even in preparation for the 1991 Census, the enumeration of mixed-race did not feature prominently. When concerns did surface, the issue of how to count multiracial people was a problem the bureaucracy shied away from. For example, during the Standing Committee's review of the 1989 Draft Census Order Roger Freeman, the Parliamentary Under-Secretary for Health, responded to a Member's concern about the enumeration of mixed-race people by arguing "It would be too complicated – and unnecessary – to include it as a question to which we need a specific answer."[87]

The 1991 Census of England, Wales and Scotland instructed that if respondents were descended from more than one ethnic or racial

[86] Interview with Working Group member, April 2009.

[87] Standing Committee Reports, Fourth Standing Committee on Statutory Instruments, &C., vol. VII, December 19, 1989.

group, they should choose "the group to which the person considers he/she belongs" or tick the "Any other ethnic group" category and write a response in the space provided on the form. Contrary to OPCS's assertion that "people of mixed descent often preferred not to be distinguished as a separate group,"[88] of the 740,000 persons who provided a description in the free-text field, nearly one-third, or 240,000 people, wrote in mixed-origins descriptions. These were greater numbers than the population for three groups counted separately on the census form (Chinese, Bangladeshi, and Black-African). Comparisons with the data on "mixed-race" from the Labour Force Survey revealed that around two-thirds of the mixed-race population chose to write in descriptions rather than select one of the designated categories.[89] Government officials and academic communities acknowledged the need to find more accurate methods to collect meaningful data on this growing population.[90]

There was no lobby to adjust the census to count mixed-race and no champion for the cause emerged – the shift from mixed-race as a problem to an acknowledgment of the multiracial population of Britain was, in the words of one working group member, a matter of common sense.[91] The ethnic question subgroup proposed to enumerate mixed-race on the 2001 Census and, in stark contrast to the United States, there was unanimous support within the ethnic question subgroup and the Content, Question Testing and Classification Working Group and from government departments and the CRE. Peter Aspinall's report on the ethnic subgroup consultation makes the case for inclusion based on demand

[88] Sillitoe and White, "Ethnic Group and the British Census," 149.

[89] Peter Aspinall, "The Conceptualisation and Categorisation of Mixed Race/Ethnicity in Britain and North America: Identity Options and the Role of the State," *International Journal of Intercultural Relations* 27, no. 3 (2003): 278. Ethnicity data in Great Britain are also available from two other surveys: the Labour Force Survey and the General Household Survey. However, both these surveys are too small to give estimates at a local level and their coverage is not as encompassing as in the census. It is also interesting to note that the collection of ethnic data was introduced in these surveys in the early 1980s without any public or political debate.

[90] Martin Bulmer, "The Ethnic Group Question in the 1991 Census of the Population," in *Ethnicity in the 1991 Census. Volume One: Demographic Characteristics of the Ethnic Minority Populations*, eds. David Coleman and John Salt (London: HMSO, 1996), 33–62; David Owen, *Towards 2001: Ethnic Minorities and the Census* (University of Warwick: Centre for Research in Ethnic Relations, 1996); Peter Aspinall, "Children of Mixed Parentage: Data Collection Needs." *Children & Society* 14, no. 3 (2000): 207–216.

[91] Interview with ethnicity question subgroup member, April 2009.

from within the group,[92] the increasing size of the group, and the need for analytical clarity, particularly when the data are being used for service provision. The ONS immediately accepted the subgroup's business case and recommendation to count mixed-race. The only concerns recorded in this instance were by census users who were apprehensive about the effects on the quality and comparability of the ethnic group data from 1991. The inclusion of mixed-race categories in the 2001 Census simply was not a contentious issue – though it was a significant development in and of itself.

With the substantive question of whether or not to include some provision to classify multiracials largely decided, the subgroup discussions focused on more semantic issues, such as whether the label should read "mixed-race" when the question itself referred to ethnicity, the order of labels within the category (whether the category should read "White and Black Caribbean" or "Black Caribbean and White"), the placement of the larger mixed category within the ethnic question, and the use of the generic label of "Asian" when the black subgroups were divided into Black-Caribbean and Black-African.[93] A multiple response approach to enumerating mixed-race was never seriously considered. ONS representatives suggested this was because multi-ticking represented "a failure of the question" – respondents tick more than one box when they are confused or when instructions are unclear.[94] A member of the ethnicity question subgroup noted that when a two-tier question on ethnic ancestry and ethnic group that required multi-ticking was tested, "people were very confused by multi-ticking."[95] Moreover, the stand-alone categories required less tabulation – and therefore less human resources of the state – than the complicated analyses required when multiple responses are permitted.

[92] Of the three arguments, "demand from within the group" is clearly the weakest. The report relies heavily on evidence from the United States, where multiracial organizations were lobbying the federal government for classificatory changes to the 2000 Census. Aspinall notes that the evidence of a similar consciousness or demand in Britain was "piecemeal." Aspinall, *Development of an Ethnic Group Question.*

[93] Note that the label in the 2001 Census simply reads "Mixed" with no further qualifier. The category was eventually placed second, after "White," to ensure that respondents did not overlook the category, though some argue that this position is also an effort to avoid the historical stigma of the "half-caste." Barry Kosmin, "Ethnic and Religious Questions in the 2001 UK Census of Population Policy Recommendations," Institute for Jewish Policy Research, Policy Paper No. 2 (1999).

[94] Interview with ONS representative, April 2009.

[95] Interview with member of ethnic question subgroup, April 2009.

The addition of the mixed-race categories were viewed by many to be the most important and significant modification to the 2001 ethnic question, one which "largely reflected the change in society between 1991 and 2001 ... what had largely not been acceptable in 1991 was now seen as being a very important issue."[96] As one ONS representative put it, "it was broadly accepted I think that there had been an underlying change in the structure of society and that the mixed group was necessary. And it was very broadly supported. I can't recall any opposition to the inclusion of a mixed race category at all."[97] The census testing program demonstrated that the question was acceptable to the mixed-race people themselves.[98] Neither the House of Commons nor the House of Lords witnessed any substantial debate over the changes to the ethnic question.[99] In short, there were few objections to the decision to count mixed-race – from within the government, the media, or the public at large. The inclusion of multiracial categories aligned well with the state's promotion of multiracial multiculturalism; in contrast to the conceptualization of mixed-race as a problem of racial enumeration, the inclusion of mixed-race categories on the census was considered an uncontroversial addition that reflected changing societal norms.

The 2001 Census of England and Wales thus asked a direct question on race, in which mixed-race was offered as a viable identity choice (Figure 6.2).[100] However, in contrast to the "mark one or more" approach utilized to enumerate mixed-race in Canada and the United States, Great Britain provided its respondents with a stand-alone "mixed" ethnic designation as one of five "coarse" classifications – White, Mixed, Asian or Asian British, Black or Black British, and Chinese or Other Ethnic Group. These coarse classifications were further divided into more specific ethnic groups; for example, the "mixed" category consisted of four options: "White and Black Caribbean," "White and Black African," "White and Asian," and a free-text space for "Any other Mixed

96 Interview with ONS representative, April 2009.

97 Interview with ONS representative, April 2009.

98 Aspinall, "The Conceptualisation and Categorisation of Mixed Race/Ethnicity."

99 *Hansard*, House of Commons, Standing Committees. Session 1999–2000. Vol. X, Sixth Standing Committee on Delegated Legislation, February 2, 2000; *Hansard*, House of Lords, Vol. 609, February 16, 2000. cols. 1305–1338.

100 In Scotland, the census offered a box to check for "Any Mixed Background," with an additional write-in space, and in Northern Ireland the category was labeled "Mixed ethnic group," also with an additional free-text space.

8 What is your ethnic group?

Choose ONE section from A to E, then ✓ the appropriate box to indicate your cultural background.

A White

- ☐ British ☐ Irish
- ☐ Any other White background, *please write in*

B Mixed

- ☐ White and Black Caribbean
- ☐ White and Black African
- ☐ White and Asian
- ☐ Any other Mixed background, *please write in*

C Asian or Asian British

- ☐ Indian ☐ Pakistani
- ☐ Bangladeshi
- ☐ Any other Asian background, *please write in*

D Black or Black British

- ☐ Caribbean ☐ African
- ☐ Any other Black background, *please write in*

E Chinese or other ethnic group

- ☐ Chinese
- ☐ Any other, *please write in*

SPECIMEN

FIGURE 6.2: Census of England and Wales, 2001

Background."[101] In 2001, more than 670,000 people in Britain chose to identify as "Mixed," representing approximately 1.4 percent of the English and Welsh population. The largest mixed-race demographic was White and Black Caribbean (237,420), followed by White and Asian (189,015), Other mixed (155,688), and White and Black African (78,911).[102] This represents a dramatic increase from the previous count of 240,000 based on write-in descriptions from the 1991 Census.

(IN)VISIBLE MINORITIES IN CANADA

Why did the similar ideational impulses and institutional structures in Canada and Great Britain not lead to the same policy outcome? In the Canadian context, multiracial multiculturalism was embodied by the recognition that the massive demographic changes in the country had contributed to complicated identities, a bureaucratic desire to allow respondents to racially self-identify, and an acknowledgment that race continued to be a controversial subject. In institutional terms, policy legacies, a far more centralized statistical system, and a tight policy network constrained the policy alternatives at the schematic state's disposal.

As demonstrated in Chapter 5, the promotion of official multiculturalism normatively preconditioned census politics in Canada. At the end of the twentieth century mixed-race was part of this multicultural diversity, and its enumeration was, according to one policymaker, "a recognition, as we've always had in Canada, or at least in the census, that there is diversity. And there's racial diversity as well, it's not just ethnic diversity. And wanting to allow people to provide those responses."[103] Another civil servant involved in the design of the 1996 question relayed that although "there was clearly a cost in terms of response burden," the addition of a direct question on race was "reflecting the incredible changes in the country."[104] This balancing act between attaining quality data and

[101] Note the specific concern with individuals of white/non-white racial backgrounds. According to ONS representatives, the number of non-white mixes (for example, Black-African and Asian) simply did not warrant specific categories; however, one cannot help but notice the continued lack of consideration of mixes that do not involve the white majority. On this topic, see Minelle Mahtani and April Moreno, "Same Difference: Towards a More Unified Discourse in 'Mixed Race' Theory," in *Rethinking Mixed Race*, eds. David Parker and Miri Song (London: Pluto Press, 2001), 65–75.

[102] HM Government, *Census of the Population, 2001*(London: HMSO, 2001).

[103] Interview with Statistics Canada representative, October 2009.

[104] Interview with Statistics Canada representative, October 2009.

recognizing/showcasing racial diversity was achieved through the imperative of racial legibility, turning complex, nested, and multiple identities into something that could be quantified, ordered, and counted.

It is precisely because of the complexity of racial identities that policymakers deemed it necessary and critical to give respondents the opportunity to choose for themselves. Since the 1986 and 1991 ethnic origins questions specifically requested respondents to mark as many groups as applicable, Statistics Canada developed a strategy to handle cases of multiple reporting for those designated as visible minority. In situations in which the respondent identified him or herself as a constituent of one visible minority group and one white group (for example, Chinese and English), Statistics Canada would assign the individual to the visible minority group, somewhat ironically echoing the same protocol used to designate mixed-race people as non-white in the censuses of the early twentieth century. To deal with multiple responses that involved two or more visible minority groups, the category "multiple visible minority responses" was used for data output.

However, in the planning stages of the 1996 Census the Canadian state had become uncomfortable with explicitly assigning identities, even though doing so would be (and, in the not-so-distant past, had been) within the very nature of the census. As one public servant put it, "The idea was to give people the opportunity. Because again, we didn't want to be the ones to decide who exactly was a visible minority. So when in doubt, allow them to respond and then if necessary look at the response patterns and make sense of those."[105] The shifting of responsibility for the classification of racial identity from the state to the respondent was, according to another public servant, one of the driving forces behind the 1996 question on race:

> there was a very strong feeling that we needed to get away from these decisions that were being made by bureaucrats. We needed to get people closer to the measure that they would see themselves in. Because we were still making decisions and we were assigning people. We needed to give them the choice to say yes, I belong to this group.[106]

Mixed-race was on the bureaucracy's radar during its discussions of how to design the race question. Statistics Canada's consultations with other government departments, provincial governments,

[105] Interview with Statistics Canada representative, October 2009.

[106] Interview with Statistics Canada representative, October 2009.

municipalities, multicultural organizations, private industry, and other stakeholders revealed a demand for information on mixed-race children.[107] The Interdepartmental Working Group then made three important decisions: first, the "population group" question would include the racial designation "white"; second, respondents would be instructed to mark more than one category, if applicable; and third, respondents would be instructed to *not* print "mixed-race" or "biracial" in the free-text field.[108] All three policy outputs supported the schematic state's tendency to address racial issues indirectly. Prohibiting "biracial" or "mixed-race" as a response provided Statistics Canada with more sensitive data, but simultaneously ensured that census responses, like the question instructions, avoided the terminology of race. The inclusion of "white" made the question about population group rather than visible minority status and gave everyone a box to check, thus avoiding (some) of the inevitable allegations that racial minorities were getting special treatment.

More importantly, because the implementation of Question 19 was controversial enough on its own, the government made attempts to minimize the potential criticisms that would undoubtedly arise if respondents were forced to choose only one racial affiliation. As Chief Statistician Ivan Fellegi argued to the press and public, respondents "are encouraged to mark as many categories as apply, or they can write their own response in the space provided. No one is asked to fit him or herself into a single category."[109] In light of Canada's established policy of allowing multiple responses to the ethnic question, necessitating a single answer for the race question would have been both problematic and unpalatable. In normative terms, permitting multiple responses and the enumeration of mixed-race people in 1996 made multicultural sense; in other words, the reconceptualized ideal of a Canadian multiculturalism that acknowledged and endorsed racial diversity dictated census practices for counting mixed-race.

There were also institutional drivers for the state to configure a taxonomy that included multiracialism. The use of a multiple response approach to enumerate mixed-race was institutionally path-dependent.

[107] Statistics Canada, *1996 Census Consultation Report.*

[108] Statistics Canada, *1996 Census Guide and Reasons Why the Questions Are Asked* (Ottawa: Statistics Canada, 1996).

[109] Ivan P. Fellegi, "Chief Statistician: Why the Census Is Counting Visible Minorities," *Globe and Mail*, April 26, 1996: A21.

Multiple responses had been permitted and analyzed for the ethnic question since 1981. Unlike the United States Census Bureau, which had to develop new tabulation procedures to analyze multiple responses to a single question, the algorithm needed to tabulate multiple responses was already well-established in Statistics Canada. The multiple response approach was a policy option with low costs.

The tight policy network also limited minority group participation. Statistics Canada sought out "target populations" for focus group and survey testing and invited public comment at every stage of the census development program.[110] These consultations with racial minorities were particularly important during the testing phase of census development, but the groups were not included in any substantial way as part of the deliberations over questionnaire design or the preferred approach to counting race or mixed-race. Policymakers were very clear that "we drive the process," and though consultations with the Canadian Ethnocultural Council and the Canadian Race Relations Foundation[111] did occur, the purpose was so as to "not surprise our respondents" with unfamiliar terminology, inaccurate group labels, or offensive language. Maintaining a certain distance from political demands from above (Members of Parliament) and below (interest groups or ethno-racial organizations) was perceived as important "to allow Statistics Canada to maintain its political objectivity – this has become part of our culture of impartiality."[112]

The institutional constraints that arose from the policy legacies of employment equity and the centralized structure of the statistical system were therefore paramount. Though the legislation itself defines visible minorities as a designated group, it does not identify which racial groups are to be included under this generic label. Decisions about which groups should count as visible minorities were handed down over time from department to department, from the categories used in the Department of Citizenship and the Abella Report in the 1980s through to the tabulation of visible minority status for employment

[110] Interview with Statistics Canada representative, October 2009.

[111] This organization features similar circumstances as the CRE in Britain in that the Canadian Race Relations Foundation was created and is funded by the state. However, it is significantly less politicized than Britain's Commission for Racial Equality (subsumed under the Equality and Human Rights Commission in 2007), does not have state-devolved responsibility for monitoring circumstances of racial discrimination and does not report to the government.

[112] Interview with Statistics Canada representative, October 2009.

equity purposes in the 1990s. The use of the ten designated visible minority groups, standardized by and throughout the schematic state, made Statistics Canada less likely to adopt the British model of using stand-alone multiracial categories. When asked why Canada opted for a multiple response approach instead of stand-alone categories, a representative of Statistics Canada responded:

> No, I don't think that decision was ever really considered because it would be too restrictive here. First of all, in terms of employment equity, there are many different groups. So it's not as if we had just black and Chinese and South Asian, we had a whole bunch of groups to consider; a larger number, and so then you get into which ones do you put down, which ones do you not, and then people are upset if their group isn't shown. Even which examples you show beside the box becomes a major, major consideration. So, there was never any discussion about having a certain number of mixed groups shown in the question itself.[113]

Rather than debating whether or not to count mixed-race identities or the best-suited approach for doing so, which was somewhat of a foregone conclusion given normative concerns about single responses and institutional path dependencies, the Interdepartmental Working Group was far more concerned with the question of which "mixes" should count for employment equity purposes.

The dilemma was two-fold. First, the very notion of visible minority is based on broad generalizations about the relationships between race, racial visibility, and racial disadvantage. As in Britain and the United States, anti-discrimination legislation in Canada refers to race rather than a particular set of racial groups, which is problematic when not all racial groups are disadvantaged equally. This leads to the second dilemma, about whether or not, in a schematic premised on racial visibility, mixed-race people should count as visible minorities. Not all groupings of "white and" are used for employment equity purposes:

> there was concern for example, that some of what we call the borderline groups – the ones where there are boundary questions as to whether or not they are visible minorities. Latin American and white – was that person telling us that there were of mixed Latin American and white background, in other words one parent was white and one was Latin American, or were they telling us that they were in fact white from Latin America? So it was those types of ambiguities. So, for the boundary questions, Latin American and also West Asian and Arab. The other groups when the response was "white and black" or "white and Chinese," they

[113] Interview with Statistics Canada representative, October 2009.

were counted as visible minorities for employment equity purposes. And only for that variable. But for employment equity, that decision was made by the interdepartmental working group.[114]

The borderline groups complicated the already convoluted relationship between mixed-race and employment equity categories. In the Canadian scheme, being a racial minority depended on corporeal visibility in a multicultural framing in which "race" is consistently equated with "not white." Though the schematic was less rigid in some ways than the American ethno-racial pentagon in, for example, its inclusion of Latin American as a visible minority group, its organizational pattern provided no clear answer about mixed-race and the so-called borderline groups that challenged state projects of legibility.

Canada is racially diverse and becoming even more so. Projections indicate that three in ten Canadians could be a visible minority by 2031[115] and both mixed-race unions and the mixed-race population are on the rise. In 2001, 3.2 percent of the Canadian population, or 452,000 people, were in mixed unions, an increase of 35 percent from 1991.[116] The mixed-race population grew from 1.2 to 1.5 percent of the population between 2001 and 2006, an increase of 25 percent in just 5 years.[117] In spite of these demographic trajectories, issues of (mixed-)race and the census have failed to achieve the same amount of academic or public attention as they have in the United States or Great Britain. Is this simply because, as many assume, race is not a salient issue in Canada? On the contrary, the political development of questions designed to count by race suggest that the schematic state has been very concerned with assessing the size and composition of the racial population, even when it has been hesitant to directly confront the terminology of race.

CONCLUSION

Ultimately, the convergence in the decision to count mixed-race and the divergence of the methods implemented for doing so are the results of

114 Interview with Statistics Canada representative, October 2009.

115 Éric Caron Malenfant, André Lebel, and Laurent Martel, *Projections of the Diversity of the Canadian Population, 2006 to 2031* (Ottawa: Statistics Canada, 2010).

116 This increase is notable given an increase of 10 percent for all couples during the same time period. Anne Milan and Brian Hamm, "Mixed Unions," *Canadian Social Trends* no. 73 (2004): 2–6.

117 Statistics Canada, *2001 Census* (Ottawa: Statistics Canada, 2001); Statistics Canada, *2006 Census* (Ottawa: Statistics Canada, 2006).

a confluence of ideational and institutional factors. At least in the Anglophone West, there appears to be a global logic to the operation of the norm of multiracial multiculturalism, which is transnational in scope but contextualized in domestic application. Deteriorating social and legal taboos against interracial marriage and changing demographic patterns in diverse societies are important factors, but their relevance is potent because of changing transnational ideas about race and mixed-race within multicultural societies. Once perceived as problematic for racial classification schema, mixed-race identities are now acknowledged as a positive attribute of the multicultural nation. In the paradigm of multiracial multiculturalism, racial self-declaration is the unequivocally preferred approach. Policymakers expressed concern that respondents have the ability to identify as *mixed-race* if they so desired and were willing to adjust previously successful census categories in order to accommodate these issues of identity and recognition. Discourses of race, citizenship, and belonging are linked together through the census, which has become an instrument of diversity governance used by the state to promote multiculturalism and diversity as national values.

Institutions also bear relevance for the timing and interpretation of this isomorphic idea in different countries. The processes of census design in Canada, the United States, and Britain are all very bureaucratic in nature, largely driven by the imperatives and priorities of these governments. Cooperation and consensus among different departments with distinct (though overlapping) priorities and responsibilities was not only a compulsory mandate in the census design process, but was also necessary in order to ensure the population's legibility and in some cases standardization throughout the schematic state apparatus. In Canada and Britain, the bureaucratic nature of the parliamentary system of government ensured that statistical agencies remained fairly autonomous, deciding when and how the census policy network was formed and what issues were on the table for discussion. In the United States, heightened stakes arising from the saliency of race in the American cultural context, more aggressive anti-discrimination legislation, and a policy network that was blown wide open (so to speak) created incentives for political action. The review of federal classification standards also added an additional layer: though the congressional oversight of the census is a function of the American political system, the congressional committee's review of OMB racial and ethnic classification standards was not a normal decennial routine.

The varying approaches employed to count the multiracial population – multiple responses in Canada and the United States compared to the stand-alone multiracial categories in England and Wales – demonstrate that policy outcomes are the result of political compromise and contestation in specific institutional settings. The structure of and interaction of agents within policy networks, which link together state and societal actors in decision-making processes, are an important explanatory element. Who is consulted, when, and in what capacity are crucial issues that have the potential to influence final policy outcomes. These outcomes can also feed back and reshape the structure of the network and actors' preferences therein. For example, the Office for National Statistics decided to build on its 2001 program experience and made more of an effort to liaise with community organizations and local authorities in the development of the 2011 Census. Though censuses are often perceived to be neutral instruments of data collection, census policy is often the outcome of political battles. As both an arena and an actor within that arena, the state must provide a venue for groups to propose and debate policy options while acting to protect its own interests.

7

The Future of Counting by Race

There is power in numbers. In common parlance, this power is people-based: the more individuals that believe in an idea, fight for a common cause, argue a particular position, or enact peculiar identities, the better the chances an idea will spread, a cause will gain social traction, a position will become prominent, or an identity will proliferate. The formation of public policy – in Harold Lasswell's original formulation, the actualization of who gets what, when, and how[1] – relies on numbers and numeracy. Statistics are a pervasive form of state writing, a numerical prose found in forms, orders, registers, regulations, and narratives about current events in the world and how we understand them.[2] As Deborah Stone argues, any conflict over policy contains the question of how to count, measure, or evaluate a given problem, and the act of counting inevitably involves deliberate political decisions about *counting as*. Counting, she continues, begins with categorization; a process that erects boundaries of inclusion and exclusion, implies that certain characteristics must be selected and then evaluated, and establishes the criteria by which normative judgments are made.[3] Power also rests in the instrumentality of numbers – the uses to which the tallies are put in the juxtaposition of large and small, substantial and insignificant, powerful and powerless.

The Schematic State is a book about the power of numbers; more specifically, about the power-ridden purposes of counting by race, the

[1] Harold Lasswell, *Politics: Who Gets What, When and How* (New York: P. Smith, 1950).
[2] Gupta, *Red Tape*, 153–159.
[3] Deborah Stone, *Policy Paradox: The Art of Political Decision Making*, 3rd edn (New York and London: W.W. Norton, 2012), ch. 8.

political conflicts inherent in the determination and manipulation of racial classifications, and the complicated ideational, institutional, and individual sites, strategies, and stakes involved in the process of enacting and foreclosing racial legibility. Racial statistics can reveal, predict, and even obscure knowledge about the empirical world. We know, for example, that the United States is set to become a "minority-majority" country by the year 2050, in that Americans who identify as Hispanic, Black, Asian, American Indian, and Native Hawaiian and Pacific Islander will together outnumber non-Hispanic whites.[4] Driven largely by the influx of foreigners and higher birthrates among immigrants, the romanticism of the approaching mid-century is marked by a wave of uncertainty about the consequences of these unprecedented changing demographics. These numbers have already begun to fuel debate over immigration policy, the composition of the labor market, overpopulation in urban areas, ethnic ghettoization, and emerging voting patterns.[5] And yet, much depends on what is encompassed within the labels employed to make sense of these demographic projections. Putting aside for the moment the oxymoronic phraseology of a "minority-majority," the division of the American population into categorical proportions is premised on a belief in an enduring color line that pits whites against others, reflecting a historical legacy created by slavery and imperialism, reinforced by Jim Crow and the racially defined borders of the nation-state, and reinvented by mechanisms of indirect discrimination, cumulative structures of white privilege, state-sanctioned violence, individual prejudice, and public discourse. Majority rule and minority rights are basic principles of democratic governance, but the ambiguity and internal contradictions of a minority-majority (or majority-minority?) reveal a deep insecurity about what Jennifer Lee and Frank Bean have called the "diversity paradox."[6] Will these demographic changes ultimately reinforce or dismantle America's color line and all its congenital privileges and detriments?

4 Sam Roberts, "Projections Put Whites in Minority in U.S. by 2050," *New York Times*, December 17, 2009, accessed June 25, 2014, www.nytimes.com/2008/08/14/world/americas/14iht-census.1.15284537.html?_r=0

5 Sam Roberts, "In a Generation, Minorities May Be the U.S. Majority," *New York Times*, August 14, 2008, accessed June 25, 2014, www.nytimes.com/2008/08/14/washington/14census.html?pagewanted=all; Paul Taylor and the Pew Research Center, *The Next America: Boomers, Millennials, and the Looming Generational Showdown* (New York: PublicAffairs, 2014).

6 Jennifer Lee and Frank D. Bean, *The Diversity Paradox: Immigration and the Color Line in Twenty-First Century America* (New York: Russell Sage Foundation, 2010).

The basic lesson of this research is that numbers and the norms derived from them are interesting not simply for what they can and cannot they tell us about political phenomena – for instance, how many people identify with which racial or ethnic group in a given census year – but are also curious in and of themselves as objects of theoretical and empirical inquiry. Counting is not simply a matter of creating a numerical tally, and racial statistics are not derived in a normative, ideational, or societal vacuum. Rather, all statistics rely on processes of categorization and classification that are inherently, unavoidably, and consequentially political. Racial classification systems are battles over truth. The racial schemas embalmed by the state are both constitutive of and by social worlds. The power of the state to standardize and disperse its preferred order is crucial, but it is neither monolithic nor omnipotent. Classification systems are ultimately maintained by social institutions, of which government is a part but not the whole. The categories that define the boundaries of racial identities accumulate over time, layer unevenly and relationally, sometimes contradict, and when set against the dynamics of lived experience classification structures can fracture.[7] State power matters, but so too does the overall structure of political choice, which, according to Paul Starr, is "the system for adjudicating conflicting claims, its rules, presuppositions, and organizational forms," especially surrounding two main types of political choices: the problem of legitimate classification (which categories should be allowed) and the problem of legitimate interference (whether and how to use classifications to evaluate or predict individual behavior).[8] Placing the complex interplay of ideas and institutions front and center, this book is an empirical investigation into the state's construction of racial schema and the ways that these binding but boundless parameters have been institutionalized through the census.

The comparison of the United States, Great Britain, and Canada over long periods of time has served methodological and theoretical purposes. Conceptualizing race as a transnational concept linked to modernity, the Atlantic slave trade, and the governing logics of colonial rule enables an analysis that takes account of the varying intensities of nationally specific racial projects and the structures of political institutions, as well as the ways that these factors shaped the cultural and institutional translational

[7] Bowker and Star, *Sorting Things Out.*

[8] Paul Starr, "Social Categories and Claims in the Liberal State," *Social Research* 59, no. 2 (1992): 265. See also Michèle Lamont and Virag Molnár, "The Study of Boundaries in the Social Sciences," *Annual Review of Sociology* 28 (2002): 167–195.

processes distinctive to each country. Both global racial ideas and domestic interpretations thereof interactively authorize particular kinds of behaviors in relation to racial classifications and inspire, though do not wholly determine, the reconfiguration of social relationships. Much like the syncretic social processes that shaped the economic and political developments associated with neoliberalism at the end of the twentieth century,[9] the overall effect of these racial ideas did not achieve total dominance. Their influence was mediated by domestic-level institutions, conditioned by the contexts into which they were produced and/or introduced, and inflected by political actors with a range of strategies, goals, and preferences. State-driven efforts to impose racial boundaries often incited countercurrents that become the mantra of social identities and groups seeking to challenge governments' definitions of race and the composition of racial categories, sometimes in order to access the resources associated with racial identification.

In more theoretical, contradictory, and perhaps controversial terms, by tracing the evolution of racial ideas, the development of census-making and -taking institutions, and the emergence of state-sanctioned racial schematics, this project seeks to trouble dominant conceptualizations of temporality and territoriality. The dual axes of time and space are integral to the effect and affinity of the census. Seeking "to tie individuals to places within an administrative grid and then to hold them steady so that they may become objects of knowledge and government,"[10] the census requires and then reproduces individuals that are frozen in both time and space, but transportable and comparable across both in quantified form by virtue of their racial legibility. My focus on overlapping temporal periods on one hand and racial transnationalism on the other is an effort to illuminate the relativity of time and disrupt the formidable seduction of taking spatial arrangements as natural rather than political. Drawing out the tension between the chronological, national, and epistemological opens a plane of possibility and uncertainty – in Stuart Hall's conceptualization, a politics without guarantees.[11] Instead of a linear, static conception of causality, we might envision a series of overlapping, interlocking

[9] Peter Hall and Michèle Lamont, eds., *Social Resilience in the Neoliberal Era* (New York: Cambridge University Press, 2013).

[10] Curtis, *Politics of Population*, 26.

[11] Stuart Hall, "Race, The Floating Signifier," Media Education Foundation Transcript, accessed June 24, 2016, www.mediaed.org/transcripts/Stuart-Hall-Race-the-Floating-Signifier-Transcript.pdf; Paul Gilroy, Lawrence Grossberg, and Angela McRobbie, eds., *Without Guarantees: In Honour of Stuart Hall* (London: Verso, 2000).

historical moments whose tendrils extend into the distant past and the unknown future – a politics of continuity rather than disjuncture, where post-politics are not bound by parsimonious chronological order. Instead of a world of nation-states with real and imagined boundaries, we might explore the constant movement and change represented in the concept of the transnational, in which the interactive formulation and flow of ideas and logics of governing by and through race spread across those ephemeral borders and circumnavigate domestic, international, and transnational realms.

Throughout these theoretical, empirical, and epistemological terrains, three intersecting vectors shape the contours of shifting classificatory systems: the state, race, and the census. Below, I describe each intersection to examine the major developments in the racial politics of the census in the twenty-first century. At the intersection of the state and the census, or the politics of population, I explore the turn away from traditional decennial censuses in favor of smaller but continuous surveys. The second section considers the intersection of race and the (schematic) state and the challenges posed by neoliberal forms of governance. The third intersection, race and the census, examines new and potentially problematic forms of post-racial legibility that may arise from proposed changes to enumerating race, particularly on the 2020 American census. More broadly, these issues and intersections lead to a larger, crucial question: what is the future of counting by race? The answer is, of course, complicated.

STATE/CENSUS – THE POLITICS OF POPULATION

The imperative to categorize and classify populations is built into the origin of nation-states, which are themselves entities that presume a bound territory and a homogenous population therein.[12] It is in the nature of the state to classify. The common standards that are essential to the maintenance of political, social, and economic order do not arise of their own accord, but instead must be cultivated and put into place, even as the mechanisms through which standardization is achieved proliferate in markedly unstandardized forms.[13] Foucault's concepts of biopolitics

[12] Andreas Wimmer, "The Making and Unmaking of Ethnic Boundaries: A Multilevel Process Theory," *American Journal of Sociology* 113, no. 4 (2008): 991.

[13] Desmond King and Marc Stears, "How the U.S. State Works: A Theory of Standardization," *Perspectives on Politics* 9, no. 3 (2011): 509–510.

and governmentality speak to the complicated ways that these types of totalizing procedures can constitute a social entity out of the individual components that comprise it while enabling the modern state to maintain a disciplining order without the use of coercive force.[14] Bureaucracy, itself an elaborate classification,[15] is steeped in categorizing processes that employ typifications – for example, in the extensive use of forms and formulas – to create statistical narratives premised on commensurability between the lives, times, and experiences of individual citizens.[16] In liberal democracies, even the rule of law is premised on the idea of equal rights before and under the law, a principle that necessitates that laws create groups and assign consequences to being placed in one group and not another. The liberal state therefore dictates the use of social categories; in James Scott's astute formulation, to "see" like a state requires both a *vision* of the population and territory and its *division* into legible, categorical parts.[17] However, as Starr points out, this impetus does not predict what kinds of categories should be promoted.[18]

The census is one of the primary instruments of classificatory assignment made by and at the disposal of the state. Evelyn Ruppert argues that censuses do not simply construct populations, but also produce them. Through the act of taking a census, she argues, "subjects gradually, but fitfully, acquired the capacity to recognise themselves as members and parts of a whole. Producing population captures the *practice* of developing, creating and bringing this capacity into being whereas constructing population attends to the practice of assembling and representing population."[19] The census form itself, with its neatly ordered rows, columns, boxes, and free-text fields, is a schematic that places one's individuality in relation to a much larger, standardized social grid. The classification schema employed by the census is both instrumental and normative – categories cannot be

14 Foucault, "Governmentality"; Michel Foucault, *Security, Territory, Population: Lectures at the Collège de France 1977–1978*, ed. Arnold Davidson, trans. Graham Burchell (New York: Picador, 2007); see also Pierre Bourdieu, *On the State: Lectures at the Collège de France 1989–1992*, eds. Patrick Champagne et al., trans. David Fernbach (Cambridge: Polity Press, 2014).

15 Starr, "Social Categories," 272.

16 Gupta, *Red Tape*, 153–159.

17 Scott, *Seeing Like a State*; see also Pierre Bourdieu, *In Other Words: Essays towards a Reflexive Sociology*, trans. Matthew Adamson (Stanford: Stanford University Press, 1990).

18 Starr, "Social Categories," 289.

19 Evelyn S. Ruppert, "Producing Population," Working Paper No. 37, CRESC Working Paper Series (Milton Keynes: Centre for Research on Socio-Cultural Change, 2007), 3–4, emphasis in original.

brought into being without an a priori conceptualization of the underlying principles associated with the category, the criteria used to demarcate categories, and the consequences of the divisions that separate one category from another. Even the process of naming different categories can be vital to the construction of social identities; one need only consider the semantic and normative implications of identifying a particular population as "illegal aliens" instead of "undocumented workers."

Census classification schemas are lines drawn by the state, though the inspiration about where these boundaries come from and where they should lie can originate elsewhere in social, political, cultural, and transnational realms. Census-making and census-taking can also involve a range of societal actors that challenge the imposition of concepts or identities, most clearly demonstrated when social groups mobilize to challenge the schematics sanctioned by the state. But because of the centralized power and authority of the state apparatus, these lines are sewn into the social fabric with more consequences than other types of group boundaries. In his recent substantial contribution to the theorization of ethnic boundary-making processes, Andreas Wimmer notes that categories create frameworks of incentives – moral, symbolic, institutional, legal – and actors will seek to manipulate structures to change the risks and benefits of being categorized in particular ways.[20] Even when classificatory structures are imbued with the administrative veneer of state power, dominant modes of categorizing are never completely hegemonic; counter-narratives and categorical contestation are always possible modes of social resistance.[21] But it is difficult, if not impossible, to recapture a "preconceptual ignorance"[22] before classificatory standards helped define ways of thinking, visualizing, and being, and because categories are exclusive and official schema must at least give the appearance of being firm, inconsistencies and borderlands will always be problematic. Many countries face challenges with the same policy issues in these areas, struggling to count populations that are transient (travelers and the young and mobile), difficult to count (the homeless), resistant to being counted (illegal aliens and asylum seekers), have historically been undercounted (racial and ethnic minorities in urban areas), or which are often double-counted (college students, persons with two homes, children in

[20] Wimmer, "The Making and Unmaking of Ethnic Boundaries."

[21] See James Scott, *The Art of Not Being Governed: An Anarchist History of Upland Southeast Asia* (New Haven: Yale University Press, 2009).

[22] Starr, "Social Categories," 272.

joint-custody arrangements). The question of census adjustments – whether or not the bureaucracy should adjust the raw data to align them with a more accurate estimation of different population groups – has become a political hotbed in a number of countries, including the United States and Great Britain.[23]

The future of racial enumeration is, of course, linked to the future of the census. This book has focused on "traditional" censuses – that is, censuses conducted once every five or ten years wherein individuals fill out census forms and are enumerated directly. In the 1970s, Canada and the United States distinguished between the census "short form," ideally to be filled in by the entire population, and the "long form," used to collect information beyond the basic demographic characteristics and sent to a representative sample of the population, typically around 20 to 30 percent. In recent years many countries have moved away from this model of census-taking, for a number of reasons: traditional censuses are expensive; public cooperation may have faltered; and censuses may not be able to capture an increasingly transient, transnational, and mobile population. The most recent census round in 2010 demonstrates a growing trend to this effect. Among forty European countries, the Scandinavian countries and Austria counted by using population registers only. Approximately half conducted traditional censuses, while thirteen employed a mixed approach that combines data from registers, sample surveys, and other sources. France alone has adopted a rolling census, first put in action in 2004.[24]

Discussions recently concluded in Britain about abandoning its traditional census. In July 2010 Cabinet Office Minister Francis Maude announced that the 2011 Census would likely be the nation's last, arguing that other avenues of collecting information would be better, quicker, more frequent, and less expensive.[25] That same year the UK Statistics Authority requested that the National Statistician and ONS review options for the future collection of population statistics. Over the next three years, the review process, "Beyond 2011," considered an integrated population statistics system, which necessitated extensive testing of

[23] Anderson and Fienberg, *Who Counts*; Kenneth Prewitt, "Politics and Science in Census Taking," in *The American People: Census 2000*, eds. Reynolds Farley and John Haaga (New York: Russell Sage Foundation, 2005), 3–45.

[24] Paolo Valente, "Census Taking in Europe: How Are Populations Counted in 2010?" *Population and Societies*, no. 467 (2010): 1–4.

[25] Christopher Hope, "National Census to Be Axed after 200 years," *The Telegraph*, July 9, 2010, accessed July 10, 2014, www.telegraph.co.uk/news/politics/7882774/National-census-to-be-axed-after-200-years.html

methods for combining the census with additional surveys and administrative data to create a single statistical database continually updated over time, and explored the possibility of conducting an online decennial census that would replace the traditional census.[26] The ONS also commissioned an independent review of census methodology chaired by Chris Skinner, Professor of Statistics at the London School of Economics, which was published in November 2013.[27] Finally, an extensive public consultation program began in October 2011 and ONS issued the findings in early 2014.[28]

In his final recommendation to Cabinet, Sir Andrew Dilnot, the Chair of the UK Statistical Authority, concluded that there remains strong demand for a decennial census.[29] An administrative database, National Statistician Jil Matheson noted in her March 2014 recommendation, had the potential to improve the accuracy, frequency, and efficiency of population statistics and was the option of choice of many of Britain's international neighbors. This approach would make use of already existing administrative data for population statistics, as Britain already does, for example, by using the number of child benefit recipients in local settings to assure the quality of the number of children counted by the 2011 Census.[30] Some statistics, however, would not be reliably produced from administrative data sources – statistics on ethnicity would require

[26] Office for National Statistics, *The Census and the Future Provision of Population Statistics in England and Wales: Recommendation from the National Statistician and Chief Executive of the UK Statistics Authority* (London: ONS, 2014). Earlier proposals explored the possibility of creating a system similar to the American Community Survey, which would provide timelier and more up-to-date information on the population. See Office for National Statistics, *Census Strategic Development Review: Alternatives to a Census: Linkage of Existing Data Sources* (London: HMSO, 2003); Office for National Statistics, *Proposals for an Integrated Population Statistics System* (London: HMSO: 2003).

[27] Chris Skinner, John Hollis, and Mike Murphy, *Beyond 2011: Independent Review of Methodology*, October 2013, accessed July 10, 2014, www.ons.gov.uk/ons/about-ons/who-ons-are/programmes-and-projects/beyond-2011/beyond-2011–independent-review-of-methodolgy/index.html

[28] Office for National Statistics, "ONS takes a fresh look beyond 2011," News Release, October 17, 2011, accessed June 21, 2016, http://webarchive.nationalarchives.gov.uk/20160105160709/http://www.ons.gov.uk/ons/rel/mro/news-release/beyond-2011/ons-takes-a-fresh-look–beyond-2011-.html

[29] Letter from Chair of the UK Statistics Authority, Sir Andrew Dilnot CBE, to Minister for the Cabinet Office Rt. Hon. Francis Maude, MP, March 27, 2014, accessed July 10, 2014, www.ons.gov.uk/ons/about-ons/who-ons-are/programmes-and-projects/beyond-2011/beyond-2011-report-on-autumn-2013-consultation–and-recommendations/index.html

[30] Office for National Statistics, *The Census and the Future Provision of Population Statistics*, 6.

a large household survey to supplement this approach. The Skinner Report also attached a higher risk of privacy violations to the use of an administrative database, though public opinion polls indicated that when provided with reassurances regarding security and privacy, the majority of the public supported ONS using administrative data from other government departments to produce statistics.[31] An approach that accepted the "natural evolution" from a paper to an online census, on the other hand, would mirror the trends in other comparable countries – for example, the report noted, in Canada 54 percent of respondents completed the census online, compared to 16 percent in England and Wales that same year.[32] The three month public consultation resulted in more than 700 responses from government, local authorities, public bodies, private industries, non-profit organizations, academics, genealogists, and individual citizens. Among other key messages, the consultations revealed that the statistics for small geographic areas and small populations that can only be produced by a full decennial census were regarded as "essential to local decision making, policy making and diversity monitoring in fulfillment of legally binding public duties."[33] The National Statistician ultimately recommended, and the UK Statistics Authority endorsed, an approach that combined data from an online census in 2021, with the acknowledgment that special care would be required for those who are unable to complete a census online, and the increased use of administrative data and surveys to improve statistics between decennial censuses. However, this solution may be temporary: the new "Census Transformation Programme" will decide how statistics are procured and provided after 2021.

Unlike Britain, the decennial census has a constitutionally entrenched place in the United States. Beginning in the 1990s, however, congressional and stakeholder demands for more up-to-date data than the ten-year cycle could provide prompted Census Bureau efforts to design a continuous measurement survey. In 1994 the Bureau established a Continuous Measurement Office tasked with developing all materials, procedures, questionnaires, and methods for the new program. The Census Bureau conducted extensive consultations with data users, researchers, stakeholders, and experts within and outside the state as well as a comprehensive testing program between 1995 and 2003. Proponents argued that an ongoing survey is an improvement over the census long-form in that it offers greater flexibility, divides a nationwide workload into manageable

[31] Ibid., 7. [32] Ibid., 9. [33] Ibid., 8.

pieces, can capture the demographic complexities of American life in a timelier manner, and is generally more efficient and effective.[34] The implementation of the American Community Survey (ACS) in 2010 replaced the long-form of the decennial census. The short form contained only that information constitutionally mandated as necessary to fully enumerate the population to apportion the House of Representatives.[35] The questions on Hispanic origin (question 8) and race (question 9) were included on the short form, sent to every American household.

In recent years, however, there have been several unsuccessful attempts to either defund or completely eliminate the ACS. In 2012 the Republican-controlled House of Representatives voted to eliminate the survey altogether. "This is a program that intrudes on people's lives, just like the Environmental Protection Agency or bank regulators," argued Representative Daniel Webster (R-FL), the bill's sponsor. He continued: "We're spending $70 per person to fill this out. That's just not cost effective ... What really promotes business in this country is liberty, not demand for information."[36] With some levelling charges that the survey is invasive and unnecessary,[37] legislators also considered making the ACS voluntary. Speaking before the Committee on Oversight and Government Reform, sociologist and former Director of the Census Bureau Robert M. Groves suggested that Canada's experience in replacing its mandatory census long-form with a voluntary survey (discussed further below) served as a cautionary tale, stating:

> In 2003, we briefed the subcommittee on the findings [of the voluntary ACS experiment] ... In addition, in 2011 Statistics Canada completed a voluntary survey that is similar to the ACS. Some of the things that we have learned from

[34] See U.S. Census Bureau, *Meeting 21st Century Demographic Data Needs – Implementing the American Community Survey: July 2001. Report 1: Demonstrating Operational Feasibility* (Washington D.C.: U.S. Census Bureau, 2001); Mark Mather, Kerri L. Rivers, and Linda A. Jacobsen, "The American Community Survey," *Population Bulletin* 60, no. 3 (2005); Deborah H. Griffin and Preston Jay Waite, "American Community Survey Overview and the Role of External Evaluations," *Population Research Policy Review* 25, no. 3 (2006): 201–223.

[35] U.S. Census Bureau, *Meeting 21st Century Demographic Data Needs*, 1.

[36] Catherine Rampell, "The Beginning of the End of the Census?" *The New York Times*, May 19, 2012, accessed July 16, 2013, www.nytimes.com/2012/05/20/sunday-review/the-debate-over-the-american-community-survey.html?_r=0

[37] Carl Bialik, "Census Gets Questions on Mandatory Queries," *Wall Street Journal*, March 30, 2012, accessed July 16, 2013, http://online.wsj.com/news/articles/SB10001424052702303404704577311540585680300

our test and Canada's experience lead us to believe that there would be major negative impacts if the ACS were a voluntary survey.[38]

The most recent effort, spearheaded by Representative Jeff Duncan (R-SC) in April 2013, proposed to eliminate the ACS along with any other small surveys not directly related to the decennial census.[39] Though the bill died when the 113th Congress came to an end, funding cuts continue to impact the ability of the Census Bureau to produce timely and robust data. The 2013 budget provided the Bureau with discretionary funding of $858 million, $112 million (or 11 percent) below President Obama's request of $970 million. According to the Census Director's blog, these reductions "undermine the ACS's ability to serve as a test bed for the 2020 Census and will likely delay planned ACS content and instrument research and testing."[40] For now, the ACS will continue to exist, but not without political battles to keep the survey alive.

In contrast, the government of Canada suddenly announced in June 2010 that it would eliminate the mandatory long-form of the census, which features questions on race and ethnicity, in the name of protecting the privacy rights of Canadians. The Conservative government framed the change as necessary in order to safeguard the privacy of Canadians. According to the Prime Minister's Office, "The government made this decision because we do not believe Canadians should be forced, under threat of fines, jail, or both, to disclose extensive private and personal information."[41] The official statement from Minister of Industry Tony Clement reiterated that the long-form was abandoned because of privacy concerns:

In the past, the Government of Canada received complaints about the long-form census from citizens who felt it was an intrusion of their privacy. The government does not think it is necessary for Canadians to provide Statistics Canada with the number of bedrooms in their house, or what time of day they leave for work, or how long it takes them to get there. The government does not believe it is

[38] Robert M. Groves, *The Pros and Cons of Making the American Community Survey Voluntary*, Statement to the Committee on Oversight and Government Reform, United States House of Representatives, March 2012.

[39] United States Congress, HR 1638: Census Reform Act of 2013, United States House of Representatives, https://beta.congress.gov/bill/113th-congress/house-bill/1638.

[40] Tom Mesenbourg, "Census Bureau Budget Update," June 19, 2013, accessed July 14, 2014, http://directorsblog.blogs.census.gov/2013/06/19/census-bureau-budget-update-2/

[41] M. Valpy, "Harper's Census Push Months in the Making," *Globe and Mail*, July 26, 2010.

appropriate to force Canadians to divulge personal information under threat of prosecution.[42]

A voluntary National Household Survey (NHS) replaced the mandatory long-form in 2011.

The announcement incited a furor of strange bedfellows, from business to labor, who publicly opposed the change.[43] Even those organizations ideologically aligned with the Conservative Party, including the Canadian Chamber of Commerce, the Canadian Association for Business Economics, the Toronto Board of Trade, and the Canadian Marketing Association, spoke out against the decision.[44] Critics charged that the shift to a voluntary survey was driven far more by ideology than a genuine threat to privacy, especially given that Federal Privacy Commissioner Jennifer Stoddart confirmed that just three complaints about the census were filed between 2000 and 2010. The fact that no one had ever been sent to prison for failing to complete a census form and that the government received only 166 complaints for the 2011 Census out of 12 million forms led many to assume some kind of ulterior motive for this abrupt change.[45] Political scientist Paul Saurette, for example, argues that this development was part of Prime Minister Stephen Harper's longer-term ideological goal to cultivate an enduring set of conservative principles that underlay public policy in Canada.[46] Unlike the development of the ACS or "Beyond 2011," which were decades in the making, this decision caught even Statistics Canada by surprise. The Chief Statistician, Munir Sheikh, resigned over the

[42] Tony Clement, *Statement on 2011 Census*, Minister of Industry, Science and Technology, July 2010, accessed June 21, 2016, www.marketwired.com/press-release/statement-on-2011-census-1289664.htm

[43] At last count, more than 400 organizations had publicly denounced the decision. Many of their letters to the government detailing the negative effects of this change can be found here: http://datalibre.ca/census-watch/

[44] Debra Thompson, "The Politics of the Census: Lessons from Abroad," *Canadian Public Policy* 36, no. 3 (2010): 377–382.

[45] John Ibbitson, "Survey Says: Government Still Not Listening on the Census," *The Globe and Mail*, July 27, 2010, accessed June 21, 2016, www.theglobeandmail.com/news/politics/survey-says-government-still-not-listening-on-census/article1387919/

[46] Paul Saurette, "When Smart Parties Make Stupid Decisions," *Mark News*, July 23, 2010. See also Michael Darroch and Gordon Darroch, "Commentary: Losing Our Census," *Canadian Journal of Communication* 35, no. 4 (2010): 609–617; William Ramp and Trevor W. Harrison, "Libertarian Populism, Neoliberal Rationality, and the Mandatory Long-Form Census: Implications for Sociology," *Canadian Journal of Sociology* 37, no. 3 (2012): 273–294; Michael Yeo, "The Rights of Science and the Rights of Politics: Lessons from the Long-Form Census Controversy," *Canadian Journal of Sociology* 37, no. 3 (2012): 295–317.

government's insinuation that Statistics Canada was firmly behind the decision, publicly stating that a voluntary survey simply cannot be a substitute for the mandatory census.

The questions on ethnicity and race, along with other questions about immigrants, Aboriginal people, and income levels, were not included on the eight-question mandatory short form. Though the NHS was sent to more households – a third, rather than the 20 percent sample of the long-form census – at the time Statistics Canada predicted a 50 percent response rate for the NHS. The data, released in May 2013, are based on a country-wide response rate of 68.6 percent,[47] a far cry from the 94 percent response rate of the 2006 Census. Even with its efforts to mitigate the problems of replacing the mandatory census form with a voluntary survey, the agency issued strong warnings about the validity and comparability of NHS data.[48] The selection bias of respondents compounds the problem. As Green and Milligan state, "rather than sampling from all the adults in Canada, we are sampling from the population of adults who chose to respond to a survey."[49] Already undercounted in mandatory surveys, visible minority and Aboriginal population groups were caught in the inevitable sampling errors of the NHS. The margins were missed and as a result Canada appears "less variant, less unequal, and more middling."[50]

During their 2015 federal election campaign the Liberal Party of Canada vowed to "immediately" restore the long-form census; once gaining power the new government kept its campaign promise just one day after the Prime Minister Justin Trudeau and his Cabinet were sworn into office. Trudeau stated that his party is "committed to a government that functions based on evidence and facts and long-form censuses are an important part of making sure we're serving constituents in our communities."[51] When Census Day came in May 2016, Canadians were apparently so enthusiastic about filling out their short- and long-form censuses

[47] Statistics Canada, "National Household Survey: Final Response Rates," accessed July 15, 2014, www12.statcan.gc.ca/nhs-enm/2011/ref/about-apropos/nhs-enm_r012.cfm?Lang=E. Note that the weighed response rates are 77.2 percent.

[48] Statistics Canada, "NHS: Data quality," accessed July 15, 2014, www12.statcan.gc.ca/NHS-ENM/2011/ref/about-apropos/nhs-enm_r005-eng.cfm

[49] David A. Green and Kevin Milligan "The Importance of the Long Form Census to Canada," *Canadian Public Policy* 36, no. 3 (2010): 384.

[50] Darroch and Darroch, "Commentary: Losing our Census," 612.

[51] Kathleen Harris, "Mandatory Long-Form Census Restored by New Liberal Government," CBC News, November 5, 2015, accessed June 21, 2016, www.cbc.ca/news/politics/canada-liberal-census-data-1.3305271

that the high volume of those attempting to complete their censuses online crashed the Statistics Canada website.[52]

STATE/RACE – THE SCHEMATIC STATE

All modern states seek to establish some degree of coherence on the core elements of life without which the maintenance of social, economic, and political order would be impossible.[53] One of the most pervasive ways that states have viewed, divided, and categorized their populations is through the prism of race. No matter how much more convenient it would be to simply adopt a definition of race that aligns with the one provided by the state, the comparative project undertaken in this book demonstrates how dominant conceptualizations of race, which often become entrenched in state-driven classificatory structures, have shifted over time and can vary between places, even within the short decade between censuses. These "statistical races," former Census Bureau Director and political scientist Kenneth Prewitt argues, "are not accidents of history. They have been deliberately constructed and reconstructed by the government. They are the tools of government, with political purposes and policy consequences – more so even than the biological races of the nineteenth century or the socially constructed races from twentieth-century anthropology or what are termed *identity races* in our current times."[54]

Statistical races may be an invention of state bureaucracy, but the concept of race itself requires a more complicated conceptualization. Race has always existed both through and beyond the imperatives of state classification, brought into being through the multitude of governing practices that require social, legal, economic, and political demarcations to mark and maintain unequal entry and access points to personhood, privilege, privacy, property, protection, and prosperity. Though several notable scholars of comparative politics, including Andreas Wimmer and Rogers Brubaker,[55] have made a persuasive case that race should be

[52] John Bowman, "Canadians' 'Enthusiasm' for Census Brings Down StatsCan Website," CBC News, May 3, 2016, accessed June 21, 2016, www.cbc.ca/news/trending/census-2016-nerds-1.3563808

[53] King and Stears, "How the U.S. State Works," 509.

[54] Kenneth Prewitt, *What is Your Race? The Census and Our Flawed Efforts to Classify Americans* (Princeton and Oxford: Princeton University Press, 2013), 4 (emphasis in original).

[55] Rogers Brubaker, "Ethnicity, Race, and Nationalism," *Annual Review of Sociology* 35 (2009): 21–42; Wimmer, "The Making and Unmaking of Ethnic Boundaries." Conversely, see Winant, "Race, Ethnicity, and Social Science," and Michael Hanchard

subsumed under a broader concept of ethnicity, throughout this book race is examined as an analytically distinct concept. Indeed, one of the telling insights that arises from the preceding analysis is the various ways that the discursive shift to ethnicity has, at different times and in different places, worked to foreclose serious and more substantive discussions about the prevalence of systemic racism, the pervasive power of white privilege, and the extent that race is tangled and nested with other forms of identity, including ethnicity, gender, class, sexuality, and religion.

There is much to be gained in analytical terms, I have suggested, by focusing on racial transnationalism, particularly in the manifestation of macro-level ideational shifts – what I have called "moments" – in which global understandings of the meaning of race and racial difference, the legitimate ends of governing structures that organize and engage racial concepts, and the appropriate means of achieving these ends have changed over time, driven by forces that were *interactively* domestic, international, and transnational. By tracing the evolution of racial worldviews over time, this study shows how these transnational ideas informed, but did not predetermine, modes of racial governance of which the census is but one example – albeit one defined by its support of and connection to many other racial projects: slavery, immigration policy, colonialism, human rights, anti-discrimination laws, models of multiculturalism, and multiracialism.

To query the role of the census in the construction of race and racial boundaries, as this book has attempted to do, leads directly to the doorstep of the state. If politics concern the relationship between state and society, racial politics have historically involved efforts of the state to manage and control racial populations, immediately bringing to mind the histories of white settler societies and imperial powers and the colonies they controlled, which have been saturated with racial anxieties. Policies, laws, and regulations designed to maintain a racialized social, political, and economic order permeated the lives of those whose superficial morphological characteristics betrayed a status of privilege or subjugation. The racialization of politics also continues in contemporary times. The transnational flows of people and ideas have created multiracial and multicultural societies around the world. Pervasive transnational norms of human rights, the end of *de jure* discrimination in liberal democracies, and the widespread implementation of anti-discrimination protections in

and Erin Aeran Chung, "From Race Relations to Comparative Race Politics: A Survey of Cross-National Scholarship on Race in the Social Sciences," *Du Bois Review* 1, no. 2 (2004): 319–343.

both domestic and international realms have largely failed to eradicate racism and racial disadvantage. Laws and policies continue to invoke racial classifications in human rights codes, government programming, and diversity governance, and the redistributive function of the welfare state can work to solidify or erode racial stratification through either government action or inaction. The invocation or avoidance of race can alter voting behavior or electoral patterns, and the recent Obamafication of the American political landscape has made race a more obvious element of elite politics. Politics is also racial for the ways in which social groups use, challenge, and transform race to converse with the state. Race informs how people form preferences, articulate interests, and build coalitions. More importantly, as one of the most powerful social signifiers of identity and difference, race works to connect and divide the lives of individuals, encompassing fundamental experiences of self and belonging, consciousness and recognition.

Given the extraordinary role of the state in defining and manipulating racial categorizations and classification schema, what does it mean to see like/be like a racial state? In an age when the normative imperative of human rights is long established in the international sphere and states take pride in their legislative prohibitions of racial discrimination, do we believe in the benign state – the last great hope that non-whites have to combat a racially stratified society – that protects its citizenry from the social injustices of racial prejudice and disadvantage? Or are we still faced with the sinister state of old, which actively ascribes the racial characteristics it then uses to hierarchically order society and maintain a national, if not global, system of white supremacy? Is the state a monolith with well-defined interests, an arena where iron triangles are forged, or a fragmented collection of autonomous entities that fight political battles over policy outputs? Should the concept of the state be abandoned altogether, drawing our focus instead to the ideological preferences and governing practices that support racial orders and racial alliances?[56]

The lens of racial census politics over time and space provides insight into the ways that the state is neither inherently sinister nor benign, but is

[56] Compare Omi and Winant, *Racial Formation*, Anthony Marx, *Making Race and Nation: A Comparison of the United States, South Africa and Brazil* (Cambridge: Cambridge University Press, 1998), Lieberman, "Ideas, Institutions, and Political Order," King and Smith, "Racial Orders," and Jennifer Hochschild, Vesla Weaver, and Traci Burch, *Creating a New Racial Order: How Immigration, Multiracialism, Genomics, and the Young can Remake Race in America* (Princeton and Oxford: Princeton University Press, 2012).

instead fundamentally *schematic*. As suggested above, it is in the nature of the state to create meaningful and legible social categories. Like other forms of standardization, the racial categories and classification rules in the census and many other areas of law, administration, and policy help to regulate and calibrate social life by imbuing social concepts with power and legitimacy. Standards and schematics are etymologically laudable in the ways that they help set goals, benchmarks, and aspirations, but they also serve as means of suppressing or erasing individuality,[57] at worst akin to being "treated like a number" by a faceless, nameless agent of bureaucratic control. As an instrument of statecraft, the purpose of the census is to make the population legible – at times *racially* legible – a premise I examine in more detail below. Racial legibility is a powerful, sometimes subtle, sometimes explicit means of organizing social life, and as such there are inevitable normative dimensions of creating racial schematics. Much depends, however, on the specific consequences, both intended and unintended, of how rules of racial classifications and the construction of racial boundaries are put to use in the regulation of racial orders.

The concept of a schematic state implicates the operation of state power on two concurrent fronts. As an arena where agents, social groups, and state agencies wage battle over competing interests and ideas in census categorizations, agreement over final policy outputs is forged through negotiation. Policy entrepreneurs, particularly those in powerful institutional positions that can leverage their political or social capital (for example, Joseph-Charles Taché, Margaret Thatcher, Tom Sawyer, Newt Gingrich), are highly influential. Agents, however, always operate within political structures and institutions that can constrain and enable the potential for policy change. The centralization of authority and the horizontal organization of a nation's statistical system, the autonomy of statistical agencies to operate free of political or societal influence, and the protocols of census administration (including the policy feedback effects that arise from traditions of racial enumeration) shape the conditions under which change may occur. The categorical imperatives that arise from prominent racial projects of the state also provide institutional incentives to count by race or to draw racial boundaries in specific ways.

The official racial schematic promoted by the census renders these political battles over policy outputs invisible and simultaneously creates

[57] Stefan Timmermans and Steven Epstein, "A World of Standards but not a Standard World: Toward a Sociology of Standards and Standardization," *Annual Review of Sociology* 36 (2010): 71.

an image of the state as a single, coherent, unitary actor. State-backed racial fictions can appear to be very real – and sometimes very troubling – to those who must abide by their demands, in part because any technocratic attempt to solidify race will always be insufficient to capture the messy realities of racial identity and identification. These contradictions are not aberrations of an incomplete system of racial classification, but are inherent to all racial schema because the definition of race has never been monopolized by state power. For example, Richard Iton's articulation of a black fantastic refers to the "minor-key sensibilities generated from the experiences of the underground, the vagabond, and those constituencies marked as deviant – notions of being that are inevitably aligned within, in conversation with, against, and articulated beyond the boundaries of the modern" – an acknowledgment that the division between what is often understood as the formal realm of politics and informal realm of popular culture has created "governmentalities and conventional notions of the political, the public sphere, and civil society that depend on the exclusion of blacks and other nonwhites from meaningful participation on their ongoing reconstitution as raw material for the naturalization of modern arrangements."[58] From a more transnational purview, Paul Gilroy's conceptualization of the Black Atlantic "provides an invitation to move into the contested spaces between the local and the global in ways that do not privilege the modern nation state and its institutional order over the sub-national and supra-national networks and patterns of power, communication and conflict that they work to discipline, regulate and govern."[59] By transforming the concept of space to include communicative circuitry rather than a fixed idea of place, diasporic ripples of racial consciousness enable dispersed populations to converse, interact, and sometimes synchronize even as struggles for civil rights or post-colonial aspirations take different forms on the shores of the Atlantic Anglosphere.[60]

More concretely, the micro-level discrepancies between imposed racial identity – the race others ascribe to me – and the ways I choose to self-identify on the census, on immigration forms, or on employment records speak to the difficulties of fully capturing the dynamism, and the unrealized im/possibilites of race. For example, one of the biggest controversies

[58] Iton, *In Search of the Black Fantastic*, 16–17.

[59] Paul Gilroy, "Route Work: The Black Atlantic and the Politics of Exile," in *The Post-Colonial Question: Common Skies, Divided Horizons*, eds. Iain Chambers and Lidia Curti (London and New York: Routledge, 1996), 22.

[60] Ibid., 17–29.

concerning the 2010 American census was not about whether a question on race should appear, but instead concerned what answer President Barack Obama provided on his census form. His choice to identify as black rather than check more than one box puzzled some and enraged others. Abigail Thernstrom, conservative political scientist and vice-chair of the United States Commission on Civil Rights, decried in the *Wall Street Journal* that in identifying as black, Obama "disowned his white mother, and, by extension, his maternal grandparents who acted as surrogate parents for much of his boyhood."[61] By doing "what was expected of him," John Judis of *The New Republic* wrote, the President "confirmed an enduring legacy of American racism."[62] George Rodriguez of the *L.A. Times* argued that Obama missed a historic opportunity to articulate a more nuanced racial vision for America and also bucked a trend: in April 2011, the Census Bureau confirmed that the number of Americans who identified as more than one race on the census grew by 32 percent over the past decade.[63]

The state interactively mediates among these forces – transnational, domestic, societal – in formulating racial schematics, which fix and bind inputs that are themselves moving targets. The ground under the multicultural and multiracial moments, for example, is shifting. In 2010, political elites of several European countries proclaimed, in quick succession, that multiculturalism was a failed state experiment. Speaking at the Munich Security Conference in February 2011, British Prime Minister David Cameron said multiculturalism was partially to blame for the rise of home-grown terrorism. "Under the doctrine of state multiculturalism," he claimed,

> we have encouraged different cultures to live separate lives, apart from each other and apart from the mainstream. We've failed to provide a vision of society to which they feel they want to belong. We've even tolerated these segregated communities behaving in ways that run completely counter to our values ... when a white person holds objectionable views, for instance, we rightly condemn them. But when equally unacceptable views or practices come from

[61] Abigail Thernstrom, "Obama's Census Identity," *The Wall Street Journal*, April 16, 2010, accessed November 10, 2011, http://online.wsj.com/article/SB10001424052702303720604575169783989253108.html

[62] John B. Judis, "Census Nonsense," *The New Republic*, April 7, 2010, accessed June 21, 2016, www.newrepublic.com/article/74334/census-nonsense

[63] Gregory Rodriguez, "President Obama: At Odds with Clear Demographic Trends toward Multiracial Pride," *LA Times* April 4, 2011, accessed November 10, 2011, www.latimes.com/news/opinion/commentary/la-oe-rodriguez-column-obama-race-20110404,0,3716973.column

someone who isn't white, we've been too cautious frankly – frankly, even afraid – to stand up to them.[64]

The multicultural project was attacked along similar lines by German Chancellor Angela Merkel and French President Nicolas Sarkozy, who made similar remarks about their countries. The "hands-off tolerance" throughout Europe has encouraged the rise of extreme Muslim groups, they argued; rather than state-driven multiculturalism, governments should be more concerned with fostering a strong national identity.

In practice, many observers suggest there is a growing retrenchment of multicultural policies.[65] Christian Joppke argues that a number of states that had previously been committed to multiculturalism are now replacing old policies with more centrist policies of civic integration. This trend is particularly prominent in Europe, which has begun a wholesale retreat from multiculturalism because of widely held beliefs that the inherent shortcomings of these policies are responsible for the socio-economic marginalization and self-segregation of immigrants and their children.[66] The most telling example comes from the Netherlands, which abandoned its multicultural policies of the 1980s in favor of compulsory, borderline coercive programs to ensure immigrant assimilation into Dutch society and culture by the 2000s.[67] Even Will Kymlicka, one of the most prominent proponents of liberal multiculturalism, admits that its Canadian version is "under attack today, more than ever."[68]

The unsettling of multicultural norms is paralleled by more substantive and more consequential challenges to the relationship between race and the state posed by the resurgence of color-blind and invention of post-racial ideologies. These arguments have most often and most destructively been used to attack affirmative action policies, a racial project that rests on a foundation of racial classification and enumeration. The ethical value of color-blindness, once used as a weapon by NAACP counsel Thurgood

[64] David Cameron, Speech at Munich Security Conference, February 5, 2011, accessed November 5, 2011, www.number10.gov.uk/news/pms-speech-at-munich-security-conference/

[65] Rogers Brubaker, "The Return of Assimilation? Changing Perspectives on Immigration and its Sequels in France, Germany and the United States," *Ethnic and Racial Studies* 24, no. 4 (2001): 531–548; Joppke, "The Retreat of Multiculturalism."

[66] Joppke, "The Retreat of Multiculturalism," 247–254.

[67] Ellie Vasta, "From Ethnic Minorities to Ethnic Majority Policy: Multiculturalism and the Shift to Assimilationism in the Netherlands," *Ethnic and Racial Studies* 30, no. 5 (2007): 713–740.

[68] Will Kymlicka, *Finding Our Way: Rethinking Ethnocultural Relations in Canada* (Toronto: Oxford University Press, 1998), 16.

Marshall in arguing for the end of racial segregation in *Brown v. Board of Education*, is now used by opponents of affirmative action to dismantle what they see as a regime of special treatment. "The way to stop discrimination on the basis of race," Justice Roberts argued in *Parents Involved v. Seattle*, "is to stop discriminating on the basis of race." Roberts' logic in this case, widely criticized by critical race theorists and a clear example of what Ian Haney Lopez calls "racial jujitsu," effectively co-opts the moral force of the civil rights movement, deploys that power to attack attempts at racial redress by defining racism as any and all use of race, and simultaneously defends racial hierarchies by defining non-racism as all interactions not explicitly predicated on race – no matter how racialized their consequences.[69] In the 2013 decision *Fisher v. University of Texas at Austin*, the Supreme Court reaffirmed the scrutiny of any use of racial classifications in public policy: any consideration of race must serve a compelling government interest; while the educational benefits of a diverse student body in institutions of higher education meet the definition of a compelling interest, redressing past circumstances of racial discrimination does not; and workable, race-neutral alternatives that could produce the same outcome should be considered before turning to racial classifications. More recently, a starkly divided court ruled in *Schuette v. Coalition to Defend Affirmative Action* that Michigan voters could ban race-conscious university admissions policies. In response to the majority opinion in this case and the tendency of conservative justices to underplay the realities of racial formations, Justice Sotomayor countered that "the way to stop discrimination on the basis of race is to speak openly and candidly on the subject of race, and to apply the Constitution with eyes open to the unfortunate effects of centuries of racial discrimination."[70]

Color-blind ideologies demand a removal of the state from racial affairs insofar as government action can be used to rectify persistent and structural inequality – hence the attack on affirmative action. These developments are connected to and compounded by the neoliberal turn at the end of the twentieth century, largely defined by the prominence of market ideologies that challenge underlying principles of state intervention and the delivery of public goods and services.[71] In fact, as a set of policies, multiculturalism has

[69] Lopez, "Is the 'Post' in Post-Racial," 815–817.

[70] *Schuette v. Coalition to Defend Affirmative Action* 572 U.S. ___ (2014), at 45–46.

[71] Mark Blyth, *Great Transformations: Economic Ideas and Institutional Change in the Twentieth Century* (Cambridge: Cambridge University Press, 2002).

been a target of neoliberal change.[72] Once rooted in a commitment to remedying racial disadvantages and promoting an egalitarian conception of nationhood and citizenship, the neoliberalization of multiculturalism is indifferent to progressive equality-seeking components of diversity, focusing instead on the creation of a cosmopolitan, global, self-sufficient market actor[73] or even commodifying diversity, racialized experiences, and cultural affinities.[74] Significantly altering the relationship between government and knowledge by recasting governing activities as nonpolitical and nonideological problems as in need of technical and bureaucratically efficient solutions, creating dominant scripts of personhood that focus on individuality and market productivity as the most important signifiers of self-worth, and generating support for neoliberal reforms via the representation of brown and black bodies as the problematic, ungovernable, economically deficient exception to market productivity, neoliberalism relies on ideas about race at the same time that it invigorates racial subjectivities.[75] These forms of racial governance create more insidious methods for disciplining by race in, for example, the generation of systemic racial disparities through the neoliberal paternalism of poverty governance and mass incarceration.[76] Building on Iton's formulation of a haunting "duppy state" that marks "the potent afterlife, mocking persistence, and resurgence – rather than remission – of coloniality,"[77] the dark side of the schematic state (the *scheming*

[72] Matt James, "Neoliberal Heritage Redress," in *Reconciling Canada: Critical Perspectives on the Culture of Redress*, eds. Jennifer Henderson and Pauline Wakeham (Toronto: University of Toronto Press, 2013), 31–45.

[73] Will Kymlicka, "Neoliberal Multiculturalism?" in *Social Resilience in the Neoliberal Era*, eds. Peter Hall and Michèle Lamont (New York: Cambridge University Press, 2013), 99–125.

[74] Yasmeen Abu-Laban and Christina Gabriel, *Selling Diversity: Immigration, Multiculturalism, Employment Equity and Globalization* (Peterborough: Broadview Press, 2002).

[75] Jodi Melamed, "The Spirit of Neoliberalism: From Racial Liberalism to Neoliberal Multiculturalism," *Social Text* 24, no. 4 (2006): 1–24; Aihwa Ong, *Neoliberalism as Exception: Mutations in Citizenship and Sovereignty* (Durham and London: Duke University Press, 2006); Wacquant, *Punishing the Poor*; Soss et al., *Disciplining the Poor*; Lester K. Spence, *Stare in the Darkness: The Limits of Hip Hop and Black Politics* (Minneapolis and London: University of Minnesota Press, 2011); Hall and Lamont, *Social Resilience in the Neoliberal Era*; Wendy Brown, *Undoing the Demos: Neoliberalism's Stealth Revolution* (Cambridge: MIT Press, 2015); Spence, *Knocking the Hustle*.

[76] Wacquant, *Punishing the Poor*; Michelle Alexander, *The New Jim Crow: Mass Incarceration in the Age of Colorblindness* (New York: The New Press, 2010); Soss et al., *Disciplining the Poor*.

[77] Iton, *In Search of the Black Fantastic*, 135.

state) implicates the extent to which state power operates by maintaining centuries-old vestiges of white supremacy and racial domination. The schematic state is a normative state, in both senses of the phrase.

CENSUS/RACE – THE POSSIBILITY AND PERIL OF RACIAL LEGIBILITY

From the nineteenth to the mid-twentieth century, racial classifications in the census and other areas of law and policy were employed to serve what Desmond King and Rogers Smith have called a racially ascriptive American ideological tradition;[78] an ideational, if not ideological, tradition shared by Canada and Britain's colonial governing logic during the same time period, as demonstrated in Chapter 3. Fast-forward to the twenty-first century and racial statistics are widely accepted as an appropriate means for monitoring circumstances of racial disadvantage. In Europe, data collection has been sanctioned by the various equality bodies of the European Union and many countries now collect heterogeneous forms of racial or ethnic data. Of the forty-one countries covered by Patrick Simon's review of the collection of ethnic statistics in Europe, country of birth and citizenship are almost universally gathered by thirty-nine countries, while twenty-two collect data on ethnicity, usually termed by reference to nationality. Even those nineteen countries that do not collect ethnic data directly use country of birth and citizenship as ethnic proxies; in addition, six countries in northern Europe have an additional question on parents' place of birth.[79] Of the seventy-one millennium-round censuses conducted in the British Commonwealth, fifty inquired into citizenship or nationality, while forty-three featured questions on race or ethnicity.[80] On a global scale, a recent quantitative analysis of censuses in 151 countries between 1995 and 2004 found that when ethnicity is operationalized to include terms such as ethnic group, descent, ancestry, race, indigenous, tribe, language, mother tongue, nationality, and national origins, more than 70 percent of national censuses featured some form of ethnic enumeration. Ethnic statistics are being produced in all parts of the world: 59 percent of countries in Europe;

[78] Smith, *Civic Ideals*; King and Smith, *Still a House Divided.*

[79] Patrick Simon, *"Ethnic" Statistics and Data Protection in the Council of Europe Countries: Study Report, European Commission against Racism and Intolerance* (Strasbourg: Council of Europe, 2007).

[80] Anthony J. Christopher, "Questions of Identity in the Millennium Round of Commonwealth Censuses," *Population Studies* 60, no. 3 (2006): 344–347.

68 percent in Africa and Asia, respectively; 86 percent in North America; and 93 percent of Oceania.[81] Tellingly, the common conclusion amongst these disparate studies of the collection of ethnic and racial statistics – including my own – is the lack of worldwide consensus about what, exactly, ethnicity and race are, and how best to measure them.

All census classifications, however, are a means of making the population racially legible, often in accordance with nationally specific cultural repertoires. The creation, promotion, and manipulation of racial classification schema is a central type of social regulation; it is through the state's articulation of racial categories that they become "actionable objects" (for example, *the* multiracial population), fixed in time and space.[82] But legible outputs are never set in stone once and for all. With the symbolic, legal, and political elements of census politics at play, actors inside and outside the state engage in an interpretive struggle over the boundaries of race. Social groups have often mobilized to add, alter, or amend the census classifications through "census activism," which I define as a form of contentious politics in which individuals and/or groups strategically target the census, either at the planning stage or while it is being carried out, in order to force the government to accommodate a wide variety of concerns related to the officially recognized and promoted racial and ethnic schematic of the nation. Since at least the multicultural moment and the implementation of self-enumeration, three major types of census activism emerge from the comparison of the United States, Canada, and Great Britain.

First, *minority mobilization for racial counting* refers to situations when minorities seeking material benefits or symbolic recognition mobilize and lobby the government for inclusion on the census. This activism can occur in order to create a new question on race or ethnicity on the census, or where a question already exists, to advocate for the creation of new racial categories or a reimagining of racial classification rules. The creation of a Hispanic origin question on the United States census in 1970, the addition of several Asian categories in 1980 and 1990, and the efforts of the mixed-race social movement during the federal review process in the 1990s are prime examples, as are the lobby efforts on behalf of the Irish to

[81] Tahu Kukutai and Victor Thompson, "'Inside Out': The Politics of Ethnically Enumerating the Nation by Ethnicity," in *Social Statistics and Ethnic Diversity: Cross-National Perspectives in Classifications and Identity Politics*, eds. Patrick Simon, Victor Piché, and Amelie Gagnon (Cham: Springer International Publishing, 2015), 39–51.

[82] Ruppert, "Producing Population."

gain inclusion in the ethnic question on the 2001 Census of England and Wales. Clearly, not all minority mobilizations have been successful at achieving their goals. Political opportunity structures and the potential for coalition-building can be important factors that influence a lobby's strategies and targets. Much also depends on the mobilization of racial capital, including how well categorical claims align with the established racial schematic and cultural understandings of what race is and how it should be operationalized in public policy. Movements may seek to make categories and coherent identities through their claims; what matters is not necessarily the cohesiveness of the identity group itself, but, rather, the extent to which the identity being promoted is a recognizable constituency, given nationally specific racial repertoires and dominant scripts of racial legibility.

A second, less obvious form of census activism occurs when *racial majorities mobilize by refusing to be counted* in accordance with the established racial schematic during the execution of the census. In essence, this activism is a form of protest embedded in the exercise of interdependent power, "the ability to exert power over others by withdrawing or threatening to withdraw from social cooperation."[83] The "Count me Canadian!" campaign of the early 1990s, alongside similar mobilizations of majoritarian group identities during the same time period in New Zealand and Australia, result in what Tahu Kukutai and Robert Didham call patterns of "national naming," when the highest reported ethnic origins and ancestry groups on the census self-identify *as* the nation.[84] The precise reasons why racial majorities mobilize in this way are difficult to discern. Individuals may choose to identify with the nation as a way of rejecting racial and ethnic distinctions, or it could be part of a genuine belief in a post-racial world. It could also be a passive normalization of white privilege, a rejection of state-sanctioned multiculturalism policies, or an ideologically charged strategy to diminish minority group rights in these settler societies. For example, the refrain "we are all New Zealanders" has been prominent during the same times when Maori indigenous groups made claims to distinctiveness and about the persistence of racial inequality.[85] Finally,

[83] Francis Fox Piven, "Can Power from Below Change the World? 2007 Presidential Address," *American Sociological Review* 73, no. 1 (2008): 5.

[84] Tahu Kukutai and Robert Didham, "In Search of Ethnic New Zealanders: National Naming in the 2006 Census," *Social Policy Journal of New Zealand* 36 (2009): 46–62; Tahu Kukutai and Robert Didham, "Re-making the majority? Ethnic New Zealanders in the 2006 Census," *Ethnic and Racial Studies* 35, no. 8 (2012): 1427–1446.

[85] Kukutai and Didham, "In Search of Ethnic New Zealanders."

national naming could be a reconfiguration of ethnicity[86] or an evolving indigenous category[87] for second-, third-, or even fourth-generation citizens who feel a stronger connection to their national identification than their ethnic or ancestral origins. Respondents who demand this form of recognition by partaking in majority mobilization may have quite different reasons for doing so and, indeed, may not view their actions as activism at all. The census is an individual, or at least household-based, exercise. However, the cumulative effect of these coordinated actions – essentially, the challenge to established racial and ethnic schematics – can be quite consequential.

The final form of census activism occurs when *minorities mobilize against racial counting* in order to avoid the state's gaze. A different exercise of interdependent power, minority mobilization requires protestors to "break the rules" in order to leverage their subordinate position. For example, the 1979 campaign against Britain's census test question in Haringey and several Indian bands' refusal to cooperate with the Canadian census of 1981 were catalyzed by minority anxieties about the racial knowledge being accrued by the state and the consequences of being officially categorized in particular ways. Just as not counting by race can rearticulate a race-neutral or color-blind image of the nation, refusing to be counted can serve political and symbolic purposes when minorities remain highly suspicious of the state's intentions.

In order to construct legible racial schema, the state mediates between transnational and domestic forces. Racial legibility, therefore, is an interactive and dynamic process subject to changing conceptualizations of race, understandings of racial discrimination (both inflammatory and preventative), and aspirations for the racial composition of the nation. In Canada, the protocol of census administration that includes and orders racial designations according to the population counts of the previous census works in some ways to affirm racial legibility by virtue of response order effects,[88] which increases the likelihood that respondents will choose the categories presented at the top of the list thereby reifying the general distributive patterns of racial diversity, and in other ways enables a racial taxonomy that can morph alongside shifting societal trends in racial identification. For example, the racial categories of Question 19 on the 2006 Census and the 2011 NHS were identical, save three minor changes: in 2006 the "Chinese" category was listed second, but after census data revealed larger numbers of

[86] Ibid. [87] Pryor et al., "Measuring Ethnicity."

[88] Allyson Holbrook, "Response Order Effects," in *Encyclopedia of Survey Research Methods*, ed. Paul J. Lavrakas (Thousand Oaks: Sage Publications, 2008), 756.

- White
- South Asian *(e.g., East Indian, Pakistani, Sri Lankan, etc.)*
- Chinese
- Black
- Filipino
- Latin American
- Arab
- Southeast Asian *(e.g., Vietnamese, Cambodian, Malaysian, Laotian, etc.)*
- West Asian *(e.g., Iranian, Afghan, etc.)*
- Korean
- Japanese

Other — *Specify*

FIGURE 7.1: Canadian National Household Survey, 2011

the "South Asian" population group ("e.g. East Indian, Pakistani, Sri Lakan, etc.") the order of the groups in the 2011 NHS reflected this shift and listed "South Asian" second, following "White," and "Chinese" third; the "Arab" category, ranked eighth in 2006, surpassed the "Southeast Asian" category and was ranked seventh in 2011; and a "Korean" category was added after 2006 census data revealed the population to be 142,000, or 2.8 percent of the visible minority population (Figure 7.1).[89]

Great Britain's 2011 Census featured a new national identity question that was developed in response to public criticism of the 2001 ethnic question, which featured headings such as "Black/Black British" and "Asian/Asian British" but included a "British" closed box under the heading "White" – in effect, white respondents could *choose* to identify

[89] Statistics Canada, *Profile of Ethnic Origin and Visible Minorities for Canada, Provinces, Territories, Census Divisions and Census Subdivisions, 2006 Census*, accessed June 25, 2014, www12.statcan.ca/census-recensement/2006/dp-pd/prof/rel/Rp-eng.cfm?LANG=E&APATH=3&DETAIL=0&DIM=0&FL=A&FREE=0&GC=0&GID=0&GK=0&GRP=1&PID=92623&PRID=0&PTYPE=89103&S=0&SHOWALL=0&SUB=0&Temporal=2006&THEME=80&VID=0&VNAMEE=&VNAMEF=

15 How would you describe your national identity?
Tick all that apply
English
Welsh
Scottish
Northern Irish
British
Other, write in

FIGURE 7.2: Census of England and Wales, 2011 – Nationality Question

as British and non-white respondents could not. To challenge the state's established schematic, in England and Wales 70,000 people wrote in "Black British" under the "Other Black" free-text field.[90] Public and political concerns were also expressed in Wales about the lack of a Welsh option under the "White" heading, especially when contrasted with the 2001 Census of Scotland, which included a "Scottish" option.[91] In the final recommendation to include a national identity question that directly precedes the ethnic question (Figure 7.2), ONS revealed:

> Evidence also suggests that respondents are happier to express their ethnic group if they can also express their national identity. Without this opportunity there is a risk that proportions of ethnic minority populations could refuse to answer the ethnic group question or the census as a whole. Due to the close association of these questions, the introduction and development of the national identity question has formed part of the decision making process on the ethnic question.[92]

The 2011 Census also added "Gypsy/Irish Traveller" under the "White" heading and "Arab" under the "Other ethnic group" heading (Figure 7.3). Qualitative assessments based on the strength of need for information, the

[90] Office for National Statistics, *Final Recommended Questions for the 2011 Census in England and Wales: Ethnic Group* (London: ONS, 2009), 11.

[91] Office for National Statistics, *Consultation Summary Report of Responses to the 2011 Census Stakeholders Consultation 2006/07: Ethnic Group, National Identity, Religion and Language, England and Wales* (London: ONS, 2007), 43.

[92] Office for National Statistics, *Final Recommended Questions*, 11.

lack of alternative sources of information, the clarity and quality of the information collected and acceptability to respondents, and the comparability with 2001 data led ONS to conclude that these groups had the highest priority for inclusion.[93] Previous estimates of the population size of both these groups varied widely, but while Arabs consistently wrote in varying terms in the "Other ethnic group" free-text field, write-in responses for Gypsy/Irish Traveller were consistently low, presumably because of an unwillingness to identify with designations that have historically been discriminated against.[94]

Even more dramatic changes are afoot for the 2020 American census. In his influential book, *What Is Your Race?*, former Census Bureau Director Kenneth Prewitt calls for a radical change in how the American government queries race on the census. He argues that the problem of the twenty-first century is not just the color line, but how the color line intersects with the "nativity line," the "messy, fluid, overlapping issues that separate by color and by place of birth."[95] Both the color line and the nativity line suffer from "statistical deficiencies": while immigration statistics are insufficiently detailed and fail to provide information on the integration of the second-generation population into American society, statistics on race and ethnicity cannot encapsulate the growing disparities within racial groups, which are becoming as great as disparities between non-white and white groups.[96] Ultimately, Prewitt contends that the eventual abandonment of racial classification is the only way to bring a post-racial society into being.

Leaving Prewitt's assessment about the best way to achieve a post-racial society aside for the moment, his concerns that the census largely fails to encapsulate America's growing and complicated diversity are echoed by many. In the weeks leading up to the 2010 Census, Arab-American groups launched a media campaign called "Check it right; you ain't white!" Omar Masry, a city planner for Irvine, California, and campaign organizer, pointed to the racial profiling and discrimination often faced by Arab-Americans and the power of highlighting their group identity on the census form; as he told CNN in May 2010, "we're being profiled anyway, so why don't we take pride in ourselves and gain

93 Ibid., 43. See also Office for National Statistics, *Information Paper: Deciding which Tick-Boxes to add to the Ethnic Group Question in the 2011 England and Wales Census* (London: ONS, 2009).

94 Ibid., 18–19, 23–24.

95 Prewitt, *What Is Your Race?*, 154.

96 Ibid., 188–192. See also, for example, Christina M. Greer, *Black Ethnics: Race, Immigration, and the Pursuit of the American Dream* (Oxford and New York: Oxford University Press, 2013).

16 What is your ethnic group?

Choose **one** section from A to E, then tick **one** box to best describe your ethnic group or background

A White

- [ ] English/Welsh/Scottish/Northern Irish/British
- [ ] Irish
- [ ] Gypsy or Irish Traveller
- [ ] Any other White background, write in

B Mixed/multiple ethnic groups

- [ ] White and Black Caribbean
- [ ] White and Black African
- [ ] White and Asian
- [ ] Any other Mixed/multiple ethnic background, write in

C Asian/Asian British

- [ ] Indian
- [ ] Pakistani
- [ ] Bangladeshi
- [ ] Chinese
- [ ] Any other Asian background, write in

D Black/African/Caribbean/Black British

- [ ] African
- [ ] Caribbean
- [ ] Any other Black/African/Caribbean background, write in

E Other ethnic group

- [ ] Arab
- [ ] Any other ethnic group, write in

FIGURE 7.3: Census of England and Wales, 2011 – Ethnicity Question

advantage from it?"[97] Campaign organizers encouraged Arab-Americans to check the "some other race" box and write in their ancestries, and in the summer of 2012 the Arab American Institute followed up with a letter to the Census Bureau and OMB signed by thirty advocacy groups, asking for the creation of a Middle East and North African category.[98] The strategy of using "some other race" to build a racial constituency was also employed by more than 19 million Hispanics, representing about one-third of the total Hispanic population and a 24 percent increase in this reporting trend from the previous census.[99] An additional 13 percent did not answer the race question at all.[100] As Nicholas Jones, Chief of the Census Bureau's Racial Statistics Branch, explains, the "some other race" category was intended to be a small residual category for those respondents who did not identify with the OMB's standard racial classifications.[101] The fact that this category has grown rapidly since 1980 into the third largest racial group behind the "White" and "Black" categories speaks to the need, the Bureau contends, to reconsider the American racial schematic.

In 2010 the Census Bureau launched an extensive research program, the Census Alternative Questionnaire Experiment (AQE), to examine different formats for enumerating race and ethnicity in order to increase reporting in the standard OMB classifications, elicit detailed reporting of racial and ethnic groups, lower non-response rates, and increase the accuracy and reliability of census data.[102] According to Robert Groves, Director of the Census Bureau from 2009 to 2012, the research was also driven by an attempt to keep pace with the moving picture of American

97 John Blake, "Arab- and Persian-American campaign: 'Check it right' on census," *CNN*, May 14, 2010, accessed August 3, 2014, www.cnn.com/2010/US/04/01/census.check.it .right.campaign/

98 Haya El Nasser, "Arabs, Hispanics seeking better US Census recognition," *Aljazeera America*, December 17, 2013, accessed July 27, 2014, http://america.aljazeera.com/art icles/2013/12/17/arabs-hispanics-seekingbetteruscensusrecognition.html

99 Sharon R. Ennis, Mararys Rios-Vargas, and Nora G. Albert, *The Hispanic Population: 2010*, U.S. Census Bureau, Population Division (Washington D.C.: U.S. Census Bureau, 2011); Mararys Ríos, Fabián Romero, and Roberto Ramírez, *Race Reporting Among Hispanics: 2010*, U.S. Census Bureau Population Division Working Paper (Washington D.C.: U.S. Census Bureau, 2014).

100 Ríos et al., *Race Reporting Among Hispanics*, 9.

101 U.S. Department of Commerce, *Results of the 2010 Census Race and Hispanic Origin Alternative Questionnaire Experiment News Conference*, George Washington University, August 8, 2012, p. 20. Transcript available at: www.census.gov/2010cen sus/news/press-kits/aqe/aqe.html

102 Karen Humes, *2010 Census Alternative Questionnaire Experiment: Race and Hispanic Origin Treatments* (Washington D.C.: U.S. Census Bureau, 2009).

diversity and to "keep up with the concepts and the words that the public uses to describe racial and ethnic groups."[103] The experiment had three components: first, a mailout/mailback questionnaire that 488,604 household units received in lieu of the 2010 Census; second, the Census Bureau conducted telephone re-interviews of a 20 percent sample of the mail respondents about three months after the 2010 Census to assess the consistency, accuracy, and reliability of the answers provided by asking a series of questions about how people self-identify and collecting more information about their racial and ethnic backgrounds; and third, a series of sixty-seven focus groups with nearly 800 people across twenty-six cities in the United States were held to complement the first two quantitative survey methods and aid in understanding how people self-identify in the ways that they do. Together, these components were the largest and most extensive multi-method effort to explore alternative designs for racial and ethnic enumeration in American history.[104]

The AQE included seventeen different questionnaire designs[105] across three research areas. The first research area tested modified examples of the race and Hispanic origin questions, explored whether the removal of the term "Negro" from the "Black, African Am., or Negro" category would affect response rates, and tested a modified Hispanic origin question that permitted multiple responses. The second area explored several different approaches for combining the race and Hispanic origin queries into a single question. The third research area focused on ways to clarify the Asian and Native Hawaiian and Other Pacific Islander checkbox categories and ways to limit the use of the term "race" in the race question.

One of the most important findings of these experiments was that the combined question approach lowered non-response rates and responses in the "some other race" category. In designs in which race and Hispanic origin questions were separated, non-response rates to the race question ranged from 3.5 percent to 5.7 percent and non-response rates to the Hispanic origin question ranged from 4.1 percent to 5.4 percent. In comparison, designs that included race and Hispanic origin in the same

103 U.S. Department of Commerce, *Results of the 2010 Census Race and Hispanic Origin Alternative Questionnaire Experiment.*

104 Elizabeth Compton, Michael Bentley, Sharon Ennis, and Sonya Rastogi, *2010 Census Race and Hispanic Origin Alternative Questionnaire Experiment: Final Report*, 2010 Census Planning Memoranda Series (Washington D.C.: U.S. Census Bureau, 2013).

105 The AQE also included two control panels and fifteen experimental treatment panels. These different questionnaires are included in Compton et al., *2010 Census Race and Hispanic Origin Alternative Questionnaire Experiment: Final Report*, 106–122.

combined question (Figure 7.4) had non-response rates between 0.6 percent and 1.2 percent. The combined question designs also reduced the proportions that identified as "some other race" from 7 percent in the separate question formats to under 0.5 percent, largely due to Hispanics being able to "find their identity" within the race question. The combined question format therefore demonstrated a more accurate reflection of how Hispanics self-identify, and there were also few negative effects on the reporting of other groups. The combined question also led to higher reporting of multiple origins of both Hispanic and non-Hispanic respondents and other groups maintained consistent responses and response rates. In addition, testing revealed that the removal of the descriptor "Negro" had no negative effects on the data produced for the black population. Finally, the research demonstrated that when test designs included write-in spaces, black and white respondents were more likely to provide more detailed reporting on how they self-identify. The Census Bureau plans to explore the most optimal use of examples in this particular format, as well as strategies for collecting these data through other means.[106]

The focus groups provided feedback about the current 2010 Census question design and the alternative formats tested in the AQE. One concern that focus groups expressed consistently was that racial and ethnic groups were not "treated equally" on the 2010 Census or on the alternative design that included a separate Hispanic origin question. Respondents viewed this separation as unfair, with some concerned that Hispanics were being singled out for either discriminatory or advantageous treatment. Participants also commented that all groups should be able to write in their ethnic and racial identities and that the equal treatment of different groups required that all groups be provided with the same opportunity to identify with more detail, should they choose to do so. Additionally, some focus group participants felt that the inclusion of examples such as Egyptian or Lebanese under the "White" racial category was inaccurate and that a separate category should be added to encapsulate people of Middle Eastern and Northern African descent.[107] Given these AQE results, the Census Bureau recommended further testing of the combined race and Hispanic origin question to refine detailed Asian and detailed Hispanic reporting, as well as continued research into the optimal use of examples for each race and origin response category. In the end, the

[106] Ibid., 71–78.

[107] U.S. Department of Commerce, *Results of the 2010 Census Race and Hispanic Origin Alternative Questionnaire Experiment*, 24–25.

8. What is Person 1's race or origin? *Mark* ☒ *one or more boxes* **AND** *write in the specific race(s) or origin(s).*

☐ White — *Print origin(s), for example, German, Moroccan, Portuguese, Middle Eastern, Russian, and so on.*

☐ Black, African Am., or Negro — *Print origin(s), for example, African American, Haitian, Nigerian, and so on.*

☐ Hispanic, Latino, or Spanish origin — *Print origin(s), for example, Mexican, Puerto Rican, Cuban, Argentinean, Colombian, Dominican, Nicaraguan, Salvadoran, Spaniard, and so on.*

☐ American Indian or Alaska Native — *Print name of enrolled or principal tribe(s), for example, Sioux, Aleut, Mayan, and so on.*

☐ Asian — *Print origin(s), for example, Asian Indian, Chinese, Filipino, Japanese, Korean, Vietnamese, Hmong, Laotian, Thai, Pakistani, Cambodian, and so on.*

☐ Native Hawaiian or Other Pacific Islander — *Print origin(s), for example, Native Hawaiian, Guamanian or Chamorro, Samoan, Fijian, Tongan, and so on.*

☐ Some other race or origin — *Print race(s) or origin(s).*

FIGURE 7.4: United States Census Bureau Alternative Question Experiment, combined Hispanic origin and race question, X3 experimental panel

AQE is but the first in a series of steps to be taken in preparation for the 2020 Census. Beyond the continuing research into different wording and question format, any change to the census questionnaire would first have to be approved by the OMB and submitted to Congress by 2017.

Depending on what Congress ultimately decides to do, the proposed changes to a combined race and Hispanic origin question have the potential to provide more detailed, accurate, and reliable racial data. Moreover, the focus groups' feedback about perceptions of the signals of racial equity inherent in the presentation of categorical options for self-identification on the census implicate the continued symbolic function of the census as a mechanism through which social groups seek and attain recognition and validation from the state. Racial legibility is still largely driven by the legislative foundations and policy imperatives that necessitate the collection of racial statistics in the United States, some of which have been challenged in recent years, but it also must adhere to social demands that the racial taxonomies resonate with perceptions about whether and how people see themselves in the measure and in relation to other social groups. The proposals being tested by the Census Bureau do not go as far as Ken Prewitt's ultimate recommendations: (1) that the questions on race and ethnicity in the decennial census be abandoned, in favor of using the ACS, which is a less public venue and would avoid sending the same kind of signal about the significance of race in American culture and society, to collect the data required for government policy and programming; (2) to phase this change in incrementally by using "generational turnover" strategically, with the aim that "the generation born in 2060 will be the first in the nation's history to know a truly postracial America"; and (3) introduce a major modification in 2020 without disrupting current policy uses by implementing a question on race that includes a Hispanic category, following it with a question on national origins, and adding a question on parental place of birth to the ACS. Using this strategy, Prewitt recommends dropping the race question in 2040 and revisiting the usefulness of the national origins question in 2060.[108]

The fundamental question of race and the census is precisely, unavoidably, this: does counting by race help or hinder progress toward a post-racial world? In one sense, post-racialism refers to the real and

[108] Prewitt, *What Is Your Race?*, 195–208. Note that Prewitt's book was published well before the AQE results were released. Prewitt also acknowledges that if racial disparities persist, particularly for the African American and American Indian populations, a separate question just on these groups may have to be retained.

substantial shifts in attitudes about race between this generation and its predecessors. There is little doubt that American society has witnessed a fundamental change in norms about race. Lawrence Bobo and his colleagues' analysis of longitudinal data from the General Social Survey demonstrates that the "Jim Crow era commitment to segregation, explicit white privilege, revulsion against mixed marriages, and the categorical belief that blacks were inherently and biologically inferior to whites [has] collapsed. Broad support for equal treatment, integration, and a large measure of tolerance supplanted these views."[109] This cohort change, Jennifer Hochschild, Vesla Weaver, and Traci Burch argue, is so powerful that it might just transform the American racial order.[110] In another sense, post-racialism is a rhetorical or discursive strategy that can be used to speak to an already-present social reality in which racial boundaries are disintegrating and the prejudices of old are quickly disappearing. Intermarriage, often perceived as a litmus test for racial integration, has increased dramatically over the past fifty years. In 1970, three years after the Supreme Court's decision in *Loving v. Virginia* overturned the miscegenation laws blanketing the South, just 4 percent of newlyweds were interracial couples; by 2011, this number increased to 15.5 percent.[111] The multiracial population, another perceived indicator of eroding racial boundaries, is young and growing in all three countries of this study. Great Britain's mixed-race population is among the fastest growing ethnic group in Britain, with over 1 million Britons identifying as "mixed" on the 2011 Census of England and Wales and nearly 1 in 10 people living in inter-ethnic relationships.[112] Mixed-race unions have also increased in Canada, from 3.1 percent of all couples in 2001 to 4.0 percent in 2011.[113] In the United States, the population reporting more than one race grew from about 6.8 million

[109] Lawrence D. Bobo, Camille Z. Charles, Maria Krysan, and Alicia D. Simmons, "The *Real* Record on Racial Attitudes," in *Social Trends in American Life: Findings from the General Social Survey since 1972*, ed. Peter V. Marsden (Princeton: Princeton University Press, 2012), 74.

[110] Hochschild et al., *Creating a New Racial Order*, 113–138.

[111] Taylor and Pew Research Center, *The Next America.*

[112] Louise Eccles, "Britain's Mixed Race Population Leaps over One Million as Research Reveals Prejudices have Sharply Dropped," *The Daily Mail Online*, 9 December 2012, accessed July 31, 2014, available at: www.dailymail.co.uk/news/article-2245406/Jessica-Ennis-hailed-face-todays-Britain-census-figures-reveal-mixed-race-rise.html; Office for National Statistics, *What Does the 2011 Census Tell Us about Inter-Ethnic Relationships?* (London: ONS, 2014).

[113] Anne Milan, Hélène Maheaux, and Tina Chui, "A Portrait of Couples in Mixed Unions, Statistics Canada," *Canadian Social Trends* no. 89 (2010): 70–80.

people to 9 million people between 2000 and 2010.[114] Post-racialism has even found traction in popular culture, as National Geographic rolled out a series of portraits of mixed-race people in a 2013 series called "The Changing Face of America" and major American brands, such as Coke, Chevy, and Cheerios, featured advertisements during the 2014 Superbowl and Olympics aimed at this "new America" – diverse, cosmopolitan, tolerant, with an "us" that incorporates and appreciates those formerly labeled as "them." In short, both dimensions are hopeful interpretations of a post-racial social ideal that we are moving closer toward and may one day reach.

But there are clear indicators that post-racialism is just that – a wishful ideal, not a reality. Intermarriage rates have increased, but the incorporative power of intermarriage works differently across racial groups. For example, in the United States rates of intermarriage with whites is much lower for the black population than for Asians and Latinos and blacks are far less likely to identify as "two or more races."[115] In *The Diversity Paradox*, Jennifer Lee and Frank Bean point to the troubling possibility that the American color line is actually a divide not between whites and non-whites, but between those who identify or are identified as black and non-blacks.[116] Evidence also points to the racialization of the gap between the rich and poor in both Britain and Canada: minority groups are much more likely to be in poverty in Britain, with an income of less than 60 percent of the median household income[117] and Canadian racial minorities are more likely to be unemployed or employed in positions with job insecurity, low wages, and few social benefits.[118] Though attitudes about race are quite different in this century than they were for most of the last, new trends of "racial resentment," the broader beliefs that enable the expression of subtle racial hostility or implicit racial bias without violating democratic norms of racial egalitarianism, suggest that racism has simply

[114] Jones and Bullock, *The Two or More Races Population.*

[115] Lee and Bean, *The Diversity Paradox*, 83–120.

[116] Ibid. See also Eduardo Bonilla-Silva, "From Bi-Racial to Tri-Racial: Towards a New System of Racial Stratification in the USA," *Ethnic and Racial Studies* 27, no. 6 (2004): 931–950.

[117] Institute of Race Relations, "Poverty Statistics," accessed July 28, 2014, www.irr.org.uk/research/statistics/poverty/

[118] Grace-Edward Galabuzi, *Canada's Economic Apartheid: The Social Exclusion of Racialized Groups in the New Century* (Toronto: Canadian Scholars' Press, 2006); Keith Banting and Debra Thompson, "The Puzzling Persistence of Racial Inequality in Canada," American Political Science Association Presidential Task Force on Racial and Economic Inequality in the Americas (Washington D.C.: APSA, 2016).

taken a different form that bleeds into public opinions about policy areas such as health care and affirmative action.[119] And while Will Kymlicka and Keith Banting have found that a more diverse populace does not necessarily lead to a retrenchment of the welfare state,[120] Robert Putnam argues that increased ethno-racial diversity does, at least in the short run, erode social solidarity and social capital as those of all races in ethnically or racially diverse neighborhoods "hunker down."[121]

More critically, post-racialism is, in the words of legal scholar Sumi Cho, "a twenty-first century ideology that reflects a belief that due to the significant racial progress that has been made, the state need not engage in race-based decision-making or adopt race-based remedies, and that civil society should eschew race as a central organizing principle of social action."[122] The "post-" in post-racial is crucial. Far more than the ideology of color-blindness, which views any expression of race as racism, post-racialism implies that race and racism are artifacts of a world history we are now beyond. It signals transcendent and unidirectional racial progress – away from the racist past and the era of civil rights, and toward a cosmopolitan, egalitarian future. The "racial" in post-racial, then, refers to the racial domination inherent in white supremacy, colonialism, and Jim Crow, as well as the racial remedies of the civil rights era, suggesting the two forms of racialism are morally equivalent and therefore equally problematic. Policies that differentiate by race, even when used to rectify circumstances of disadvantage, are posited by the post-racial norm as overly divisive to an otherwise and increasingly progressive society. As a new, twenty-first century ideology, post-racialism is discursively distant from the structures and strictures of white supremacy, racism, race-consciousness, and more conservatively color-blind strategies, enabling post-racialism to be employed as

[119] David C. Wilson and Darren W. Davis, "Reexamining Racial Resentment: Conceptualization and Content," *ANNALS of the American Academy of Political and Social Science* 634, no. 1 (2011): 117–133; Antoine J. Banks and Nicholas A Valentino, "Emotional Substrates of White Racial Attitudes," *American Journal of Political Science* 56, no. 2 (2012): 286–297; Bobo et al., "The *Real* Record on Racial Attitudes"; Michael Tesler, "The Spillover of Racialization into Health Care: How President Obama Polarized Public Opinion by Racial Attitudes and Race," *American Journal of Political Science* 56, no. 3 (2012): 690–704.

[120] Keith Banting and Will Kymlicka, eds., *Multiculturalism and the Welfare State: Recognition and Redistribution in Contemporary Democracies* (New York: Oxford University Press, 2006).

[121] Robert D. Putnam, "*E Pluribus Unum*: Diversity and Community in the Twenty-First Century," The 2006 Johan Skytte Prize Lecture, *Scandinavian Political Studies* 30, no. 2 (2007): 137–174.

[122] Sumi Cho, "Post-Racialism," *Iowa Law Review* 94, no. 5 (2009): 1594.

a liberal, socially palatable alternative that appeals to the "universalism" of racial indifference and negates the enduring persistence of racial inequality.[123]

The meaning of post-racialism, the uses to which these aspirations are put, and their relationship with processes of racial legibility warrant careful and critical consideration along three lines. First, racial legibility as cemented through the census does not only differentiate, as some proponents of post-racial ideology suggest; it also creates equivalencies that are central to liberal democratic rule. Historian Bruce Curtis writes that

> it is only on the grounds of constructed and enforced equivalencies that one body comes to equal another, that each death, birth, marriage, divorce, and so on, comes to be the equivalent of any other. It is only on the grounds of such constructed equivalencies that it is possible for statistical objects to emerge in the form of regularities and to become the objects of political practice.[124]

The AQE focus group criticism that groups were not "treated equally" on the census speaks to the symbolic function these equivalencies serve. Just as distinctions can be used to create illiberal racial hierarchies, equivalencies are fundamental to liberal ideas about common personhood, the equal moral worth of individuals, and the rule of law.

Second, the belief that the post-racial ideal is somehow in tension with racial legibility confuses the technocratic, legislative, and policy basis for racial census classifications with the real, lived experiences of race, giving primacy to the former at the expense of the latter. Race cannot simply be wished away, as Justice Sotomayor argued in her powerful dissent in *Schuette*, worth quoting at length:

> Race matters. Race matters in part because of the long history of racial minorities' being denied access to the political process. Race also matters because of persistent racial inequality in society – inequality that cannot be ignored and that has produced stark socioeconomic disparities. And race matters for reasons that really are only skin deep, that cannot be discussed another way, and that cannot be wished away. Race matters to a young man's view of society when he spends his teenage years watching others tense up as he passes, no matter the neighborhood where he grew up. Race matters to a young woman's sense of self when she states her hometown, and then is pressed, "No, where are you *really* from?" regardless of how many generations her family has been in the country. Race matters to a young person addressed by a stranger in a foreign language, which he does not understand because only English was spoken at home. Race matters because of the

[123] Ibid., 1600–1604; see also Lopez, "The 'Post' in Post-Racial."

[124] Bruce Curtis, "Foucault on Governmentality and Population: The Impossible Discovery," *Canadian Journal of Sociology* 27, no. 4 (2002): 529.

slights, the snickers, the silent judgments that reinforce that most crippling of thoughts: "I do not belong here."

In my colleagues' view, examining the racial impact of legislation only perpetuates racial discrimination. This refusal to accept the stark reality that race matters is regrettable. The way to stop discrimination on the basis of race is to speak openly and candidly on the subject of race, and to apply the Constitution with eyes open to the unfortunate effects of centuries of racial discrimination. As members of the judiciary tasked with intervening to carry out the guarantee of equal protection, we ought not sit back and wish away, rather than confront, the racial inequality that exists in our society. It is this view that works harm, by perpetuating the facile notion that what makes race matter is acknowledging the simple truth that race *does* matter.[125]

At base, post-racialism relies on the idea that racial progress is unidirectional – we are moving away from the explicit racism of the past and toward a future in which the signifier of race plays no role in determining one's socio-economic status, educational attainment, or life chances. We are far from living in such a post-racial moment; a decade and a half into the twenty-first century, we remain "suspended uncomfortably" between the collapse of an explicitly hierarchical and institutionalized racial order and a post-racial social order that may or may not be on the horizon.[126] Further, the ways in which Jim Crow and colonialism continue to haunt contemporary racial dynamics, morphing into new evasive forms that are hard to prove and even harder to address through government action, calls this linear reasoning into question. Just as racial legibility cannot, on its own, create hierarchical racial dynamics, nor can its avoidance unilaterally diminish or rectify their structural effects.

Third, and finally, post-racialism is a hegemonic device that, when layered on top of color-blindness, laissez-faire racism, or the conflation of race and culture, can be a powerful weapon in foreclosing other possibilities or different interpretations of the nature, meaning, and prevalence of race and racism in a given society. Derived from Lacanian psychoanalysis, Barnor Hesse writes that foreclosure

makes certain expressions impossible, insofar as the locutions that would allow that expression have already been denied any existence within valorized discourse ... the 'action of foreclosure' is repetitive and quotidian because its proscription of particular discursive terms, themes or questions is never finalized; the

[125] *Schuette v. Coalition to Defend Affirmative Action.*

[126] Lawrence D. Bobo, "Somewhere between Jim Crow and Post-Racialism: Reflections on the Racial Divide in America Today," *Dædalus, the Journal of the American Academy of Arts & Sciences* 140, no. 2 (2011): 11–36.

conventional, hegemonic or normalizing discourse remains ever threatened by what has in effect been *constitutively foreclosed.*[127]

For example, post-racial vernacular truncates the meaning of racism by suturing it to individual bigotry, rather than structures of privilege and subjugation. Racial classifications thus become the moral equivalent of instances of racial discrimination, so toxic to the (post-racial) society that, "like chemotherapy, they should be utilized only when absolutely necessary and, even then, must be used as sparingly as possible."[128] Viewed in this light, racial legibility is, as I have intoned, a form of foreclosure. It is a convenient but spurious shorthand for capturing the messy fluidity of race, one that divorces race from its transnational origins, circulations, and effects and its intrinsic connection to the powers and practices of modernity and colonial rule. As an anchor for racial legibility, the racial schematic of the census becomes authoritative by limiting and negating other modes of racial identification and other possibilities of being and becoming through race.

There are no easy solutions to this quandary. It is, however, unlikely that ending the enumeration of race on the census will hasten the end of racial discrimination. It is much more likely that a premature end to counting by race will deprive us of the accurate and reliable data needed to create sound public policy. Moreover, the evolution of the census from an instrument of state surveillance that enabled the management and control of racial bodies and populations to the use of census data to defend human rights speaks to the powerful symbolic role of the census as a means though which social groups may seek and attain recognition from the state as well as a public proclamation that diversity and equality are important state-endorsed goals. Given the deepening of different, more subtle forms of racial inequality that exist in conjunction with the rise of a post-racial epoch, a counter-language is required:[129] a discourse of escapology[130] that can break free of the confines of static conceptions of time and space and expose racial legibility as one set of processes, among many others, through which race is socially, legally, and politically constructed. The aim of *The Schematic State* is precisely this. It is an examination of the political development of racial categories and rules of racial classification

[127] Hesse, "Escaping Liberty," 290, emphasis in original.
[128] Cho, "Post-Racialism," 1617.
[129] See Lawrie Balfour, "Unthinking Racial Realism: A Future for Reparations?" *Du Bois Review* 11, no. 1 (2014): 43–56.
[130] Hesse, "Escaping Liberty"; Richard Iton, "Still Life," *small axe* 40 (2013): 22–39.

on national censuses in the United States, Great Britain, and Canada that exposes the census as inherently, unavoidably political. It is also an exploration of both the role of race in shaping politics and the role of politics in making race – at the heart of the project is an answer to the question of how the racial categories that came to be institutionalized and bound by state power are made shiny and official by the veneer of institutional and democratic legitimacy that both hides and enshrines the fragile, shifting, contested, transnational, and power-enmeshed ideas, norms, and material realities that mark the concept of race.

APPENDIX

List of Interviews and Archival Sources

INTERVIEWS

This research includes primary source material derived from approximately twenty semi-structured interviews with current or former civil servants and political elites, all of whom were selected based on their involvement in the design of the race question on the censuses of the United States, Great Britain, or Canada during the 1990s and the 2000s. Since the census is a large enterprise comprised of many questions on a number of different topics, I found through the course of this research that only a few policymakers in each country had extensive knowledge of the design of questions on race or ethnicity – in effect, the policy sphere was rather small. To expand my number of respondents I used snowball interview techniques, which often proved very helpful for accessing interviewees who had taken other positions in the government or retired from the civil service altogether. As source material, the information provided in the interviews was largely original. That is, interviewees often filled in the gaps in the historical narrative by providing "insider" information that was otherwise not available. Whenever possible, I triangulated interview data with publicly available and internal government documents accessed through "freedom of information" or "access to information" requests – though it sometimes took years from when I requested the information to actually receive the (sometimes highly redacted) documents. I also used interview data as a "check" against other interview data. For example, I asked a number of different participants in the same policymaking process the same question and when I received the same response consistently I judged the information to be reliable and included it in this study. When there was conflict between interviewee responses, rather than make assumptions about which version was more accurate I took efforts to flag apparent contradictions in the text (for example, Chapter 5 details the disagreement about whether Statistics Canada chose not to enumerate by race on the 1991 Census because of financial constraints or because of an aversion to including something so explicitly racial). I have classified all interviews with civil servants as anonymous, regardless of whether anonymity was requested by the interviewee, since the civil servants in some countries were much more hesitant to have their quotations attributed to them than in others. All interviews were conducted in-person by the author unless otherwise indicated.

LIST OF INTERVIEWS

United States

Representative of Office of Management and Budget, Washington D.C., February 13, 2009

Representative of Office of Management and Budget, Washington D.C., February 13, 2009

Representative of Office of Management and Budget, Washington D.C., February 13, 2009

Representative of the Census Bureau, Washington D.C., February 13, 2009

Representative of the Census Bureau, Washington D.C., February 13, 2009

Representative of the Census Bureau, Washington D.C., February 19, 2009 (follow-up)

Tom Sawyer, Former Chair, Subcommittee on Census, Statistics, and Postal Personnel, Committee on Post Office and Civil Service, House of Representatives, Columbus OH, February 23, 2009

Great Britain

Ethnic Question Working Group member, Canterbury, England, April 6, 2009

Representative of the Office for National Statistics, Titchfield, England, April 15, 2009

Ethnic Question Working Group member, London, England, April 20, 2009

Ethnic Question Working Group member, London, England, April 22, 2009

Ethnic Question Working Group member, London, England, April 23, 2009 (email communication)
Representative of the Office for National Statistics, Titchfield, England, April 24, 2009

Canada

Representative of Statistics Canada, Ottawa, ON, October 19, 2009
Former employee of Statistics Canada, Ottawa, ON, October 20, 2009
Former employee of Statistics Canada, Ottawa, ON, October 21, 2009
Representative of Statistics Canada, Ottawa, ON, October 21, 2009
Former employee of Statistics Canada, Ottawa, ON, October 21, 2009
Former employee of Statistics Canada, Toronto, ON, October 28, 2009 (follow-up)
Former Chief Statistician Dr. Ivan Fellegi, phone interview, February 2, 2011

ARCHIVAL SOURCES

This research includes primary source material from the National Archives of Canada (NAC) in Ottawa, Ontario, and the National Archives of the United Kingdom/Public Records Office (PRO) in Kew, Richmond, England. Archival research in the United States was not necessary, in part because of the wealth of publicly available information from Census Reports, Congressional Records, and the first-hand published accounts of Superintendents of the Census Office and Directors of the Census Bureau, but also because the history of the American census has been extensively and painstakingly documented by a number of scholars, including Margo Anderson, Melissa Nobles, Sharon Lee, Alice Robbin, Victoria Hattam, Jennifer Hochschild, and Brenna Powell. Archival records are rarely complete or comprehensive. Whenever possible, I attempted to triangulate archival data with other publicly available source material, including supplemental archival data, primary accounts, parliamentary debates, and secondary research. As such, this list of archival files, which only includes material that actually appears in the text, is much shorter than the complete list of archives I consulted while at the National Archives of the United Kingdom/Public Records Office in March and April of 2009 and the National Archives of Canada in November and December 2010.

LIST OF ARCHIVAL SOURCES

Great Britain

CAB 128/63/14. Cabinet: Minutes (CM and C Series). Conclusion. Former Reference CM (78) 14. April 13, 1978.

PREM 13/2703. Prime Minister's Office: Correspondence and Papers, 1964–1970. HOME AFFAIRS. Possible sample of census of population in 1966: 1968 pre-test of 1971 census; suggestions to set up committee to examine population growth in UK. February 15, 1965 – September 10, 1969.

PREM 16/1689. Prime Minister's Office: Correspondence and Papers, 1974–1979. IMMIGRATION. Immigration policy: Home Secretary's parliamentary statement on immigration statistics in response to Select Committee on immigration report. Government Statistical Service draft article on New Commonwealth and Pakistani population statistics. March 31, 1978 –November 21, 1978.

PRO HO 376/175. Home Office: Racial Disadvantage (RDI Symbol Series) Files. 1971 Census: possibility of including questions on ethnic origins. 1966–1968.

PRO HO 376/123. Home Office: Racial Disadvantage (RDI Symbol Series) Files. Collection of statistics on Immigrants. 1968–1969.

PRO HO 376/124. Home Office: Racial Disadvantage (RDI Symbol Series) Files. Collection of statistics on basis of colour or ethnic origin. 1969–1970.

PRO HO 376/223. Home Office: Racial Disadvantage (RDI Symbol Series) Files. 1981 Census: consultation between Home Office and ethnic minority groups about the inclusion of questions on nationality and ethnicity in the 1981 Census. March 12, 1979 – January 3, 1980.

RG 26/436. Office of Population Censuses and Surveys and predecessors, Statistical Branch: Population and Medical Statistics: Correspondence and Papers. POPULATION STATISTICS. Immigration and ethnic origin statistics: coloured population of Great Britain; policy. 1975–1976.

RG 40/397. Central Office of Information, Social Survey Division: Social Survey: Registered Files. ADMINISTRATION FILES. Question wording tests for the 1991 Census: ethnicity, religion and language. 1984–1986.

Canada

NAC RG2 vol. 148, file D-25-3-C. Privy Council Office of Canada. Department of Trade and Commerce. Dominion Bureau of Statistics. Census, 1951.

NAC RG2 vol. 2744. Cabinet Conclusions, 1959.

NAC RG31 Accession 1989–90/133, box 29, file 7267. Nationality, Orientals and Others.

NAC RG31 Accession 1989–90/133, box 29, file 7267. Racial Origins Inquiries, 1932–34.

NAC RG31 vol. 1417. Records of the Assistant Dominion Statistician, Dr. R.H. Coats' Material, Dominion Statistician, 1918–1942. Census Material 1891–1940.

NAC RG31 vol. 1517, file 123. Records of the Assistant Dominion Statistician, Walter Duffet. 1961 Census – Origin or Ethnic Question.

Bibliography

Aarim-Heriot, Najia. *Chinese Immigrants, African Americans, and Racial Anxiety in the United States, 1848–82*. Urbana and Chicago: University of Illinois Press, 2003.

Abu-Laban, Yasmeen. "Welcome/STAY OUT: The Contradiction of Canadian Integration and Immigration Policies at the Millennium." *Canadian Ethnic Studies* 30, no. 3 (1998): 190–211.

Abu-Laban, Yasmeen, and Christina Gabriel. *Selling Diversity: Immigration, Multiculturalism, Employment Equity, and Globalization*. Toronto: University of Toronto Press, 2002.

Abu-Laban, Yasmeen, and Daiva Stasiulis. "Ethnic Pluralism under Siege: Popular and Partisan Opposition to Multiculturalism." *Canadian Public Policy* 18, no. 4 (1992): 365–386.

Acharya, Amitav. "How Ideas Spread: Whose Norms Matter? Norm Localization and Institutional Change in Asian Regionalism." *International Organization* 58, no. 2 (2004): 239–275.

Adams, Mark B., ed. *The Wellborn Science: Eugenics in Germany, France, Brazil and Russia*. New York: Oxford University Press, 1990.

Agassiz, Elizabeth Cary, ed. *Louis Agassiz: His Life and Correspondence*. London: Macmillan and Company, 1885.

Agassiz, Louis. "Sketch of the Natural Provinces of the Animal World and Their Relation to the Different Types of Man." In *Types of Mankind: or, Ethnological Researches, Based upon the Ancient Monuments, Paintings, Sculptures, and Crania of Races, and upon Their Natural, Geographical, Philological, and Biblical History*, edited by J. Nott and G. Gliddon, lviii–lxxvi. Philadelphia: Lippincott, Grambo, 1854

Alexander, Michelle. *The New Jim Crow: Mass Incarceration in the Age of Colorblindness*. New York: The New Press, 2010.

Alfred, Taiaiake. *Wasa'se: Indigenous Pathways of Action and Freedom*. Peterborough: Broadview Press, 2005.

Andersen, Chris. "From Nation to Population: The Racialisation of 'Métis' in the Canadian Census." *Nations and Nationalisms* 14, no. 2 (2008): 347–368.

"Underdeveloped Identities: The Misrecognition of Aboriginality in the Canadian census." *Economy and Society* 42, no. 4 (2013): 626–650.

"Métis": Race, Recognition, and the Struggle for Indigenous Peoplehood. Vancouver: University of British Columbia Press, 2014.

Anderson, Benedict. *Imagined Communities: Reflections on the Origins and Spread of Nationalism*, 2nd edn. London and New York: Verso, 1991.

Anderson, Margo J. *The American Census: A Social History.* New Haven: Yale University Press, 1988.

"The Census and the Federal Statistical System: Historical Perspectives." *ANNALS of the American Academy of Political and Social Science* 631 (2010): 152–162

Anderson, Margo, and Stephen E. Fienberg. *Who Counts?: The Politics of Census-Taking in Contemporary America.* New York: Russell Sage Foundation, 1999.

Angers, François-Albert. "Between Ourselves." *L'Action Nationale*, vol. XLVII, no. 9–10. Montreal, May–June 1959.

Ansell, Amy Elizabeth. *New Right, New Racism: Race and Reaction in the United States and Britain.* New York: New York University Press, 1997.

Appadurai, Arjun. "Number in the Colonial Imagination." In *Orientalism and the Postcolonial Predicament*, edited by Carol A. Breckenridge and Peter van der Veer. 314–340. Philadelphia: University of Pennsylvania Press, 1993.

Modernity at Large: Cultural Dimensions of Globalization. Minneapolis: University of Minnesota Press, 1996.

Aspinall, Peter J. *The Development of an Ethnic Group Question for the 2001 Census: The Findings of a Consultation Exercise with Members of the OPCS 2001 Census Working Subgroup.* London: United Medical and Dental Schools, 1996.

"Children of Mixed Parentage: Data Collection Needs." *Children & Society* 14, no. 3 (2000): 207–216.

"The Conceptualisation and Categorisation of Mixed Race/Ethnicity in Britain and North America: Identity Options and the Role of the State." *International Journal of Intercultural Relations* 27, no. 3 (2003): 269–296.

Back, Les, Michael Keith, Azra Khan, Kalbir Shukra, and John Solomos. "New Labour's White Heart: Politics, Multiculturalism and the Return of Assimilation." *The Political Quarterly* 73, no. 4 (2002): 445–454.

Backhouse, Constance. *Colour-Coded: A Legal History of Racism in Canada: 1900–1950*. Toronto: University of Toronto Press, 1999.

Bailey, Stanley, and Edward Telles, "Multicultural versus Collective Black Categories: Examining Census Classification Debates in Brazil." *Ethnicities* 6, no. 1 (2006): 74–101.

Balfour, Lawrie. "Unthinking Racial Realism: A Future for Reparations?" *Du Bois Review* 11, no. 1 (2014): 43–56.

Ballard, Roger. "Negotiating Race and Ethnicity: Exploring the Implications of the 1991 Census." *Patterns of Prejudice* 30, no. 3 (1996): 3–33.

"The Construction of a Conceptual Vision: 'Ethnic Groups' and the 1991 UK Census." *Ethnic and Racial Studies* 20, no. 1 (1997): 182–194.

Balibar, Etienne. "Is There a Neo-Racism?" In *Race, Nation, Class: Ambiguous Identities*, by Etienne Balibar and Immanuel Wallerstein, 17–28. New York and London: Verso, 1991.

Banks, Antoine J, and Nicholas A Valentino. "Emotional Substrates of White Racial Attitudes." *American Journal of Political Science* 56, no. 2 (2012): 286–297.

Bannerji, Himani. "The Paradox of Diversity: The Construction of a Multicultural Canada and 'Women of Color'." *Women's Studies International Forum* 23, no. 5 (2000): 537–560.

Banting, Keith, and Will Kymlicka, eds. *Multiculturalism and the Welfare State: Recognition and Redistribution in Contemporary Democracies*. New York: Oxford University Press, 2006.

Banting, Keith and Debra Thompson. "The Puzzling Persistence of Racial Inequality in Canada." *American Political Science Association Presidential Task Force on Racial and Class Inequalities in the Americas*. Washington D.C.: APSA, 2016.

Banton, Michael. *Racial and Ethnic Competition*. Cambridge: Cambridge University Press, 1983.

International Action Against Racial Discrimination. Oxford: Oxford University Press, 1996.

The International Politics of Race. Oxford and Malden: Blackwell Publishers, 2002.

Barkan, Elazar. *The Retreat of Scientific Racism: Changing Concepts of Race in Britain and the United States between the World Wars*. Cambridge: Cambridge University Press, 1992.

Barry, Brian. *Culture and Equality: An Egalitarian Critique of Multiculturalism*. Cambridge: Polity Press, 2001.

Bashford, Alison, and Phillippa Levine, eds. *The Oxford Handbook of the History of Eugenics*. Oxford and New York: Oxford University Press, 2010.

Baum, Bruce. *The Rise and Fall of the Caucasian Race: A Political History of Racial Identity*. New York and London: New York University Press, 2006.

Baumgartner, Frank R., and Bryan D. Jones. "Agenda Dynamics and Policy Subsystems." *Journal of Politics* 53, no. 4 (1991): 1044–1074.

Agendas and Instability in American Politics. Chicago: University of Chicago Press, 1993.

Beaud, Jean-Pierre, and Jean-Guy Prévost. "Statistics as the Science of Government: The Stillborn British Empire Statistical Bureau, 1918–20." *Journal of Imperial and Commonwealth History* 33, no. 3 (2005): 369–391.

Béland, Daniel, and Robert Henry Cox, eds. *Ideas and Politics in Social Science Research*. Oxford: Oxford University Press, 2011.

"Introduction: Ideas and Politics." In *Ideas and Politics in Social Science Research*, edited by Daniel Béland and Robert Henry Cox. New York: Oxford University Press, 2011.

Bell, Derrick. "Brown v. Board of Education and the Interest-Convergence Dilemma." *Harvard Law Review* 93 (1980): 518–533

Benedict, Ruth. *Race: Science and Politics*. New York: Modern Age Books, 1940.

Bennett, Claudette. "Exploring the Consistency of Race Reporting in Census 2000 and the Census Quality Survey." *Annual Meeting of the American Statistical Association*. San Francisco, 2003.

Berg, Manfred, and Simon Wendt, eds. *Racism in the Modern World: Historical Perspectives on Cultural Transfer and Adaptation*. New York and Oxford: Berghahn Books, 2011.

Berman, Sheri. "Ideas, Norms, and Culture in Political Analysis." *Comparative Politics* 33, no. 2 (2001): 231–250.

Bhambra, Gurminder K. "Historical Sociology, International Relations and Connected Histories." *Cambridge Review of International Affairs* 23, no. 1 (2010): 127–143.

Bhrolcháin, Maire Ni. "The Ethnicity Question for the 1991 Census: Background and Issues." *Ethnic and Racial Studies* 13, no. 4 (1990): 542–567.

Bialik, Carl. "Census Gets Questions on Mandatory Queries." *Wall Street Journal*, March 30, 2012. Accessed July 16, 2013, http://online.wsj.com/news/articles/SB10001424052702303404704577311540585680300

Blake, John. "Arab- and Persian-American campaign: 'Check it right' on census." *CNN*, May 14, 2010. Accessed August 3, 2014, www.cnn.com/2010/US/04/01/census.check.it.right.campaign/

Bleich, Erik. *Race Politics in Britain and France: Ideas and Policymaking Since the 1960s*. New York: Cambridge University Press, 2003.

"Institutional Continuity and Change: Norms, Lesson-drawing, and the Introduction of Race-conscious Measures in the 1976 British Race Relations Act." *Policy Studies* 27, no. 3 (2006): 219–234.

Blyth, Mark. *Great Transformations: Economic Ideas and Institutional Change in the Twentieth Century*. Cambridge: Cambridge University Press, 2002.

Bobo, Lawrence D. "Somewhere between Jim Crow & Post-Racialism: Reflections on the Racial Divide in America Today." *Daedalus* 140, no. 2 (2011): 11–36.

Bobo, Lawrence D. and Ryan A. Smith. "From Jim Crow to Laissez-Faire Racism: The Transformation of Racial Attitudes," In *Beyond Pluralism: The Conception of Groups and Identities in America*, edited by Wendy F. Katkin, Ned Landsman, and Andrea Tyree, 182–220. Urbana: University of Illinois Press, 1998.

Bobo, Lawrence D, Camille Z. Charles, Maria Krysan, and Alicia D. Simmons. "The Real Record on Racial Attitudes." In *Social Trends in American Life: Findings from the General Social Survey since 1972*, edited by Peter V. Marsden, 38–83. Princeton: Princeton University Press, 2012.

Bonilla-Silva, Eduardo. "From Bi-racial to Tri-racial: Towards a New System of Racial Stratification in the USA." *Ethnic and Racial Studies* 27, no. 6 (2004): 931–950.

Racism without Racists: Color-Blind Racism and the Persistence of Racial Inequality in the United States, 3rd edn New York: Rowman & Littlefield Publishers, 2010.

Borstelmann, Thomas. *The Cold War and the Color Line: American Race Relations in the Global Arena*. Cambridge: Harvard University Press, 2002.

Bourhis, Richard Y. "Measuring Ethnocultural Diversity Using the Canadian Census." *Canadian Ethnic Studies* 35, no. 1 (2003): 9–32.

Bourdieu, Pierre. *In Other Words: Essays Towards a Reflexive Sociology*. Stanford: Stanford University Press, 1990.

On the State: Lectures at the Collège de France 1989–1992. Eds. Patrick Champagne, Remi Lenoir, Franck Poupeau, and Marie-Christine Rivière. Trans. David Fernbach. Cambridge: Polity Press, 2014.

Bowker, Geoffrey C., and Susan Leigh Star. *Sorting Things Out: Classification and Its Consequences*. Cambridge, MA: The MIT Press, 1999.

Bowman, John. "Canadians' 'Enthusiasm' for Census Brings Down StatsCan Website." CBC News, May 3, 2016. Accessed June 21, 2016, www.cbc.ca/news/trending/census-2016-nerds-1.3563808

Boxhill, Walton O. *Limitations to the Use of Ethnic Origin Data to Quantify Visible Minorities in Canada*. Ottawa: Statistics Canada, 1984.

Making Tough Choices in Using Census Data to Count Visible Minorities in Canada. Ottawa: Statistics Canada, 1990.

Boyd, Monica. "Canadian, Eh? Ethnic Origins Shifts in the Canadian Census." *Canadian Ethnic Studies* 31, no. 3 (1999): 1–19.

Boyd, Monica, Gustave Goldmann, and Pamela White. "Race in the Canadian Census." In *Race and Racism: Canada's Challenge*, edited by Leo Driedger and Shiva Halli, 33–54. Montreal: McGill-Queen's University Press, 2000.

Bratter, Jenifer. "Will 'Multiracial' Survive to the Next Generation?: The Racial Classification of Children of Multiracial Parents." *Social Forces* 86, no. 2 (2007): 821–849.

Brown, Jacqueline Nassy. *Dropping Anchor, Setting Sail: Geographies of Race in Black Liverpool*. Princeton: Princeton University Press, 2005.

"The Racial State of the Everyday and the Making of Ethnic Statistics in Britain." *Social Text* 27, no. 1 (2009): 11–36.

Brown, Michael K., Martin Carnoy, Elliott Currie, Troy Duster, David B. Oppenheimer, Marjorie M. Shultz, and David Wellman. *Whitewashing Race: The Myth of a Color-Blind Society*. Berkeley: University of California Press, 2003.

Brown, Wendy. *States of Injury: Power and Freedom in Late Modernity*. Princeton: Princeton University Press, 1995.

Undoing the Demos: Neoliberalism's Stealth Revolution. Cambridge: MIT Press, 2015.

Brubaker, Rogers. "The Return of Assimilation? Changing Perspectives on Immigration and its Sequels in France, Germany, and the United States." *Ethnic and Racial Studies* 24, no. 4 (2001): 531–548.

"Ethnicity, Race, and Nationalism." *Annual Review of Sociology* 35 (2009): 21–42.

Bryant, Barbara, and William Dunn. *Moving Power and Money: The Politics of Census Taking*. New York: New York Strategist Publications, 1995.

Bulmer, Martin. "A Controversial Census Topic: Race and Ethnicity in the British Census." *Journal of Official Statistics* 2, no. 4 (1986): 471–480.

"The Ethnic Group Question in the 1991 Census of Population." In *Ethnicity in the 1991 Census. Volume One: Demographic Characteristics of Ethnic Minority Populations*, edited by David Coleman and John Salt, 33–62. London: HMSO, 1996.

Caballero, Chamion. *'Mixed-Race Projects': Perceptions, Constructions, and Implications of Mixed-Race in the UK and USA*. Unpublished dissertation. Bristol: University of Bristol, 2004.

Calliste, Agnes. "Race, Gender and Canadian Immigration Policy: Blacks from the Caribbean, 1900–1932." *Journal of Canadian Studies* 28, no. 4 (1993): 131–148.

Canada. *Fourth Census of Canada, 1901. Instructions to Chief Officers, Commissioners, and Enumerators*. Ottawa: Government Printing Bureau, 1901.

Ninth Census of Canada, 1951. Volume X: General Review and Summary Tables. Ottawa: Queen's Printer, 1956.

Equality Now! Report of the Special Committee on Visible Minorities in Canadian Society. Ottawa: Supply and Services Canada, 1984.

Royal Commission on Equality in Employment. Ottawa: Supply and Services Canada, 1984.

Citizens' Forum on Canada's Future, Report to the People and Government of Canada. Ottawa: Minister of Supply and Services Canada, 1991.

Canada. Department of Agriculture. *Census of Canada, 1870–71*. Ottawa: I.B. Taylor, 1871.

Canada. Department of Indian Affairs and Northern Development. *Statement of the Government of Canada on Indian Policy (The White Paper)*. Ottawa: Queen's Printer, 1969.

Canada. Dominion Bureau of Statistics. *Fifth Census of Canada, 1911. Instructions to Officers, Commissioners and Enumerators*. Ottawa: Government Printing Bureau, 1911.

Sixth Census of Canada, 1921. Instructions to Commissioners and Enumerators. Ottawa: Government Printing Bureau, 1921.

Seventh Census of Canada, 1931. Instructions to Commissioners and Enumerators. Ottawa: King's Printer, 1931.

Eighth Census of Canada, 1941. Instructions to Commissioners and Enumerators. Ottawa: King's Printer, 1941.

Eighth Census of Canada, 1941. Administrative Report of the Dominion Statistician. Ottawa: King's Printer, 1941.

Census of Canada, 1951. Instructions to Commissioners and Enumerators. Ottawa: King's Printer, 1951.

Canada. Indian Registration and Band Lists Directorate. *The Indian Act, Past and Present: A Manual on Registration and Entitlement Legislation*. Ottawa: Indian Registration and Band Lists Directorate, 1991.

Carpenter, Daniel P. *The Forging of Bureaucratic Autonomy: Reputation, Networks, and Policy Innovation in Executive Agencies, 1862–1928*. Princeton: Princeton University Press, 2001.

Carroll, Joseph. "Most Americans Approve of Interracial Marriages." Gallup News Service. Accessed May 5, 2014, www.gallup.com/poll/28417/most-americans-approve-interracial-marriages.aspx

Carter, Bob, Clive Harris, and Shirley Joshi. 1987. "The 1951–1955 Conservative Government and the Racialisation of Black Immigration." *Immigrants and Minorities* 6, no. 3 (1987): 335–347.

Chambers, Iain, and Lidia Curti, eds. *The Post-Colonial Question: Common Skies, Divided Horizons*. London and New York: Routledge, 1996.

Checkel, Jeffrey. "The Constructivist Turn in International Relations Theory." *World Politics* 50, no. 2 (1998): 324–348.

"Norms, Institutions and National Identity in Contemporary Europe." *International Studies Quarterly* 43, no. 1 (1999): 84–114.

Chhibber, Pradeep, and Ken Kollman. *The Formation of National Party Systems: Federalism and Party Competition in Britain, Canada, India, and the United States*. Princeton: Princeton University Press, 1994.

Cho, Sumi. "Post-Racialism." *Iowa Law Review* 94, no. 5 (2009): 1589–1645.

Cho, Sumi, Kimberle Williams Crenshaw, and Leslie McCall. "Toward a Field of Intersectionality Studies: Theory, Applications, and Praxis." *Signs* 38, no. 4 (2013): 785–810.

Choldin, Harvey M. "Statistics and Politics: The 'Hispanic Issue' in the 1980 Census." *Demography* 23, no. 3 (1986): 403–418.

Looking for the Last Percent: the Controversy over Census Undercounts. New Brunswick: Rutgers University Press, 1994.

Christopher, Anthony J. "Race and the Census in the Commonwealth." *Population, Space and Place* 11 (2005): 103–118.

"Questions of Identity in the Millennium Round of Commonwealth Censuses." *Population Studies* 60, no. 3 (2006): 343–352.

"The Quest for a Census of the British Empire, c. 1840–1940." *Journal of Historical Geography* 34 (2008): 268–285.

Clement, Tony. *Statement on 2011 Census*. Minister of Industry, Science and Technology, July 2010. Accessed June 21, 2016, www.marketwired.com/press-release/statement-on-2011-census-1289664.htm

Clément, Dominique. *Canada's Rights Revolution: Social Movements and Social Change, 1937–82*. Vancouver: University of British Columbia Press, 2008.

Coats, Robert Hamilton. "Beginnings in Canadian Statistics." *The Canadian Historical Review* 27, no. 2 (1946): 109–130.

Cohen, Patricia Cline. *A Calculating People: The Spread of Numeracy in Early America*. Chicago: University of Chicago Press, 1982.

Cohn, Bernard. "The Census, Social Structure and Objectification in South Asia." In *An Anthropologist Among the Historians and Other Essays*, 224–254. Delhi: Oxford University Press, 1987.

Commission for Racial Equality. *1981 Census: Why the Ethnic Question Is Vital. A Discussion Document*. London: Commission for Racial Equality, 1980.

Community Relations Commission. *Review of the Race Relations Act*. London: HMSO, 1975.

Compton, Elizabeth, Michael Bentley, Sharon Ennis, and Sonya Rastogi. *2010 Census Race and Hispanic Origin Alternative Questionnaire Experiment: Final Report*. 2010 Census Planning Memoranda Series. Washington D.C.: U.S. Census Bureau, 2013.

Connerly, Ward. *Creating Equal: My Fight Against Racial Preferences*, rev. edn. New York: Encounter Books, 2007.

Cooper, Frederick. "What Is the Concept of Globalization Good For? An African Historian's Perspective." *African Affairs* 100, no. 399 (2001): 189–213.

Cooper, Frederick, and Ann Laura Stoler. "Between Metropole and Colony: Rethinking a Research Agenda." In *Tensions of Empire: Colonial Cultures in a Bourgeois World*, edited by Frederick Cooper and Ann Laura Stoler, 1–56. Berkley: University of California Press, 1997.

Cornell, Stephen E., and Douglas Hartmann. *Ethnicity and Race: Making Identities in a Changing World*, 2nd edn. Thousand Oaks: Pine Forge Press, 2007.

Cortell, Andrew P., and James W. Davis. "How Do International Institutions Matter? The Domestic Impact of International Rules and Norms." *International Studies Quarterly* 40, no. 4 (2000): 451–478.

Coulthard, Glen. *Red Skin, White Masks: Rejecting the Colonial Politics of Recognition*. Minneapolis: University of Minnesota Press, 2014.

Crenshaw, Kimberlé, Neil Gotanda, Gary Peller, and Kendall Thomas, eds. *Critical Race Theory: The Key Writings that Formed the Movement*. New York: The New Press, 1995.

Curtis, Bruce. "The Canada 'Blue Books' and the Administrative Capacity of the Canadian State, 1822–67." *Canadian Historical Review* 74, no. 4 (1993): 535–565.

The Politics of Population: State Formation, Statistics, and the Census of Canada, 1840–1875. Toronto: University of Toronto Press, 2001.

"Foucault on Governmentality and Population: The Impossible Discovery." *Canadian Journal of Sociology/Cahiers canadiens de sociologie* 27, no. 4 (2002): 505–533.

D'souza, Dinesh. *The End of Racism: Principles for a Multiracial Society*. New York: The Free Press, 1995.

DaCosta, Kimberly McClain. "Multiracial Identity: From Personal Problem to Public Issue." In *New Faces in a Changing America:*

Multiracial Identity in the 21st Century, edited by Loretta I. Winters, and Herman L. DeBose, 68–84. Thousand Oaks: Sage Publications, 2003.

Making Multiracials: State, Family, and Market in the Redrawing of the Color Line. Stanford: Stanford University Press, 2007.

Dahl, Robert A. *Who Governs?: Democracy and Power in an American City*. New Haven: Yale University Press, 1961.

Daniel, G. Reginald. *More than Black? Multiracial Identity and the New Racial Order*. Philadelphia: Temple University Press, 2002.

Darroch, Michael, and Gordon Darroch. "Commentary Losing Our Census." *Canadian Journal of Communication* 35, no. 4 (2010): 609–617.

Davis, F. James. *Who Is Black? One Nation's Definition*. University Park: Pennsylvania State University Press, 1991.

de Gobineau, Joseph Arthur. *The Moral and Intellectual Diversity of Races, with Particular Reference to Their Respective Influence in the Civil and Political History of Mankind*. Philadelphia: J.B. Lippincott, 1856.

Dikötter, Frank. *The Discourse of Race in Modern China*. London: Hurst, 1992.

Dobbin, Frank, Beth A. Simmons, and Geoffrey Garrett. "The Global Diffusion of Public Policies: Social Construction, Coercion, Competition, or Learning?" *Annual Review of Sociology* 33 (2007): 449–472.

Dolowitz, David P., and David Marsh. "Learning from Abroad: The Role of Policy Transfer in Contemporary Policy-Making." *Governance* 13, no. 1 (2000): 5–24.

Donnelly, Jack. *Universal Human Rights in Theory and Practice*, 3rd edn. Ithaca: Cornell University Press, 2013.

Downes, Bryan T. "A Critical Reexamination of Social and Political Characteristics of Riot Cities." *Social Science Quarterly* 51, no. 2 (1970): 349–360.

Doyle, Jamie Mihoko, and Grace Kao. "Are Racial Identities of Multiracials Stable? Changing Self-identification among Single and Multiple Race Individuals." *Social Psychology Quarterly* 70, no. 4 (2007): 405–423.

Du Bois, W.E.B. *The Conservation of Races*. The American Negro Academy Occasional Papers, No. 2. Washington D.C.: American Negro Academy, 1897.

"The Twelfth Census and the Negro Problems." *The Southern Workman* 29, no. 5 (1900): 305–309.

Dudziak, Mary L. "Desegregation as a Cold War Imperative." *Stanford Law Review* 41, no. 1 (1988): 61–120.

"The Little Rock Crisis and Foreign Affairs: Race, Resistance, and the Image of American Democracy." *Southern California Law Review* 70, no. 6 (1997): 1641–1716.

Cold War Civil Rights: Race and the Image of American Democracy. Princeton: Princeton University Press, 2000.

"Brown as a Cold War Case." *The Journal of American History* 91, no. 1 (2004): 32–42.

Dunnell, Karen. "Evolution of the United Kingdom Statistical System." United Nations Statistics Division, 2007. Accessed August 15, 2013, http://unstats.un.org/unsd/statcom/statcom_seminar/UK%20paper%20for%20UNSC%20final.pdf.

Eccles, Louise. "Britain's Mixed Race Population Leaps over One Million as Research Reveals Prejudices have Sharply Dropped." *The Daily Mail Online*, December 9, 2012. Accessed July 31, 2014, www.dailymail.co.uk/news/article-2245406/Jessica-Ennis-hailed-face-todays-Britain-census-figures-reveal-mixed-race-rise.html

Eckler, A. Ross. *The Bureau of the Census.* New York: Praeger, 1972.

Edmonston, Barry, Juanita Tamayo Lott, and Joshua Goldstein. *Spotlight on Heterogeneity: The Federal Standards for Racial and Ethnic Classification, Summary of a Workshop.* Washington D.C.: National Academy Press, 1996.

Edmonston, Barry, Sharon M Lee, and Jeffrey S Passel. "Recent Trends in Intermarriage and Immigration and Their Effects on the Future Racial Composition of the US Population." In *The New Race Question: How the Census Counts Multiracial Individuals*, edited by Joel Perlmann, and Mary C. Waters, 227–255. New York: Russell Sage Foundation, 2002.

Elgersman Maureen G. *Unyielding Spirits: Black Women and Slavery in Early Canada and Jamaica.* New York: Garland Publishing, 1999.

Ennis, Sharon R., Mararys Rios-Vargas, and Nora G. Albert. *The Hispanic Population: 2010*, U.S. Census Bureau, Population Division. Washington D.C.: U.S. Census Bureau, 2011.

Epp, Charles R. *The Rights Revolution: Lawyers, Activists, and Supreme Courts in Comparative Perspective.* Chicago: University of Chicago Press, 1998.

Essed, Philomena. *Understanding Everyday Racism: An Interdisciplinary Theory.* Newbury Park: Sage Publications, 1991.

European Statistical System Committee. *European Statistics Code of Practice for the National and Community Statistical Authorities.* Luxembourg: Eurostat, 2012.

Evinger, Suzann. "How to Record Race." *American Demographics* 18, no. 5 (1995): 36–41.

Farley, Reynolds. "Identifying with Multiple Races: A Social Movement that Succeeded but Failed?" In *The Changing Terrain of Race and Ethnicity*, edited by Maria Krysan and Amanda E. Lewis, 123–148. New York: The Russell Sage Foundation, 2004.

Fellegi, Ivan P. "Chief Statistician: Why the Census Is Counting Visible Minorities." *The Globe and Mail*, 26 April (1996): A21.

Fields, Barbara Jeanne. "Slavery, Race and Ideology in the United States of America." *New Left Review* 181, no. 1 (1990): 95–118.

Finnemore, Martha, and Kathryn Sikkink. "International Norm Dynamics and Political Change." *International Organization* 52, no. 4 (1998): 887–917.

Finnemore, Martha. "Norms, Culture, and World Politics: Insights from Sociology's Institutionalism." *International Organization* 50, no. 2 (1996): 325–347.

Fitzpatrick, Peter. "Racism and the Innocence of Law." *Journal of Law and Society* 14, no. 1 (1987): 119–132.

Forbes, Jack D. *Africans and Native Americans: The Language of Race and the Evolution of Red-Black Peoples*, 2nd edn. Urbana: University of Illinois Press, 1993.

Ford, Christopher A. "Administering Identity: The Determination of 'Race' in Race-Conscious Law." *California Law Review* 82 (1994): 1231–1285.

Foucault, Michel. "Governmentality." In *The Foucault Effect: Studies in Governmentality*, edited by Graham Burchell, Colin Gordon, and Peter Miller, 87–104. Chicago: University of Chicago Press, 1991.

Security, Territory, Population: Lectures at the Collège de France 1977–1978. Ed. Arnold Davidson. Trans. Graham Burchel. New York: Picador, 2007.

Fowler, David. *Northern Attitudes Towards Interracial Marriage: Legislation and Public Opinion in the Middle Atlantic and the States of the Old Northwest, 1780–1930*. New York and London: Garland Publishing, Inc., 1987.

Fredrickson, George M. *The Black Image in the White Mind: The Debate on Afro-American Character and Destiny, 1817–1914*. New York: Harper & Row Publishers, 1971.

Racism: A Short History. Princeton: Princeton University Press, 2002.

Fryer, Roland G. "Guess Who's Been Coming to Dinner? Trends in Interracial Marriage over the 20th Century." *Journal of Economic Perspectives* 21, no. 2 (2007): 71–90.

Füredi, Frank. *The Silent War: Imperialism and the Changing Perception of Race*. New Brunswick: Rutgers University Press, 1998.

Furrow, Matthew. "Samuel Gridley Howe, the Black Population of Canada West, and the Racial Ideology of the 'Blueprint for Radical

Reconstruction'." *Journal of American History* 97, no. 2 (2010): 344–370.

Galabuzi, Grace-Edward. *Canada's Economic Apartheid: The Social Exclusion of Racialized Groups in the New Century*. Toronto: Canadian Scholars' Press, 2006.

George, Alexander L. and Andrew Bennett. *Case Studies and Theory Development in the Social Sciences*. Cambridge, MA: MIT Press, 2005.

Gilroy, Paul. *There Ain't no Black in the Union Jack: The Cultural Politics of Race and Nation*. London: Hutchinson, 1987.

The Black Atlantic: Modernity and Double Consciousness. London and New York: Verso, 1993.

"Route Work: The Black Atlantic and the Politics of Exile." In *The Post-Colonial Question: Common Skies, Divided Horizons*, edited by Iain Chambers and Lidia Curti, 17–29. London and New York: Routledge, 1996.

Postcolonial Melancholia. New York: Columbia University Press, 2005.

Gilroy, Paul, Lawrence Grossberg, and Angela McRobbie, eds. *Without Guarantees: In Honour of Stuart Hall*. London: Verso, 2000.

Glazer, Nathan. *We Are All Multiculturalists Now*. Cambridge: Harvard University Press, 1998.

Affirmative Discrimination: Ethnic Inequality and Public Policy. New York: Basic Books, 1975.

Glazer, Nathan, and Ken Young, eds. *Ethnic Pluralism and Public Policy: Achieving Equality in the United States and Britain*. Lexington: Lexington Books, 1983.

Goldberg, David Theo. *The Racial State*. Malden: Blackwell Publishing, 2002.

The Threat of Race: Reflections on Racial Neoliberalism. Malden: Blackwell Publishing, 2009.

Goldstein, Joshua R., and Ann Morning. "Back in the Box: The Dilemma of Using Multiple-Race Data for Single-Race Laws." In *The New Race Question: How the Census Counts Multiracial Individuals*, edited by Joel Perlmann and Mary C. Waters, 119–136. New York: Russell Sage Foundation, 2002.

Gossett, Thomas F. *Race: The History of an Idea in America*, new edn. New York: Oxford University Press, 1997.

Gould, Stephen Jay. *The Mismeasure of Man*. New York and London: W.W. Norton & Company, 1981.

Graham, Hugh Davis. *The Civil Rights Era: Origins and Development of National Policy 1960–1972*. New York: Oxford University Press, 1990.

"The Origins of Official Minority Designation" In *The New Race Question: How the Census Counts Multiracial Individuals*, edited by Joel Perlmann and Mary C. Waters, 288–299. New York: Russell Sage Foundation, 2002.

Green, David and Kevin Milligan. "The Importance of the Long Form Census to Canada." *Canadian Public Policy* 36, no. 3 (2010): 383–388.

Green, Joyce, ed. *Making Space for Indigenous Feminism*. Black Point: Fernwood Pub, 2007.

Greer, Christina M. *Black Ethnics: Race, Immigration, and the Pursuit of the American Dream*. Oxford and New York: Oxford University Press, 2013.

Griffin, Deborah H, and Preston Jay Waite. "American Community Survey Overview and the Role of External Evaluations." *Population Research and Policy Review* 25, no. 3 (2006): 201–223.

Grob, Gerald N. *Edward Jarvis and the Medical World of Nineteenth Century America*. Knoxville: University of Tennessee Press, 1978.

Groves, Robert M. *The Pros and Cons of Making the American Community Survey Voluntary*. Statement to the Committee on Oversight and Government Reform, United States House of Representatives, March 2012.

Gupta, Akhil. *Red Tape: Bureaucracy, Structural Violence, and Poverty in India*. Durham and London: Duke University Press, 2012.

Gwyn, Richard. "Census Focus on Race a Step Backward." *The Toronto Star*, May 19, 1996: F3.

Haas, Peter M. "Introduction: Epistemic Communities and International Policy Coordination." *International Organization* 46, no. 1 (1992): 1–35.

Hacker, Jacob S. "The Historical Logic of National Health Insurance: Structure and Sequence in the Development of British, Canadian, and US Medical Policy." *Studies in American Political Development* 12, no. 1 (1998): 57–130.

Hacking, Ian. *The Taming of Chance*. Cambridge: Cambridge University Press, 1990.

Hall, Catherine. *Civilising Subjects: Metropole and Colony in the English Imagination, 1830–1867*. Chicago and London: University of Chicago Press, 2002.

Hall, Peter A. *Governing the Economy: The Politics of State Intervention in Britain and France*. Oxford: Oxford University Press, 1986.

ed. *The Political Power of Economic Ideas: Keynesianism Across Nations*. Princeton: Princeton University Press, 1989.

Hall, Peter A., and Michèle Lamont, eds. *Social Resilience in the Neoliberal Era*. New York: Cambridge University Press, 2013.

Hall, Stuart. "Race, The Floating Signifier." Mediation Education Foundation Transcript. Accessed June 24, 2016, www.mediaed.org/transcripts/Stuart-Hall-Race-the-Floating-Signifier-Transcript.pdf

Hampshire, James. *Citizenship and Belonging: Immigration and the Politics of Demographic Governance in Postwar Britain*. New York: Palgrave Macmillan, 2005.

Hanchard, Michael, and Erin Aeran Chung. "From Race Relations to Comparative Race Politics: A Survey of Cross-National Scholarship on Race in the Social Sciences." *Du Bois Review* 1, no. 2 (2004): 319–343.

Hancock, Ange-Marie. "When Multiplication Doesn't Equal Quick Addition: Examining Intersectionality as a Research Paradigm." *Perspectives on Politics* 5, no. 1 (2007): 63–79.

Hansen, Randall. *Citizenship and Immigration in Post-War Britain: The Institutional Origins of a Multicultural Nation*. Oxford: Oxford University Press, 1999.

Hansen, Randall, and Desmond King. *Sterilized by the State: Eugenics, Race, and the Population Scare in Twentieth-Century North America*. New York: Cambridge University Press, 2013.

Harris, Kathleen. "Mandatory Long-Form Census Restored by New Liberal Government." CBC News, November 5, 2015. Accessed June 21, 2016, www.cbc.ca/news/politics/canada-liberal-census-data-1.3305271

Haque, Eve. *Multiculturalism Within a Bilingual Framework: Language, Race, and Belonging in Canada*. Toronto: University of Toronto Press, 2012.

Hattam, Victoria. "Ethnicity and the Boundaries of Race: Rereading Directive 15." *Daedalus* 134, no. 1 (2005): 61–69.

In the Shadow of Race: Jews, Latinos, and Immigrant Politics in the United States. Chicago: University of Chicago Press, 2007.

Hawkins, Freda. *Canada and Immigration: Public Policy and Public Concern*. Montreal: McGill-Queens University Press, 1972.

Critical Years in Immigration: Canada and Australia Compared. Kingston and Montreal: McGill-Queen's University Press, 1989.

Henry, Frances, and Carol Tator. *The Colour of Democracy: Racism in Canadian Society*, 4th edn. Toronto: Harcourt Brace Canada, 2010.

Her Majesty's Government. *1991 Census of the Population (Census White Paper)*, Cm 430, London: HMSO, 1988.

The 2001 Census of Population (Census White Paper), Cm 4253. London: HMSO, 1999.

Census of the Population, 2001. London: HMSO, 1999.

Her Majesty's Government. Parliament. *Ethnic and Racial Questions in the Census, Volume I: Report together with Proceedings of the*

Committee. Second Report from the Home Affairs Committee, Session 1982–83. HC 33-I. London: HMSO, 1983.

The Government Reply to the Second Report of the Home Affairs Committee Session 1982–83 HC 33-I: *Ethnic and Racial Questions on the Census*. London: HMSO, 1984.

Her Majesty's Government. Select Committee on Race Relations and Immigration. *The Organisation of Race Relations Administration*. London: HMSO, 1975.

Hernández, Tanya Katerí. "'Multicultural Discourse': Racial Classifications in an Era of Color-Blind Jurisprudence." *Maryland Law Review* 57, no. 1 (1998): 97–173.

Hesse, Barnor. "Introduction: Un/Settled Multiculturalisms." In *Un/settled Multiculturalisms: Diasporas, Entanglements, Transruptions*, edited by Barnor Hesse, 1–30. London and New York: Zed Books, 2000.

"Racialized Modernity: An Analytics of White Mythologies." *Ethnic and Racial Studies* 30, no. 4 (2007): 643–663.

"Self-Fulfilling Prophecy: The Postracial Horizon." *South Atlantic Quarterly* 110, no. 1 (2011): 155–178.

"Escaping Liberty: Western Hegemony, Black Fugitivity." *Political Theory* 42, no. 3 (2014): 288–313.

Hillygus, D. Sunshine, Norman H. Nie, Kenneth Prewitt, and Heili Pals. *The Hard Count: The Political and Social Challenges of Census Mobilization*. New York: Russell Sage Foundation, 2006.

Hindell, Keith. "The Genesis of the Race Relations Bill." *The Political Quarterly* 36, no. 4 (1965): 390–405.

Hirschman, Charles. "The Origins and Demise of the Concept of Race." *Population and Development Review* 30, no. 3 (2004): 385–415.

Hochschild, Jennifer L., and Brenna Marea Powell. "Racial Reorganization and the United States Census 1850–1930: Mulattoes, Half-Breeds, Mixed Parentage, Hindoos and the Mexican Race." *Studies in American Political Development* 22, no. 1 (2008): 59–96.

Hochschild, Jennifer, and Vesla Mae Weaver. "'There's No One as Irish as Barack O'Bama': The Policy and Politics of American Multiracialism." *Perspectives on Politics* 8, no. 3 (2010): 737–759.

Hochschild, Jennifer L., Vesla M. Weaver, and Traci R. Burch. *Creating a New Racial Order: How Immigration, Multiracialism, Genomics, and the Young can Remake Race in America*. Princeton: Princeton University Press, 2012.

Hodes, Martha. *White Women, Black Men: Illicit Sex in the Nineteenth Century South*. New Haven: Yale University Press, 1997.

Holbrook, Allyson. "Response Order Effects." In *Encyclopedia of Survey Research Methods*, edited by Paul J. Lavrakas, 756. Thousand Oaks: Sage Publications, 2008.

Hollinger, David. *Postethnic America: Beyond Multiculturalism*, rev. edn. New York: Basic Books, 2000.

Hooker, Juliet. "Indigenous Inclusion/Black Exclusion: Race, Ethnicity and Multicultural Citizenship in Latin America." *Journal of Latin American Studies* 37, no. 2 (2005): 285–310.

Hope, Christopher. "National Census to be Axed After 200 years." *The Telegraph*, July 9, 2010. Accessed July 10, 2014, www.telegraph.co.uk/news/politics/7882774/National-census-to-be-axed-after-200-years.html

Horne, Gerald. *Black and Red: WEB Du Bois and the Afro-American Response to the Cold War, 1944–1963*. Albany: SUNY Press, 1986.

Howe, Samuel G. *The Refugees from Slavery in Canada West: Report to the Freedmen's Inquiry Commission*. Boston: Wright and Potter Printers, 1864.

Humes, Karen. *2010 Census Alternative Questionnaire Experiment: Race and Hispanic Origin Treatments*. Washington D.C.: U.S. Census Bureau, 2009.

Huxley, Julian, and Alfred Haddon. *We Europeans: A Survey of "Racial" Problems*. New York and London: Harper, 1935.

Ibbitson, John. "Survey Says: Government Still Not Listening on the Census." *The Globe and Mail*, July 27, 2010. Accessed June 21, 2016, www.theglobeandmail.com/news/politics/survey-says-government-still-not-listening-on-census/article1387919/

Ignatiev, Noel. *How the Irish Became White*. New York: Routledge, 1995.

Ingersoll, Thomas N. *To Intermix with Our White Brothers: Indian Mixed Bloods in the United States from the Earliest Times to the Indian Removals*. Albuquerque: University of New Mexico Press, 2005.

Inglis, Christine. "Multiculturalism: New Policy Responses to Diversity." Policy Paper No. 4, UNESCO Management of Social Transformation. Accessed April 15, 2014, www.unesco.org/most/pp4.htm

Iton, Richard. *In Search of the Black Fantastic: Politics and Popular Culture in the Post-Civil Rights Era*. New York: Oxford University Press, 2008.

"Still Life." *small axe* 40 (2013): 22–39

Jacobson, Matthew Frye. *Whiteness of a Different Color: European Immigrants and the Alchemy of Race*. Cambridge: Harvard University Press, 1998.

James, Matt. "Neoliberal Heritage Redress." *In Reconciling Canada: Critical Perspectives on the Culture of Redress*, edited by Jennifer Henderson and Pauline Wakeham, 31–45. Toronto: University of Toronto Press, 2013.

Jedwab, Jack. "Coming to Our Census: The Need for Continued Inquiry into Canadians' Ethnic Origins." *Canadian Ethnic Studies* 35, no. 1 (2003): 35–50.

Jones, Branwen Gruffydd. "Race in the Ontology of International Order." *Political Studies* 56, no. 4 (2008): 907–927.

Jones, Nicholas A. *We the People of More than One Race in the United States*. Census 2000 Special Reports. Washington D.C.: U.S. Census Bureau, 2005.

Jones, Nicholas A., and Jungmiwha Bullock. *The Two or More Races Population: 2010*. Census Brief. Washington D.C.: U.S. Census Bureau, 2012.

Joppke, Christian. "Multiculturalism and Immigration: A Comparison of the United States, Germany, and Great Britain." *Theory and Society* 25, no 4 (1996): 449–500.

Immigration and the Nation-State: the United States, Germany, and Great Britain. Oxford and New York: Oxford University Press, 1999.

"The Retreat of Multiculturalism in the Liberal State: Theory and Policy." *The British Journal of Sociology* 55, no. 2 (2004): 237–257.

Selecting by Origin: Ethnic Migration in the Liberal State. Cambridge: Harvard University Press, 2005.

Jordan, Winthrop D. *White over Black: American Attitudes toward the Negro, 1550–1812*. Chapel Hill: University of North Carolina Press, 1968.

Judis, John B. "Census Nonsense." *The New Republic*, April 7, 2010. Accessed June 21, 2016, www.newrepublic.com/article/74334/census-nonsense

Katznelson, Ira. *Black Men, White Cities: Race, Politics, and Migration in the United States, 1900–30, and Britain, 1948–68*. Chicago: University of Chicago Press, 1976.

"Strong Theory, Complex History: Structure and Configuration in Comparative Politics Revisited." In *Comparative Politics: Rationality, Culture, and Structure*, edited by Mark Irving Lichbach, and Alan S. Zuckerman, 81–112, 2nd edn. New York: Cambridge University Press, 2009.

Kelley, Ninette, and Michael Trebilcock. *The Making of the Mosaic: A History of Canadian Immigration Policy*, 2nd edn. Toronto: University of Toronto Press, 2010.

Kelly, Karen. *Collecting Census Data on Canada's Visible Minority Population: A Historical Perspective*. Ottawa: Statistics Canada, 1995.

Kennedy, Joseph Camp Griffith. "The Origin and Progress of Statistics." *Journal of American Geographical and Statistical Society* 2 (1860): 92–120.

Kertzer, David I., and Dominique Arel. "Censuses, Identity Formation, and the Struggle for Political Power." In *Census and Identity: The Politics of Race, Ethnicity, and Language in National Censuses*, edited by David I. Kertzer, and Dominique Arel, 1–42. Cambridge: Cambridge University Press, 2002.

Kevles, Daniel J. *In the Name of Eugenics: Genetics and the Uses of Human Heredity*, rev. edn. Cambridge: Harvard University Press, 1995.

King, Desmond S. *In the Name of Liberalism: Illiberal Social Policy in the USA and Britain*. Oxford and New York: Oxford University Press, 1999.

Making Americans: Immigration, Race, and the Origins of Diverse Democracy. Cambridge: Harvard University Press, 2000.

King, Desmond S. and Rogers M. Smith. "Racial Orders in American Political Development." *American Political Science Review* 99, no. 1 (2005): 75–92.

Still a House Divided: Race and Politics in Obama's America. Princeton: Princeton University Press, 2011.

King, Desmond, and Marc Stears. "How the US State Works: A Theory of Standardization." *Perspectives on Politics* 9, no. 3 (2011): 505–518.

Kirkham, Della. "The Reform Party of Canada: A Discourse on Race, Ethnicity and Equality." In *Racism and Social Inequality in Canada: Concepts, Controversies and Strategies of Resistance*, edited by Vic Satzewich, 243–267. Toronto: Thompson Educational Publishing Inc., 1998.

Klinkner, Philip A., and Rogers M. Smith. *The Unsteady March: The Rise and Decline of Racial Equality in America*. Chicago: University of Chicago Press, 1999.

Klotz, Audie. *Norms in International Relations: The Struggle against Apartheid*. Ithaca: Cornell University Press, 1995.

Knill, Christoph. "Introduction: Cross-National Policy Convergence: Concepts, Approaches and Explanatory Factors." *Journal of European Public Policy* 12, no. 5 (2005): 764–774.

Knowles, Valerie. *Strangers at Our Gates: Canadian Immigration and Immigration Policy, 1540–1990*. Toronto: Dundurn Press, 1992.

Kollman, Kelly. "Same Sex Unions: The Globalization of an Idea." *International Studies Quarterly* 51, no. 2 (2007): 329–357.

Kosmin, Barry. "Ethnic and Religious Questions in the 2001 UK Census of Population Policy Recommendations." Institute for Jewish Policy Research, Policy Paper No. 2, 1999.

Kralt, John. "Ethnic Origins in the Canadian Census, 1871–1986." In *Ethnic Demography: Canadian Immigrant, Ethnic and Cultural*

Variations, edited by Shiva S. Halli, Frank Trovato, and Leo Driedger, 13–29. Montreal and Kingston: McGill-Queen's University Press, 1990.

Kukutai, Tahu. "Building Ethnic Boundaries in New Zealand: Representations of Maori Identity in the Census." In *Indigenous Peoples and Demography: the Complex Relation Between Identity and Statistics*, edited by Per Axelsson and Peter Sköld, 33–54. Oxford: Berghahn Books, 2011.

Kukutai, Tahu, and Robert Didham. "In Search of Ethnic New Zealanders: National Naming in the 2006 Census." *Social Policy Journal of New Zealand* 36 (2009): 46–62.

"Re-Making the Majority? Ethnic New Zealanders in the 2006 Census." *Ethnic and Racial Studies* 35, no. 8 (2012): 1427–1446.

Kukutai, Tahu, and Victor Thompson. "'Inside Out': The Politics of Ethnically Enumerating the Nation by Ethnicity." In *Social Statistics and Ethnic Diversity: Cross-National Perspectives in Classifications and Identity Politics*, edited by Patrick Simon, Victor Piché and Amélie Gagnon, 39–61. Cham: Springer Publishing International, 2015.

Kymlicka, Will. *Multicultural Citizenship: A Liberal Theory of Minority Rights*. Oxford: Clarendon Press, 1995.

Finding Our Way: Rethinking Ethnocultural Relations in Canada. Toronto: Oxford University Press, 1998.

"Comments on Shachar and Spinner-Halev: An Update from the Multiculturalism Wars." In *Multicultural Questions*, edited by Christian Joppke and Stephen Lukes, 112–131 (Oxford: Oxford University Press, 1999).

Politics in the Vernacular: Nationalism, Multiculturalism, and Citizenship. Oxford: Oxford University Press, 2001.

"American Multiculturalism and the Nations Within." In *Political Theory and the Rights of Indigenous Peoples*, edited by Duncan Ivison, Paul Patton, and Will Sanders, 216–236 (New York: Cambridge University Press, 2000).

Multicultural Odysseys: Navigating the New International Politics of Diversity. Oxford: Oxford University Press, 2007.

"Neoliberal Multiculturalism?" In *Social Resilience in the Neoliberal Era*, edited by Peter Hall and Michèle Lamont, 99–125. New York: Cambridge University Press, 2013.

Lake, Marilyn, and Henry Reynolds. *Drawing the Global Colour Line: White Men's Countries and the International Challenge Racial Equality*. Cambridge: Cambridge University Press, 2008.

Lamont, Michèle, and Virág Molnár. "The Study of Boundaries in the Social Sciences." *Annual Review of Sociology* 28 (2002): 167–195.

Larson, Edward John. *Sex, Race, and Science: Eugenics in the Deep South*. Baltimore: Johns Hopkins University Press, 1995.

Lasswell, Harold Dwight. *Politics: Who Gets What, When, How*. New York: P. Smith, 1950.

Lauren, Paul Gordon. *Power and Prejudice: The Politics and Diplomacy of Racial Discrimination*, 2nd edn. Boulder: Westview Press, 1996.

Lawrence, Bonita. "Gender, Race, and the Regulation of Native Identity in Canada and the United States: An Overview." *Hypatia* 18, no. 2 (2003): 3–31.

Layton, Azza Salama. "International Pressure and the U.S. Government's Response to Little Rock." *The Arkansas Historical Quarterly* 56, no. 3 (1997): 257–272.

Lee, Jennifer, and Frank D Bean. "America's Changing Color Lines: Immigration, Race/ethnicity, and Multiracial Identification." *Annual Review of Sociology* 30 (2004): 221–242.

The Diversity Paradox: Immigration and the Color Line in Twenty-first Century America. New York: Russell Sage Foundation, 2010.

Lee, Sharon M. "Racial Classifications in the U.S. Census: 1890–1990." *Ethnic and Racial Studies* 16, no. 1 (1993): 75–94.

Leech, Kenneth. *A Question in Dispute: The Debate about an "Ethnic" Question in the Census*. London: Runnymede Trust, 1989.

Leslie, John, and Ron Maguire. *The Historical Development of the Indian Act*. Ottawa: Department of Indian Affairs and Northern Development, 1978.

Lester, Anthony, and Geoffrey Bindman. *Race and Law*. London: Longman, 1972.

Li, Peter S. *The Chinese in Canada*. Toronto: Oxford University Press, 1988.

Lieberman, Robert C. "Ideas, Institutions, and Political Order: Explaining Political Change." *American Political Science Review* 96, no. 4 (2002): 697–712.

Lieberson, Stanley. "The Enumeration of Ethnic and Racial Groups in the Census: Some Devilish Principles." In *Challenges of Measuring an Ethnic World: Science, Politics and Reality*, Proceedings of the Joint Canada-United States Conference on the Measurement of Ethnicity, April 1–3, 1992, 29–34. Washington D.C.: U.S. Government Printing Office, 1993.

Lieberson, Stanley, and Mary C. Waters. *From Many Strands: Ethnic and Racial Groups in Contemporary America*. New York: Russell Sage Foundation, 1988.

Liss, Julia E. "Diasporic Identities: The Science and Politics of Race in the Work of Franz Boas and W.E.B. Du Bois, 1894–1919." *Cultural Anthropology* 13, no. 2 (1998): 127–166.

Lopez, Ian Haney. *White by Law: The Legal Construction of Race*. New York: New York University Press, 1996.

"Is the 'Post' in Post-Racial the 'Blind' in Colorblind?" *Cardozo Law Review* 32, no. 3 (2010): 807–831.

Loveman, Mara. "Whiteness in Latin America: Measurement and Meaning in National Censuses (1850–1950)." *Journal de la Société des Américanistes* 95, no. 2 (2009): 207–234.

National Colors: Racial Classification and the State in Latin America. New York: Oxford University Press, 2014.

Lowance, Mason I., Jr., *A House Divided: The Antebellum Slavery Debates in America, 1776–1865*. Princeton and Oxford: Princeton University Press, 2003.

Lowndes, Joseph E., Julie Novkov, and Dorian Warren, eds. *Race and American Political Development*. New York: Routledge, 2008.

MacKinnon, Catharine A. *Toward a Feminist Theory of the State*. Cambridge, MA: Harvard University Press, 1989.

MacLennan, Christopher. *Toward the Charter: Canadians and the Demand for a National Bill of Rights, 1929–1960*. Montreal and Kingston: McGill-Queen's University Press, 2003.

Mahtani, Minelle, and April Moreno. "Same Difference: Towards a More Unified Discourse in 'Mixed Race' Theory." In *Rethinking Mixed Race*, edited by David Parker and Miri Song, 65–75. London: Pluto Press, 2001.

Makkonen, Timo. *Measuring Discrimination: Data Collection and EU Equality Law*. Luxembourg: Office for Official Publications of the European Communities, 2007.

Malenfant, Éric Caron, André Lebel, and Laurent Martel. *Projections of the Diversity of the Canadian Population, 2006 to 2031*. Ottawa: Statistics Canada, 2010.

Marsh, David, and R.A.W. Rhodes, eds. *Policy Networks in British Government*. Oxford: Claredon Press, 1992.

Marsh, David, and J.C. Sharman. "Policy Diffusion and Policy Transfer." *Policy Studies* 30, no. 3 (2009): 269–288.

Marsh, David, and Martin Smith. "Understanding Policy Networks: Towards a Dialectical Approach." *Political Studies* 48, no. 1 (2000): 4–21.

Marx, Anthony W. *Making Race and Nation: A Comparison of South Africa, the United States, and Brazil*. Cambridge: Cambridge University Press, 1998.

Mather, Mark, Kerri L. Rivers, and Linda A. Jacobsen. "The American Community Survey." *Population Bulletin* 60, no. 3 (2005).

Mathieu, Sarah-Jane. "North of the Colour Line: Sleeping Car Porters and the Battle against Jim Crow on Canadian Rails, 1880–1920." *Labour/Le Travail* 47 (2001): 9–41.

North of the Color Line: Migration and Black Resistance in Canada, 1870–1955. Chapel Hill: University of North Carolina Press, 2010.

McAdam, Doug. *Political Process and the Development of Black Insurgency, 1930–1970*. Chicago: University of Chicago Press, 1982.

"On the International Origins of Domestic Political Opportunities." In *Social Movements and American Political Institutions*, edited by Anne N. Costain and Andrew S. McFarland, 251–267. New York: Rowman and Littlefield Publishers, 1998.

McClain, Paula D., and Joseph Stewart Jr., *Can We All Get Along? Racial and Ethnic Minorities in American Politics*, 5th edn. Boulder: Westview Press, 2010.

McDonald, Laughlin, and John A. Powell. *The Rights of Racial Minorities: The Basic ACLU Guide to Racial Minority Rights*, 2nd edn. Carbondale: Southern Illinois University Press, 1993.

McKenney, Nampeo R., and Arthur R. Cresce. "Measurement of Ethnicity in the United States: Experiences of the U.S. Census Bureau." In *Challenges of Measuring an Ethnic World: Science, Politics and Reality*. Proceedings of the Joint Canada-United States Conference on the Measurement of Ethnicity, April 1–3, 1992, 173–221. Washington D.C.: U.S. Government Printing Office, 1993.

McLaren, Angus. *Our Own Master Race: Eugenics in Canada, 1885–1945*. Toronto: Oxford University Press, 1990.

McRoberts, Kenneth. *Misconceiving Canada: The Struggle for National Unity*. Toronto: Oxford University Press, 1997.

Meer, Nasar, and Tariq Modood. "The Multicultural State We're In: Muslims, 'Multiculture' and the 'Civic Rebalancing' of British Multiculturalism." *Political Studies* 57, no. 3 (2009): 473–497.

Melamed, Jodi. "The Spirit of Neoliberalism from Racial Liberalism to Neoliberal Multiculturalism." *Social Text* 24, no. 4 (2006): 1–24.

Mesenbourg, Tom. "Census Bureau Budget Update." Census Director's Blog, June 19, 2013. Accessed July 14, 2014, http://directorsblog.blogs.census.gov/2013/06/19/census-bureau-budget-update-2/

Messina, Anthony M. *Race and Party Competition in Britain*. Oxford: Oxford University Press, 1989.

Mettler, Suzanne. *The Submerged State: How Invisible Government Policies Undermine American Democracy*. Chicago: University of Chicago Press, 2011.

Meyer, John, John Boli, George M. Thomas, and Francisco O. Ramirez. "World Society and the Nation-State." *American Journal of Sociology* 103, no. 1 (1997): 144–181.

Migdal, Joel S. *State in Society: Studying How States and Societies Transform and Constitute One Another*. Cambridge and New York: Cambridge University Press, 2001.

Milan, Anne, and Brian Hamm. "Mixed Unions." *Canadian Social Trends* no. 73 (2004): 2–6.

Milan, Anne, Hélène Maheaux, and Tina Chui, "A Portrait of Couples in Mixed Unions, Statistics Canada." *Canadian Social Trends* no. 89 (2010): 70–80.

Miles, Robert. "The Riots of 1958: Notes on the Ideological Construction of 'Race Relations' as a Political Issue in Britain." *Immigrants and Minorities* 3, no. 3 (1984): 252–275.

Miles, Robert, and Annie Phizacklea. *White Man's Country: Racism in British Politics*. London: Pluto Press, 1984.

Mills, Charles W. *Blackness Visible: Essays on Philosophy and Race*. Ithaca: Cornell University Press, 1998.

The Racial Contract. Ithaca: Cornell University Press, 1997.

Mills, Sean. *The Empire Within: Postcolonial Thought and Political Activism in Sixties Montreal*. Montreal and Kingston: McGill-Queen's University Press, 2010.

Mitchell, Timothy. "The Limits of the State: Beyond Statist Approaches and Their Critics." *American Political Science Review* 85, no. 1 (1991): 77–96.

Modood, Tariq. *Multicultural Politics: Racism, Ethnicity, and Muslims in Britain*. Minneapolis: University of Minnesota Press, 2005.

Multiculturalism: A Civic Idea. Cambridge: Polity Press, 2005.

Montagu, Ashley. *Man's Most Dangerous Myth: The Fallacy of Race*. Walnut Creek: AltaMira Press, 1942.

Moran, Rachel. *Interracial Intimacy: The Regulation of Race and Romance*. Chicago and London: University of Chicago Press, 2001.

Morning, Ann. "Ethnic Classification in Global Perspective: A Cross-National Survey of the 2000 Census Round." *Population Research and Policy Review* 27, no. 2 (2000): 239–272.

Morris, Aldon. *The Scholar Denied: W.E.B. Du Bois and the Birth of Modern Sociology*. Oakland: University of California Press, 2015.

Morton, Samuel. *Crania Americana; or, A comparative View of the Skulls of Various Aboriginal Nations of North and South America: To Which Is Prefixed an Essay on the Varieties of the Human Species*. London: J. Dobson, 1839.

Myrdal, Gunnar. *An American Dilemma, Volume 2: The Negro Problem and Modern Democracy*. 20th Anniversary Edition. New York: Harper and Row, 1962.

Nasser, Haya El. "Arabs, Hispanics Seeking Better US Census Recognition." *Aljazeera America*, December 17, 2013. Accessed July 27, 2014, http://america.aljazeera.com/articles/2013/12/17/arabs-hispanics-seekingbetteruscensusrecognition.html

National Research Council. *Principles and Practices for a Federal Statistical Agency*, edited by Constance F. Citro and Miron L. Straf. 5th edn. Washington D.C.: The National Academies Press, 2013.

Neal, Sarah. "The Scarman Report, the Macpherson Report and the Media: How Newspapers Respond to Race-Centred Social Policy Interventions." *Journal of Social Policy* 32, no. 1 (2003): 55–74.

Ngai, Mae M. *Impossible Subjects: Illegal Aliens and the Making of Modern America*. Princeton: Princeton University Press, 2004.

Nichols, Roger L. *Indians in the United States and Canada: A Comparative History*. Lincoln: University of Nebraska Press, 1998.

Nobles, Melissa. *Shades of Citizenship: Race and the Census in Modern Politics*. Stanford: Stanford University Press, 2000.

Norwood, Janet L. *Organizing to Count: Change in the Federal Statistical System*. Washington D.C.: Urban Institute Press, 1995.

Nott, Josiah C. "Diversity of the Human Race." *Debow's Review* 10, no. 2 (1851): 113–132.

Nott, Josiah C., and G.R. Gliddon. *Types of Mankind: Or, Ethnological Researches, Based upon the Ancient Monuments, Paintings, Sculptures, and Crania of Races, and Upon their Natural, Geographical, Philological, and Biblical History*. Philadelphia: Lippincott, Grambo, 1854.

Nova Scotia. *Census of St. John Island: Populations, Sexes, Religions, Origins*. 1767.

Novkov, Julie L. *Racial Union: Law, Intimacy, and the White State in Alabama, 1865–1954*. Ann Arbor: University of Michigan Press, 2008.

O'Connor, Julia S., Ann Shola Orloff, and Sheila Shaver. *States, Markets, Families: Gender, Liberalism and Social Policy in Australia, Canada, Great Britain and the United States*. Cambridge: Cambridge University Press, 1999.

Office for National Statistics. *Census Strategic Development Review: Alternatives to a Census: Linkage of Existing Data Sources*. London: HMSO, 2003.

Proposals for an Integrated Population Statistics System. London: HMSO: 2003.

Consultation Summary Report of Responses to the 2011 Census Stakeholders Consultation 2006/07: Ethnic Group, National

Identity, Religion and Language, England and Wales. London: ONS, 2007.

Information Paper: Deciding which Tick-Boxes to Add to the Ethnic Group Question in the 2011 England and Wales Census. London: ONS, 2009.

Final Recommended Questions for the 2011 Census in England and Wales: Ethnic Group. London: ONS, 2009.

"ONS Takes a Fresh Look beyond 2011," News Release, October 17, 2011. Accessed June 21, 2016, http://webarchive.nationalarchives.gov.uk/20160105160709/http://www.ons.gov.uk/ons/rel/mro/news-release/beyond-2011/ons-takes-a-fresh-look–beyond-2011-.html

The Census and the Future Provision of Population Statistics in England and Wales: Recommendation from the National Statistician and *Chief Executive of the UK Statistics Authority*. London: ONS, 2014.

What Does the 2011 Census Tell Us about Inter-Ethnic Relationships? London: ONS, 2014.

Office of Management and Budget. "Race and Ethnic Standards for Federal Statistics and Administrative Reporting." Statistical Directive No. 15, 1977.

"Guidelines for Federal Statistical Activities." *Federal Register* 53, no. 12 (1988): 1542–1552.

"Standards for the Classification of Federal Data on Race and Ethnicity." *Federal Register* 59, no. 110 (1994): 29831–29835.

"Standards for the Classification of Federal Data on Race and Ethnicity." *Federal Register* 60, no. 166 (1995): 44677–44693.

"Recommendations from the Interagency Committee for the Review of the Racial and Ethnic Standards to the Office of Management and Budget Concerning Changes to the Standards for the Classification of Federal Data on Race and Ethnicity." *Federal Register* 62, no. 131 (1997): 36873–36946.

"Revisions to the Standards for the Classification of Federal Data on Race and Ethnicity." *Federal Register* 62, no. 210 (1997): 58781–58790.

Office of Population Censuses and Surveys. "Country of Birth and Colour." *Population Trends* 2 (1975): 2–8.

Tests of an Ethnic Question. OPCS Monitor CEN 80/2, 1980.

Census 1981: General Report, England and Wales. London: HMSO, 1990.

Ethnicity in the 1991 Census: Volume One: Demographic Characteristics of the Ethnic Minority Populations. London: HMSO, 1996.

Looking towards the 2001 Census, Occasional Paper 46. London: OPCS, 1996.

Office of Population Censuses and Surveys and General Register Office for Scotland. "Major steps towards the 1991 Census." *1981 … 1991 Census Newsletter*, no. 4. December 17, 1987.

"Coverage in the 1991 Census." *Census Newsletter* 32, no. 3 (1995).

"New OPCS Area Classifications." *Census Newsletter* 33, no. 16 (1995).

Omi, Michael, and Howard Winant. *Racial Formation in the United States: From the 1960s to the 1990s*, 2nd edn. New York and London: Routledge, 1994.

Ong, Aihwa. *Flexible Citizenship: The Cultural Logics of Transnationality*. Durham: Duke University Press, 1999.

Neoliberalism as Exception: Mutations in Citizenship and Sovereignty. Durham: Duke University Press, 2006.

Orren, Karen, and Stephen Skowronek. *The Search for American Political Development*. New York: Cambridge University Press, 2004.

Orloff, Ann Shola, *The Politics of Pensions: A Comparative Analysis of Britain, Canada, and the United States, 1880–1940*. Madison: University of Wisconsin Press, 1993.

Outlaw, Lucius. "Toward a Critical Theory of 'Race'." In *Anatomy of Racism*, edited by David Theo Goldberg, 58–82. Minneapolis: University of Minnesota Press, 1990.

Owen, David. *Towards 2001: Ethnic Minorities and the Census*. Centre for Research in Ethnic Relations: University of Warwick, 1996.

Panke, Diana, and Ulrich Petersohn. "Why International Norms Disappear Sometimes." *European Journal of International Relations* 18, no. 4 (2012): 719–742.

Pant, Rashmi. "The Cognitive Status of Caste in Colonial Ethnography: A Review of Some Literature on the North West Provinces and Oudh." *Indian Economic and Social History Review* 24 (1987): 145–162.

Parekh, Bhikhu C. *Rethinking Multiculturalism: Cultural Diversity and Political Theory*. Harvard University Press, 2000.

The Future of Multi-Ethnic Britain: Report of the Commission on the Future of Multi-Ethnic Britain. London: Profile Books, 2000.

Pascoe, Peggy. *What Comes Naturally: Miscegenation Law and the Making of Race in America*. Oxford: Oxford University Press, 2009.

Patriarca, Silvana. *Numbers and Nationhood: Writing Statistics in Nineteenth-Century Italy*. Cambridge: Cambridge University Press, 1996.

Patrias, Carmela. "Socialists, Jews, and the 1947 Saskatchewan Bill of Rights." *Canadian Historical Review* 87, no. 2 (2006): 265–292.

Patrias, Carmela, and Ruth A Frager. "'This Is Our Country, These Are Our Rights': Minorities and the Origins of Ontario's Human Rights Campaigns." *Canadian Historical Review* 82, no. 1 (2001): 1–35.

Paul, Kathleen. *Whitewashing Britain: Race and Citizenship in the Postwar Era*. Ithaca: Cornell University Press, 1997.

Peabody, Norbert "Cents, Sense, Census: Human Inventories in Late Precolonial and Early Colonial India." *Comparative Studies in Society and History* 43, no. 4 (2001): 819–850.

Perlmann, Joel, and Mary C. Waters, eds. *The New Race Question: How the Census Counts Multiracial Individuals*. New York: Russell Sage Foundation, 2002.

Peters, B. Guy, Jon Pierre, and Desmond S. King. "The Politics of Path Dependency: Political Conflict in Historical Institutionalism." *Journal of Politics* 67, no. 4 (2005): 1275–1300.

Pierson, Paul. "Path Dependency, Increasing Returns, and the Study of Politics." *American Political Science Review* 94, no. 2 (2000): 251–267.

Politics in Time: History, Institutions, and Social Analysis. Princeton: Princeton University Press, 2004.

Piven, Frances Fox. "Can Power from Below Change the World?" *American Sociological Review* 73, no. 1 (2008): 1–14.

Porter, Robert. "The Eleventh United States Census." *Journal of the Royal Statistical Society* 57, no. 4 (1894): 643–677.

Porter, Theodore M. *The Rise of Statistical Thinking, 1820–1900*. Princeton: Princeton University Press, 1986.

Potvin, Maryse. "The Role of Statistics on Ethnic Origin and 'Race' in Canadian Anti-Discrimination Policy." *International Social Science Journal* 57, no. 163 (2005): 27–42.

Potvin, Maryse, and Sophie Latraverse. *Comparative Study on the Collection of Data to Measure the Extent and Impact of Discrimination in a Selection of Countries: Final Report on Canada*. Lyon, FR: European Commission, Employment and Social Affairs DG, 2004.

Preston, Sarah. *The Colonial Blue Books: A Major Resource in the Royal Commonwealth Society Library*. Reproduced from the *Bulletin of the Friends of Cambridge University Library* no. 26–27 (2006). Accessed March 11, 2014, www.lib.cam.ac.uk/deptserv/rcs/rcs_op_project/FriendsofCULibraryarticle.htm

Prewitt, Kenneth. "Politics and Science in Census Taking." In *The American People: Census 2000*, edited by Reynolds Farley and John Haaga, 3–45. New York: Russell Sage Foundation, 2005.

"The U.S. Decennial Census: Politics and Political Science." *Annual Review of Political Science* 13 (2010): 237–254.

What Is Your Race?: The Census and Our Flawed Efforts to Classify Americans. Princeton: Princeton University Press, 2013.

Pryor, Edward T., Gustave J. Goldmann, Michael Sheridan, and Pamela White. "Measuring Ethnicity: Is 'Canadian' an Evolving

Indigenous Category?" *Ethnic and Racial Studies* 15, no. 2 (1992): 214–235.

Pullinger, John. "The Creation of the Office for National Statistics." *International Statistical Review* 65, no. 3 (1997): 291–308.

Putnam, Robert D. "E pluribus unum: Diversity and Community in the Twenty-First Century. The 2006 Johan Skytte Prize Lecture." *Scandinavian Political Studies* 30, no. 2 (2007): 137–174.

Race Relations Board. *Report of the Race Relations Board for 1966–67*. London: HMSO, 1967.

Report of the Race Relations Board for 1974. London: HMSO, 1975.

Rallu, Jean-Louis, Victor Piché, and Patrick Simon. "Démographie et Ethnicité: Une Relation Ambiguë." In *Démographie: Analyse et Synthèse*, edited by G. Caselli, J. Vallin, and G. Wunsch, 481–516. Paris: Institut National d'Etudes Démographiques, 2004.

Ramp, William, and Trevor W. Harrison. "Libertarian Populism, Neoliberal Rationality, and the Mandatory Long-form Census: Implications for Sociology." *Canadian Journal of Sociology* 37, no. 3 (2012): 273–294.

Rampell, Catherine. "The Beginning of the End of the Census?" *The New York Times*, May 19, 2012. Accessed July 16, 2013, www.nytimes.com/2012/05/20/sunday-review/the-debate-over-the-american-community-survey.html?_r=0

Rasmussen, Ken. "Administrative Reform and the Quest for Bureaucratic Autonomy, 1867–1919." *Journal of Canadian Studies* 29, no. 3 (1994): 45–62.

Ringelheim, Julie. "Collecting Racial or Ethnic Data for Antidiscrimination Policies: A U.S.-Europe Comparison." *Rutgers Race and the Law Review* 10, no. 1 (2009): 39–142.

Ríos, Mararys, Fabián Romero, and Roberto Ramírez. *Race Reporting Among Hispanics: 2010*, U.S. Census Bureau Population Division Working Paper. Washington D.C.: U.S. Census Bureau, 2014.

Risse, Thomas, Stephen C. Ropp, and Kathryn Sikkink, eds. *The Power of Human Rights, International Norms and Domestic Change*. New York: Cambridge University Press, 1999.

Robbin, Alice. "Classifying Racial and Ethnic Group Data in the United States: The Politics of Negotiation and Accommodation." *Journal of Government Information* 27 (2000): 139–156.

"The Politics of Representation in the US National Statistical System: Origins of Minority Population Interest Group Participation." *Journal of Government Information* 27, no. 4 (2000): 431–453.

Roberts, Dorothy. *Killing the Black Body: Race, Reproduction, and the Meaning of Liberty*. New York: Vintage, 1997.

Roberts, Sam. "In a Generation, Minorities May Be the US Majority." *New York Times*, August 14, 2008. Accessed June 25, 2014, www.nytimes.com/2008/08/14/washington/14census.html?pagewanted=all

"Projections Put Whites in Minority in US by 2050." *The New York Times*, December 17, 2009. Accessed June 25, 2014, www.nytimes.com/2008/08/14/world/americas/14iht-census.1.15284537.html?_r=0

Rodriguez, Clara E. *Changing Race: Latinos, the Census, and the History of Ethnicity in the United States*. New York: New York University Press, 2000.

Rodriguez, Gregory. "President Obama: At Odds with Clear Demographic Trends toward Multiracial Pride." *LA Times* April 4, 2011. Accessed November 10, 2011, www.latimes.com/news/opinion/commentary/la-oe-rodriguez-column-obama-race-20110404,0,3716973.column

Roediger, David. *The Wages of Whiteness: Race and the Making of the American Working Class*. New York: Verso, 1991.

Working toward Whiteness: How America's Immigrants Became White; the Strange Journey from Ellis Island to the Suburbs. New York: Basic Books, 2005.

Rose, Eliot, Joseph Benn et al. *Colour and Citizenship: A Report on British Race Relations*. London: Printed for the Institute of Race Relations by Oxford University Press, 1969.

Ross, Dorothy. *The Origins of American Social Science*. Cambridge: Cambridge University Press, 1991.

Rueschemeyer, Dietrich. "Can One or a Few Cases Yield Theoretical Gains?" In *Comparative Historical Analysis in the Social Sciences*, edited by James Mahoney and Dietrich Rueschemeyer, 305–336. New York: Cambridge University Press, 2003.

Ruppert, Evelyn S. "Producing Population." Working Paper No. 37. CRES Working Paper Series. Milton Keyes: CRES, 2007.

Ryder, N.B. "The Interpretation of Origin Statistics." *The Canadian Journal of Economics and Political Science* 21, no. 4 (1955): 466–479.

Sabatier, Paul A., and Hank C. Jenkins-Smith, eds. *Policy Change and Learning: An Advocacy-Coalition Approach*. Boulder: Westview Press, 1993.

Sawer, Marian. "Gender, Metaphor, and the State." *Feminist Review* 52 (1996): 118–134.

Sabbagh, Daniel, and Ann Morning. *Comparative Study on the Collection of Data to Measure the Extent and Impact of Discrimination in a Selection of Countries: Final Report on the United States*. Lyon, FR: European Commission, Employment and Social Affairs DG, 2004.

Santamaria, Ulysses, and Kristin Couper. "The Making of the Multi-Racial Society in the United Kingdom: Strategies and Perspectives." *Social Science Information* 24, no. 1 (1985): 145–159.

Satzewich, Vic. "Racism and Canadian Immigration Policy: The Government's View of Caribbean Migration, 1962–1966." *Canadian Ethnic Studies* 21, no. 1 (1989): 77–97.

Saurette, Paul. "When Smart Parties Make Stupid Decisions." *The Mark News*, July 23, 2010.

Scarman, Leslie G. *The Brixton Disorders 10–12 April 1981. Report of an Inquiry by the Rt. Hon. The Lord Scarman OBE*. London: HMSO, 1981.

Schor, Paul. "Mobilising for Pure Prestige? Challenging Federal Census Ethnic Categories in the USA (1850–1940)." *International Social Science Journal* 57, no. 183 (2005): 89–101.

Schmidt, Vivien A. "Discursive Institutionalism: The Explanatory Power of Ideas and Discourse." *Annual Review of Political Science* 11 (2008): 303–326.

Schweber, Libby. *Disciplining Statistics: Demography and Vital Statistics in France and England, 1830–1885*. Durham and London: Duke University Press, 2006.

Scott, Corrie. "How French Canadians Became White Folks, or Doing Things with Race in Quebec." *Ethnic and Racial Studies* 39, no. 7 (2016): 1280–1297.

Scott, James C. *Seeing Like a State: How Certain Schemes to Improve the Human Condition Have Failed*. New Haven and London: Yale University Press, 1998.

The Art of Not Being Governed: An Anarchist History of Upland Southeast Asia. New Haven: Yale University Press, 2009.

Seigel, Micol. *Uneven Encounters: Making Race and Nation in Brazil and the United States*. Durham and London: Duke University Press, 2009.

Seltzer, William. "Excluding Indians Not Taxed: Federal Censuses and Native-Americans in the 19th Century." Paper presented at the 1999 Joint Statistical Meetings. Baltimore, 1999.

Shachar, Ayelet. *Multicultural Jurisdictions: Cultural Differences and Women's Rights*. Cambridge: Cambridge University Press, 2001.

Sharma, Aradhana, and Akhil Gupta, eds. *The Anthropology of the State: A Reader*. Malden: Blackwell Publishing, 2006.

Shipan, Charles R., and Craig Volden. "The Mechanisms of Policy Diffusion." *American Journal of Political Science* 52, no. 4 (2008): 840–857.

Shull, Steven A. *A Kinder, Gentler Racism?: The Reagan-Bush Civil Rights Legacy*. Armonk: M.E. Sharpe, 1993.

Siebert, Wilbur H. *The Underground Railroad: From Slavery to Freedom*. New York and London: Macmillan, 1898.

Sikkink, Kathryn. "The Power of Principled Ideas: Human Rights Policies in the United States and Western Europe." In *Ideas and Foreign Policy: Beliefs, Institutions and Political Change*, edited by Judith Goldstein and Robert O. Keohane, 139–170. Ithaca: Cornell University Press, 1993.

Sil, Rudra, and Peter J. Katzenstein. "Analytic Eclecticism in the Study of World Politics: Reconfiguring Problems and Mechanisms across Research Traditions." *Perspectives on Politics* 8, no. 2 (2010): 411–431.

Sillitoe, Ken. *Ethnic Origins I: An Experiment in the Use of a Direct Question about Ethnicity, for the Census*. Office of Population Censuses and Surveys, Occasional Paper No. 8. London: OPCS, 1978.

Ethnic Origins II: An Experiment in the Use of a Direct Question about Ethnicity, for the Census. Office of Population Censuses and Surveys, Occasional Paper No. 9. London: OPCS, 1978.

Ethnic Origins III: An Experiment in the Use of a Direct Question about Ethnicity, for the Census. Office of Population Censuses and Surveys, Occasional Paper No. 10. London: OPCS, 1978.

Developing Questions on Ethnicity and Related Topics for the Census. Office of Population Censuses and Surveys, Occasional Paper 36. London: OPCS, 1987.

Sillitoe, Ken, and Philip H. White. "Ethnic Group and the British Census: The Search for a Question." *Journal of the Royal Statistical Society. Series A (Statistics in Society)* 155, no. 1 (1992): 141–163.

Simmons, Beth A., Frank Dobbin, and Geoffrey Garrett. "Introduction: The International Diffusion of Liberalism." *International Organization* 60, no. 4 (2006): 781–810.

Simmons, Beth A., and Zachary Elkins. "The Globalization of Liberalization: Policy Diffusion in the International Political Economy." *American Political Science Review* 98, no. 1 (2004): 171–189.

Simon, Patrick. "The Measurement of Racial Discrimination: The Policy Use of Statistics." *International Journal of Social Science* no. 183 (2005): 9–25.

"Ethnic" Statistics and Data Protection in the Council of Europe Countries. Strasbourg: Council of Europe, 2007.

"The Choice of Ignorance: The Debate on Ethnic and Racial Statistics in France." *French Politics, Culture & Society* 26, no. 4 (2008): 7–31.

Singh, Nikhil Pal. *Black Is a Country: Race and the Unfinished Struggle for Democracy*. Cambridge: Harvard University Press, 2004.

Skerry, Peter. *Counting on the Census?: Race, Group Identity, and the Evasion of Politics*. Washington D.C.: Brookings Institution Press, 2000.

Skinner, Chris, John Hollis, and Mike Murphy. *Beyond 2011: Independent Review of Methodology*. October 2013. Accessed July 10, 2014, www.ons.gov.uk/ons/about-ons/who-ons-are/programmes-and-projects/beyond-2011/beyond-2011–independent-review-of-methodolgy/index.html

Skogstad, Grace D., ed. *Policy Paradigms, Transnationalism, and Domestic Politics*. Toronto: University of Toronto Press, 2011.

"Policy Networks and Policy Communities: Conceptualizing State-Societal Relationships in the Policy Process." In *The Comparative Turn in Canadian Political Science*, edited by Linda White, Richard Simeon, Robert Vipond, and Jennifer Wallner, 205–220. Vancouver: UBC Press, 2008.

Skrentny, John David. *The Ironies of Affirmative Action: Politics, Culture, and Justice in America*. Chicago: University of Chicago Press, 1996.

"The Effect of the Cold War on African-American Civil Rights: America and the World Audience, 1945–1968." *Theory and Society* 27, no. 2 (1998): 237–285.

The Minority Rights Revolution. Cambridge: Harvard University Press, 2002.

Slaughter, Anne-Marie. *A New World Order*. Princeton: Princeton University Press, 2005.

Small, Stephen. *Racialised Barriers: The Black Experience in the United States and England in the 1980's*. London: Routledge, 1994.

Small, Stephen, and John Solomos. "Race, Immigration and Politics in Britain Changing Policy Agendas and Conceptual Paradigms 1940s–2000s." *International Journal of Comparative Sociology* 47, nos.3–4 (2006): 235–257.

Smedley, Audrey. *Race in North America: Origin and Evolution of a Worldview*, 3rd edn. Boulder: Westview Press, 2007.

Smith, Richard Saumarez. "Rule-by-Records and Rule-by-Reports: Complementary Aspects of the British Imperial Rule of Law." *Contributions to Indian Sociology* 19, no. 1 (1985): 153–176.

Smith, Rogers M. "Beyond Tocqueville, Myrdal, and Hartz: The Multiple Traditions in America." *American Political Science Review* 87, no. 3 (1993): 549–566.

Civic Ideals: Conflicting Visions of Citizenship in U.S. History. New Haven: Yale University Press, 1997.

Political Peoplehood: The Roles of Values, Interests, and Identities. Chicago: University of Chicago Press, 2015.

Solomos, John. *Race and Racism in Britain*, 3rd edn. London: Palgrave Macmillan, 2003.

Soss, Joe, Richard C. Fording, and Sanford F. Schram. *Disciplining the Poor: Neoliberal Paternalism and the Persistent Power of Race*. Chicago: University of Chicago Press, 2011.

Soysal, Yasemin Nuhoğlu. *Limits of Citizenship: Migrants and Postnational Membership in Europe*. Chicago: University of Chicago Press, 1994.

Spektorowski, Alberto. "The Eugenic Temptation in Socialism: Sweden, Germany, and the Soviet Union." *Comparative Studies in History and Society* 46, no. 1 (2004): 84–106.

Spence, Lester K. *Stare in the Darkness: The Limits of Hip-Hop and Black Politics*. Minneapolis: University of Minnesota Press, 2011.

Knocking the Hustle: Against the Neoliberal Turn in Black Politics. Brooklyn: punctum books, 2015.

Spencer, Ian R.G. *British Immigration Policy Since 1939: The Making of Multi-Racial Britain*. London: Routledge, 1997.

Spencer, Rainier. *Spurious Issues: Race and Multiracial Identity Politics in the United States*. Boulder: Westview Press, 1999.

Reproducing Race: The Paradox of Generation Mix. Boulder and London: Lynne Rienner Publishers, 2011.

Squires, Catherine R. *Dispatches from the Color Line: The Press and Multiracial America*. Albany: SUNY Press, 2007.

Stanton, William. *The Leopard's Spots: Scientific Attitudes toward Race in America, 1815–59*. Chicago: University of Chicago Press, 1960.

Starr, Paul. "The Sociology of Official Statistics." In *The Politics of Numbers*, edited by William Alonso and Paul Starr, 7–58. New York: Russell Sage Foundation, 1987.

"Social Categories and Claims in the Liberal State." *Social Research* 59, no. 2 (1992): 263–295.

Stasiulius, Daiva. "Symbolic Representation and the Numbers Game: Tory Policies on 'Race' and Visible Minorities." In *How Ottawa Spends: The Politics of Fragmentation, 1991–92*, edited by Frances Abele, 229–267. Ottawa: Carleton University Press, 1991.

Statistics Canada. *Census of the Population, 1986*. Ottawa: Statistics Canada, 1986.

1991 Census Consultation Report. Ottawa: Statistics Canada, 1988.

1991 Census, Content of Questionnaire. Ottawa: Statistics Canada, 1991.

1991 Census Highlights. Ottawa: Statistics Canada, 1994.

1996 Census Consultation Report. Ottawa: Statistics Canada, 1996.

1996 Census Guide and Reasons Why the Questions Are Asked. Ottawa: Statistics Canada, 1996.

Content of the Questionnaire, the 1996 Population Census. Ottawa: Statistics Canada, 1996.

2001 Census. Ottawa: Statistics Canada, 2001.

2006 Census. Ottawa: Statistics Canada, 2006.

Statistics Canada and United States Bureau of the Census. *Challenges of Measuring an Ethnic World: Science, Politics and Reality*. Proceedings of the Joint Canada-United States Conference on the Measurement of Ethnicity, April 1–3, 1992. Washington D.C.: U.S. Government Printing Office, 1993.

Stavo-Debauge, Joan, and Sue Scott. *Comparative Study on the Collection of Data to Measure the Extent and Impact of Discrimination in a Selection of Countries: Final Report on England*. Lyon, FR: European Commission, Employment and Social Affairs DG, 2004.

Stears, Mark. "The Liberal Tradition and the Politics of Exclusion." *Annual Review of Political Science* 10 (2007): 85–101.

Stepan, Nancy. *The Idea of Race in Science: Great Britain, 1800–1960*. Oxford: Macmillan, 1982.

The Hour of Eugenics: Race, Gender, and Nation in Latin America. Ithaca: Cornell University Press, 1991.

Stevens, Jacqueline. "Beyond Tocqueville, Please!" *American Political Science Review* 89, no. 4 (1995): 987–995.

Stigler, Stephen M. *The History of Statistics: The Measurement of Uncertainty before 1900*. Cambridge: Harvard University Press, 1986.

Stoler, Ann Laura. *Carnal Knowledge and Imperial Power: Race and the Intimate in Colonial Rule*. Berkeley: University of California Press, 2002.

Along the Archival Grain: Epistemic Anxieties and Colonial Common Sense. Princeton: Princeton University Press, 2009.

Stone, Deborah. *Policy Paradox: The Art of Political Decision Making*, 3rd edn. New York and London: W.W. Norton, 2012.

Street, Harry, Geoffrey Howe, and Geoffrey Bindman. *Anti-Discrimination Legislation: The Street Report*. London: Political and Economic Planning, 1967.

Tan, Seng, and Amitav Acharya, eds. *Bandung Revisited: The Legacy of the 1955 Asian-African Conference for the International Order*. Singapore: National University of Singapore Press, 2008.

Tanser, H.A. "Intelligence of Negroes of Mixed Blood in Canada." *The Journal of Negro Education* 10, no. 4 (1941): 650–652.

Tarnopolsky, Walter S. *The Canadian Bill of Rights*, 2nd rev. edn. Toronto: McClelland and Stewart, 1975.

Discrimination and the Law in Canada. Toronto: R. De Boo, 1982.

Taylor, Charles. "The Politics of Recognition." In *Multiculturalism: Examining the Politics of Recognition*, edited by Amy Gutmann, 25–73. Princeton: Princeton University Press, 1994.

Taylor, Paul, and Pew Research Center. *The Next America: Boomers, Millennials, and the Looming Generational Showdown*. New York: PublicAffairs, 2014.

Tesler, Michael. "The Spillover of Racialization into Health Care: How President Obama Polarized Public Opinion by Racial Attitudes and Race." *American Journal of Political Science* 56, no. 3 (2012): 690–704.

Thelen, David. "The Nation and Beyond: Transnational Perspectives on United States History." *Journal of American History*, 86, no. 3 (1999): 965–975.

Thelen, Kathleen. "Historical Institutionalism in Comparative Politics." *Annual Review of Political Science* 2 (1999): 369–404.

Thelen, Kathleen, and Sven Steinmo, eds. *Structuring Politics: Historical Institutionalism in Comparative Politics*. Cambridge: Cambridge University Press, 1992.

Thernstrom, Abigail. "Obama's Census Identity." *The Wall Street Journal*, April 16, 2010. Accessed November 10, 2011, http://online.wsj.com/article/SB10001424052702303720604575169783989253108.html

Thernstrom, Stephan, and Abigail Thernstrom. *America in Black and White: One Nation, Indivisible*. New York: Simon and Schuster, 1999.

Thobani, Sunera. *Exalted Subjects: Studies in the Making of Race and Nation in Canada*. Toronto: University of Toronto Press, 2007.

Thompson, Debra. "Racial Ideas and Gendered Intimacies: The Regulation of Interracial Relationships in North America." *Social and Legal Studies* 18, no. 3 (2009): 353–371.

"The Politics of the Census: Lessons from Abroad." *Canadian Public Policy* 36, no. 3 (2010): 377–382.

"What Lies Beneath: Equality and the Making of Racial Classifications." *Social Philosophy and Policy* 31, no. 2 (2015): 114–136.

Thompson, Jonathan. *"We Are All Black": Contrast, Uhuru and the African-Canadian Press, 1969–1970*. Unpublished M.A. Thesis. Kingston: Queen's University, 2008.

Tichenor, Daniel J. *Dividing Lines: The Politics of Immigration Control in America*. Princeton: Princeton University Press, 2002.

Tillery Jr, Alvin B. *Between Homeland and Motherland: Africa, U.S. Foreign Policy, and Black Leadership in America*. Ithaca: Cornell University Press, 2011.

Timmermans, Stefan, and Steven Epstein. "A World of Standards but not a Standard World: Toward a Sociology of Standards and Standardization." *Annual Review of Sociology* 36 (2010): 69–89.

Titley, E. Brian. *A Narrow Vision: Duncan Campbell Scott and the Administration of Indian Affairs in Canada*. Vancouver: University of British Columbia Press, 1986.

Triadafilopoulos, Triadafilos. "Building Walls, Bounding Nations: Migration and Exclusion in Canada and Germany, 1870–1939." *Journal of Historical Sociology* 17, no. 4 (2004): 385–427.

Becoming Multicultural: Immigration and the Politics of Membership in Canada and Germany. Vancouver: University of British Columbia Press, 2012.

Troper, Harold Martin. "The Creek-Negroes of Oklahoma and Canadian Immigration, 1909–11." *The Canadian Historical Review* 53, no. 3 (1972): 272–288.

Tully, James. "Indigenous Peoples Struggles for and of Freedom." In *Political Theory and the Rights of Indigenous Peoples*, edited by Duncan Ivison, Paul Patton, and Will Sanders, 36–59. Cambridge: Cambridge University Press, 2000.

Tyrrell, Ian R. *Transnational Nation: United States History in Global Perspective since 1789*. New York: Palgrave Macmillan, 2007.

United Nations. *Principles and Recommendations for Population and Housing Censuses*. Statistical Paper M/67. New York: United Nations, 1980.

Manual on Human Rights Reporting under Six Major International Human Rights Instruments. Geneva: United Nations, 1997.

Principles and Recommendations for Population and Housing Censuses. Statistical Paper M/67/Rev. 1. New York: United Nations, 1998.

World Conference against Racism, Racial Discrimination, Xenophobia, and Related Intolerance, Declaration. Geneva: United Nations, 2002.

Principles and Recommendations for Population and Housing Censuses. Statistical Paper M/67/Rev. 2. New York: United Nations, 2008.

UNESCO. *The Race Question*. Paris: UNESCO, 1950.

The Race Concept: Results of an Inquiry. Paris: UNESCO, 1952.

Proposals on the Biological Aspects of Race. Paris: UNESCO, 1964.

United Nations Statistics Division. *Fundamental Principles of Official Statistics*. New York: United Nations Statistical Division, 2013. http://unstats.un.org/unsd/dnss/gp/FP-New-E.pdf (accessed September 25, 2013).

United States. *Review of Federal Measurements of Race and Ethnicity*. Hearings before the Subcommittee on Census, Statistics and Postal

Personnel of the Committee on Post Office and Civil Service, House of Representatives, 103rd Congress, 1st session. Washington D.C.: US Government Printing Office, 1994.

Federal Measures of Race and Ethnicity and the Implications for the 2000 Census. Hearings before the Subcommittee on Government Management, Information and Technology, of the House Committee on Government Reform and Oversight, 105th Congress. Washington D.C.: U.S. Government Printing Office, 1997.

United States Bureau of the Census. *Negro Population 1790–1915.* Washington D.C.: U.S. Government Printing Office, 1918.

United States Census Bureau. *Findings on Questions on Race and Hispanic Origin Tested in the 1996 National Content Survey.* Population Division Working Paper No. 16. Washington D.C.: Bureau of the Census, 1996.

Results of the 1996 Race and Ethnic Targeted Test. Population Division Working Paper No. 18. Washington D.C.: Bureau of the Census, 1997.

Meeting 21st Century Demographic Data Needs – Implementing the American Community Survey: July 2001. Report 1: Demonstrating Operational Feasibility Washington D.C.: U.S. Census Bureau, 2001.

Historical Census Statistics on Population Totals by Race, 1790 to 1990, and by Hispanic Origin, 1970 to 1990, for the United States, Regions, Divisions, and States. United States – Race and Hispanic Origin: 1790 to 1990, Working Paper Series No. 56. Washington D.C.: United States Census Bureau, 2002.

United States Census Office. *Population of the United States in 1860: Compiled from the Original Returns of the Eighth Census.* By Joseph C.G. Kennedy. Washington D.C.: Government Printing Office, 1864.

The Statistics of the Population of the United States. Washington D.C.: Government Printing Office, 1872, xiii.

United States Congress. *Report of the Ninth Census.* U.S. House of Representatives, 41st Congress, 2nd Session. Washington D.C.: Government Printing Office, 1870.

Enumeration of the Chinese Population of the United States. U.S. House of Representatives, 51st Congress, 1st Session. Washington D.C.: Government Printing Office, 1890.

United States Department of Commerce. *Results of the 2010 Census Race and Hispanic Origin Alternative Questionnaire Experiment News Conference*, George Washington University. August 8, 2012, www.census.gov/2010census/news/press-kits/aqe/aqe.html

United States Federal Interagency Committee on Education. *Report of the Ad Hoc Committee on Racial and Ethnic Definitions.*

Washington D.C.: U.S. Department of Health, Education, and Welfare, National Institute of Education, 1975.

United States General Accounting Office. *Statistical Agencies: A Comparison of the United States and Canadian Statistical Systems*. Report to Congressional Requesters, GAO/GGD-96–142. Washington D.C.: U.S. GAO, 1996.

United States House of Representatives. 28th Congress, 1st Session. *House Reports* Volume III, no. 580.

Valente, Paolo. "Census Taking in Europe: How are Populations Counted in 2010?" *Population and Societies* no. 467 (2010): 1–4.

Valpy, M. "Harper's Census Push Months in the Making." *Globe and Mail*, July 26, 2010.

Valverde, Mariana. *The Age of Light, Soap and Water: Moral Reform in English Canada, 1885–1925*. Toronto: University of Toronto Press, 1991.

Van Kirk, Sylvia. "From 'Marrying-In' to 'Marrying-Out': Changing Patterns of Aboriginal/Non-Aboriginal Marriage in Colonial Canada." *Frontiers: A Journal of Women Studies* 23, no. 3 (2002): 1–11.

Vasta, Ellie. "From Ethnic Minorities to Ethnic Majority Policy: Multiculturalism and the Shift to Assimilationism in the Netherlands." *Ethnic and Racial Studies* 30, no. 5 (2007): 713–740.

Vitalis, Robert. *White World Order, Black Power Politics: The Birth of American International Relations*. Ithaca: Cornell University Press, 2015.

Von Eschen, Penny M. *Race Against Empire: Black Americans and Anti-Colonialism, 1937–1957*. Ithaca: Cornell University Press, 1997.

Vucetic, Srdjan. "Anglobal Governance?" *Cambridge Review of International Affairs* 23, no. 3 (2010): 455–474.

The Anglosphere: A Genealogy of Racialized Identity in International Relations. Stanford: Stanford University Press, 2011.

Wacquant, Loïc. *Punishing the Poor: The Neoliberal Government of Social Insecurity*. Durham: Duke University Press, 2009.

Walker, Barrington. *Race on Trial: Black Defendants in Ontario's Criminal Courts, 1858–1958*. Toronto: University of Toronto Press, 2010.

Walker, Francis A. "The Indian Question." *North American Review* 116, no. 239 (1873): 329–388.

Walker, James W. St. G. *Black Loyalists: The Search for a Promised Land in Nova Scotia and Sierra Leone, 1783–1870*. Toronto: University of Toronto Press, 1992.

"Race," Rights and the Law in the Supreme Court of Canada: Historical Case Studies. Waterloo: Wilfred Laurier University Press, 1997.

Wallenstein, Peter. *Tell the Court I Love my Wife: Race, Marriage, and Law: An American History*. New York: Palgrave Macmillan, 2002.

Wallman, Katherine K. "Data on Race and Ethnicity: Revising the Federal Standard." *The American Statistician* 52, no. 1 (1998): 31–33.

Watts, Robs. "Making Numbers Count: The Birth of the Census and Racial Government in Victoria, 1835–1870." *Australian Historical Studies* 34, no. 121 (2003): 26–47.

Wayne, Michael. "The Black Population of Canada West on the Eve of the American Civil War: A Reassessment Based on the Manuscript Census of 1861." *Histoire Sociale/Social History* 28, no. 56 (1995): 465–485.

Weaver, Sally M. *Making Canadian Indian Policy: The Hidden Agenda, 1968–1970*. Toronto: University of Toronto Press, 1981.

White, Pamela. "Challenges in Measuring Canada's Ethnic Diversity." In *Twenty Years of Multiculturalism: Successes and Failures*, edited by Stella Hryniuk, 163–182. Winnipeg: St. John's College Press, 1992.

White, Pamela, Jane Badets, and Viviane Renaud. "Measuring Ethnicity in Canadian Censuses." In *Challenges of Measuring an Ethnic World: Science, Politics and Reality*, 223–269. Proceedings of the Joint Canada-United States Conference on the Measurement of Ethnicity, April 1–3, 1992. Washington D.C.: U.S. Government Printing Office, 1993.

White, Philip H., and David L. Pearce. "Ethnic Group and the British Census." In *Challenges of Measuring an Ethnic World: Science, Politics and Reality*. Proceedings of the Joint Canada-United States Conference on the Measurement of Ethnicity, April 1–3, 1992, 271–306. Washington D.C.: U.S. Government Printing Office, 1993.

Willcox, Walter F. "Development of International Statistics." *The Milbank Memorial Fund Quarterly* 27, no. 2 (1949): 143–153.

"The Development of the American Census Office since 1890." *Political Science Quarterly* 29, no. 3 (1914): 438–459.

Williams, Dorothy. *The Road to Now: A History of Blacks in Montreal*. Montreal: Vehicule Press, 1997.

Williams, Kim. "From Civil Rights to the Multiracial Movement." In *New Faces in a Changing America in the 21st Century*, edited by Loretta I. Winters and Herman L. DeBose, 85–98. Thousand Oaks: Sage Publications, 2003).

Mark One or More: Civil Rights in Multiracial America. Ann Arbor: University of Michigan Press, 2006.

Williams, Robert A. *The American Indian in Western Legal Thought: Discourses of Conquest*. New York: Oxford University Press, 1990.

Williamson, Joel. *New People: Miscegenation and Mulattoes in the United States*. New York: The Free Press, 1980.

Wilson, David C., and Darren W. Davis. "Reexamining Racial Resentment: Conceptualization and Content." *The ANNALS of the American Academy of Political and Social Science* 634, no. 1 (2011): 117–133.

Wimmer, Andreas. "The Making and Unmaking of Ethnic Boundaries: A Multilevel Process Theory." *American Journal of Sociology* 113, no. 4 (2008): 970–1022.

Winant, Howard. "Race and Race Theory." *Annual Review of Sociology* 26 (2000): 169–185.

The World Is a Ghetto: Race and Democracy Since World War Two. New York: Basic Books, 2001.

The New Politics of Race: Globalism, Difference, Justice. Minneapolis: University of Minnesota Press, 2004.

"Race, Ethnicity, and Social Science." *Ethnic and Racial Studies* 38, no. 13 (2015): 2176–2185.

Winks, Robin W. "Negro School Segregation in Ontario and Nova Scotia." *Canadian Historical Review* 50, no. 2 (1969): 164–191.

The Blacks in Canada: A History, 2nd edn. Montreal and Kingston: McGill-Queen's University Press, 1997.

Woolf, Stuart. "Statistics and the Modern State." *Comparative Studies in Society and History* 31, no. 3 (1989): 588–604.

Worley, Claire. "'It's Not about Race. It's about the Community': New Labour and 'Community Cohesion'." *Critical Social Policy* 25, no. 4 (2005): 483–496.

Worton, David A. *The Dominion Bureau of Statistics: A History of Canada's Central Statistical Office and Its Antecedents, 1841–1972*. Montreal and Kingston: McGill-Queen's University Press, 1998.

Wright, Carroll D., and William O. Hunt. *The History and Growth of the United States Census*. Washington D.C.: Government Printing Office, 1900.

Wright, Lawrence. "One Drop of Blood." *The New Yorker* 25 (1994): 46–55.

Wright, Richard, Serin Houston, Mark Ellis, Steven Holloway, and Margaret Hudson. "Crossing Racial Lines: Geographies of Mixed-Race Partnering and Multiraciality in the United States." *Progress in Human Geography* 27, no. 4 (2003): 457–474.

Yeo, Michael. "The Rights of Science and the Rights of Politics: Lessons from the Long-Form Census Controversy," *Canadian Journal of Sociology* 37, no. 3 (2012): 295–317.

Young, Iris Marion. *Justice and the Politics of Difference*. Princeton: Princeton University Press, 1990.

Young, Robert J.C. *Colonial Desire: Hybridity in Theory, Culture and Race*. London and New York: Routledge, 1995.

Index

CPSIA information can be obtained
at www.ICGtesting.com
Printed in the USA
LVOW10*1808230617
539172LV00007B/51/P